DAY OF THE MATCH

DAY OF THE MATCH

A HISTORY OF FOOTBALL IN 366 DAYS

Scott Murray and Rowan Walker

BOXTREE

First published 2008 by Boxtree
an imprint of Pan Macmillan Ltd
Pan Macmillan, 20 New Wharf Road, London N1 9RR
Basingstoke and Oxford
Associated companies throughout the world
www.panmacmillan.com

ISBN 978-0-7522-2678-1

A CIP catalogue record for this book is available from
the British Library.

Printed by CPI Mackays, Chatham ME5 8TD

Visit www.panmacmillan.com to read more about all our books and to buy them. You will also find features, author interviews and news of any author events, and you can sign up for e-newsletters so that you're always first to hear about our new releases.

JANUARY

HIBERNIAN 5-6 HEARTS: THE TRUTH
IS STRANGER THAN FICTION
(1940)

Commentators are often accused of being utterly incapable of describing what's going on in front of their noses, but in the case of BBC broadcaster Bob Kingsley, that really was the case during this New Year's Day Edinburgh derby.

Easter Road was enveloped in the mother of all pea-soupers. Under normal circumstances the game would not have gone ahead as the players, referee and 14,000 spectators could not see much further than ten feet in front of them, but with the match to be broadcast on the radio for overseas soldiers, it was decided that a postponement might have alerted the Germans to weather conditions in Edinburgh.

This caused a massive problem for Kingsley, who was under strict instruction to commentate as though it was a beautiful sunny day. He put in place a relay of runners between his commentary position and the pitch in an attempt to garner some idea of what was going on, but it proved futile. Instead he simply invented a fantastic fictional match packed with outrageous goals, saves and near misses.

Yet Kingsley's ad-libbed riffs, sadly now lost in the ether, were nothing compared to the actual match. Hibernian went into the break 3-2 up, only for the referee to realise he had blown up on 43 minutes. The teams returned to play out an extra two minutes, during which Hearts scored twice. In the second half, Hibs went 3-5 down only to peg it back to 5-5, with John Cuthbertson scoring a hat-trick, but Hearts striker Tommy Walker's last-minute strike secured an amazing 6-5 away win. The servicemen abroad had no idea whatsoever what was going on, but then neither did the crowd, many of whom only realised the match had ended ten minutes after the final whistle.

THE SECOND IBROX DISASTER KILLS 66
(1971)

There had already been one major disaster at Rangers' Ibrox stadium. In 1902, six minutes into the Scotland vs England home international, 26 people died and 517 were injured when twenty square yards of wooden planks in the West Tribune Stand gave way, sending spectators tumbling fifty feet to the ground. Amazingly, after a short break the game was restarted and finished 1-1, after several stoppages to allow the injured and dead to be transported across the pitch, although the result would later be declared void by the English and Scottish FAs.

Nearly 70 years later, tragedy would again befall the stadium at the end of the traditional New Year's 'Old Firm' derby. As the crowd began to leave the ground after the match, 66 people were crushed to death on Stairway 13 as crash barriers collapsed. A myth persists to this day that the crush occurred after fans who had left before the final whistle turned back when a roar went up to greet Colin Stein's late equaliser for Rangers. This is untrue; while Stein did indeed score to force a 1-1 draw, the accident happened after the final whistle. A subsequent inquiry suggested fans may have lost balance as a result of someone bending down to pick up a scarf, hat or coin.

The disaster had been a major accident waiting to happen. Ten years earlier, a barrier had collapsed on the same stairway, killing two fans, while there were a further 32 injuries on the stairwell during the next decade. The 1971 disaster was the final straw for Rangers. Ibrox was effectively razed to the ground and rebuilt as an all-seater stadium. Archibald Leitch's famous 1929 facade apart, Ibrox is unrecognizable from the ground of the early 1970s.

JANUARY 3

GEORGE BEST FAILS TO TURN UP FOR TRAINING AT MANCHESTER UNITED
(1974)

Best had already 'retired' from football twice, leaving Manchester United in the summer of 1972 to sun himself in Marbella, then coming back for the start of the following season only to miss training so often he would be transfer-listed by December and bow out again soon after.

But when Tommy Docherty lured Best back to Old Trafford in September 1973, the initial signs were good. He played eleven times between October and January, scoring twice, though the 28-year-old was operating nowhere near the level of his mid-60s pomp. 'He is little more than a sad parody of the player he was,' reported the *Guardian* after a bearded and overweight Best waddled through a dismal 3-0 defeat at QPR on January 1, 1974. Nevertheless, according to Docherty's assistant Paddy Crerand, Best had 'done exceptionally well since he came back and has not once stepped out of line'.

When Best failed to turn up for training two days after the QPR debacle, few thought the game would turn out to be his last for the club. 'Because it is Best and it has happened before, people think there may be something seriously wrong,' insisted Crerand. 'In fact George could be ill or there could be some other reasonable explanation.'

Best did show up for work on January 4, but was dropped for the following game. Three more no-shows in eight days moved Docherty to place the matter in the hands of the directors. Within the month Best had severed his ties with United and been arrested for stealing the reigning Miss World's fur coat to boot. He was later cleared, but there wasn't much more good news for anyone concerned, as Best would end the season at Dunstable Town, while United would be relegated.

BURNLEY 0-1 WIMBLEDON: A PIVOTAL CUP TIE
(1975)

It was one of the biggest cup shocks of all time, and would send the two competing teams heading in opposite directions. Burnley had won the league as recently as 1960 and reached the FA Cup final of 1962. Wimbledon were winning honours around that time too, albeit on a more modest scale. They had won the Isthmian League three years running between 1962 and 1964 as well as the FA Amateur Cup in 1963.

By the time they were drawn away to Burnley in the third round of the 1975 FA Cup, Wimbledon were major players in the Southern League, but that was still five divisions below their hosts. It was a shock of seismic proportions, therefore, when Wimbledon became the first non-league side to win away at a top-division club in the cup since North Eastern League's Darlington eliminated Sheffield Wednesday, at Hillsborough, in 1920.

Wimbledon's heroics continued in the next round at champions Leeds. Goalkeeper Dickie Guy saved a Peter Lorimer penalty in an incredible scoreless draw against a team who reached that season's European Cup final. But the run ended in the subsequent Plough Lane replay. The tie was settled when future boss Dave Bassett deflected a Johnny Giles shot into his own net.

Burnley ended the season tenth, but suffered relegation the season after. By 1986/87, they needed a final-day win against Tranmere to avoid becoming the first club to be automatically relegated from the league. That same 1986/87 season saw top-flight Wimbledon knock champions Everton out of the FA Cup. A year later they won it.

JANUARY 5

THE FIFA WORLD CLUB CHAMPIONSHIP
IS BORN, THE FA CUP DIES A LITTLE
(2000)

Since 1960, the holders of the European Cup and the Copa Libertadores (its South American equivalent) had played off to decide the Intercontinental Cup, with the winners claiming the unofficial title of 'world club champions'. However by the turn of the millennium it was clear FIFA's four other 'continents' required representation, so a broader worldwide tournament was launched.

The 2000 FIFA World Club Championship was, in truth, a sprawling mess. Invitations were seemingly handed out at random. For example, while Manchester United, reigning European and Intercontinental Cup holders, represented Europe, so too did Real Madrid, Intercontinental Cup winners of 1998. Vasco da Gama competed as South American champions, but 1999 Brazilian league winners Corinthians did too, as hosts.

Real Madrid won the first game, 3-1 against Asian Super Cup winners Al Nassr. Nicolas Anelka scored the tournament's first ever goal. A goalless final would be won by Corinthians, who beat Vasco 4-3 on penalties. Manchester United crashed out in the first round, beating only South Melbourne of Oceania, a failure viewed by most back home with schadenfreude as the club had opted out of the 2000 FA Cup, while holders, in order to compete in Brazil. The criticism was a tad unfair, as United were under unwelcome pressure from the FA, who wanted them to help curry world favour in a futile bid for England to host the 2006 World Cup.

The FIFA World Club Championship was put in storage until 2005, since when only the champions of the six governing bodies have been allowed to compete for the re-titled FIFA World Club Cup.

ARSENAL MANAGER HERBERT
CHAPMAN DIES SUDDENLY
(1934)

The last game ever seen by inspirational manager Herbert Chapman featured the Arsenal third XI playing at Guildford on the cold, foggy night of Wednesday January 3 1934. 'I don't get the chance to see the lads very often,' he said, ignoring the club doctor's advice to stay in bed after picking up what appeared to be a heavy cold watching Sheffield Wednesday, who were due to visit Highbury on the upcoming Saturday.

Upon returning from Guildford, Chapman's condition had worsened considerably and he retired to bed. By 3 a.m. on Saturday Chapman had died of pneumonia. The first Cliff Bastin and the rest of the Arsenal team heard of the news was walking to Highbury for the match. Bastin said: 'It seemed just too bad to be true. He had been loved by us all.' The game against Wednesday went ahead after a short silence, Arsenal somehow holding out for a 1-1 draw.

Whoever was rounding up the sports news in the following day's *Observer* wasn't too adept at spotting a 'top line' story as the news was hidden away in the third paragraph of a page-28 report carrying the headline 'Stockport Score Thirteen Goals'. Admittedly Stan Milton of Halifax had set an unwelcome league record in a Third Division North match by conceding 13 goals – *on his debut for the club*. The newspaper commented: 'In the First Division Arsenal have shown tremendous tenacity in clinging to a slight lead, but their followers are excusably anxious about the future. The manager of the club has passed away.' Arsenal did indeed show anxiety, losing their next three games, but caretaker manager Joe Shaw steadied the ship and the team won the league, in a delicious tribute, ahead of second-placed Huddersfield, Chapman's previous club.

JANUARY 7

REAL MADRID 5-0 BARCELONA: LAUDRUP'S FIVE IN A ROW
(1995)

Despite playing alongside talents as stellar as Hristo Stoichkov, Pep Guardiola, Ronald Koeman and Romário, Danish winger Michael Laudrup was the true heartbeat of Barcelona's early 1990s side. The famous 'Dream Team' won four *La Liga* titles in a row from 1990/91 to 1993/94 and the club's first European Cup in 1992.

Barça were undoubtedly fortunate during that run of consecutive titles, having three gifted to them on the final day of the season. In 91/92, Real Madrid tossed away a two-goal lead at lowly Tenerife to lose, repeating the trick a year later with a 2-0 defeat at the same venue. Then in 93/94 Miroslav Djukic missed a late penalty which would have secured a first ever title for Deportivo La Coruña. Each time, Barcelona were on hand to take advantage of their rivals' nightmares.

Still, you make your own luck, which is exactly what manager Johan Cruyff did when he signed Laudrup from Juventus in 1989. The Dream Team were there to capitalise because they played exquisite attacking football. Cruyff would make himself a hostage to fortune, however, during the 93/94 season. Having just bought Romário, Cruyff marginalised Laudrup – despite Laudrup starring in an early-season 5-0 win over Real Madrid – partly because of UEFA's three-foreigner rule, partly because the two had fallen out. Having sat out both the second *El Clasico* match (against Real) of the campaign and Barça's capitulation in the European Cup final to AC Milan, Laudrup demanded a transfer. To Real Madrid.

The script wrote itself. Laudrup's next appearance in an *El Clasico* match saw him enjoy a second consecutive 5-0 win, but this time in a Real shirt. And sure enough, he would go on to add an unprecedented fifth title in a row as Real won *La Liga* at the end of his debut season.

JANUARY 8

KEEGAN RESIGNS AS NEWCASTLE MANAGER
(1997)

Suffering a hangover from the previous season, when they blew a 12-point lead to hand the Premiership to Manchester United, Newcastle United started the 1996/97 campaign badly. They were trounced 4-0 in the Charity Shield by United, then lost two of their opening three league games. But the club had just spent a world-record £15m on Alan Shearer, whose partnership up front with Les Ferdinand began to bear fruit. The team's form soon picked up and when United came to St James' Park in October, the Charity Shield defeat was avenged in a 5-0 rout which sent them to the top of the league. 'It's undoubtedly the most enjoyable day I have had as a manager,' smiled Kevin Keegan.

By the morning of January 8, Newcastle were five points behind leaders Liverpool, but had a game in hand. They had just won their last two league games 7-1 and 3-0, against Spurs and Leeds, and were still in both the FA and UEFA Cups. So it was a shock when, later that day, Keegan resigned as manager. 'It was my decision and my decision alone,' he said. 'I offered my resignation at the end of last season but was persuaded to stay. I feel I have taken the club as far as I can and that it would be in the best interests of all concerned if I resigned.'

Kenny Dalglish replaced him a week later, just as he had done as a player at Liverpool, but this succession was not so successful. Momentum was immediately lost; Dalglish's first league game saw Newcastle throw away a 2-0 lead at Southampton by conceding two goals in the last two minutes. In the very next game they were knocked out of the FA Cup at home by relegation-bound Nottingham Forest. Newcastle would still scrape to second in the league, but the dream was over and the defensive Dalglish was gone before 1998 was out. The 'Toon Army' spent the next eleven years getting through five more managers and dreaming of Keegan's return.

JANUARY 9

CHARLTON 1-1 MAIDSTONE: A MIDDLEWEIGHT BOUT
(1979)

With four minutes to go of their third-round FA Cup tie against Southern League Premier Division Maidstone United, Charlton Athletic of the Second Division were being embarrassingly held at home. At which point, Mike Flanagan burst forward into the Maidstone half, with most of the opposition caught up the other end. His strike partner Derek Hales made a run to one side, midfielder Keith Peacock joined up on the other and a gilt-edged opportunity to escape with a face-saving win presented itself. Flanagan hesitated, fatally. By the time he eventually slipped the ball beyond the last Maidstone player towards Hales, his partner was flagged offside and the chance was gone.

Hales and Flanagan exchanged words and strutted towards each other. Hales, a self-styled 'fiery' character, wasted no time in flinging a punch. 'He wasn't the kind of guy to see what the other fellow would do,' said Peacock, who watched in stunned disbelief as Flanagan retaliated to spark an unprecedented fistfight between two team mates. The impromptu middleweight bout ended when the referee sent both Hales (11st 2lbs) and Flanagan (11st 8lbs) off to reduce Charlton to nine men. The team held on for the draw and went on to win the replay 2-1, albeit without either suspended player.

'This is the most serious breach of discipline in the history of the club,' said manager Andy Nelson after the game. 'I am so angry if I do anything in haste I might regret it.' The club did act with too much haste. Hales, seen as the aggressor, was sacked three days later, but within the month had to be reinstated by law. Flanagan was transferred to Crystal Palace, only to return five years later to link up once again with Hales. All this for one misplaced pass? 'There was more to it than that,' was Hales's enigmatic, tight-lipped reply.

JANUARY 10

RONALDO TAKES THE STAND IN THE 'NIKE' TRIAL
(2001)

Approximately six hours before the 1998 World Cup final was due to kick off, Brazilian striker Ronaldo suffered a mysterious fit. Not that he knew it; he was asleep at the time and had to be told what happened by worried team mate Leonardo a couple of hours later, as he joined the squad for the pre-match meal. Whisked off to hospital for tests, Ronaldo's name was taken off the teamsheet, only to be put back on again less than an hour before the match. He arrived at the Stade de France dressed in his kit, having been given the all-clear by doctors. Ronaldo played dismally and Brazil were trounced 3-0 by France.

It was a strange affair and one that will likely never be explained away to anyone's satisfaction. That didn't stop Brazilian Communist congressman Aldo Rebelo from trying to get to the truth. Rebelo was holding an inquiry into the nature of Nike's $160m contract with the CBF and the amount of influence the firm held on the team. As it had been rumoured that Nike insisted Ronaldo play against France despite the striker's poor health, Ronaldo was forced to take the stand. Exactly what his testimony achieved is a moot point. 'You had a role ... in marking Zidane?' he was asked. He replied: 'Is this really going to help? ... I don't remember ... Whoever should have marked him didn't mark him very well, right?' Then he was quizzed as to why Brazil did not win the final. 'Because we let in three goals. Because we lost!' As for Nike's influence, Ronaldo explained that all the company ever asked from him was to 'preferably score a few goals with their boots.'

The inquiry would find evidence of corruption in the sport, but Nike were not implicated. As for congressman Rebelo, in 2006 he became Brazil's first Communist president for a single day, when both the president and vice president were out of the country.

BECKHAM SIGNS FOR LA GALAXY – THEN SALVAGES
HIS GALACTICO PRIDE
(2007)

David Beckham's *La Liga* debut for reigning champions Real Madrid in September 2003 couldn't have gone much better. Beckham scored his first goal for the club after less than three minutes, as his new club started the season with a 2-1 win over Real Betis. But the Galactico experiment at the Bernabéu was beginning to turn sour. Despite the presence of Beckham, Ronaldo, Raúl, Figo, Esteban Cambiasso and Fernando Morientes at the club, Real finished fourth in the league that season, seven points behind eventual champions Valencia.

The following two seasons would be equally frustrating for Beckham and Real. Real finished runners up both times behind Barcelona, four points off the pace in 2004/05 and an embarrassing twelve behind their rivals the year after. When, midway through the following season, Beckham announced he would be leaving for Major League Soccer club LA Galaxy that summer, Real were trailing yet again in *La Liga*, two points behind Barcelona and five behind leaders Sevilla. The club were enduring their longest trophy-less period for over half a century. This period coincided with Beckham's arrival, so it looked like his time in Spain would be defined by failure – especially as Real coach Fabio Capello responded to Beckham's announcement by saying he would not pick him for the remainder of the season.

Beckham impressed Capello with his attitude by knuckling down in training. Within a month he had won a recall to the team, scoring on his comeback against Real Sociedad. On June 17, Real ended their trophy drought, pipping Barcelona to the title with a 3-1 last-day win over Real Mallorca. Cynics would point out that Real Madrid were losing the must-win Mallorca match until Beckham was subbed – the man who replaced him, Jose Antonio Reyes, scored twice – but for persevering Beckham deserved his Hollywood ending.

ENGLAND NAME THEIR FIRST EVER FOREIGN MANAGER
(2001)

'If we don't get results, they will try to hang me. But if I was an Englishman they would try to hang me.' So joked Sven Goran Eriksson, upon arriving at the headquarters of the FA in 2001. Eriksson had arrived fresh from Lazio, where he had won the Roman club's first *Scudetto* since 1974. The Swede was the first foreigner to become England boss.

For a football nation with notoriously insular attitudes, it was a brave appointment by go-getting FA chief executive Adam Crozier, but one that initially paid off. Nine months into his tenure, Eriksson presided over one of England's most famous victories, a rampant 5-1 World Cup qualifier win in Germany. The result juxtaposed nicely with his predecessor Kevin Keegan's final game in charge (a flaccid 1-0 home defeat against the same team).

Expectation was heightened accordingly, but England could only reach the quarter-finals of the 2002 World Cup. The Germans had since regrouped and made the final, maintaining their record of going further than the English in every tournament since 1966. The pattern continued throughout Eriksson's reign; qualification would be achieved effortlessly, but England would always come up short in the finals.

After being caught on camera discussing other job opportunities, Eriksson fell on his sword early in 2006, before a frankly abysmal campaign in that year's World Cup, its nadir for England a risible struggle to overcome lowly Trinidad and Tobago. Despite often lurid revelations about his private life, the nation never quite bayed for the hanging he feared on his arrival. Eriksson went on to partially repair his reputation in England after a solid spell at Manchester City. Crozier, meanwhile, joined the Royal Mail; buying the right stamp to post a letter would soon require a degree in advanced mathematics.

JANUARY 13

BRIGHTON 1-1 CORINTHIANS: CORINTHIANS'
FA CUP DEBUT
(1923)

Formed in 1882, the Corinthians were the last great bastions of amateur football in England. Modelled in part on Scotland's Queen's Park, whose motto was 'the game for the game's sake', Corinthians generally recruited from the top universities and followed their own set of rules. If some – possibly romantic – sources are to be believed, any players given a red card would never play for the club again. If they were awarded a penalty they would refuse to take it; if they conceded one, the goalkeeper would stand aside to let the opponent roll it into the net.

In an era of Scottish dominance, it was hoped that Corinthians would provide a pool of amateur players to both challenge Queen's Park, and strengthen the full England team. From 1883 to 1890, 22 of the 50 English caps awarded against Scotland went to players who had played at some point for the club, and although ultimately England's resurgence was due to more and more professional players coming into the national side, the Corinthians nonetheless enjoyed some big successes at club level: they won the Sheriff of London Shield in 1900, beating Aston Villa 2-1 to gain their first trophy, and four years later hammered Manchester United 11-3, still United's record defeat. Their greatest achievement was beating FA Cup holders Bury 10-3 in 1904. Bury had beaten Derby 6-0 in the final.

In 1922/23 the Corinthians finally deigned to enter the FA Cup, playing home games at the Crystal Palace. They took Brighton to a second replay and a year later beat Blackburn Rovers 1-0. Their tie at home to Newcastle United in 1927 drew a crowd of 56,000 and was the second-ever match covered live by BBC radio, but the glory days were over. In 1936, the Crystal Palace burned down leaving them homeless and by 1939 they had merged with the Casuals. Their spirit, in name at least, lives on in the Isthmian League.

JANUARY 14

WALSALL 2-0 ARSENAL – THE GREATEST
GIANT-KILLING ACT OF ALL
(1933)

'When the history of our club comes to be written, there can be little doubt that January 14, 1933 will be given prominence in it as a Red Letter Day.' Rarely can there have been more prescient words in a programme than the ones printed in Walsall's, ahead of the club's third-round FA Cup tie against Herbert Chapman's Arsenal in 1933.

In 1930, Arsenal had won the FA Cup. In 1931, they were league champions. In 1932, they were runners up in both competitions. When they arrived at Fellows Park in early January 1933, they were top of the First Division and on their way to another title, having registered some stupendously silly scorelines, including 6-1 vs Sunderland, 8-2 vs Leicester, 7-1 vs Wolves and 9-2 vs Sheffield United.

Walsall stood tenth in Division Three (North) behind teams such as Gateshead, Accrington Stanley, Barrow, Southport and Stockport County (who had recently beaten them 5-0).

What followed defied the form book, to say the least. Whilst it is true that Chapman had decided to play some of his reserves in the match, the team still boasted both Alex James and David Jack, Britain's first £10,000 player. Jack was joined up front by a nervous reserve called Charlie Walsh, who spent most of the afternoon getting in the way of his partner. At one point Walsh accidentally tackled Jack as he prepared to shoot. With half an hour to go, Walsall's Gilbert Alsop headed home a corner. Five minutes later, Alsop was scythed down by Tommy Black in the area. Bill Sheppard's spot kick made it two and with Arsenal impotent up front, the most sensational result in the Cup's 61-year history was sealed. Chapman was not a happy man. Neither Walsh nor Black ever played for the club again.

WORCESTER CITY 2-1 LIVERPOOL: FARCE
USHERS IN THE SHANKLY ERA
(1959)

The Liverpool side of Billy Liddell and Albert Stubbins were the first post-war league champions, landing the title on an exciting last day which saw them pip Manchester United and Wolverhampton Wanderers by a point. After that title win the club went into a steep decline. They reached the 1950 FA Cup final, only to be outplayed by Arsenal and lose 2-0; their title-winning manager George Kay had to retire through ill health in 1951; and by 1954, under Don Welsh, they had suffered relegation for the first time in over half a century.

They would not find it easy to get back to the top flight. After a non-descript first season in the Second Division, when they finished mid-table, the next four seasons would see them finish third, third, fourth and fourth, agonisingly just out of reach of the promotion places each time (before play-offs were introduced). It wasn't considered good enough for a club which had won five titles. Welsh was sacked in 1956 and his replacement Phil Taylor would follow him out of the door within three years.

The result that effectively did for Taylor was the most embarrassing in the club's history. Drawn away at Worcester City in the third round of the 1959 FA Cup, they performed abysmally on a wet, bald pitch at St George's Lane. Worcester's teenage striker Tommy Skuse opened the scoring for the Southern League side and Liverpool's Dick White lobbed into his own net to gift them a second. Liverpool's futile reply was a hotly disputed Geoff Twentyman penalty, which only seemed to heighten their embarrassment. Worcester were not short of quality – their captain Roy Paul had lifted the FA Cup for Manchester City three years earlier – but this result was still considered beyond the pale. When Taylor's men started the next season sluggishly, he was sacked in November. Still, there was a silver lining. The man lined up to replace him was Bill Shankly.

JANUARY 16

QUEEN'S PARK FINALLY CONCEDE A GOAL –
AFTER EIGHT YEARS
(1875)

'Tonight at half past eight o'clock a number of gentlemen met at No.3 Eglinton Terrace for the purpose of forming a football club.' So ran minutes taken on July 9, 1867 in Glasgow, as the Queen's Park Football Club was founded. Nobody present could have thought it would take nearly eight years before they conceded their first goal.

Queen's Park were utterly dominant in their early years, playing a 2-2-6 formation that pressed other teams back, even if it didn't necessarily result in a goal for themselves. Invited to play in the first FA Cup in 1871, though Queen's Park didn't win the competition, their goal remained intact. Given a bye to the semi-finals, they drew 0-0 with eventual winners Wanderers, but could not afford to stay to contest a replay and were forced to scratch.

They then walked the first ever Scottish Cup in 1873/74, beating Dumbreck 7-0, Eastern Glasgow 1-0, Renton 2-0 and Clydesdale Glasgow 2-0. The following season's Scottish Cup initially saw the run continue. Wins over Western Glasgow (1-0) and West End Glasgow (7-0) lined up a March semi-final against Clydesdale. Before that tie, their proud record would be ended, by Vale of Leven, during a Hampden 'friendly' abandoned after Vale, a goal up, disputed a Queen's equaliser and stormed off. The invincible aura was gone, and in the cup semi-final Clydesdale became the first team to score two against Queen's. Queen's salvaged a draw, won the replay and then the cup.

After a third successive Scottish Cup win in 1876, Queen's finally tasted competitive defeat in 1877, losing a quarter-final to...Vale of Leven. They soon came back, winning the trophy seven more times between 1880 and 1893. Only Rangers and Celtic have a better record.

JANUARY 17

'SONS OF BEN' FORMED: THE SUPPORTERS CLUB WITHOUT A TEAM
(2007)

The football scene in Philadelphia has always been infused with a rebel spirit. The city's North American Soccer League (NASL) franchise in the late 1970s and early 1980s, the Philadelphia Fury, boasted a team featuring such maverick talents as Frank Worthington and Peter Osgood and a boardroom that was literally rock and roll: Rick Wakeman; Peter Frampton; the tour manager of the Rolling Stones and the owners of Chrysalis and A&M Records. Such an attitude lingered on and in 2007 the most out-there supporters association in the world was formed: The Sons of Ben, a group of Philadelphia football fans…who didn't have a team to support.

The main aim of The Sons of Ben, named after US Founding Father Benjamin Franklin and founded on the anniversary of his birthday, was simple: to agitate for a Major League Soccer (MLS) franchise. Within a year they had over 2,000 members and nearly 3,000 pledges to buy a season ticket. They quickly also realised there was another benefit of clubbing together. Just because Philadelphia didn't have a team, it didn't mean The Sons of Ben couldn't do what every other set of supporters in the world do and taunt opposing supporters. That November, they went to the MLS Cup final featuring New England Revolution and Houston Dynamo with the sole purpose of drumming up a rivalry with New England fans. They succeeded, coming under attack from a hail of open drinks cartons after taunting supporters of the four-time MLS Cup runners-up with the catchy song: 'We've won as many cups as you and we don't have a team.'

That song will become redundant in 2010 as, happily for The Sons of Ben, in 2008 the MLS granted Philly its 16th franchise. Having already annoyed New England fans (and the New York Red Bulls, and DC United) excitement is guaranteed even before a ball is kicked.

JANUARY 18

LAZIO STAR SHOT DEAD WHILE PRETENDING TO ROB JEWELLER
(1977)

The Lazio squad of the 1970s were a notorious bunch. At a post-match banquet in Rome held after a Fairs Cup tie against Arsenal in 1970, a brawl broke out between both teams when the English side took umbrage at the leather purses the Italians had given them as gifts. Three years later, after being knocked out of the UEFA Cup by Ipswich Town, Lazio's players threw punches, as well as objects which had been thrown onto the pitch by the crowd, at Bobby Robson's team, before chasing them back to their dressing room. Ipswich were forced to barricade themselves in for over an hour before they felt able to come out.

The Ipswich debacle meant Lazio were banned from Europe for three years, which would prove costly. After landing the club's first *Scudetto* at the end of that 1973/74 season, they were nonetheless unable to compete in the European Cup. It was a self-inflicted setback and it was to be followed by a tragic one, as title-winning coach Tommaso Maestrelli was diagnosed with stomach cancer in 1975 and died a year later.

After that came a setback that was both self-inflicted and tragic. Early in 1977, the club's 28-year-old box-to-box midfield star, Luciano Re Cecconi – a surname which, incidentally, means 'King of the Big Blind Ones' – went into a Rome jewellery shop with two friends and decided to play a practical joke. Entering the shop, he screamed: 'Stop! This is a robbery!' His next – and last – words were uttered after the jeweller, who had his back to the shop, had spun round and shot him. 'It's a joke, it's a joke,' gasped Re Cecconi. Within 30 minutes he was dead, the Lazio dream gone with him.

JANUARY 19

'PROFESSIONAL' PRESTON DISQUALIFIED
FROM FA CUP
(1884)

Since its inception in 1863, the London-based Football Association had considered amateurism to be one of the game's fundamental principles. Nobody should get paid for playing what was, after all, only a game. Clubs from the rich industrial north, however, did not agree. Teams like Preston North End, Blackburn, Bolton and Darwen argued that players needed to be compensated for the time they took off work. Furthermore, their teams were full of top-quality Scottish players, who were not going to move away from home without reward for their sacrifice. The FA, however, would not budge from their lofty position and amateurism remained.

The problem was not going to go away, however hard the metropolitan elite attempted to ignore it. The situation reached crisis point after the fourth round of the 1883/84 FA Cup, when the amateur side Upton Park visited Preston. Upton Park came away with a 1-1 draw, but before a replay could be contested they complained to the FA that Preston were fielding professionals. Preston had certainly been paying their players, spending over £1,000 a year on wages. Though at the time this was not proved, they were found guilty of importing players and finding them suspiciously highly-paid work, so were disqualified from that season's competition as a result.

The FA then introduced a residency test, designed to halt the flood of 'pseudo-professional' imports. More than 30 clubs from the north were up in arms. At the very least, players had to be compensated for loss of earnings. The clubs decided to pursue the possibility of first setting up a rival Northern Football Association, then a British Football Association with clubs from the midlands and Scotland. Eventually the FA relented, sensing the tide was not going to turn back and a year later, on July 20, 1885, professionalism was legalised.

GARRINCHA'S SAD DECLINE: THE LITTLE BIRD
DIES AGED 49
(1983)

Nobody did more to ensure Brazil won their first two World Cups than Garrincha. After mixed success for the *Seleção* in the first two games in the 1958 tournament, he was thrown into the side for the third, against USSR. As someone once said, the Soviets may have been able to put a man in space, but they couldn't mark Garrincha: within 40 seconds he had stripped two Russian defenders down the right and hammered a shot against the near post. Brazil's campaign was kick-started. Less than 20 seconds later, Pelé hit a post again. Two more minutes elapsed when the Russians, completely disoriented by the opening salvo, were split right down the middle by Didi's ball to Vavá, who scored. Re-energized, Brazil went on to win the cup in style.

Four years later, Pelé limped out of the 1962 competition injured, so it was down to Garrincha to put on a one-man show. He set up the winner against a Spanish side featuring Ferenc Puskás, scored twice in the quarter-final versus England and netted two more in the semi-final against Chile. Garrincha had succumbed to a heavy fever by the time the final came round, but still played to help Brazil retain their trophy.

By that time the sport was taking its toll. His famously bent legs were causing him serious cartilage problems. In 1964 he had a corrective operation, but was never the same thereafter. He retired from international football after Brazil's unsuccessful 1966 World Cup, and while he played on at club level until 1972, his best days were long gone. Always a heavy drinker, he hit the bottle with determination after a car he was driving crashed and killed the mother of his wife, the singer Elza Soares, in 1969. Eight years later Soares divorced him after he hit her in a drunken rage. By 1983 his drinking had reached prodigious levels and after a binge on the morning of January 19, he admitted himself to hospital feeling ill. Having slipped into a coma soon after, the 'Little Bird' died at 6 a.m. the following morning.

JANUARY 21

THE STRIKE THAT NEVER WAS AND THE END
OF THE MAXIMUM WAGE
(1961)

In 1957, Fulham striker Jimmy Hill became the chairman of the Professional
Footballer's Association (PFA). Hill immediately put a proposal to the floor:
the Football League's maximum wage limit of £20 a week should be
scrapped; as should the retain-and-transfer system, which denied a player the
option to leave a club once his contract was up.

Action was not immediately forthcoming, but the climate had definitely
changed. 'John Charles and Jimmy Greaves were going out to Italy and
earning vastly different money,' explained Hill. 'In the end we'd have lost all
of our top-class players to other places who had no maximum wage, so it had
to end.' When in 1960 Newcastle's George Eastham refused to re-sign a
contract and was denied his wish to transfer to Arsenal, the PFA's troops
finally mobilised. The League once again refused to budge on either point, so
a ballot was taken and in November the PFA called for a strike to begin on
January 21.

Negotiating positions became entrenched. The League repeatedly gave
'unequivocal assurances' that they would not agree to the PFA's demands, but
public opinion was against them. There was also pressure from bookmakers,
whose businesses would have suffered from a strike. On January 18, the
action was called off with three days to spare. The League gave in, abolishing
both the wage cap and retain-and-transfer system – though they would renege
on the latter, a situation which would not be resolved until Eastham won a
court case in 1963.

Fulham chairman Tommy Trinder had special cause to rue the agreement.
He had previously gone on record to say he'd pay striker Johnny Haynes
£100 a week, if only he could. 'Poor old Tom was lumbered,' laughed Haynes
years later, 'but I give him credit. He stood by it and paid me £100 a week.'

ARSENAL 1-1 SHEFFIELD UNITED: ENGLISH
FOOTBALL'S FIRST RADIO COMMENTARY
(1927)

George Allison is primarily remembered for managing Arsenal to two league championships and an FA Cup during the 1930s. But he began his career as a journalist, initially joining Arsenal as the editor of their matchday programme before becoming a club director. It was in the media rather than management that Allison first made his mark in the public consciousness, however, when in 1927 he became one of the first ever sports commentators.

The BBC had just become a public corporation at the beginning of the year and with their Royal Charter came the right to cover major sporting events. Allison became aware of the chance to commentate as the BBC planned to use Highbury – only a couple of miles from their Alexandra Palace headquarters – as the venue of its first trial broadcast. He would not, however, get behind the mic to deliver the historic first commentary. The honour of describing Arsenal's league game against Sheffield United fell to former Harlequins rugby player Henry 'Teddy' Wakelam.

To accompany the broadcast, that week's *Radio Times*, along with several other newspapers, printed a plan of the pitch divided into eight numbered squares. Wakelam, who described the action, was joined by co-commentator C.A. Lewis, whose job it was to call out the number of whichever square the ball happened to be in at the time. This system, devised by groundbreaking BBC producer Lance Sieveking, is believed to be the origin of the phrase 'back to square one'.

The match was only heard by a select few in the London region – as was the first FA Cup commentary a week later between Corinthians and Newcastle United – but that year's FA Cup final would reach the entire nation. By then Allison was behind the mic, presumably talking through gritted teeth as Arsenal were shocked by Cardiff City.

JANUARY 23

AUSTRIA'S LEGENDARY 'PAPER MAN' FOUND DEAD IN HIS FLAT
(1939)

Matthias Sindelar, 'der Papierene', was the cutting edge of the greatest international team of the early 1930s: Austria's 'Wunderteam'. They announced themselves by trouncing a highly regarded Scotland 5-0 in May 1931, before going on to cut a swathe through Europe over the next year, beating their arch-rivals Germany 6-0 and 5-0; Switzerland 2-0 and 8-1; Hungary 8-2 (after a 2-2 draw) and Italy 2-1.

Sindelar was the star of the side, a wiry striker who scored 27 goals in 43 appearances for his country. The 1934 World Cup probably came too late for the Wunderteam, although pre-tournament friendlies saw wins over Switzerland (3-2), Hungary (5-2) and Italy (4-2). At the World Cup, Austria made the semi-finals but Sindelar was overpowered by Italy midfielder Luis Monti and they lost by a single goal. A bitter third-place play-off against Germany was also lost, defender Karl Sesta showboating by sitting on the ball, only to be robbed of it and forced to watch in horror as the decisive goal flew in.

By the time the next World Cup came round, Austria had been swallowed up by the Anschluss and Sindelar had reportedly refused to play for the new 'Greater Germany' team. His final game for Austria was against Germany in the infamous April 1938 'Alliance Game'; in a 2-0 win, he scored the first and, if some sources are to be believed, celebrated the other by dancing in front of the Nazi dignitaries (though naturally there was no mention of such a display in the Nazi paper *Völkischer Beobachter*).

Less than a year after the Alliance Game Sindelar was found dead, gassed in his flat alongside his girlfriend of ten days. Did the Nazis punish him for his defiance? Possibly. Yet neither he nor his companion were Jewish; his 'refusal' to play for Germany could have meant little anyway, as he was 35 and essentially finished by then – and the flats he lived in were known to have defective chimneys. Still the conspiracy theories remain and we will never know for sure.

JANUARY 24

KETTERING TYRES DRIVE THE SHIRT
SPONSORSHIP VANGUARD
(1976)

When former Wolverhampton Wanderers striker Derek Dougan joined Southern League Kettering Town as manager in December 1975, he was given the freedom to run the club exactly as he pleased. 'He will be responsible for the running of the team and affairs off the field, such as administrative work and advertising,' explained chairman John Nash, who possibly didn't quite know what he was letting himself in for.

Within a month of Dougan's appointment, he had negotiated a £4,000 deal with local garage Kettering Tyres, and in a Southern League game against Bath City on January 24, 1976, Kettering ran out with the firm's name across their chests, becoming the first club in Britain to carry shirt sponsorship. The move drew opprobrium from the FA, who immediately wrote to Dougan – already known in football's corridors of power as a troublemaker in his role as chairman of the Professional Footballer's Association – ordering him to pack it in. 'I can find no mention of this clause in the rule books and until it appears I shall ignore the FA's request,' said Dougan defiantly, pointing out the FA's hypocrisy in allowing the England national team to run about in tracksuits advertising Admiral sports clothing on the back.

The FA fought hard and Dougan was eventually forced to back down, but not before he had changed the wording on the shirts to 'Kettering T', which he claimed stood for Town and not Tyres. A couple of months later the threat of a £1,000 fine was considered too much for a small club like Kettering and the letters were removed.

Along with Derby and Bolton, the club put forward an official proposal to the FA on shirt sponsorship, which was accepted in June 1977. Sadly Kettering could not subsequently find a sponsor, but Derby would begin the season wearing shirts sponsored by Saab, with many of the players driving their cars. Whether the Derby squad got their free wheels balanced at the relatively local Kettering Tyres is not recorded.

CRYSTAL PALACE 1-1 MANCHESTER UNITED:
SIMMONS 0-1 CANTONA
(1995)

Eric Cantona was an accident waiting to happen. By the age of 25 he had allegedly punched one team mate in the eye; shoved his boots in the face of another; been banned from the French national team for calling the coach a 'sack of shit'; received a suspension for flinging his shirt at a referee and upon being suspended again for throwing the ball at another ref, carefully addressed each member of the disciplinary hearing as an 'idiot', before retiring from football in a fit of pique.

Having come out of retirement and arrived at Manchester United via Leeds in 1992, he appeared to have calmed down. Only relatively, though – on the subs' bench at Galatasaray in 1993 he punched the Turkish side's reserve goalkeeper, then received a red card for calling the referee a cheat – but such episodes were trifles compared to what had gone before. And nothing compared to what was about to follow at Selhurst Park.

Few recall the match particulars now. David May gave United the lead just after half-time and Gareth Southgate equalised with eleven minutes to go. Everyone remembers that evening for the drama just after May's goal. Cantona was sent off for a kick at Richard Shaw. As he walked towards the dressing rooms, Crystal Palace fan Matthew Simmons rushed down to the front of the stand to scream abuse. Simmons claimed he had simply chirruped, 'It's an early bath for you!' Cantona leapt over the hoardings and crumped both his feet into Simmons's chest.

Iconic, but costly. Cantona was banned until October, leaving new signing Andy Cole to lead the line in the title chase with Blackburn Rovers. Cole missed two chances to convert a winner from six yards on the final day of the season at West Ham and Blackburn won the title by a point.

JANUARY 26

TEN IMPRISONED FOR MATCH-FIXING CONSPIRACY
(1965)

Sheffield Wednesday's 2-0 loss at Ipswich Town on December 1, 1962 looked like a predictable result. Ipswich were the reigning champions and had beaten Wednesday the previous season 2-1 at Portman Road and 4-1 away at Hillsborough. But all was not as it seemed.

Wednesday striker David 'Bronco' Layne had recently watched a match at his old club Mansfield Town, after which he had a chat with Mansfield player Jimmy Gauld. Gauld informed him that some players were placing bets on matches they were involved in. The seed and idea sown, Layne later mentioned the scam to team mates Tony Kay and Peter Swan. Kay was soon to win the league after a transfer to Everton, while Swan was a defender thought of by Alf Ramsey as 'top of the list' and a near-certainty for England's 1966 World Cup team. 'Give me £50 and I'll get you twice your money,' said Layne – and so the bets were placed.

'We lost the game fair and square though I don't know what I'd have done if we'd been winning,' Swan later admitted. 'It would have been easy for me to give away a penalty or score an own goal.' Kay played a blinder and was named man-of-the-match in the *Sunday People* – a savage irony, as it would be that newspaper that broke the scandal two years later in 1964, when Gauld sold his confession for £7,000.

Ten men in all were subsequently found guilty of conspiracy to defraud. Gauld was sentenced to four years in prison. 'You have befouled professional football and corrupted your friends and acquaintances,' said the judge. Kay, Swan and Layne were given four months. 'The greater your distinction in football, the greater your fall,' was the verdict. All three were banned by the FA for life. Though the ban was lifted seven years later, their careers were effectively over by that time.

BARBADOS 3-2 GRENADA: BOTH TEAMS
TRY TO SCORE OWN GOALS
(1994)

For such a young competition, the Caribbean Cup has suffered more than its fair share of travails. Its second staging, in 1990, was abandoned before completion. Not because St Maarten, Cayman Islands, French St Martin, Anguilla and British Virgin Islands were drawn together in a preliminary group which nobody seems certain was ever played or not; nor because Tropical Storm Arthur, a 70mph near-whirlwind, swung close to the host islands of Trinidad and Tobago. It was abandoned because hours before the scheduled final between the hosts and Jamaica, radical Islamic group Jamaat al Muslimeen stormed the Trinidadian parliament and overthrew the government, taking the prime minister hostage for six days before surrendering.

Despite the coup at the cup, the tournament's most infamous incident came three years later, in a final preliminary group match between Barbados and Grenada. Barbados needed to beat their opponents by two clear goals to qualify for the next round and at 2-0 up with seven minutes to go were on course. However, at that point Grenada pulled one back and Barbados were heading out.

Strangely for a league system, all drawn games went to sudden-death extra-time, where a goal would count double in the goals-for column. So with three minutes remaining, Barbados whacked one into their own net in order to enforce an extra period where they had a chance to restore their two-goal cushion in one fell swoop. Hilariously, this meant a goal for Grenada during the last three minutes at either end would see them through, so Barbados were forced to defend both nets until the final whistle. Barbados managed it and were rewarded by scoring the winner four minutes into extra-time. Much good it did them; they went out in the first round of the final stages.

JANUARY 28

LUTON 2-6 MAN CITY: LAW SCORES
ALL SIX – BUT STILL LOSES
(1961)

The rain in Luton had been torrential all day, and the saturated Kenilworth Road pitch was in a hell of a state. There seemed little chance of Luton's fourth-round FA Cup tie with Manchester City taking place, but the cloud cover broke and the game went ahead. Luton were soon happy that it had as within 18 minutes Alec Ashworth had put them 2-0 up.

A minute later, the game began to turn, Manchester City striker Denis Law pulling one back. It was to be the beginning of an outstanding personal performance. By half-time he had completed his hat-trick and then scored another three between the 51st and 66th minutes. Law's joy was to last approximately 180 seconds. The driving rain had by now returned and was turning an already heavy pitch into a total quagmire. Three minutes after making it 6-2, with Luton in total disarray, the referee abandoned the game. Law was dismayed – none of his goals would count in the record books – but in truth there was little option as in some places the water on the pitch was ankle deep.

Four days later the game was replayed on what was described in the *Guardian* as a 'pudding-like' pitch. The newspaper reported: 'When the players came out to begin the encounter they sank in places to below the welts of their boots, leaving prints as clear as an Abominable Snowman's.' With the sun shining this time, Luton again raced into a two-goal lead with Ashworth again scoring the opener, Jim Fleming the second. This time, however, there would be no comeback. Law pulled one back which did count in the record books before half-time, but another Ashworth goal in the second half sealed a 3-1 Luton win. 'It's not every day that you score six goals,' recalled Law, 'and I never did it again. The most I managed in a game that counted was four, which I got a couple of times. But then the heavens opened. Obviously it wasn't meant to be.'

YEOVIL 2-1 SUNDERLAND: THE BANK
OF ENGLAND BROKEN
(1949)

When Sunderland came to Southern League Yeovil Town's The Huish ground to play a fourth-round FA Cup tie, nobody expected anything other than an easy win for the First Division club. Sunderland were fast acquiring a reputation as the most ambitious club in the country. They would soon be known as 'The Bank of England' thanks to their outrageously high spending in the transfer market and had paid a record £20,500 on the great inside-forward Len Shackleton. Part-time Yeovil, meanwhile, had a weekly wage bill of less than £100 per week.

Yeovil had two things in their favour: their sloping pitch, which was eight feet higher at one end than the other, and player-manager Alec Stock's egg, sherry and glucose punch which they would consume before matches. That seemed to do the trick: Sunderland didn't perform for the first half hour, by which time Stock had hammered home a shot on the turn. The visitors proceeded to pepper the home goal, only to find goalkeeper Dickie Dyke – who had only played for the club once before – in inspired form. Ex-England player Jackie Robinson eventually scrambled an equaliser with 15 minutes left, forcing extra-time, but Yeovil would not relent. After 104 minutes, in thick fog, Ray Wright pounced on a bizarre overhead clearance by Shackleton and fed Eric Bryant for the winner.

The result was seen at the time as the biggest shock in football's history. To put it into context, Yeovil were trounced 8-0 by Manchester United in the next round. The fact the victory came about as a result of an error by the game's most expensive player was a fact not lost on many. This would not be the last indignity heaped upon 'The Bank'. Eight years later, having won nothing despite their heavy spending, they were found guilty of making illegal payments to players. The season after that they tasted relegation for the first time since joining the League in 1891.

JANUARY 30

HODDLE TELLS *THE TIMES*: WHAT YOU SOW, YOU REAP
(1999)

Glenn Hoddle was statistically the most successful England manager since Sir Alf Ramsey and his 1998 World Cup squad one of the very few to come home from a tournament to bouquets not brickbats. Yet he was sacked less than three years into his reign.

The 1998 World Cup campaign was a success for Hoddle, albeit a qualified one. England made it to the finals with a tactically savvy 0-0 draw in Italy and were unlucky to go out on penalties in the second round against Argentina when down to ten men. Sol Campbell had a potential winner disallowed nine minutes from time after Alan Shearer's off-the-ball transgression. On the flip side, though, was Hoddle's controversial reluctance to play Michael Owen and David Beckham in the early matches. He picked them only when it was too late to win the group and avoid that difficult second-round Argentina showdown, arguably heaping so much pressure on Beckham that he snapped.

Nonetheless, Hoddle was highly regarded, but publication of his World Cup diaries saw him break dressing-room *omertá*. As well as irritating several members of his squad, it laid bare his poor man-management. At one point he told Beckham to stop practising free kicks because 'you are not good enough to do that skill'. He arguably should have gone then. When, soon after, he gave an interview to *The Times* explaining his views on reincarnation, the die was cast: 'You and I have been physically given two hands and two legs and half-decent brains. Some people have not been born like that for a reason. The karma is working from another lifetime. What you sow, you have to reap.' On ITV's *This Morning* the Monday after, Prime Minister Tony Blair opined it would be 'very difficult for him to stay'. It was, and 24 hours later Hoddle was dismissed by the FA. What Hoddle had reaped, he had sown.

JANUARY 31

GHANA 0-2 IVORY COAST: ELEPHANTS
SENT TO MILITARY CAMP
(2000)

The 2000 African Nations Cup did not start well for Ivory Coast. The team were expected to progress from their group, but started disastrously, drawing 1-1 with little-fancied minnows Togo in their opening match. They were then thrashed 3-0 in their second game by Cameroon, one of the strongest nations on the continent, the tournament hosts and eventual champions – a result which meant they needed to win by three clear goals against Ghana in the final group game to progress.

They gave it a good shot. Bonaventure Kalou put Ivory Coast one up just before half-time and Donald-Olivier Sie scored a second with six minutes to play. Despite piling on the pressure the Elephants couldn't score the crucial third goal. They were going home, expecting, as all disappointed squads do, to receive a hot reception on their return. But nobody was expecting the reprisals coming their way.

When Italy were knocked out of the 1966 World Cup they had been pelted with rotten tomatoes. Ivory Coast's punishment was to be sent to military boot camp for three days. 'I asked that you should be taken there so you could reflect for a while,' said General Robert Guei, who had taken over the country in a military coup the previous Christmas Eve. 'You behaved unworthily. You should have avoided us such shame. Next time you will stay there for military service. You will be sent to the barracks until a sense of civic pride gets into your heads.'

Kalou's next high-profile goal came in the 2006 World Cup, the deciding penalty in a 3-2 win over Serbia and Montenegro. The team again headed home after the first round, but this time to a heroes' welcome. General Guei had been killed in the continuing civil war in 2002.

FEBRUARY 1

THE BIRTH OF STANLEY MATTHEWS, FOOTBALL'S KNIGHT
(1915)

From Matt Busby to Alex Ferguson via Tom Finney and Geoff Hurst, plenty of famous footballing figures have been knighted for their services to the sport. But only one man has been given such an honour while still playing the game. Stanley Matthews joined his hometown club Stoke City as a precocious 15-year-old winger in 1930, and in his first full season the club were promoted from the Second Division. Though in his time there Stoke would never feature at the business end of a title race, they did finish fourth twice: once in 1935/36, the second time in the first season after World War II. At which point, aged 32, he bade his leave of manager Bob McGrory, with whom he'd had several disputes over money, and left for Blackpool.

There were to be no league challenges at Bloomfield Road either. Blackpool finished as high as second in 1955/56, but they were 11 points behind Manchester United and never in it; but that wasn't really the point as the FA Cup was the big prize back then. After losing in the 1948 and 1951 finals, Matthews would have his day in 1953 against Bolton, his wing-play helping Blackpool come back from 3-1 down to win 4-3 in the last minute. 'It would be a fitting gesture if this modest, unassuming star – the perfect gentleman both on and off the field – was given the knightly accolade of Sir Stanley,' enthused a prescient *Sunday Express*, albeit jumping the gun by 12 years.

Matthews' England career never quite took off, despite the fact that both fans and Press loved him. The selectors dropped him for the first two games of the ill-fated 1950 World Cup campaign, meaning Matthews avoided the USA debacle, but he did return for the 1954 competition, at the age of 39. In 1961, he returned to Stoke, struggling in the Second Division, where history repeated itself, Matthews leading the club to promotion in his first full season. In the 1965 New Year Honours List Matthews was knighted, four months before he bowed out as the oldest player ever to feature in the top flight.

CATANIA 1-2 PALERMO: ITALY STOPS
AFTER MURDER OF POLICEMAN
(2007)

Two killings in six days at separate stadiums cast a gloomy shadow over an Italy still revelling in their 2006 World Cup victory, seven months previously. The first death came when an official was kicked in the neck trying to break up a fight at an amateur game in the southern town of Luzzi; the second involved the death of a policeman at the Serie A Sicilian derby between Catania and Palermo and prompted a nationwide football ban.

The problems began long before kick off when rowdy Palermo fans were admitted late into the Stadio Massimino. Palermo went one up through Andrea Caracciolo. Catania fans disputed the goal and started throwing firecrackers and homemade bombs onto the pitch. The police fired back with tear gas, and on 58 minutes the referee suspended play. Forty minutes later the players were back on. Catania's Fabio Caserta was quick to equalise, but in the 83rd minute David Di Michele scored a controversial winner. After the game rioting fans spilled out onto the streets of Catania. More than 100 people were injured. 38-year-old policeman Filippo Raciti received a blow to his liver from a sharp object thrown by a fan and later bled to death in hospital.

'Football cannot last for much longer,' raged Palermo coach Francesco Guidolin. For the first time in Serie A history, play was suspended for a week. Catania were forced to play the remainder of the season at a neutral ground. Politicians and football authorities vowed to tighten up stadium security after Raciti's murder, which had highlighted the tensions between police and Ultra fan groups.

In November that year, Italian police and fans clashed again when Lazio fan Gabriele Sandri was hit by a stray bullet from an officer's gun while asleep in the back of a car outside a petrol station. Lazio fans were pictured with a banner: 'For Raciti you stopped the league, but the death of a fan doesn't matter.'

BOCA JUNIORS 5-2 RIVER PLATE: THE INSTANT
SUPERCLASICO SUPERSTAR
(1974)

Carlos María García Cambón wasn't a man to hang around. In his debut season as a professional footballer, the 20-year-old striker helped his team Chacarita Juniors to their one and only league title, the 1969 Metropolitano championship. Five seasons later he had earned himself a transfer to Boca Juniors – where he would make even more of an instant impact.

Thrown into the first team for his debut against Boca's fierce rivals River Plate, García Cambón took all of two minutes to open his account, latching onto a long ball and smashing it past River Plate keeper Ubaldo Fillol. That would have been enough to endear him to a packed Bombonera, but the new signing was far from finished. He scored three more goals, the last two turning a precarious 3-2 lead into one of the biggest routs in the history of the *Superclasico* derby.

Whether it should be considered the greatest individual performance in a *Superclasico* is a moot point. Diego Maradona scored a hat-trick in a 3-0 Boca win in April 1981, a game which went a long way to deciding that year's Metropolitano and one which saw Maradona beat the same defender twice during the same mazy dribble before waltzing round the unfortunate Fillol – once again the fall guy – and dinking the ball into the net. In November 1977 River Plate's Pedro González scored a last-minute winner after embarking on a 40-yard Maradona-esque run to secure a 2-1 victory which effectively landed the league. But García Cambón's debut is the only time a single player has ever scored four in a *Superclasico*, and is arguably the greatest debut in the history of South American football.

FEBRUARY 4

GUN-TOTING JOURNALIST BECOMES BRAZIL MANAGER
(1969)

During 1968, the Brazilian national side was a shambles. They lost matches against West Germany, Czechoslovakia, Mexico (twice) and Paraguay. With the 1970 World Cup looming on the horizon, five defeats in a calendar year was not a good sign. The press were getting on the team's back, so in what can either be taken as a stroke of genius or an act of insanity, CBF president João Havelange decided to give the managerial job to journalist João Saldanha.

Although some considered it a cynical move designed to stifle newspaper criticism of the team – the rationale being that other hacks wouldn't attack one of their own – it wasn't quite the leftfield appointment it may have seemed. Saldanha, a former Botafogo player turned writer, had been asked to step in as coach of his former club in 1957 and managed to lead them to the state championship.

Saldanha was an immediate success on the field, winning each of his first thirteen games in charge, including a World Cup qualifying campaign which saw Brazil score 23 goals while conceding only two. Off the pitch, however, there were problems. He suggested Pelé could not see properly out of one of his eyes, so should be dropped. He refused to bow to pressure from Brazilian president Emilio Medici to play the military dictator's favourite striker Dario, declaring: 'I don't choose the president's ministry and he can't choose my front line.' When his predecessor as coach, Dorival Yustrich, criticised his managerial skills, Saldanha went looking for him to discuss the matter, toting a loaded pistol.

Accused of being emotionally unstable, in early 1970 he was replaced by Mario Zagallo, who would lead the team Saldanha had crafted to the most famous of all World Cup victories.

HEREFORD 2-1 NEWCASTLE: 'MAC THE MOUTH' SILENCED
(1972)

'Radford... now Tudor's gone down for Newcastle... Radford again... oh what a goal! What a goal! Radford the scorer, Ronnie Radford, and the crowd, the crowd are invading the pitch! And now it will take some time to clear the field.' It was the goal which launched the career of 26-year-old trainee BBC commentator John Motson. Motson had been sent to cover the fourth-round FA Cup replay between Southern League Hereford United and top-flight Newcastle United, a match which had been pencilled in for a brief slot at the end of *Match of the Day*.

The shock result meant it would become the lead match. Hereford had already stunned Newcastle in an amazing 2-2 draw at St James' Park. Brian Owen hit the roof of the Newcastle net after only 17 seconds. Newcastle came back and even took the lead, but Hereford player-boss Colin Addison ensured the replay with a 20-yard shot. 'This was my greatest thrill in football,' said Addison after the match. It wasn't to be his greatest thrill for long.

Malcolm Macdonald announced in his newspaper column that in the replay at Edgar Street he would beat Ted McDougall's record of nine goals in a single FA Cup match, but in the event he only scored one, a header with eight minutes to play. Macdonald's goal looked like being enough, but three minutes later Radford unleashed his 35-yard screamer. Ricky George grabbed a second for Hereford in extra-time to win the tie, a heroic effort in which their right back Roger Griffiths had played for 70 minutes with a cracked fibula.

In a neat symmetry it was the first time a non-league side had beaten a top-flight club since Yeovil knocked out Newcastle's rivals Sunderland in 1949. Macdonald later denied having promised to score ten. 'My paper saw it as an opportunity to get one over a rival,' was his none-too-convincing explanation.

FEBRUARY 6

EIGHT 'BUSBY BABES' PERISH AT MUNICH
(1958)

Manchester United had swaggered into the semi-finals of the European Cup. After beating Red Star Belgrade 2-1 at Old Trafford in their quarter-final first leg, they travelled to Yugoslavia for the return and had the tie wrapped up by half-time. Dennis Viollet put United up within 90 seconds, the same player had a header disallowed on fourteen minutes, Bobby Charlton scored a 30-yard screamer to make it 2-0 on 30 minutes, then added another a minute later after Duncan Edwards caused mayhem in the Red Star area. Red Star scored three in the second half to draw level, but it would not have been enough as they had needed four to force a play-off. The 'Busby Babes' would get another chance to break Real Madrid's stronghold on the European Cup and claim their place in history.

The Babes would indeed be guaranteed their place in history, but in the most tragic way imaginable. In the wake of the Superga disaster, many clubs divided their teams in two and sent the parties off in separate aircrafts. United did not. Their return flight from Belgrade stopped to refuel at Munich, where it was snowing. The pilot aborted two attempts to take off for the second leg of the journey. On the third, the plane could not pick up enough speed for lift-off due to the amount of slush on the runway and skidded off at 157mph into a nearby house. Upon impact, 21 of the plane's 44 passengers were killed, including seven of the United team: Geoff Bent, Roger Byrne, Eddie Colman, Mark Jones, David Pegg, Tommy Taylor and Billy Whelan. Byrne was the oldest at only 28. Duncan Edwards survived the crash, but died 15 days later.

Red Star Belgrade responded to the tragedy by asking UEFA for Manchester United to become 'Honorary Champions' of Europe. Their request was not granted. In May, United won the first leg of their semi-final against Milan 2-1, but lost the return 4-0. Real Madrid went on to retain the cup.

FEBRUARY 7

ORYX DOUALA 2-1 STADE MALIEN: THE FIRST CLUB CHAMPIONS OF AFRICA
(1964)

When Ghana became the first black African country to gain independence in 1957, the country's head of state, Kwame Nkrumah, decided that sport – and in particular, football – was a way of establishing national pride and unity in a fledgling state. He sent his best coaches to pick up tips in Europe in the hope of building a strong Ghana team and was rewarded when the Black Stars won the 1963 African Cup of Nations. Nkrumah's plan worked. 'It united the whole country,' said striker Joseph Agyeman-Gyau years later. 'Nkrumah was to tell the whole world that we can do things for ourselves and achieve positive results.'

Ghana had also, in 1960, drawn 3-3 with a Real Madrid side featuring Ferenc Puskás and Alfredo di Stéfano in a friendly in Accra, only being denied a win by a last-minute Real equaliser. That result drove Nkrumah to press for an African Champions Cup (ACC), a suggestion which became reality in late 1963. Fourteen teams contested a preliminary tournament which saw four group winners advance to the knock-out finals, to be held, naturally enough, in Ghana. The host nation's Real Republicans were hot favourites to win, but Cameroonian champions Oryx Douala beat them 2-1 in the semi-finals, rendering the final a sparsely attended affair. Oryx beat Stade Malien of Mali 2-1 and were presented with the Kwame Nkrumah Trophy.

There would be no ACC in 1965 as debate raged over the best way to organise the competition, but a knockout format was agreed in time for Stade Abidjan of Ivory Coast to beat Real Bamako of Mali in a two-legged final in 1966. The title has been contested ever since, becoming the African Champions League in 1997. Teams no longer play for the Kwame Nkrumah Trophy, however, as the trophy was awarded to Hafia Conakry of Guinea in 1977 when the club became the first to win the title three times.

FEBRUARY 8

CELTIC 1-3 INVERNESS CALEDONIAN THISTLE:
VIDUKA GOES BALLISTIC
(2000)

John Barnes's first three matches as Celtic manager were won 5-0, 3-0 and 6-0. The results didn't signify much as they were recorded against the worst Aberdeen team in living memory, St Johnstone and Cwmbran. By the time the Scottish Cup came round in February, Barnes was in serious trouble. Celtic trailed Rangers by ten points in the league, had been knocked out of the UEFA Cup and were playing dismally.

Inverness Caledonian Thistle were only in their sixth year of existence, after Highland League clubs Caledonian FC and Inverness Thistle merged to gain entry to the Scottish League. The new club had performed well, finishing in a higher position each season than the one before and winning two promotions along the way. Nevertheless, the Caley Jags were still a division below Celtic and nobody seriously expected them to spring a surprise as they travelled to Parkhead in the cup.

What followed was the most embarrassing debacle in Celtic's history. Trailing 2-1 at half-time, Celtic self-destructed in the changing room, with Mark Viduka and assistant manager Eric Black in a nose-to-nose row, after the striker criticised the efforts of team mates Stephane Mahe and Oliver Tebily. Viduka then, in a fit of pique, flung his boots into the corner and refused to come out for the second half. An ageing Ian Wright replaced Viduka for the second period, during which Inverness scored a third to put the tin lid on Celtic's nightmare.

Normally the result, which saw Barnes off after a mere eight-month reign, would be remembered for that amazing changing room bust-up. Thanks to the *Sun* newspaper, what went down in folklore instead was 'Super Caley Go Ballistic, Celtic Are Atrocious' – a reworking of the *Liverpool Echo*'s 1976 Ian Callaghan-inspired 'Super Cally Is Fantastic, QPR Atrocious'.

FEBRUARY 9

TREVOR FRANCIS BECOMES BRITAIN'S FIRST £1M PLAYER
(1979)

Nottingham Forest's actual outlay on Britain's first £1m footballer was substantially less than the price on the tag. Expenditure on the balance sheet allowed the avoidance of a large corporation tax bill, plus a rebate on the previous year's payments to boot. Nevertheless, despite Forest effectively laying out only £400,000 in ready cash, a million-pound player is a million-pound player, whichever way you spin it. Especially as, at the time, the British transfer record was £516,000, paid by West Bromwich Albion for Middlesbrough's David Mills.

Football had come a long way since Sunderland striker Alf Common became the first £1,000 player on February 14, 1905 by moving to Middlesbrough. It was another eight years before a £2,000 fee was paid (George Utley leaving Barnsley for Sheffield United in 1913). It took until 1928 for Arsenal to break the £10,000 barrier, by signing David Jack from Bolton. Those signings were all world as well as British records, but when River Plate spent £23,000 on Bernabe Ferreyra in 1932, the world-record transfer fee would not be broken by a British club again until Newcastle signed Alan Shearer for £15m in 1996.

Jimmy Greaves narrowly avoided becoming Britain's first £100,000 player in November 1961, Spurs boss Bill Nicholson agreeing a fee with Milan of £99,999 for precisely that reason. A year later Manchester United would have no such worries, splashing out £115,000 on Torino's Denis Law. By the time Forest broke the British seven-figure barrier 17 years later, Giuseppe Savoldi had already moved from Bologna to Napoli for £1.2m in 1975. Three years after that, Paolo Rossi left Juventus for Vicenza for £1.75m. The Francis deal was money well spent in comparison, though, as within four months of joining Forest, he scored the winning goal in the European Cup final against Malmo.

FEBRUARY 10

ARGENTINA 2-0 BRAZIL: A TEN-YEAR HIATUS BEGINS
(1946)

Argentina and Brazil first competed in two unofficial friendlies in Buenos Aires in 1914. Argentina won the first encounter 3-0, Brazil's *Seleção* the second 1-0 a week later. Their rivalry has bubbled along nicely ever since. Prior to a match in 1920, an Argentinian newspaper published a derogatory article about the Brazilian side which led to several of their players dropping out. Brazil fielded only seven players for the match, so Argentina did likewise (and won 3-1). In the final of the 1937 South American Championship, Brazil walked off the pitch. Brazil were trailing 2-0 with only seconds remaining, but claimed their players had been racially abused.

In January 1939, a staging of an irregular tournament between the two countries, the Copa Roca, took some thirteen months to complete. An initial 5-1 victory for Argentina was soon followed by a controversial 3-2 Brazilian win, sealed after a hotly disputed last-minute penalty resulted in the entire Argentinian side flouncing off and Brazil converting the kick with no opposing keeper in goal. As a result of the brouhaha that followed, it took over a year to stage a third match, which was drawn, then Argentina finally won the tournament with a 3-0 win in the fourth match.

Things really got out of hand after another Copa Roca game in 1945 saw Brazil win 6-2, when their striker Ademir Menezes fractured Argentinian Jose Batagliero's leg. When the sides next met, in the 1946 South American Championship decider in Buenos Aires, all hell broke loose. Brazilian Jair Rosa Pinto went in studs-up on José Salomón, breaking the Argentine's leg in two places. Salomón's team mate Juan Fonda squared up to Jair. Chico rushed in to grab Fonda by the shirt, at which point four Argentinians descended on Chico and began to give him a royal shoeing. A crowd invasion took place and after the police waded in to the crowd, the teams retreated to the changing rooms. Eventually order was restored, the teams coming out to complete the match, which Argentina won 2-0.

With relations soured, the countries did not play again for ten years until they were finally drawn together in the 1956 South American Championship. Things have never been quite as heated since.

THE ORIGINAL CONTINENTAL CHAMPIONSHIP BEGINS
(1948)

Conmebol's blue riband club competition, the Copa Libertadores, was launched in 1960 as a direct response to the success of the European Cup, which had been in existence since 1955. Yet South America can nevertheless claim the world's first ever continental champions, thanks to a one-off 1948 tournament organised by Chile's Colo Colo.

Having won Chile's 1947 championship, Colo Colo invited six other teams to compete for the Copa de Campeones in order to find the best club in South America. Colo Colo were joined by the national champions of Uruguay and Argentina, Nacional and River Plate; the Peruvian runners up Municipal and from countries with no national championships, Litoral of Bolivia; Emelec of Ecuador and Vasco da Gama of Brazil. The tournament, a round-robin league, would open with a 2-2 draw between Colo Colo and Emelec and be decided when Vasco da Gama held River Plate in the last round of matches to secure the title from the Argentinian side by one point.

The victorious Vasco line-up included Albino Friaça, who would go on to score Brazil's goal in their 2-1 defeat to Uruguay in the final match of the 1950 World Cup along with Barbosa, Brazil's goalkeeper and scapegoat for that infamous game. Whether having been crowned the world's first ever continental champions made up in later years for the pain of their defeat in the 'Fateful Final' is unknown, but highly unlikely.

While a success on the pitch, the Copa de Campeones was a financial disaster, and the idea was canned until UEFA proved such a tournament was workable. In 1960 Conmebol tried again, when Peñarol of Uruguay won the first title with a team built around Alberto Spencer. Spencer, with 54 goals, is still the all-time leading Copa Libertadores scorer.

FEBRUARY 12

ROBERT HOYZER ARRESTED FOR MATCH-FIXING SCANDAL IN GERMANY
(2005)

When Regionalliga side SC Paderborn took on Bundesliga giants SV Hamburg in the first round of the DFB-Pokal (the German FA Cup) in August 2004, nobody expected them to win. Less so when Christian Rahn and Emile Mpzena had put Hamburg 2-0 by the half-hour mark. But by half-time Paderborn had remarkably levelled the score. Mpzena had been sent off five minutes after his goal for Hamburg disputing a very questionable Paderborn penalty, which Guido Spork converted; then minutes later Rene Mueller made it 2-2. Paderborn scored again on the hour through Daniel Cartus, before Spock scored another soft penalty eight minutes from time. The amazing result when referee Robert Hoyzer blew the final whistle was 4-2 to Paderborn. A month later, Hamburg manager Klaus Toppmoller was sacked.

It was soon revealed that the amazing result was no accident. Referee Hoyzer, once described by the Hamburger Abendblatt newspaper as possessing a 'fashion model's body' and could be 'the brother of Richard Gere', had fixed the match. Toppmoller was outraged, claiming Hoyzer had cost him his job (although Hamburg had already lost their first two league games that season). After a series of investigations, Hoyzer admitted the tie was one of a series of games he had fixed in return for cash from three Croatian brothers who ran a gambling ring from sports bar Café King in Berlin. Hoyzer received up to £14,000 a game – with the odd plasma TV thrown in.

After being given a lifetime refereeing ban, Hoyzer was arrested the following February and jailed for two years in November, much to the embarrassment of the DFB, who had previously called him 'a huge talent with splendid prospects'. Not since the Bundesliga matchfixing scandal of 1971 had German football been so exposed; on the eve of Germany's 2006 World Cup, it couldn't have come at a worse time.

FEBRUARY 13

ARSENAL 2-1 SHEFFIELD UNITED:
KANU'S NIGHTMARE DEBUT
(1999)

Nwankwo Kanu only needed 12 minutes to make his mark in English football. Having recently completed a £4.5m transfer from Internazionale to Arsenal, the Nigerian striker came on in the 64th minute of his new club's fifth-round FA Cup tie against Sheffield United at Highbury. He was soon to instigate one of the biggest brouhahas the world's oldest football tournament had ever seen.

With a quarter of an hour to go, Sheffield United's Lee Morris went down with cramp, so his goalkeeper Alan Kelly kicked the ball out of play so he could receive treatment. Sporting convention dictated that Arsenal should return possession to the Blades once Kelly was up and running again, which is what Ray Parlour did when he threw the ball back into the United half towards Kelly. Kanu, however, seemingly unaware of the unwritten rule, latched onto Parlour's throw, raced down the right wing and crossed to Marc Overmars in the centre who, with the majority of both teams' players standing stunned in the centre circle, scored a tap-in.

Cue bedlam. As Kanu looked on in bemusement, United manager Steve Bruce twice gestured for his players to return to the dressing room, though striker Graham Stuart eventually talked him out of taking the team off the pitch. Arsenal keeper David Seaman offered to let United score directly from the kick off, but the referee threatened to send the entire home team off if that happened. After a seven-minute hiatus, the match resumed and ended in a 2-1 win for Arsenal.

'I have never felt so angry and bitter,' said Bruce after the match, but within 19 minutes of full-time Arsenal manager Arsene Wenger offered to replay the tie. 'Kanu is new to this country and did not know what was going on,' he said. 'Now he has got the whole world on his back. We did not want to win a game like that, it is not the Arsenal way.' The players returned ten days later, where the 2-1 scoreline was replicated. Despite Arsenal's largesse, United still harboured some resentment, as they had been 14 minutes from taking the tie to a replay at Bramall Lane. 'We were still disappointed,' admitted Kelly. Arsenal went on to reach the semi-final, which they lost to Manchester United by a brilliant goal from Ryan Giggs.

FEBRUARY 14

PRESTON NORTH END 1-0 SHEFFIELD WEDNESDAY: DOOLEY LOSES A LEG
(1953)

Derek Dooley was in the form of his life. The Sheffield Wednesday striker had scored 46 times in 30 matches in 1951/52, a total which amounted to 46% of his club's goals that season as they won the Second Division championship. By February the following season he had continued scoring at an outstanding rate. A powerful 23-year-old who was adding some subtleties to his game during his first season in top-flight football, Dooley had amassed 16 goals from his first 20 games of the new season and was being talked of as a real prospect. However his 21st game of that campaign would be his last ever.

Valentine's Day 1953 was a lovely one for Preston North End. A second half goal from Tom Finney gave them a 1-0 victory over Wednesday at Deepdale and sent them to the top of the league. By the time the final whistle blew, however, Dooley was already in Preston Royal Infirmary, his right shinbone having been snapped in two places after challenging North End keeper George Thompson for a 50-50 ball. Dooley's leg was reset and cast in plaster, but before he left hospital he complained he could no longer feel his toes. The cast was removed and a scratch was found on the back of his leg. Gas gangrene had set in, the surgeon assuming it had 'entered from the soil through abrasions'. Despite a police car whisking anti-gangrene serum to Preston from Manchester, it was too late as four days after the match, in order to save his life, surgeons were forced to amputate the leg above the knee. 'I shall have to think about the future,' said a surprisingly chipper Dooley six days later. 'I hope it will be something in football.'

Dooley went on to become Wednesday Manager in 1971 only to fall out bitterly with the club after they sacked him in 1973 – on Christmas Eve. Within months he joined arch-rivals Sheffield United as Commercial Manager.

FEBRUARY 15

REPUBLIC OF IRELAND 1-0 ENGLAND:
THE LANSDOWNE ROAD RIOT
(1995)

Since taking over as England coach from the hapless Graham Taylor in January 1994, Terry Venables had yet to taste defeat in the role, but performances in a series of Wembley friendlies had not been impressive. Apart from a 5-0 win over Greece, England had drawn against Norway and Romania, and laboured to wins over Denmark, USA and Nigeria. For the first quarter of their first match of 1995, a minor humiliation looked on the cards. England were being played off the park by the Republic of Ireland at Lansdowne Road and were already a goal down as a result of David Kelly's 22nd-minute strike. Their on-the-field travails were, however, about to pale into insignificance.

With 27 minutes played, England supporters in the top tier of the West Stand began to rip out the wooden seats and hurl them into the tier below and onto the pitch. The referee led the players off. England captain David Platt gestured to the rioting fans in the hope they would calm down and was nearly hit with a lump of wood. The match was abandoned as the Irish police waded into the melee wielding truncheons, applied liberally to the skulls of the troublemakers. Fifty people were injured as a result of the riot. Venables described the events as 'an embarrassment', while Ireland manager Jack Charlton was even more forthright: 'I hate this. We've never had anything like this in this country. When I played for England I never experienced anything like this before. The English should be ashamed about what went on tonight.'

There would be concerns that England would lose the right to host Euro '96, but their fans happily got their house in order by the tournament, which passed off without a major incident. The England team also improved as the year went on, thrashing a Hong Kong League XI 1-0.

FEBRUARY 16

EGYPT 4-0 ETHIOPIA: THE FIRST AFRICAN CHAMPIONS
(1957)

The first ever African Nations Cup was a disorganised shambles. Held to mark the foundation of the Confederation of African Football – which had been agreed upon by representatives of Egypt, Sudan, Ethiopia and South Africa in a Lisbon hotel room in June 1956 – the championship was to be played in a brand-new stadium in Khartoum. A draw was made pairing the four founder members into two semi-finals: Egypt would play Sudan, while Ethiopia would take on South Africa.

The federation insisted that South Africa field a multi-racial side. South Africa, pursuing its policy of apartheid, refused, insisting they would only send either an all-white or an all-black team. This stance was unacceptable to the federation who refused to budge, so South Africa withdrew. The withdrawal meant the inaugural African Nations Cup would be contested by only three teams. A proposal was submitted to reorganise the competition into a round-robin mini-league, but Ethiopia refused it, successfully arguing that they were entitled to a bye into the final as a result of South Africa's withdrawal. Much good it did them: Egypt beat the hosts Sudan 2-1 in the only semi-final, before spanking the Ethiopians 4-0 in the final – 'El Diba' (Mohammed Dhiab Attar) scoring all four.

With many African nations still colonised or too poor to compete, the tournament took a while to grow. In 1959 the same three teams competed. This time a round-robin system was used. Ethiopia were again thrashed 4-0 by Egypt, who then won the decider against Sudan with an injury-time goal. Ethiopia went on to gain revenge over Egypt in the 1962 final with a 4-2 extra-time win at home. Soon the tournament caught on, in part thanks to Ghana and Tunisia's exciting teams of the 1960s. By 1968, 15 nations had entered the competition, bringing with them a need for pre-qualification. The cup had arrived.

FEBRUARY 17

REAL MADRID 0-5 BARCELONA: CRUYFF, BARÇA'S VERY OWN DI STÉFANO
(1974)

In 1955, Real Madrid stole Alfredo di Stéfano right from under Barcelona's noses, then went on to win five European Cups in a row with him at the centre of their team. To say it rankled in the Catalan capital would be a huge understatement. So when Barcelona, who had lined up a million-pound transfer for Johan Cruyff in August 1974 then dithered over paying the world-record price, heard Real were sniffing around the Ajax superstar with a £1m cheque, they bit the bullet and signed their man. It would not be long before Cruyff would appear as historically significant a signing as Di Stéfano had been two decades before.

In Cruyff's first season, Barcelona won *La Liga* for the first time in fourteen years. To neutrals, the highlight was obvious, Cruyff's legendary 'Impossible Goal' against champions Atlético Madrid which saw him backheel a right-wing cross coming towards him at head height into the top-left corner of the net. But the Barça faithful had bigger fish to fry.

When Cruyff visited Real Madrid's Bernabéu for the first time in a Barça shirt, his performance would mark, if not the best night in Barcelona's history, then certainly the worst in Real's.

Real had countered Cruyff's signing by landing an icon of their own in Gunther Netzer. At the Bernabéu, Netzer would not get a kick. Cruyff dictated all aspects of the play, prompting from the centre, dribbling down either wing, even tackling back when necessary. He set up three goals and scored another with a languid, mazy run in a 5-0 win. It was the signature performance of Barça's first title season since the days of di Stéfano's Real. But it was also the signature performance of Cruyff's entire four-season stay at Barça. His team made no mark in Europe, and won no more league titles. Somehow, Real still had the last laugh.

FEBRUARY 18

HAVING QUIT VILLA, RON SAUNDERS TAKES OVER AT BIRMINGHAM
(1982)

Ron Saunders was Aston Villa's most successful manager for 70 years. Under his management the club won the Second Division title and the League Cup in 1975, the League Cup again in 1977 and in 1981 their first league championship since 1910. Having taken Villa to the quarter-finals of the European Cup the following season, Saunders asked Villa's majority shareholder Ron Bendall for a more secure rolling contract, which would reward him for his efforts with a payoff should he ever be sacked. Bendall refused, so Saunders resigned.

The move would benefit neither party in the long run, though Villa did not realise this immediately. Eight days after quitting Villa Park, Saunders took another job – at Villa's fierce rivals Birmingham City. The very first game of his reign was a 1-0 home defeat by, of course, Villa, yet what followed must have been even harder for Saunders to bear. As City battled against relegation, albeit successfully, Villa reached the European Cup final and beat Bayern Munich 1-0. It was the team Saunders built, but it was new boss Tony Barton who enjoyed the glory (although in a revealing slip, the official programme claimed Villa's manager was not Barton, but club kitman Roy McLaren).

Saunders's career at City was a failure. The club escaped relegation again the following season, dramatically winning five of their last six games to stay up, but finally succumbed the year after. Saunders won instant promotion back to the top flight, but quit in 1986 after an FA Cup home defeat by non-league Altrincham. Villa, meanwhile, suffered relegation in 1987, a mere five years after becoming champions of Europe; their post-Saunders adventures had been equally as hapless as Saunders's post-Villa ones. A fact their fans would later admit in song: 'We won the league, we won the cup and Ronnie Bendall fucked it up.'

FEBRUARY 19

MANCHESTER UNITED 3-0 SHEFFIELD WEDNESDAY: AFTER MUNICH
(1958)

After beating Arsenal 5-4 at Highbury on February 1, Manchester United were third in the First Division and still in the FA Cup. For a club who had only been denied a league and cup double the season before by a controversial defeat in the FA Cup final against Aston Villa, when Peter McParland barged into goalkeeper Ron Wood, breaking his cheekbone and rendering him unconscious, the chance for another double was on.

Munich changed all that. In the immediate wake of the disaster, the FA agreed to postpone United's upcoming fifth-round FA Cup tie with Sheffield Wednesday, but when the rearranged fixture finally came round it still seemed too soon. Only thirteen days earlier, survivor Harry Gregg, passed fit to play in goal, had pulled a crying baby from the wreckage of the plane. The other playing survivor from the crash, Bill Foulkes, lined up alongside Gregg in a team cobbled together by Matt Busby's assistant Jimmy Murphy, who was holding the fort while the manager lay gravely ill in hospital. There were 11 blank spaces in the programme's teamsheet that day. Stan Crowther was signed a mere 30 minutes before kick-off. In front of a 60,000 crowd, United won 3-0. Twenty-year-old debutant Shay Brennan, who would go on to win the European Cup with United in 1968, scored twice. For many there was little to celebrate, Gregg and Foulkes admitting to feeling 'empty'. Within two days, Duncan Edwards was dead.

Their league campaign fell to pieces as they lost eight of their fourteen games post-Munich. They won only one game and finished ninth. They did reach the FA Cup final, losing controversially once again as Bolton's Nat Lofthouse shoulder-charged Gregg into the net for his second goal. There was to be no trophy, never mind a double. For once, it really didn't matter.

FEBRUARY 20

SILVIO BERLUSCONI BUYS MILAN
(1986)

'Il Golden Boy' of Italian football, playmaker Gianni Rivera, was pretty much the only good thing about AC Milan in the 1970s. The historic club struggled through the decade with only a Cup Winners Cup and three Coppa Italias to show for their efforts. The final season of the decade offered new hope. Milan finally landed their tenth *Scudetto* and with it the right to wear a *stella* (star) on their shirts in 1978/79, but it was a mirage. Rivera left to pursue a career in politics and at the end of the following season the *Rossoneri* had been relegated to Serie B for the very first time. Milan president Felice Colombo had attempted to influence a game against Lazio in the 'Totonero' match-fixing scandal.

Though Milan bounced back to Serie A after just one season, a dismal performance the following year saw them back in Serie B. This time their humiliation had come about due to their inadequacies on the pitch. Just as their decline was symbolised by the exit of Rivera, so another political figure would assist their rebirth, media tycoon and property entrepreneur Silvio Berlusconi, who announced his plans to take over the club in 1986. With Milan rudderless in mid-table, things could surely only get better. And they did, pretty much instantly.

Berlusconi's first step was to appoint little-known Arrigo Sacchi of Serie B side Parma as coach. Sacchi would transform Milan into a glamorous and attacking side, albeit with one of the best defences in the world. The front line was led by three Dutchmen: Ruud Gullit, Marco van Basten and Frank Rijkaard. At the back there was world-class home-grown talent in Franco Baresi and Paolo Maldini. The team was propelled to unprecedented success. Under Sacchi the 1987/88 Serie A title was followed by two European Cups. After Sacchi, Fabio Capello led the club to a hat-trick of *Scudetto*s in the early 1990s, culminating in the majesty of the 1994 Champions League final thrashing of Barcelona, arguably the best performance in a European final since Real Madrid's 1960 Hampden show.

Berlusconi was unstoppable too. In 1994 he founded the Forza Italia party and within two months had been elected president. His party, of course, had been named after a football chant.

FEBRUARY 21

GEORGE GRAHAM LEAVES ARSENAL IN WAKE OF BUNGS SCANDAL
(1995)

Christmas '91 was a very merry one for George Graham. On December 23, the Arsenal manager was presented with a 'Winner Takes All' style briefcase full of crisp banknotes by Norwegian agent Rune Hauge. Believing the money to be an 'unsolicited gift', a thank you for advising Hauge over the potential transferring of Scandinavia's top talent to Premier League clubs, Graham accepted the £140,000 and thought nothing more of it. He also thought nothing of it when Hauge gifted him another £280,000 in August the following year.

The Inland Revenue, however, took slightly more interest. Money had also been paid by Hauge into an Irish bank account belonging to a member of Graham's coaching staff, Steve Burtenshaw. Arsenal, having been asked by the taxman what Burtenshaw was up to, quizzed Burtenshaw and subsequently Graham about the money. Though the payments had been made after Arsenal had purchased Swedish winger Anders Limpar, Norwegian defender Pål Lydersen and Danish midfielder John Jensen in deals brokered by Hauge, both men denied any wrongdoing. Graham insisted he still considered his cash a 'gift', while Burtenshaw claimed he had been paid to head up a 'scouting network' for Hauge, independent of his work with Arsenal.

The club accepted the duo's claims and Graham paid £420,000 back to Arsenal as a gesture of goodwill, but the climate was against them. The FA were in the middle of an investigation into possible bungs in transfer deals and Graham was one of the individuals under scrutiny. Arsenal dismissed both men, saying they had 'failed to act in the best interests of the club'. Graham was banned for a year by the FA before taking over at Leeds. One of the most successful managerial reigns at Highbury had come to a sorry, shabby end.

FEBRUARY 22

KENNY DALGLISH RESIGNS AS LIVERPOOL MANAGER
(1991)

The Liverpool players had sensed 'something in the air' that morning, and assumed it was the announcement of a surprise big signing. 'Nobody remotely guessed the gaffer was going to call it a day,' said Ronnie Whelan after Kenny Dalglish administered the biggest shock to Anfield's collective system since Bill Shankly retired on July 12, 1974.

Liverpool were top of the league and still in the FA Cup when Dalglish resigned, though their position belied the team's poor form. Their cup run was more of a stagger: they needed two games apiece to get past Second Division sides Blackburn and Brighton, then relinquished the lead four times in a tumultuous 4-4 fifth-round replay at Everton. Their recent league record was even worse with only two wins from seven before Dalglish left. Peter Beardsley was being regularly left out of the team and new signings David Speedie and Jimmy Carter didn't pass muster.

'The biggest problem was the pressure I was putting myself under in my desire to be successful,' said a tearful Dalglish. 'I felt it would be wrong to mislead everybody into thinking everything was fine.' He had kept Liverpool at the top for fourteen years as player then manager. There was also the impact of Hillsborough on Dalglish as he had reportedly gone to every funeral.

Liverpool succumbed to Everton in the cup, then Arsenal in the title race after a frankly surreal run of form. One week they beat Derby 7-1 away before losing 3-1 to QPR at home; two successive away fixtures returned a 5-4 win at Leeds and then a 4-2 tonking by Chelsea. Meanwhile the pundits wondered who would take over. Alan Hansen, John Toshack, Phil Neal and Jack Charlton were mooted, but Graeme Souness of Rangers got the call. 'I believe he is making the biggest mistake of his life,' said Ibrox chairman David Murray. 'Time will tell.'

FEBRUARY 23

QUEEN'S PARK 4-0 THIRD LANARK: VALE OF LEVEN EXPELLED FROM CUP
(1884)

Vale of Leven, from the small Dunbartonshire town of Alexandria, won three Scottish Cups in a row from 1877 to 1879, one of only four clubs to have ever achieved such a hat-trick (the others being Queen's Park, Aberdeen and Rangers). They enjoyed a fair a bit of luck during that run. The 1877 final ended in a 1-1 draw and a pitch invasion, after Rangers scored an extra-time goal which wasn't spotted by the referee. There were no nets at that time, and the ball clanked off a spectator behind the goal and back to the Vale goalkeeper, who made out he had saved the shot. Vale won the replay 3-2. Then, a year after retaining their trophy against Third Lanark, they were awarded the 1879 cup after a 1-1 draw with Rangers. Rangers had a good goal ruled out for offside and refused to contest a replay as they were still in a lather of righteousness over what had happened to them two years earlier.

Vale's luck finally ran out in 1884. Having reached the final against Queen's Park, they announced the day before the match that they could not play as several of their players were 'hors de combat' (diplomatic speak for 'injured'). In addition, one of their team had suffered a family bereavement. They enquired, could the match be rearranged? It could not. The Scottish FA were unimpressed at such a request being made at such short notice and turned them down, arranging instead a friendly between Queen's Park and Third Lanark, before which Queen's Park, as finalists, were awarded the trophy by default. Vale of Leven did not let it lie and threw a petulant wobbly the following week by refusing to play a scheduled game against Partick Thistle. Thistle's president Joseph Halley had sat on the Scottish FA committee which denied Vale's cup final request.

Vale lost the following season's cup final, this time on the pitch, 3-1 against near neighbours Renton. They also lost the 1890 final to Queen's Park and that was to be the end of their love affair with the cup. Vale were founder members of the Scottish League in 1890, but fell out of it within two seasons, failing to win a match in 1891/92. That year Celtic won the Scottish Cup and the big boys were slowly taking over.

DEATH OF WILLIAM 'WILLY' GARBUTT, FIRST ITALIAN MANAGER
(1964)

Willy Garbutt was a far bigger influence on the Italian game than back at home in his native England. Though he spent his early days playing for Reading, Stockport and Blackburn Rovers, his big move was to Genoa in 1912 when, at 29, he was appointed manager of the club – the first person to hold such a title in Italian professional football. It is said he was spotted by future Italy coach Vittorio Pozzo on a visit to England.

Garbutt was quick to introduce some of the habits he had picked up in England. Among them were structured warm-ups, hot showers in the dressing rooms and the dubious practise of enticing players away from rivals with under-the-counter cash inducements. Genoa had won six national titles from 1898 to 1904, but had been in the doldrums since. Garbutt soon led them to victory again. They won the northern championship in 1913 and when north-and-south play-offs were reintroduced after the war, back-to-back *Scudetto*s in 1923 and 1924. In between, he was called back to England and sent to France to fight in World War I.

In 1928 Garbutt took up the managerial post at Roma, though he would not enjoy the same success he had at Genoa. After spells with Napoli, AC Milan and Atlético Madrid, he finally returned to Genoa in 1938, but when war broke out, the Englishman was deemed an outcast by Mussolini's Fascists. After refusing to leave Italy he was forced into hiding near Naples, leaving his adopted daughter behind. Garbutt's final years would paint a sad picture. Though he would be eventually reunited with his daughter, his wife was killed in an Allied bombing raid. After a short, undistinguished post-war spell back at Genoa, Garbutt returned to England in 1951 and died 13 years later in Leamington Spa aged 81.

FEBRUARY 25

BARCELONA 9-0 CATALA: ALCÁNTARA'S DEBUT
(1912)

Filipino-born striker Paulino Alcántara Riestra is not a household name, but he should be. Barcelona's first 'Golden Boy', he was signed at the age of 15 by the club's founder Joan Gamper, scored a hat-trick on his debut against local rivals SC Catala, and would go on to tot up a ridiculous number of goals (346 in 357 matches) to become the club's most prolific scorer in its history. Within four years of his debut, Barça had won two Catalan championships and the Copa del Rey.

As well as possessing a powerful right foot (and not a bad left either), Alcántara also had a steady hand and hoped to qualify as a doctor. In 1916, his parents ordered him back to the Philippines to continue his studies. While there, he still managed to shine as a footballer, playing for the Bohemians of Manila and becoming their top scorer too. He also represented the Philippines at the 1917 Far Eastern Games in Tokyo, where his side thrashed Japan 15-2.

Back in Catalonia, Alcántara was sorely missed. Barça failed to win any titles and the club were keen to get him back on board. His parents, however, believed his medical career came first and forbade his return. But Alcántara was determined, and manipulated events to bribe his way back to Barça. After contracting malaria, he agreed only to take medication if he could play again in Spain.

On his return, Alcántara joined Ricardo Zamora and Josep Samitier, the three helping Barça to their glory years. In the 1922 cup final they beat Real Union 5-1 and in 1926 beat Atlético Madrid 3-2. Alcántara also played for Spain. On his debut, naturally, he scored both goals in a 2-0 win over Belgium. But the lure of medicine would prove too strong and in 1927 he left Barça aged 31 to become a doctor.

FEBRUARY 26

CHELSEA 1-0 LEICESTER: DANNY BAKER
LOSES IT AND LOSES JOB
(1997)

Football phone-in shows are usually not worth the wear and tear on your hammer, anvil and stirrup ossicles, nor the surface area of your eardrum, but as with anything else in life there is an exception that proves the rule. After referee Mike Reed awarded a decisive penalty to Chelsea when Erland Johnsen went down under a non-existent challenge in the 117th minute of a fifth-round FA Cup tie against Leicester, BBC Radio Five Live's Danny Baker embarked upon the most majestic rant on that evening's 'The Baker Line' programme.

'It was scandalous,' he began, 'an absolute scandal … football has a maggot at its golden core, and that maggot is referees … we've been at that game for two hours and the referee was bad all the way through it … what is the point of people running themselves to a standstill, what is the point of supporters investing time money and emotion, what is the point in anyone investing millions in football when the whole thing rests on some erstwhile van driver from Folkstone who's probably had a row with his wife? If this was a boxing match and the referee turned round and gave the fight to the bloke who was knocked out on the floor we would say you can't do that … most of them need a good slap round the face … hacks should doorstep this man like he's a member of Oasis … that worm should be on the phone now, Radio Five should be knocking down that ref's dressing room and [asking] do you know on behalf of all referees how bad you are?'

Baker then accused both the FA and the media in general for being 'mealy mouthed' and not really caring when games are 'ballsed up' by 'some idiot' like Reed, before upbraiding his producer for putting on callers who disagreed with him. A bravura performance that got him sacked a week later.

FEBRUARY 27

NEWTON HEATH OPEN THEIR FATEFUL BAZAAR
(1901)

Newton Heath Lancashire & Yorkshire Railway Football Club (try branding a lampshade and quilt with that name) were formed in the eponymous north-eastern suburb of Manchester in 1878. Their feats as a club were not particularly auspicious. Their first foray into the FA Cup ended in farce, when the team refused to play extra-time after a 2-2 draw against Fleetwood Rangers. They were disqualified from the competition as a result. Upon winning admission to the top tier of the newly expanded two-division Football League in 1892, they immediately finished last and had to win a Test Match relegation play-off against Second Division Small Heath to remain in the First. The next year, after finishing bottom again, they became the first top-flight club to lose such a Test Match – to Liverpool, of all clubs – and therefore the first ever Football League team to suffer relegation.

Eight more nondescript years passed. By 1901 the club were nearly £3,000 in debt and facing extinction, so decided to hold a four-day bazaar to raise money in Manchester's St James' Hall. Sadly, despite a large donation from Manchester City, the event raised hardly a penny once the cost of renting the hall had been factored in. However fate, in the shape of a St Bernard dog, had already lent a helping paw.

Newton Heath's captain, Harry Stafford, had taken his dog, Major, along to the bazaar with a collection box strapped round its neck. Major ran away. On Saturday March 1, Major had been found by wealthy local brewer John Henry Davies, who wanted to keep the dog for his daughter. Upon tracing Stafford in order to make a purchase, Davies was told of Newton Heath's predicament. By 1902, Davies, Stafford and three other businessmen had taken over the club. The consortium had one quibble. They wanted to change the team name. But what to? Manchester Central? Manchester United? Decisions, decisions…

FA OFFICIALLY RECOGNIZE WOMEN'S FOOTBALL AT LAST
(1972)

In football as in life, women had to fight like hell for equal rights. On December 5 1921, the FA had banned women's teams like the famous Dick, Kerr Ladies from using men's pitches, the normally free-thinking *Manchester Guardian* opining in an editorial: 'If there is any real desire to have women [sic] football teams the action of the FA can hardly put an end to the forming of them, nor can it prevent the teams from acquiring grounds of their own. But if it does discourage the playing of football matches by women as a public spectacle, there will be no tears shed on that score.' Women's football did mobilise itself, forming the short-lived English Ladies' FA five days after the FA ban, but the game had been dealt a savage blow from which it took decades to recover.

After the war, the tide slowly turned. In 1957 an organisation called the International Ladies Football Association organised a European championship which was won by the Manchester Corinthians and by 1969 in England, 44 clubs had formed the Women's Football Association (WFA). Within two years the FA Council had lifted the ban forbidding women playing on FA-affiliated clubs' pitches and in May 1971 the first women's FA Cup final was played, Southampton beating Stewarton and Thistle 4-1. On February 28 the following year, in the wake of a meeting between the FA Council and the WFA, the FA finally agreed to officially recognise the game.

During November 1972, 51 years after Dick, Kerr Ladies had played France in an unofficial international match (which the English team won 2-0), the first official international was played on British soil. England won again, beating Scotland 3-2. In 1991, the WFA launched a 24-strong national league. The same year FIFA staged the inaugural Women's World Cup. Within two seasons the sport was under the auspices of…the FA.

FEBRUARY 29

MIDDLESBROUGH 2-1 BOLTON: BORO'S LONG WAIT ENDS
(2004)

The idea of forming a football club in Middlesbrough was first mooted in the town's Corporation Hotel in 1876 over a dinner of tripe. The food served up that day proved to be an open goal for quipsters in the north east over the next century. While Newcastle and Sunderland wasted no time in bringing home league titles and FA Cups, it took Boro exactly 100 years to lift their first trophy. Even when they did, it wasn't one of the major pots. Jack Charlton's side beat Fulham 1-0 over two legs to lift the first ever Anglo-Scottish Cup.

Middlesbrough's wait looked to be over on April 6, 1997, when Fabrizio Ravanelli gave Bryan Robson's Boro a 1-0 extra-time lead in the Coca-Cola Cup final over Leicester City, but with two minutes to play Emile Heskey levelled the scores. A goal from Leicester's Steve Claridge defeated them in the replay ten days later. Boro went on to be relegated from the Premiership and lose the FA Cup final to Chelsea.

A year later they reached their second League Cup final, losing again to Chelsea, but it was third time lucky in League Cup finals in 2004. In the semi-final they beat Arsenal, who were undefeated in the league. Boro then landed their first ever major trophy in the final with a 2-1 win over Bolton. Even then, there was an element of farce. When scoring the decisive penalty, Boudewijn Zenden slipped and inadvertently kicked the ball twice. But the goal stood and the wait was over.

Incidentally, this leap-year date is also the date of Manchester City's last trophy, the League Cup of 1976. Unlike Boro's first, the facts around which can never change, mentioning City's 'last' trophy in a book could be construed as a hostage to fortune. However as this is Manchester City we are talking about, we will take our chances.

RAFAEL MORENO ARANZADI – 'PICHICHI' – DIES
(1922)

El Trofeo Pichichi is awarded annually to the top scorer in Spain's *La Liga*. Won over the years by the likes of Alfredo di Stéfano, Ferenc Puskás, Mario Kempes, Hugo Sánchez, Emilio Butragueño, Bebeto, Romário, Ronaldo, Raúl, Samuel Eto'o and Ruud van Nistelrooy, its roll of honour contains a healthy proportion of the greatest ever strikers to play the game. Fitting, then, that it is named after one of Spanish football's most legendary stars: Athletic Bilbao striker Rafael Moreno Aranzadi, who went by the name of 'Pichichi'.

Pichichi made his debut for Bilbao in 1911. Although born to immigrant parents, his Bilbao birthplace allowed him to turn out for the exclusively Basque side. He scored the first ever goal at their San Mames stadium, the oldest football ground still in use in Spain. In 1914 he won the first of his four Copa Del Rey finals with Bilbao, against Espana de Barcelona. The following year he scored a hat-trick in the final against Espanol. Bilbao and Pichichi made it three cups in a row, trouncing Real Madrid 4-0 in the 1916 final.

In 1920, Pichichi was a member of the Spanish side that won the silver medal at the Antwerp Olympics. It was during this run that he scored his one and only goal for Spain in the silver medal decider against Holland. Spain had gone 2-0 up, but with 22 minutes to play the Dutch had clawed a goal back. Pichichi almost immediately settled nerves with a header and the silver was Spain's.

The following year saw Pichichi claim his fourth Copa Del Ray with Bilbao, but it would be his last. The following year, aged just 29, Arandzadi died suddenly after contracting a bout of typhus. Four years after his death a bust was erected at San Mames in his honour and in 1953 the Spanish federation, along with the *Marca* newspaper, named their new top-scorer trophy after him. The title was also awarded retrospectively, all the way back to the first league in 1928/29. It is somehow fitting that the first four players to achieve Pichichi status were, like the man himself, of Basque origin.

WILLIAM MCGREGOR DECIDES TO
FORM FOOTBALL LEAGUE
(1888)

In July 1885, the Football Association, for so long stuck in a southern, public school, amateur mindset, had bowed to years of pressure applied by clubs from the industrial north and legalised professionalism. The clubs had got their way, but with their new freedom came new problems. With wages to pay, more money had to be generated. Money could only be generated by the staging of an increased number of crowd-pleasing matches. The FA Cup could only offer clubs so many of those; what they needed was regular, guaranteed, fixtures.

William McGregor, a Scottish director of Aston Villa, decided to act. On March 2, 1888, McGregor wrote to the chairmen of Blackburn, Bolton, Preston and West Bromwich Albion with a groundbreaking idea: 'Every year it is becoming more and more difficult for football clubs of any standing to meet their friendly engagements and even arrange friendly matches ... I beg to tender the following suggestion as a means of getting over the difficulty. It is that ten or twelve of the most prominent clubs in England combine to arrange home-and-away fixtures each season ... This combination might be known as the Association Football Union ... My object in writing to you at present is merely to draw your attention to the subject, and to suggest a friendly conference to discuss the matter more fully ... how would Friday 23rd March 1888 suit for the friendly conference at Anderton's Hotel, London?'

The meeting went ahead, with representatives from Accrington, Burnley, Derby, Everton, Notts County, Stoke and Wolverhampton Wanderers also in attendance. It was decided to call the new venture the Football League – not the English Football League, as it was hoped at the time Scottish clubs would also join. At a second meeting on April 17 the League was formally founded. Within five months it was up and running. McGregor's Villa racked up five League titles by the turn of the century.

MARCH 3

NOTTM FOREST 1-0 MAN CITY: CROSBY BEATS DIBBLE BY A HEAD
(1990)

In a 1971 Home International fixture between Northern Ireland and England, Gordon Banks went to launch a kick upfield. As he dropped the ball towards his boot, George Best stuck out a leg, whipped the ball into the air and headed home. It was an outrageous piece of skill, but was scandalously ruled out. Adding insult to injury, Northern Ireland went on to lose the game to an offside goal. Such goalkeeper-baiting opportunism had its day in a First Division match nearly two decades later.

It was a match that meant something as Nottingham Forest sat in fourth place with an outside chance of the title, while Howard Kendall's Manchester City were only two points clear of the relegation zone. After 52 minutes of incident-free action, Forest launched a deep cross from the right into City's box. With winger Gary Crosby scooting in from the left hoping to crash a header home, City goalkeeper Andy Dibble sprang into the air and claimed the high ball. With most of the players flooding back upfield, Dibble surveyed his distribution options, the ball resting on the platform of his right hand. One player had hung back. Crosby, who had been bundled off the pitch, came back on and from behind Dibble's right shoulder, nipped round to head the ball from the keeper's palm before passing the ball into the net. City surrounded the referee, but the goal was given. 'The ball did not leave his hand so the goal should not have stood,' spluttered Kendall afterwards, but the ball was not considered to be in Dibble's control.

It is probably just as well that the result had little bearing on the end of the season. Forest fell away into mid-table anonymity, while City easily avoided the drop. There were long-term repercussions, however. To this day, goalkeepers round the world can be seen clasping the ball to their chest, consumed by paranoia of who might be coming up behind them.

MARCH 4

QPR 3-2 WBA: THE LEAGUE CUP COMES OF AGE
(1967)

The League Cup suffered an inauspicious start when it was launched in 1960. Only 46 of the Football League's 92 member clubs deigned to enter. Although the list of participants in its first season wasn't as shabby as popular myth has it – double-chasing Spurs, Wolves and Arsenal didn't compete, but reigning champions Burnley, Manchester United and Everton did – the clubs didn't take it as seriously as they might have done. Second Division Rotherham made the first final, where they lost 3-2 to Aston Villa. The second final saw Second Division Norwich beat Rochdale, of the Fourth Division, 4-0.

The finals were played over two legs until 1965/66, when West Bromwich Albion won the last two-legged affair 5-3 on aggregate against West Ham. The top teams were still eschewing the competition, so to encourage participation the League took action. The final would be a one-off Wembley occasion with the winners qualifying for the Fairs Cup.

The plan worked, but with inevitable irony the first Wembley final would be contested by a Third Division team, Queen's Park Rangers, facing holders West Bromwich Albion. The First Division side were expected to win easily and by half-time Clive Clark's double saw them 2-0 up. QPR staged a dramatic turnaround. Roger Morgan headed home after 63 minutes, 23-year-old Rodney Marsh dropped a shoulder and clipped in off a post after 75 minutes and, having come back from the dead – you couldn't script this – Lazarus (Mark) struck the winner with nine minutes to go.

QPR had become the first third-tier team to win a major trophy. In another seemingly inevitable twist, despite winning promotion to the Second Division that same season, QPR were banned by UEFA from taking part in the Fairs Cup due to their lowly league status.

STASI CATCH UP WITH DYNAMO BERLIN 'TRAITOR' LUTZ EIGENDORF
(1983)

The Stasi liked to interfere with all aspects of life in the German Democratic Republic (DDR) and football was no exception. After World War II and Germany's partition, Erich Mielke, the Stasi state secretary, ordered East German team Dynamo Dresden to relocate to the capital and become Dynamo Berlin. Dresden's reserves and unwanted kids were allowed to continue under their old name as a husk of a club.

Under Mielke's meticulous control, Dynamo Berlin was constantly riddled with Stasi informers who would report any wrong move by a footballer or potential defection to the West. Getting found out could result in prison, a long-term ban or occasional 'accidents'. One player whose fate would be sealed thus was Lutz Eigendorf.

After a friendly against Kaiserslautern in West Germany in 1979, Eigendorf never returned to Dynamo's team hotel. He had fled to the West. He initially set up base with Eintract Braunschweig and ended up playing for, of course, Kaiserslautern. Had it not been for Mielke, he may have enjoyed a quiet life, but instead the Stasti would make it a misery. From that moment on, he was branded a 'traitor' by Mielke.

Four Stasi agents monitored him constantly – though some reports put the total of spies as high as 50 – and it was Eigendorf's outspokenness that became the nail in his coffin. After daring to criticise the DDR in an interview, he was soon involved in a mysterious car crash and died two days later. His autopsy showed a large amount of alcohol in his blood, yet Eigendorf was not a known heavy drinker and witness accounts said he'd only had a couple of drinks on the night of his death.

When the Stasi files were opened up to the public after German reunification in 1991, Eigendorf's documents suggested his crash had been set up. It was also revealed they had deliberately set up his wife with a former boyfriend.

ACCRINGTON STANLEY RESIGN MID-SEASON
(1962)

Provincial clubs haemorrhaging support to the big teams isn't solely a modern phenomenon. In 1960 Burnley had won the league and were runners up two years later, while Blackburn Rovers reached the FA Cup final in 1960. Near neighbours Accrington Stanley simply couldn't compete with the glamour. In February 1962, Stanley were marooned at the bottom of the Fourth Division, and were asked to clarify their financial position by the powers that be.

Stanley's vice-president Sam Pilkington assured Football League president Alan Hardaker that all was well, but in truth it was anything but. The club's average crowd was 2,300. The gate receipts of £300 a week nowhere near covered their expenses as they required £450 simply to cover players' wages. On Saturday March 3 Stanley lost 4-0 at Crewe. It was to be their last game. The following Monday, a meeting of creditors found the club to be £62,000 in debt and with a large National Insurance bill. The following day the club admitted defeat, notifying the League of their intention to resign their membership. It looked as good as over for Accrington Stanley.

Then came a scene straight out of the movies (or a cheap TV drama at least). A day after tendering their resignation, a mysterious potential benefactor turned up at the club with a bag containing £10,000. 'I don't want this club to go under,' he announced. Stanley withdrew their resignation, but Hardaker accepted it nonetheless. The club threatened to sue the League, but when Stanley's record that season was expunged, the battle was lost. Stanley had become only the second-ever league club to resign mid-season, after Wigan Borough baled out of the Third Division (North) in the 1931/32 campaign.

MARCH 7

RESTAURATEUR ARRESTED – SERIE A'S 'TOTONERO' SCANDAL BEGINS
(1980)

Roman restaurateur Alvaro Trinca and his greengrocer friend Massimo Cruciano were the men behind the biggest Italian football scandal of all time. They attempted to fix a series of matches in Serie A during the 1979/80 season, bribing footballers who were regulars at Trinca's 'fresh' frozen-food eaterie and making a killing betting on the outcome. They went on to ruin their own scam quite spectacularly.

While Italy's popular state-run Totocalcio pools attracted most punters, it was hard to manipulate as you could not bet on individual games. You could on the illegal tax-free 'Totonero' scene, though. Trinca and Cruciano tried to fix at least eight matches in order to coin it in on Totonero, but little went to plan. For a start, the pair underestimated the ability of footballers to throw a game. For example, in the first game they tried to fix, between Lazio and Palermo, the Rome side missed their flight to Sicily. With no team to play, Palermo were awarded the win. But for a while their bets started to come in, so the pair placed ever larger wagers.

Several players were then accepting bribes from the pair with absolutely no intention of throwing the games. Trinca and Cruciano began to lose money hand over fist, owing it to unscrupulous Totonero bookmakers who wanted the debts settled quickly. Amid death threats from irate bookmakers to their families, they panicked and hired a lawyer who unsuccessfully presented *them* as victims of fraud by the players to the Italian FA. It was a thinly-veiled blackmail. They hoped the federation would settle their debts to avoid a scandal breaking. It didn't work.

After the pair confessed to the papers, Trinca was eventually arrested and the country knew it was only a matter of days before others were charged. On March 23 the police stormed into the dressing rooms of several clubs across the country and arrested eleven players and club officials. There were 33 players charged in all. Paolo Rossi, who went on win the golden boot at the 1982 World Cup, initially received a three-year ban while Milan and Lazio were relegated to Serie B. Nobody went to prison though, as sporting fraud did not become illegal in Italy until 1986.

MERRIONGATE: THE FAI, WORLD CUP
TICKETS AND 'GEORGE THE GREEK'
(1996)

The Football Associations of England and Scotland have a rich historical stock of ridiculous decisions. The Scots turned down a chance to play in the 1950 World Cup as they hadn't won the Home International championship. The English once gave Steve McClaren a job. Few of their choices compare to those of their counterparts at the Football Association of Ireland (FAI), where high farce seems to be standard practice.

The vote to appoint a new team manager to replace Eoin Hand in 1986 was a shambles. At the last minute in the selection process, former captain Johnny Giles and ex-Liverpool manager Bob Paisley were added to a ballot already featuring Jack Charlton and Liam Tuohy. There were 18 votes which counted. Paisley, who had won three European Cups and seven league titles at Liverpool, received nine votes, while Giles, Charlton and Tuohy each had three. In the recount, with some FAI members piqued that Paisley had been introduced late in the process, all the Tuohy and Giles votes went to Charlton, while one voter crossed the floor. The result being Charlton 10, Paisley 8. When Charlton was told he had got the job, he admitted that he had forgotten he'd applied. The process was at least an improvement on the 1980 decision which saw Hand beat Paddy Mulligan by one vote. An FAI administrator admitted he only voted for Hand because he suspected Mulligan of 'throwing a bun' at him on an away trip.

Those farces pale into insignificance when compared with treasurer Joe Delaney's decision to give £296,000 of FAI money to a man going by the name of an 'agent' called 'George The Greek' in order to garner tickets for the 1994 World Cup. Amazingly, the agent turned out to be a tout. The FAI only received 314 tickets and were left with a £214,000 hole in their accounts. Delaney made up the shortfall himself, but was forced to resign, along with FAI president Louis Kilcoyne who stood down on March 8, 1996 at an Extraordinary General Meeting. 'I took what I considered a calculated risk,' admitted Delaney by way of apology. He was at least spared the indignity of having pastries thrown at him as he made his valedictory speech.

BOLTON WANDERERS 0-0 STOKE CITY:
33 KILLED AT BURNDEN PARK
(1946)

A bumper crowd had gathered at Burnden Park for a chance to see Bolton Wanderers take on Stoke City in the sixth round of the FA Cup. The excitement was palpable. Wanderers were already 2-0 up (in the only year FA Cup ties would be decided over two legs) while the great Stanley Matthews was in town. Between 50,000 and 60,000 spectators were expected, but more than 85,000 turned up. The *Bolton Evening News* noted the game was 'irresistible to football lovers of the north. There were all the signs of cup-tie enthusiasm and a spirit of great humour.'

When the teams appeared, surges in the heavily overcrowded Embankment Stand caused thousands of fans to lose their feet and fall onto the crush barriers, which collapsed under the weight. As spectators piled on top of each other, many found themselves unable to breathe and some were crushed to death. Thirty-three people died and over 500 were injured. Despite these scenes, the game continued after a short interval for fear a cancellation would lead to further chaos.

It transpired that a father trying to escape the crush with his little boy had broken open a gate, leaving it open to fans desperate to get in. Most of the crowd were unaware of the tragedy occurring further in. Within minutes, the 'glorious day' had become the biggest footballing disaster Britain had ever seen. Some reports attributed the troubles to fans who had illegally jumped barriers to get inside, but a government inquiry ran by R. Moelwyn Hughes, KC concluded 'unauthorised entry was a factor, but not a major one.'

It was believed 2,000 people over the 'safe' capacity level had gained entry into the Embankment stand. Hughes opined that 'if a lower number of people had been allowed into the stand' the disaster would not have happened. The inquiry also revealed that not all the stands and turnstiles were open, creating bottlenecks. Hughes recommended the number of fans entering future big fixtures should be monitored by 'mechanical means.'

His recommendations were, however, not backed up by legislation; clubs had the option to ignore them. The culture of complacency continued for four decades afterwards, a culture betrayed by events at an FA Cup semi-final in Sheffield in 1989. Burnden Park would not be the last tragedy of its kind.

MARCH 10

LEICESTER 1-2 WYCOMBE: THE END OF THE FOXES' GOLDEN ERA
(2001)

It took a while for Leicester City fans to warm to Martin O'Neill. After taking over as manager of the club in December 1995, the Foxes only won twice in O'Neill's first sixteen games, a run which saw City slip from third in the First Division to eighth and included a 5-0 shellacking at Manchester City in the FA Cup. There were calls for his head, but the club held firm and O'Neill turned his team's form around. Leicester scraped into the Premiership through the play-offs, then went on to reach three League Cup finals in four seasons, winning the trophy in 1997 and 2000. It was the most productive period in their history.

The 2000 win would be O'Neill's valedictory swansong. He left for Celtic in the summer, with Peter Taylor his replacement. During his first couple of months Taylor took Leicester as high as second in the Premiership, but his reign would be almost an exact mirror image of O'Neill's. The team's form suddenly went to pot, and it would be a cup tie which highlighted that things were beginning to go seriously wrong.

Leicester hosted Wycombe Wanderers in the sixth round of the FA Cup. The Second Division side were suffering an injury crisis so acute that manager Lawrie Sánchez was forced to place an advert for a striker on his club's website. Sánchez's plea had been picked up by a writer for ITV's Teletext service and spotted by the agent of Roy Essandoh, formerly of Finnish side VPS Vassa, who contacted the club and won a short-term contract. The rest of the story wrote itself: Wanderers played Leicester off the park and Essandoh scored the winner during injury-time in a 2-1 win.

Wanderers went on to give a good account of themselves in the semi-final – it took Liverpool 78 minutes to break them down, Wanderers eventually losing 2-1 – but the dream would soon be over for Essandoh. Released at the end of the season, he became an itinerant non-league player. Taylor was sacked during the following season, which saw Leicester relegated; O'Neill's Celtic, meanwhile, won the Scottish league.

FOREST COMPLAIN TO FA – AND NEWCASTLE
FACE CUP-RIOT EXIT
(1974)

After winning the FA Cup in 1955 for the third time in five seasons, Newcastle United endured nearly two decades of pain in the tournament. The holders were denied a place in the 1956 semi-finals by Sunderland, who beat them in the sixth round despite having lost a derby 6-1 earlier in the year. After that indignity, Newcastle wouldn't reach the last four again until March 9, 1974, when they finally made it after a dramatic win at St James' Park over Nottingham Forest. Forest, then of the Second Division, had gone 3-1 up only for Newcastle to storm back through Terry McDermott, John Tudor and a last-minute winner from Bobby Moncur.

Two days later, the semi-final draw paired Newcastle with Burnley, but the prize would be immediately snatched from them. Forest had appealed to the FA. When Forest's third goal, a 56th-minute penalty which saw Pat Howard sent off for protesting, had gone in, 'a fat gentleman in civvies appeared in the Forest area, waving and shouting,' reported the *Observer*. 'His chubby strivings set off a riot.' Forest's Dave Serella was punched in the face. The players had left the field for eight minutes and when they returned, Forest fell apart. Adding insult to injury, Moncur's winner was yards offside, but the linesman feared a 'lynching'. The teams were forced to replay twice at Goodison Park, the tie finally settled by a Malcolm Macdonald goal.

So Newcastle reached the semi-finals after all, despite having made heavy going of their campaign. In earlier rounds, they had been held at home by non-league Hendon and fourth division Scunthorpe United. Would their efforts be worth it? Initially it seemed so, as they beat Burnley 2-0 at Hillsborough to reach Wembley. Whether they still thought as much after the final – where in the words of David Coleman they were 'undressed' 3-0 by a rampant Liverpool – is another matter.

93 KILLED IN NEPAL HAILSTORM
STAMPEDE IN KATHMANDU
(1988)

A crowd of nearly 30,000 fans turned up to watch Nepalese side Janakpur play Muktijoddha from Bangladesh at Nepal's national stadium. The match was not to be completed. Tragedy stuck when a freak hailstorm broke out during the match. The crowds scattered for shelter towards the back of the stands, but what followed was a huge crush. With doors and exits locked fans could not escape. The melee resulted in the death of 93 people, while over 700 others were injured.

Witnesses reported that 'police at the game refused to open the gates without orders' despite the obvious crush developing in the stands. The police, however, shifted blame to the stadium officials, who the police said were responsible for all decisions. It was believed that at least 25,000 tickets were sold for the match held in the 20,000 capacity stadium, while thousands more attempted to get in without tickets.

In the aftermath of the disaster, more chaos followed as people took to the streets of Kathmandu to riot and protest over the events. As priests burned the bodies of the victims on huge funeral pyres, there were anti-police demonstrations; the Nepalese chief justice had his car pelted with stones.

The Nepalese government responded by announcing cash grants to the families of those killed. Entertainment was banned for 24 hours.

MARCH 13

LUTON TOWN 1-0 MILLWALL: RIOT LEADS TO AWAY FANS BAN
(1985)

Millwall's previous foray into the quarter-finals of the FA Cup had not been a peaceful one. Bobby Robson's Ipswich Town were the visitors to The Den that day in 1978, and their supporters' coach was greeted on arrival by an avalanche of bricks and stones. Midway through the first half, Millwall were already a goal down when fighting broke out in a corner of ground. The melee spilled out onto the pitch, forcing the game to be stopped for 18 minutes as bottles and iron bars were wielded by the mob. Forty-five people were injured and 30 were arrested. Ipswich won the match 6-1, though that hardly placated Robson. 'Turn flamethrowers on them,' he suggested after the game, though he later retracted it as a comment made 'in the heat of the moment'.

Supporter behaviour at the club's next quarter-final tie, away at Luton Town in 1985, would be even more outrageous. It turned into a riot which became the defining image of 1980s hooliganism. A suspiciously large away contingent turned up at Kenilworth Road – the cream of London's firms looking for trouble. More than 3,000 ticketless fans burst through the turnstiles. Fans invaded the pitch before the match, during and after, when Millwall's support reacted to their team's 1-0 defeat by ripping out seats and flinging them at retreating policemen. One officer was hit on the head by a concrete block and momentarily stopped breathing; his colleague was attacked as he stopped to administer the kiss of life. There were 81 people treated for injuries, 31 of them police officers. Thirty-one people were arrested and charged, though the majority of them turned out to follow clubs other than Millwall.

In the wake of the riot, the FA ordered Luton to erect barriers in front of their stands. The club refused, opting to introduce a ban on away supporters instead. They were expelled from the 1986/87 League Cup as a result.

BRAZIL PLAY IN THEIR FAMOUS YELLOW
STRIP FOR THE FIRST TIME
(1954)

Brazil expected its footballers to win the 1950 World Cup. When they didn't, everyone and everything was blamed. Even the strip, an all-white affair, wasn't spared. Most considered it lacking in national character and it was immediately jettisoned – though the replacement all-blue kit wasn't much better. So, in 1953, a competition was launched by Rio newspaper *Correio da Manha* in association with the Brazilian Sport Confederation to design a new kit for the national team. The only conditions were that it had to contain all four colours featured on the Brazilian flag: yellow; green; blue and white.

Had the second-placed entry won – from the professional designer who created the official 1950 World Cup poster – Brazil would to this day be running around in green shirts, white shorts and yellow socks. Thankfully the *Correio da Manha* chose an effort from a 19-year-old newspaper illustrator from southern Brazil instead. The prize was won by Aldyr Garcia Schlee's soon-to-be-iconic yellow shirt with green collar and cuffs, blue shorts and white socks. The kit had a happy debut. Brazil first wore it at the Maracanã on 14 March 1954 against Chile in a World Cup qualifier which they won 1-0, Baltazar da Silva scoring the *Seleção*'s first ever goal in yellow on 35 minutes.

That Schlee won a competition which was only held as a result of Brazil losing the 1950 World Cup to Uruguay was laced with irony. Despite being Brazilian, Schlee lived near the Uruguayan border and supported the Uruguay national side. Though Brazil would win the World Cup a mere four years later, their new strip played no part in the final. In their victorious 1958 final, they played home team Sweden, who also wear yellow. Brazil had to buy some blue shirts from a Stockholm shop and sew the cut-out badges from their home kits onto them.

MARCH 15

EVERTON LEAVE ANFIELD – A NEW CLUB IS BORN
(1892)

In 1878 a north Liverpool church, St Domingo's, formed a football club in order to encourage the local lads to stay good and righteous. Soon enough they had changed their name to Everton, and playing on the local Stanley Park, were drawing huge crowds. It quickly became obvious that the club needed a proper stadium, so in 1884 club president John Houlding, a local brewer, secured a plot of land south of the park – Anfield – and rented it out to the club.

In their first season at Anfield, Everton's gate receipts more than quadrupled. Houlding was making good money himself from the arrangement as Anfield was close to a pub he owned, the Sandon, which did a roaring trade on matchdays. Houlding's 'sparkling ales' were the sole beverages on sale in the ground. On the other hand Houlding was helping the club with transfer fees, wages and ground maintenance, so in 1889 he hiked the rent from £100 a year to £250. Everton were incandescent, offering Houlding only £180, and a three-year stand-off ensued. Houlding decided he wanted out, giving Everton the option to buy Anfield for £6,000. The club threw a fit of pique – they were also unhappy that the team were forced to change in the Sandon and drink from Houlding's bar – and voted to leave Anfield in October 1891, instead spending £8,090 on a nearby plot of land called Mere Green (soon to be Goodison Park).

Houlding threw his own fit of pique. Left with a ground and nobody to play in it, he decided to form a new club. Having initially tried to legally claim the Everton name for himself, he settled on a new name – Liverpool – and along with the help of one of the few staff members who had not decamped with Everton, John McKenna, imported several Scottish players. 'The Team Of All The Macs' made their way into the Football League in 1893, winning promotion to the first division in their debut season. That set up the first league game between the two clubs on October 13, 1894, a 3-0 win for Everton. Liverpool would not taste league victory against their city rivals until they won 3-1 at Anfield in September 1897.

MARCH 16

SHEFFIELD UNITED 0-3 WBA: THE SECOND BATTLE OF BRAMALL LANE
(2002)

The first ever game held at Bramall Lane ended in a fistfight. Appropriately the match, between Sheffield and Hallam, was played on Boxing Day 1862. So it was entirely fitting that the first Football League fixture to be abandoned after a team were reduced to six men was a filthy-tempered first division encounter at Sheffield United's home ground in 2002.

During a match at Bramall Lane the previous season, United defender Georges Santos had suffered a broken cheekbone after receiving an elbow in the face from Nottingham Forest midfielder Andy Johnson. Johnson had since been transferred to West Bromwich Albion and was returning to the scene of his crime for the first time since that incident. Santos was lying in wait for his prey.

Not that it needed either Santos or Johnson's presence for the match to turn sour. On nine minutes, United keeper Simon Tracey was sent off for handling the ball outside the area. By the 62nd minute West Brom were two up against the ten men. United manager Neil Warnock responded two minutes later with a double substitution, but within 90 seconds he would wish he hadn't bothered.

Substitute one, Santos, immediately took retribution on Johnson, scything him down with a sickening two-footed lunge. Santos was sent off. A melee ensued, which saw substitute two, Patrick Suffo, head-butt West Brom captain Derek McInnes. Suffo became the third United player that afternoon to see red. It could soon have been worse for United but for kind refereeing by Eddie Wolstenholme. Keith Curle should have walked for aiming punches at McInnes's head, but was shown only yellow.

On 77 minutes, Michael Brown limped off, reducing United to seven men, then five minutes later Robert Ullathorne followed him to the treatment room. With United down to six men, referee Wolstenholme had no option but to abandon the game. Some questioned whether Brown and Ullathorne had deliberately left the pitch in the hope that a replay would be sanctioned.

'There will be no replay,' said livid West Brom manager Gary Megson after the game. 'If we are called back to Bramall Lane we shall kick off then walk off the pitch.' He need not have worried, the result stood.

BOCA JUNIORS 2-2 SPORTING CRISTAL:
THE BATTLE OF BOMBONERA
(1971)

The Argentinian side Estudiantes, who ruled the roost in South America at the end of the 1960s, were infamous for getting down and dirty when the occasion demanded with a cynical approach to the game known as 'antifutbol'. They hoofed first Celtic, Manchester United and then Milan around the park during Intercontinental Cup ties at the end of the decade – but even they never got involved in anything quite as outrageous as this.

In the first-round group stage, Boca Juniors needed to win their match at home to Sporting Cristal in order to have any real chance of progression, having already lost to the Peruvian side two weeks previously. They established a 2-0 lead in their Bombonera stadium but were pegged back to 2-2. With four minutes to go, desperate Boca striker Robert Rogel went down in the Cristal area. When the referee failed to point to the spot, Boca captain Ruben Suñé attacked Cristal defender José Gallardo, who responded with a flying kick to Suñé 's face. Suñé later needed seven stitches. Boca's Ángel Rojas then kicked Cristal's Fernando Mellán in the face as he lay on the floor. It was initially thought Mellan had suffered brain damage, though he got away 'lightly' with a fractured skull. By now nineteen players were trading haymakers. All nineteen were sent off – only the two goalkeepers and Boca's Peruvian defender Julio Meléndez avoided dismissal – and the match was abandoned.

The day after, all the dismissed players were given jail sentences of 30 days each, though these were quickly rescinded after desperate diplomatic manoeuvring, the Peruvian government insisting Cristal had defended themselves 'with honour and nobility'. In a tragic postscript, it was then announced the mother of Cristal defender Orlando de la Torre had died of a heart attack while watching the melee on TV. Boca's remaining matches were not played; their opponents were awarded wins.

SWINDON 1-0 BRISTOL ROVERS: THE LONG-BALL GAME IS BORN
(1950)

Given that the long-ball game is a tactical theory in thrall to minute statistical data, it's appropriate that its genesis can be pinpointed almost to the very second. At 3.50 p.m. on March 18, 1950, as Swindon and Bristol Rovers prepared to kick off for the second half of their Third Division (South) game, accountant and former RAF wing commander Charles Reep whipped out a pad and pencil and started taking notes.

Reep had embarked on the first great statistical analysis of football. He quickly came to the conclusion that '85% of goals tend to be scored from passing sequences that involved a small number of passes, usually three or less' and that 'two thirds of goals come from balls recovered in the last third of the pitch.' Teams should, he argued, adjust their tactics accordingly. There was no point playing possession football, better instead to hoof it upfield and deal with what unfolds there. A simplification of his theories, but not by much; for hoof, read 'reacher', which is what Reep called 'a single pass from the defensive third to the attacking third of the pitch'. In other words, whack it into the danger zone often enough, and eventually you'll score.

Reep's methods were picked up by 1950s Wolverhampton Wanderers manager Stan Cullis. They were later adopted by the FA's director of coaching Charles Hughes, who ramped up the jargon (lumping the ball forwards was 'creating a Position of Maximum Opportunity' – a 'pomo'). Hughes introduced the theory to Graham Taylor. Egil Olsen, coach of the eye-wateringly crude 1990s Norway team also studied the method.

Did Reep's tactics bear fruit? Cullis's Wolves won three titles, but remain the last English champions to rely solely on the long lump. Meanwhile on June 2, 1993, Olsen's Norway played Taylor's England in a World Cup qualifier. In terms of aesthetics, it was arguably the worst game of football the tournament has ever produced. Reep was in the stands as guest of honour.

BAYER UERDINGEN 7-3 DYNAMO DRESDEN: 'DAS WUNDER VON DER GROTENBURG'
(1986)

In 1954, the excellent Dynamo Dresden team was uprooted en masse to Berlin by Erich Mielke, the head of the Stasi (the East German intelligence network), who had decided that East Germany's capital city should host the best side in the land. While that team became Berliner FC Dynamo – better known as Dynamo Berlin – Dresden were allowed to scrape about in the lower leagues with the reserves and youngsters that Mielke and his goons deemed surplus to requirements.

Amazingly Dresden regrouped and won promotion to the top flight in 1962. Then between 1971 and 1978 they landed five titles. This state of affairs threw Mielke into the hottest of funks. It was at this point he ordered the state's best players to turn out for Dynamo Berlin, who then won all ten titles between 1979 and 1988. Dresden came second in six of those seasons, though relief was usually provided by European competition, where the club would regularly perform better than Mielke's Berliners. So it seems somehow harsh, then, that despite all the indignities visited upon them at home, Dynamo Dresden's greatest humiliation would be suffered on the European stage.

Dresden had a fantastic squad in the 1985/86 season which included strikers Ulf Kirsten and Ralf Minge, and sweeper Matthias Sammer. The side won the first leg of their Cup Winners Cup quarter-final against West Germany's Bayer Uerdingen 2-0, and were 3-1 up after 58 minutes of the return at Uerdingen's Krefeld stadium. At 5-1 up on aggregate with three away goals in the bag, they looked home and dry – at which point the roof inexplicably fell in. Uerdingen scored five goals in 21 minutes to make it 5-6 on aggregate. Wolfgang Schäfer hammered the final nail in Dresden's coffin with his side's seventh four minutes from time. The shock of this unprecedented defeat may have snapped something in Dresden striker Frank Lippmann's head. Fed up of being hounded by the Stasi after a drink-driving incident the year before, he defected to West Germany that very evening.

MARCH 20

FOUNDER OF SPARTAK MOSCOW ARRESTED
FOR TRYING TO KILL STALIN
(1942)

When talented Russian football player Nikolai Starostin nutmegged his opponent in a lower league match in Georgia in the 1920s, he had no idea what an enemy he had made. Laventry Beria, the man he had outplayed so convincingly, would go on to become a very dangerous man: the head of the Russian police, the KGB, supporter of Dinamo Tbilisi and head of Dinamo Moscow.

Meanwhile in 1935, Starostin and his three brothers became involved with the left-wing footballing arm of the Moscow Sport Circle and the food-workers' union, renaming them Spartak Moscow. 'The People's Team' immediately became the foil to Dinamo Moscow, the team run and supported by Beria's secret police. Spartak were successful from the off and within two years they had won both Russian league and cup, but this success fuelled Beria's jealously. When, in 1939, they won the championship and defeated Beria's favourite team, Dinamo Tbilisi, in the cup final, Starostin's fate was effectively sealed.

On March 20, 1942, Starostin woke up with a pistol against his head. He was marched to the Lubyanka, the secret police headquarters, questioned and accused of trying to murder Stalin. The evidence was a dictionary definition of the word flimsy. Beria had provided the interrogators with a photograph of Starostin and his team within metres of Stalin at an exhibition match in Moscow's Red Square in 1936. Rumour has it that Dinamo were also due to play that day, but had pulled out for fear of hitting Stalin with a ball. Spartak played their reserve team instead, and much to Beria's annoyance, treated Stalin to quite a show.

The Starostin brothers were sent to Siberia for ten years where Nikolay entertained prison guards with tales of his time in Moscow. 'Beria was not dealing with just four men,' he recalled in his autobiography, 'but the hopes of millions of ordinary Soviet people. People saw us embodying Spartak.'

Following Stalin's death, Starostin was released and returned to Moscow. Something of a national hero, he was appointed coach of the USSR team and reunited with Spartak Moscow as their president until 1992. The state was less rewarding to Beria, who was tried for war crimes and shot dead.

ROMA 0-0 LAZIO: TOTTI SPEAKS TO RIOTING 'ULTRAS' AS POLICE ARE ROUTED
(2004)

The first half of an often fraught Lazio-Roma derby had passed by surprisingly smoothly, but four minutes into the second half, sections of the crowd began to get restless. There was talk of a young boy having been killed by a police car outside the Stadio Olimpico. In an unprecedented scene, three heads of Roma's hardcore 'Ultra' group walked past security and onto the pitch, where they proceeded to tell Roma captain Francesco Totti to put a stop to the match.

At the same time, referee Roberto Rosetti was in talks on a mobile with the Italian Football Federation. Despite announcements confirming nobody had died, the game was abandoned and the players sent off the field. Fans called police 'murderers' and fighting continued outside the stadium long into the night. A total of 155 police officers were injured, whilst 21 fans were hurt, as extensive damage was caused on the streets when rioting fans set fire to cars and motorbikes.

After the match it was reported that Totti had told his manager, Fabio Capello, that 'if we carry on, they will kill us.' This news raised questions about the Ultras and the power they wielded. Some politicians claimed it was a pre-organised act 'aimed at blackmailing the government' into bailing out several of Italy's biggest clubs. Others simply put it down to the false rumour offering an excuse to go on the rampage.

Roma played their following two home games on a neutral ground in Palermo and the derby rematch on March 28 ended peacefully in a 1-1 draw. Rather than the usual display of hostility between fans – most infamously illustrated in 1979 when Lazio supporter Vincenzo Paparelli was killed by a flare launched by a Roma fan – in this *'Derby della Capitale'*, for once it was the police on the receiving end.

CHELSEA AND CITY PLAY IN THE LEAGUE –
24 HOURS BEFORE CUP FINAL
(1986)

It was a satisfying Saturday in the First Division for both Chelsea and Manchester City. The former had won 1-0 at Southampton, a result which kept them in the title hunt. Mid-table City, who had been two goals down at Manchester United, hit back to claim a 2-2 draw which severely dented their arch-rivals' chances of winning a first championship since 1967. Their weekend's work, however, was far from complete. Less than 24 hours later, both teams would be at Wembley to contest the first ever Full Members Cup final.

The Full Members Cup had been set up to fill the void left by the post-Heysel ban on English clubs in Europe. It wasn't taken particularly seriously by the footballing cognoscenti, as the scheduling of the final proved. Neither Chelsea nor City had enjoyed a particularly fruitful decade though, both spending time in the Second Division, so a day out at a cup final was not to be sniffed at. A very healthy crowd of 68,000 obviously agreed, and despite both teams' utter lack of preparation, the final would prove to be a minor Wembley classic.

City took a tenth-minute lead through Steve Kinsey, but then Chelsea ran riot with five unanswered goals, a hat-trick for David Speedie and two for Colin Lee. At 5-1 with ten minutes to play, the game looked over, but in the last six minutes City scored through Mick McCarthy, a Doug Rougvie own goal and a Mark Lillis penalty. It wasn't quite enough for City, the game ended 5-4. 'If football is dying,' said Chelsea manager John Hollins, 'I hope it's dying like that.' Chelsea's jubilant fans, caught in the moment, sang of winning the league, though their team only claimed nine points from the last 33 and ended the season in sixth.

MARCH 23

NORTH LONDON 7-1 SOUTH LONDON:
THE FIRST LADIES' MATCH
(1895)

The formation of the first women's football club was more a political than a sporting event. Suffragette Nettie Honeyball founded the British Ladies' Football Club in north London in 1894, and said of the team: 'I founded the association with the fixed resolve of proving to the world that women are not the ornamental and useless creatures men have pictured ... I look forward to the time when ladies may sit in Parliament and have a voice in the direction of affairs.'

To this end Honeyball organised the first high-profile women's football match, a game between a north London representative XI and one from south London. A crowd of more than 10,000 at the Crouch End Athletic Ground witnessed a one-sided affair, the north winning 7-1. The match appeared to have been successful in achieving Honeyball's goals. 'The quality of the playing,' opined the *Manchester Guardian*, 'was of the mildest description', though the paper's 'Lady Correspondent' did add that 'both teams have only had a few months' practice and no real play could therefore be expected ... I imagine that women players may after some further practice develop a style of play which may be both vigorous and graceful ... I do not think that ladies football matches will attract crowds, but there seems no reason why the game should not be annexed by women for their own use.'

During April, Honeyball took the two teams on a tour of England. They played exhibition matches in Brighton, Bury, Bristol and Reading, in the latter match breaking the ground attendance record previously held by a Reading vs Luton Town match. The women's game was on the up – although it would only really take off during World War One when the Dick, Kerr Ladies team became the star draw in English football. When Dick, Kerr drew 53,000 for a Boxing Day fixture in 1920, the more small-minded of the gentlemen began to worry.

MARCH 24

NORWICH 1-0 SUNDERLAND: THE DOOMED
LEAGUE CUP FINALISTS
(1985)

Middlesbrough's 1996/97 season, when they lost both FA and League Cup finals and were relegated from the Premiership, is considered by many to be the most hapless top-flight English campaign on record. It is, however, questionable as to whether it is even the most hapless top-flight English campaign by a club from the north-east.

Admittedly in 1984/85 Sunderland did not reach the FA Cup final. But they did make the League Cup final, where they faced Norwich City. Their performance was a slapstick farce. In a 1-0 defeat, Clive Walker missed a penalty, while the only goal of the game was put through his own net by Gordon Chisholm. The team then went on to lose eight of their last twelve first division games and go down.

Amazingly the victors in the League Cup final would also suffer relegation that season – the only time the winners of a domestic trophy in England have done so – but Norwich can feel more hard done by. Having completed their fixtures, they were eight points clear of Coventry City, who were in the drop zone with three games of an extended campaign to play. Coventry were, however, midway through a 32-year residency of the top flight, during which they became adept at avoiding the drop. After 1-0 wins against bottom-of-the-league Stoke and mid-table Luton, they needed an improbable victory against league champions Everton. Everton had just won the Cup Winners Cup, lost the FA Cup final and beaten Liverpool in the space of nine days. Coventry beat Everton 4-1 and Norwich were down.

The respective qualities of the League Cup finalists would be soon borne out. Norwich came straight back up; Sunderland only narrowly avoided relegation to the third division. They went down the season after.

WALTER TULL, FIRST TOP-FLIGHT OUTFIELD BLACK PLAYER, KILLED IN BATTLE
(1918)

After years of lobbying, in 1999, fans were proudly able to unveil a memorial at Northampton's Sixfields Stadium for former player Walter Tull, born in 1888 to a Barbadian father and English mother, the first professional black outfield player in the world.

After the death of his parents, Tull was packed off to a Kent Methodist orphanage in 1897 and quickly made his name playing football. In 1908 he was recruited by amateur side Clapton FC, now known as Leyton Orient, and a year later by First Division side Tottenham Hotspur.

Despite glowing notices, Tull was dropped from the first team after seven games following racist abuse flung at him during a match at Bristol City in 1909. 'A section of the spectators made a cowardly attack in a language lower than Billingsgate (a fish market),' reported the *Football Star* newspaper. 'Let me tell these Bristol hooligans that Tull is so clean in mind and method as to be a model for all white men who play football.' Two seasons later he moved to Northampton where he played 110 matches under the legendary Herbert Chapman. His displays were enough to earn a transfer to Rangers, but he never played for the Glasgow giants.

When war broke out in 1914, Tull was one of the first to enlist and joined up with the 1st Football Battalion. He quickly moved up the ranks to Second Lieutenant, an outstanding achievement at a time when a 'colour bar' operated in the higher ranks of the British Army. After surviving six major battles he was shot in no-man's-land outside Favreuil in the Pas De Calais, France. Although his Privates tried to drag him to safety, he died instantly. Days later, his brother Edward received a letter from Tull's commanding officer: 'The battalion and company have lost a faithful officer, and personally I have lost a friend.' Unlike the Bristol City fans who had jeered him, to his fellow soldiers his colour made no odds.

MARCH 26

LIVERPOOL 2-1 MANCHESTER UNITED:
BOB PAISLEY LIFTS THE MILK CUP
(1983)

When Bill Shankly shocked Liverpool by resigning out of the blue on July 12 1974 – the very day he signed Ray Kennedy from Arsenal for a club record £180,000 – the rumour mill went into overdrive regarding the identity of his successor. The names in the frame seem shocking now. Former Liverpool player and Motherwell manager Ian St John, club captain Tommy Smith, Brighton & Hove Albion's Brian Clough (who was soon to embark on an ill-fated sojourn at Leeds) and Celtic's Jock Stein. It would be assistant manager Bob Paisley who would get the nod, two weeks after Shankly's announcement. 'This is a very proud moment for me,' he smiled shyly at the shareholders AGM, when his appointment was revealed.

Behind the scenes it was a different story. Paisley had not been keen on stepping up to the plate. At his first team meeting as manager, he told his players: 'I didn't want the job anyway.' The squad were concerned. Kevin Keegan later remembered that they had held a summit meeting where they pledged to 'help the guy become a great manager.' It soon became apparent Paisley didn't need anyone's help.

His first season was trophyless, but he made two monumental decisions. Firstly, he converted Kennedy, who had been signed as a striker but faced competition up front from Keegan and John Toshack, into a left-sided attacking midfielder. Secondly, he blooded new signings Terry McDermott and Phil Neal in the first Merseyside derby of the year. The following season saw Liverpool win a league and UEFA Cup double. The year after that, they won the league and European Cup. During his nine seasons in charge at Anfield, Paisley won three European Cups – the only manager to do so – plus six league titles and a UEFA Cup, signing Kenny Dalglish, Alan Hansen, Graeme Souness and Ian Rush along the way. Towards the end of his final season, Liverpool beat Manchester United 2-1 after extra-time in the Milk Cup final at Wembley. After the game, Paisley was leaving the pitch in his raincoat and flat cap, at which point he was stripped down to his grey suit and ordered to pick up the trophy. He refused – so Souness all but pushed him up Wembley's 39 steps to receive the acclaim he deserved.

FOWLER FINED BY UEFA – A DAY AFTER FIFA PRAISE
(1997)

In 1995, around 500 dockers working for the Mersey Docks and Harbour Company had refused to cross a picket line, and were sacked as a result. Many were reinstated soon after, but the terms of their employment contracts had been vastly altered. An industrial dispute began. Robbie Fowler and Steve McManaman had been given t-shirts supporting the striking workers, and decided to wear them under their Liverpool shirts during a Cup Winners Cup tie against Brann. McManaman advised his team mate not to lift his Liverpool shirt if he scored; better to have waited until shirts are swapped at the end of the match, when a political gesture could be made without controversy.

Some chance. 'I agreed with him 100 per cent,' said Fowler, 'and then went completely mental.' Upon scoring his second goal of the evening to seal a 3-0 victory, Fowler pulled up his strip to reveal a pastiche of Calvin Klein which bore the legend 'Support the 500 sacked doCKers'. 'I pulled down the t-shirt and ran over to all the photographers to have me picture taken!' Staunch work from Comrade Robbie.

Four days later, the halo hadn't slipped. During a crucial league match at Highbury, Fowler rushed into the Arsenal area and was upended by David Seaman. Or so the referee thought. A penalty wrongly awarded, Fowler tried to make the official change his mind. 'It was a bit fucking dippy,' reminisced Fowler, 'but I have never been a cheat.' Fowler got up and missed the kick, though Jason McAteer followed in the rebound.

'I want to congratulate you for the act of sportsmanship you demonstrated,' wrote FIFA president Sepp Blatter on March 26. A day later, UEFA were in touch as well. 'It may seem strange and a little unfair…' began their letter fining Fowler £900 for his dockers protest.

MARCH 28

REIGNING CHAMPIONS MILAN BANNED
FROM EUROPE FOR WALK-OFF
(1991)

The AC Milan side of Ruud Gullit, Marco van Basten and Frank Rijkaard dominated European football in the late 1980s and early 1990s. In the 1989 European Cup, they swept away the Real Madrid of Emilio Butragueño and Hugo Sánchez in the semi-final – their 5-0 second leg win inflicting on Real their worst-ever defeat in Europe. Milan then romped the final against Steaua Bucharest 4-0, all four goals coming before Guillit had to go off injured after an hour of play. They retained their trophy the year after, beating Real again and Bayern Munich en route to a straightforward win over Benfica in the final.

Looking to become the first three-in-a-row winners since Bayern Munich in the mid 1970s, Milan stuttered at the start of their 1990/91 campaign. They scraped through against Brugge to make the quarter-finals, but paid a heavy price. Marco van Basten was sent off, ruling him out of their quarter-final tie against an up-and-coming Marseille side starring free-scoring striker Jean-Pierre Papin and Chris Waddle, in the form of his life and arguably the most effective winger in the world. Without van Basten, Milan could only draw 1-1 in the first leg at the San Siro stadium. In the second leg on March 21, they fell behind after 75 minutes to a superb Waddle volley. With two minutes of the match to go, Marseille fans invaded the pitch thinking the referee had blown his final whistle. Then, as they were shooed back into the stands, the floodlights failed.

With the lights out, and Milan's European flame nearly extinguished, Guillit and Sacchi called the team off the pitch. Milan refused to continue and demanded a replay. The referee refused and awarded the victory to Marseille. A week later, Milan were banned from Europe for a year as a result of their protest, a sorry end to an imperious reign. Marseille went on to reach the final, where they were clinically smothered by Red Star Belgrade.

PICKLES THE DOG BECOMES A FILM STAR
(1966)

Four months before the start of the 1966 World Cup finals, the Jules Rimet Trophy was put on display at an exhibition of rare postage stamps by the Stanley Gibbons stamp company in Westminster's Central Hall. The cup was housed in a locked cabinet, and police officers patrolled the hall constantly, but the trophy was not to be guarded around the clock. It would prove to be a costly error.

On Sunday March 20, one day after the exhibition opened, the display cabinet was found open and empty by guards on their circuit of the hall. The cup had obviously been standing unguarded for quite a while as the case had not been jemmied open – the thieves had carefully removed the screws from the back of the cabinet and whipped it out before ambling off with their loot.

What unfolded thereafter was a typical British farce. A letter containing a ransom demand of £15,000 in £1 and £5 notes, which, if not met, would result in the trophy being melted down, was sent to the FA. A man called 'Jackson' then rang the FA to change the demand to £5 and £10 notes. A meeting in Battersea Park was – via coded messages in the personal ads of the *Evening News* – arranged between 'Jackson' and an undercover officer, the amusingly named Detective Inspector Charles Buggy of the Flying Squad. After 'Jackson' got paranoid, a chase ensued. Buggy caught his prey, but the man, a known petty thief called Edward Bletchley, proved not to have the cup and could not be linked to the theft.

The following Sunday, after a futile week's police work, a dog called Pickles sniffed out the Jules Rimet Trophy from under a hedge in South Norwood. Within two days the hero of the hour had been signed up by Associated London (Films) Ltd to star in a movie called *The Spy With A Cold Nose* alongside Eric Sykes and Denholm Elliot. Sadly, like many a film star before and since, Pickles would die an undignified death, hanging himself by his lead on the branches of a tree while chasing a cat in 1971.

MARCH 30

PRESTON NORTH END 3-0 WOLVES:
THE ONLY TRUE INVINCIBLES
(1889)

As a result of going through their 2003/04 Premiership campaign undefeated, Arsenal's championship-winning team that season were crowned 'The Invincibles'. But nobody really bought it. Arsene Wenger's side lost the opening game of that season, the Community Shield against Manchester United, on penalties, were beaten in the FA Cup by the same opposition and in the League Cup by Middlesbrough. In the Champions League they were defeated by Internazionale, Dynamo Kiev and Chelsea. Hardly invincible, however elastically you define the word.

Preston's side of 1888/89 were the real deal, however. The season before, William Sudell's team had won 42 consecutive matches, only to bridle at the very last jump, the 1888 FA Cup final against West Bromwich Albion. They'd beaten Hyde 26-0 along the way, still an English record, and were so sure of winning the final they asked for a photo of themselves to be taken with the trophy ahead of the game. 'Hadn't you better win it first?' asked referee and FA president Major Francis Marindin. George Woodhall's goal 13 minutes from time gave WBA a 2-1 win and ensured Preston wouldn't get their snap.

The year after, Preston's confidence was less misplaced. They romped the first season of the nascent Football League, finishing 11 points ahead of Aston Villa after winning 18 of their games, drawing the other four, and scoring 74 goals. True, unlike Arsenal, Preston's league season only compromised 22 matches, as opposed to Arsenal's 38. Arsenal were also playing in four competitions, not two. Then again Preston won the double, thrashing Wolves 3-0 in the FA Cup final, having failed to concede a goal during the entire cup run – while playing two at the back and five up front. There have been many pretenders, but only one team has ever really been able to call themselves invincible.

MARCH 31

ENGLAND 1-5 SCOTLAND: THE WEMBLEY WIZARDS
(1928)

Not much was expected of the Scotland side that travelled down to Wembley to face the 'auld enemy' in the final game of the 1928 Home Championship. The Scots had drawn their opening match 2-2 with Wales in Cardiff, then lost their next 1-0 against Northern Ireland at Hampden. In exasperation the Scottish selectors ripped it up and started again, making nine changes from the team that played the Welsh.

All but one of the side in that previous match played at home in Scotland; now eight of the team were 'Anglos', plying their trade in the English league. The biggest shocks were the omission of Celtic's Jimmy McGrory, the leading goalscorer in Scotland that season, and experienced Rangers defender Davie Meiklejohn. McGrory's place went to Huddersfield striker Alex Jackson – who at 5ft 7ins was the tallest of Scotland's five front men – while Meiklejohn was replaced by debutant Tom 'Tiny' Bradshaw, and he'd have to deal with Dixie Dean.

The portents didn't look good, but then again this was a bottom-of-the-table clash. England were in poor shape, having lost against both the Welsh and Irish. There would be no need to worry for Scotland as Preston's Alex James got them off to a flyer, setting up the opener for Jackson after three minutes and scoring a second to give Scotland a 2-0 half-time lead. In the second period Scotland's tricky ball-players gave England a dribbling masterclass. Jackson completed a hat-trick and James added another in a 5-1 rout. 'Once were counted 15 consecutive passes from Scot to Scot,' simpered the *Observer*. 'England were as helpless as small boys chasing a butterfly.'

Scotland romped the following season's championship, beating Wales 4-2, Northern Ireland 7-3 and England 1-0. They looked set fair to rule Britain for some time. Scotland being Scotland, the next time they visited Wembley, in 1930, England won 5-2.

APRIL

TOROS NEZA 0-1 JAMAICA: A BRICK-AND-BOTTLE BRAWL
(1997)

Jamaica had reached the final pool in the North and Central American qualification tournament for the 1998 World Cup, and harboured real hopes of reaching the finals for the first time in the country's history. Three teams from a six-strong group would make it to France. Mexico and the United States were hot favourites to grab two of the places, while Canada were without hope, so the final spot was expected to be a three-way contest between Jamaica, Costa Rica and El Salvador.

Jamaica had started the group solidly, holding USA to a 0-0 draw at home. With a testing fixture in Mexico City coming up, their Brazilian coach René Simões decided to do the professional thing and spend plenty of time acclimatizing in the Mexican altitude. Sadly, that would be just about the only professional decision made on the trip.

Simões arranged a game with local team Toros Neza. It descended into light farce. After 19 minutes, Toros Neza's German Arangio was scythed down by an errant Jamaican challenge. Arangio responded by getting up and driving his fist into his aggressor's face. The act provoked a full-scale melee between the two teams involving haymakers and high-kicks, which continued for five minutes – at which point several of the Jamaican team left the field and came back armed. With the Jamaicans waving bricks, broken bottles and even a chair, the referee had no option but to call the game off there and then.

'That is not normal behaviour,' one Neza player remarked after the match. 'It isn't possible that they react like this in a friendly.' Simões argued that his team simply lacked international experience. Simões himself was the man who forgot to inform the Mexican FA that his squad were setting up camp for a pre-qualifier, so the Jamaican FA were hit with a fine by FIFA. Whether the acclimatisation period was worth all the bother is a moot point. Jamaica were demolished 6-0 by Mexico. Jamaica made the finals, eventually, and went on to beat future hosts Japan 2-1 in a glorious valedictory game in Lyon.

APRIL 2

MANCHESTER UNITED 2-0 LIVERPOOL: 'KNOCKER' WEST'S 30-YEAR BAN
(1915)

Coming into Easter, Liverpool's season was petering out into mid-table nothingness. Manchester United had something to play for, though as they were staring relegation in the face and needed a win quickly. Against Liverpool at Old Trafford, United enjoyed a very Good Friday indeed, when they beat their rivals 2-0 with two goals from George Anderson. Something hadn't been quite right, though. Liverpool had looked well off the pace; even when given a free shot at goal, Jackie Sheldon's penalty was shanked hilariously wide. 'Play was scrappy, both sides shooting badly,' reported the *Guardian*. 'There was not a dangerous forward on the field.' In their next match, United were beaten 5-0 at Bradford Park Avenue.

After the Liverpool game, the referee picked up on a rumour that several players had taken odds of 7/1 on a 2-0 win. The FA launched an inquiry and eight players were found guilty of fixing the result: United's Sandy Turnball, Enoch 'Knocker' West and Arthur Whalley; Liverpool's Tom Fairfoul, Tom Miller, Bob Purcell and Sheldon – the last a former United player and ringleader of the sting.

All seven players were banned from playing for life. Turnball was killed in the Great War, but five of the remaining six had their life bans lifted by 1919 and all began playing again. The odd man out was West, who, unlike the other men, denied all accusations and had taken the matter through the courts in order to clear his name.

The FA argued that, once the scoreline was 2-0, West had spent the best part of the match booting the ball into the stands. West argued that, with relegation a real threat, he was simply doing his best to ensure United won two points. It was to no avail. West lost the case and was blackballed by the FA. He did not have his ban lifted until 1945 – when he was 59 years old.

The two points United won became very useful – they finished one point and one place ahead of relegated Chelsea. The London club didn't miss out, though as football was suspended for the war, and after restructuring Chelsea were re-elected to the top flight. West enjoyed no such reprieve.

APRIL 3

AJAX 5-0 NEC NIJMEGEN: CRUYFF HANDS THE BATON TO VAN BASTEN
(1982)

The change made by Ajax coach Kurt Linder at half-time during a run-of-the-mill Dutch League match in 1982 was a momentous one. Off went 34-year-old Johan Cruyff, to be replaced by 17-year-old debutant Marco van Basten. The greatest player in the world during the 1970s passed the baton to one of the men who would dominate European football during the late 1980s.

It wasn't quite as seamless as it sounds. Although van Basten scored a goal on his debut, he didn't immediately supplant Cruyff as figurehead of the Ajax team. Cruyff enjoyed one more season at the De Meer Stadion and spent most of it playing alongside Wim Kieft, winner of the European Golden Boot in 1981/82. Kieft and Cruyff's presence restricted van Basten to 20 appearances that season – though he would still score nine times. It was not until 1983/84, after Cruyff had left for Feyenoord, and Kieft had signed for Pisa, that van Basten really made his mark.

And how. Van Basten scored 151 goals in 172 games for Ajax between 1982 and 1987. In 1985/86 he won the European Golden Boot, having scored 37 goals in 26 games. He won three Dutch titles and scored the winning goal in the 1987 Cup Winners Cup final against Lokomotive Leipzig. His greatest achievements came after his transfer to AC Milan. At Milan van Basten made his mark in Europe, just as Cruyff had done 15 years earlier. Ninety goals in 147 Serie A appearances, two European Cups and four Serie A titles followed. He was also named European Footballer of the Year three times, a feat only Platini and – yes – Cruyff had ever managed before.

Van Basten prematurely retired from injury in 1995 due to a persistent ankle injury. Like his mentor, he was destined to be remembered for one, often repeated, piece of outrageous skill. For Cruyff it was his touchline turn against Sweden in the 1974 World Cup, for van Basten his byline volley against USSR in the final of the 1988 European Championships. At the tournament, unlike Cruyff, he actually won a major title with Holland.

APRIL 4

WEST BROM 12-0 DARWEN: ENGLAND'S BIGGEST TOP-FLIGHT WIN
(1892)

Darwen's debut season in the Football League was not the most successful on record. They started inconsistently. Their first six games saw three defeats, a draw, and two big wins – 5-2 against Accrington and a preposterous 9-3 versus Stoke. Then the heavy losses began to pile up. Notts County beat them 5-0, while Derby, Sunderland and Aston Villa all ran out 7-0 victors and Burnley scored nine without reply. Even Stoke avenged their 9-3 defeat with a 5-1 reverse.

Yet, even after those defeats, the ignominy of last place in the division could still be avoided. At the beginning of April, Darwen were only a point behind Stoke with two games in hand, and within four of West Bromwich Albion, who they were about to play twice. But the last slivers of dignity were about to slip from their grasp as West Brom won 12-0. It was a Football League record. Not so surprising then, given the League was only in its fourth season, but it is a black mark which still stands today. Amazingly Darwen took a point from West Brom in a 1-1 draw twelve days later, but it was their last of the season. 4-0 and 7-1 defeats by second-placed Preston and champions Sunderland condemned them to become founder members of the new Second Division the season after.

In 1909, Darwen's top-flight record defeat was matched by Leicester Fosse, who went down 12-0 to Nottingham Forest; although Fosse could at least point to the celebration of a team mate's wedding two days previously.

The record all-division League defeat was superseded by Halifax, who lost 13-0 to Stockport in 1934, and matched by Newport against Newcastle twelve years later. Even by the time of the Fosse result, however, Darwen had long left the League. They failed to win re-election in 1899 after embarking on a run of 18 consecutive defeats – one record which is still theirs and theirs alone.

APRIL 5

SCOTLAND 1-1 ENGLAND: THE FIRST IBROX DISASTER
(1902)

Scottish architect and engineer Archibald Leitch was a boyhood Rangers fan, and in 1899 gleefully accepted the task of drawing up a design to turn Ibrox Park into one of the largest stadiums in the country. Leitch was so happy to do his bit for the 'Light Blues' that he agreed to take on the work without being paid. Timber terraces were erected on a steel frame – council surveyors had suggested an all-steel structure would be a better option, but costs had to be kept down. In 1900, the new Ibrox was fully opened.

The largest terrace, the West Tribune Stand, could hold nearly 36,000 spectators. In its first two years of existence the stand was rarely filled, although there had been many accounts of disturbing levels of swaying. In 1902 Ibrox was selected to host the annual Scotland vs England fixture. The stadium, which had been designed to take nearly 80,000, hosted a crowd of 68,114 that day – but even that was too many. Ten minutes into the game, there was a loud crack on the packed West Tribune terrace. The timber, sodden by a heavy downpour the night before, had given way, dropping around 100 people to the ground below. There were 25 deaths, and more than 500 injuries in the ensuing crush. The game was halted for 20 minutes – but despite bodies being carried round the side of the pitch, the fixture was restarted and completed, in fear of rioting if abandoned. Scotland's goalkeeper was in tears for most of the second half.

Watching the tragedy unfold from the main stand was Leitch. Later cleared of professional wrongdoing by a Glasgow court, he wrote to Rangers begging a chance to write the wrongs of the disaster: 'I need hardly say what unutterable anguish the accident caused me, surely the most unhappy eyewitness of all.' Leitch then made it his goal to design safer, more practical football stands – and did so at more than 30 stadiums in the UK during a 40-year career. His work can still be seen at, among other places, Goodison Park, Craven Cottage and… Ibrox.

SAN JOSE CLASH 1-0 DC UNITED: MAJOR LEAGUE SOCCER KICKS OFF

(1996)

Contrary to popular myth, the US Soccer Federation was not duty bound by FIFA to create a national professional league as a condition of winning the right to host the 1994 World Cup. FIFA's member nations had little option but to award the USA the tournament, as the other options at the 1988 ballot were poor (Brazil's bid wasn't even backed by its own government). Nevertheless, the man subsequently entrusted with running the show for the USA argued that the tournament provided ideal momentum to finally – after decades of trying – establish a viable 'pro-soccer' system in the country.

Alan Rothenberg had been involved with the North American Soccer League (NASL) in the 1970s and 1980s. Rothenberg had wasted nearly $1m on the failed experiment to make a star of Johan Cruyff at the Los Angeles Aztecs. He knew of the NASL's salary excesses and its Achilles heel, small attendances. Rothenberg's new set-up, the Major Soccer League (MLS), was an ersatz socialist collective, where owners bought into a share of the MLS as a whole, shared profits and losses, and agreed to a salary cap. This allowed the league to develop without the boom and bust which ultimately killed the NASL.

The league kicked off in 1996, with ten teams competing in the first season. 31,683 watched San Jose Clash's Eric Wynalda score the first MLS goal in a 1-0 victory over future USA coach Bruce Arena's DC United. DC United ended the season as champions, winning the MLS Cup (the league title with Super Bowl-style denouement) and completing the USA's first ever double by winning the US Open Cup.

By 2006, with steadily growing support after a shaky start, the MLS was considered healthy enough to allow the introduction of the Designated Player Rule. The rule allows each franchise to make one salary-busting signing, allowing clubs to attract top world talent in order to improve standards. This is also known as the 'Beckham Rule'.

DEPORTIVO LA CORUÑA 4-0 MILAN: THE ISTANBUL HARBINGER
(2004)

In the years before the Champions League, European Cup winners had a habit of tossing away their crowns with indecent haste the season after. In 1967, Celtic were four minutes into their title defence when they conceded an away goal to Dynamo Kiev, from which they never recovered. Feyenoord lost their 1970 title at the first hurdle, crashing out on away goals to unfancied Romanians UT Arad. Ajax's three-year reign as 'Kings of Europe' ended in 1973/74, after they threw away a first round, first leg lead against CSKA Sofia. Sofia also eliminated Nottingham Forest in the opening round in 1980. Forest in turn did for Liverpool in 1978. Hamburg and Steaua Bucharest were also deposed immediately by Dinamo Bucharest in 1983 and Anderlecht in 1987 respectively.

Since the safety net of the Champions League group stage was introduced in 1993, reigning European champions have been guaranteed six or more matches to get it right. This means spectacular humiliation for the holders these days is rare. The only Champions League era side to suffer thus far are 2003 winners Milan. In the quarter-finals of the 2004 tournament, Milan travelled to Deportivo La Coruña having won their home leg 4-1. No team had ever let slip such a lead in the competition's history – but Deportivo turned the tie round by half-time, scoring three without reply through Walter Pandiani, Juan Carlos Valeron and Albert Luque. When Fran added a fourth in the second half, Milan needed two goals to progress. Visibly humiliated, they never looked like getting one.

Deportivo would lose their semi-final to eventual champions Porto, while for Milan the pain was not yet over. Having regrouped to reach the following season's final, they suffered yet another three-goal crumbling against Liverpool. If La Coruna was abject, Istanbul took sorry capitulation to another level.

APRIL 8

SOUNESS ARRIVES AT RANGERS: THE ENGLISH
REVOLUTION BEGINS
(1986)

In the 22 seasons before Graeme Souness took over at Ibrox in 1986, Rangers won three league titles. For a club of their size, stature and self-image, this was pitiful. During that period, they enjoyed one bout of success, landing three championships in four seasons between 1975 and 1978. In the fallow ten seasons before that, Jock Stein's legendary nine-in-a-row Celtic side ruled the roost. The pattern after 1978 was arguably more worrying for Rangers: not only were their 'Old Firm' rivals still racking up titles, a 'New Firm' of Aberdeen and Dundee United were doing so too. Patience was wearing thin. During 1983/84, one match at Ibrox (capacity 44,000) drew 5,000.

That would all change when Souness took office as player-manager in 1986, once he had fulfilled his contract at Sampdoria and his role as Scotland captain in Mexico '86. Souness revolutionised the Scottish game at a stroke. Taking advantage of the Heysel ban on English clubs in Europe, first he signed Terry Butcher – who turned down an offer from Manchester United – then England goalkeeper Chris Woods. By tempting England's top-drawer acts north of the border, Souness had reversed a trend which had lasted the best part of a century.

His first match as player-manager started abysmally. Souness was sent off after 34 minutes in a 2-1 loss at Hibernian. It was no harbinger of failure. Rangers ended the season champions for the first time in eight years and Ibrox was filled to capacity. Souness lifted two more titles at Rangers and kept the flow of English talent coming – Gary Stevens, Trevor Steven, Mark Hateley and Mark Walters also arrived. Ironically, Souness's signature signing, made on July 10 1989, was destined to be a Scot: Maurice Johnston.

APRIL 9

MCGUINNESS TAKES OVER FROM BUSBY AT MANCHESTER UNITED
(1969)

Manchester United's 1968 European Cup victory always had an air of finality about it. 'George Best insisted that was the end of something when it should really have been the beginning,' said Nobby Stiles years later, 'and I disagreed with him, but I now know what he meant by that remark. The general feeling was we'd done it for Matt and his beloved 'Babes'. I don't think we ever felt the same spirit again, and I don't think Matt did, either.' Less than eight months after the valedictory win, Busby announced plans to retire on January 14, 1969.

Rather than step down completely, Busby stepped upstairs and took on an 'administrative role' as General Manager, while a coach was to be appointed, to continue with the day-to-day running of the team. After nearly three months during which potential successors such as Coventry's Noel Cantwell and Derby's Brian Clough were suggested in the press, reserve team coach Wilf McGuinness was given the position on a trial basis. Within two weeks United had lost the first leg of their European Cup semi-final against Milan 2-0. Bobby Charlton pulled one back in the return, but the goal represented a great team's last act of defiance. United went out of Europe and finished the season in eleventh place.

With an ageing team shorn of motivation, George Best sick of the lack of ambition, and Busby failing to relinquish full control, United stumbled to eighth in McGuinness's first full season. It was enough to win him the job permanently. His reign only lasted four months into the new season, however. After losing a League Cup semi-final to Third Division Aston Villa, and with United fifth from bottom in the league, he was shunted back to reserve-team duty after Christmas in 1970. Busby resumed temporary control. Among the names touted in the papers to replace him this time? Don Revie and Bill Shankly. They got neither man, but appointed Frank O'Farrell.

NORTHERN IRELAND 0-0 WALES: JUVENTUS
DECIDE TO BUY CHARLES
(1957)

Juventus were going through a lean period during the mid-to-late 1950s. They hadn't won a *Scudetto* since 1952, were stranded in mid-table mediocrity, and in April 1957 were about to finish ninth in Serie A for the second season in a row. Club president (and head of Fiat) Umberto Agnelli decided it was time to act and got out his cheque book to buy two strikers: River Plate's Omar Sivori and Leeds United's John Charles.

Charles had become a sensation since joining Leeds as a 22-year-old in 1947, averaging a goal every two games – despite being occasionally deployed as a central defender. His goals helped the team to promotion in 1956 and Charles immediately took to the top flight, scoring 38 times in his first season. Towards the end of the campaign he attracted interest from European champions Real Madrid, who were said to be preparing a £70,000 bid for the player, but Agnelli had been tracking him and got in first. Charles was watched as he led the line for Wales in Belfast, in a Home Championship wooden-spoon decider. He didn't have the greatest of games, but toiled without much in the way of service. It was good enough for Juventus, who, despite being reportedly willing to spend £100,000 on Charles, settled at £65,000 with two desperate Leeds directors. 'Agnelli put the cheque on the table and when he turned back it had gone and the two directors had disappeared,' reminisced Charles years later. 'They didn't even say goodbye to me.'

Charles's £10,000 signing-on fee, in the era of the maximum wage, softened the blow. He scored two goals in his final game for Leeds, being chaired off the field, then left for Italy. In his first season at Juve, he and Sivori scored 50 league goals between them, landing the 'Old Lady's' first *Scudetto* in seven years. Two more followed in the next three seasons and Charles was on his way to becoming a Juve legend.

APRIL 11

AUSTRALIA 31-0 AMERICAN SAMOA:
A WORLD CUP RECORD
(2001)

At number 200 in the FIFA rankings, American Samoa were officially the worst team in the world, so the result of their Oceania World Cup qualifier against Australia was never going to be in doubt. Especially as FIFA had recently gone over the team's passports and discovered ten of their first team were ineligible, forcing the Samoan FA to scour local high schools for any talent it could find. With the youngest player in the team aged 15, the prospect was daunting enough. Then, two days before the match, Australia ran up a FIFA world-record international score of 22-0 against Tonga.

In fact, the game started well for American Samoa. Nicky Salapu (the only player remaining from the passport cull) tipped an Aurelio Vidmar shot over the bar. It was the goalkeeper's highlight of the evening. The visitors held out for 8 minutes, until Con Boutsianis opened the scoring direct from a corner. Nine minutes later, it was 6-0. By the 27th minute, David Zdrilic and Archie Thompson had both claimed hat-tricks and by half-time Thompson had bagged eight. The score at the interval: 16-0.

The risible mismatch continued to unfold in the second half. When Thompson, earning only his third cap, scored his eleventh on 65 minutes to make it 23-0, he broke the individual international scoring record. He ended the match with thirteen goals, a tally only matched in first-class football by Arbroath striker John Petrie in the 1885/86 Scottish Cup. Zdrilic had to make do with eight.

The stadium scoreboard read 32-0, an outrageous libel on American Samoa, who had in fact shipped one fewer. 'I couldn't see any reason why they wanted to score that many goals,' said their coach Tunoa Lui later. But Thompson had a point to prove. A point he clearly didn't make that well; he was dropped for Australia's next match.

SPURS 2-5 EVERTON: CHEDGZOY'S RULE-BENDING CORNER
(1924)

Before the laws of Association Football were tinkered with by the FA in 1923, it was illegal to score a goal direct from a corner-kick. The rules have since been changed to allow it. Huddersfield Town striker Billy Smith should have gone down in history as the first player to curl one in directly from a corner, scoring as he did in his side's 4-0 victory over Arsenal on October 11, 1924. Thanks to an eagle-eyed journalist at the *Liverpool Echo* newspaper, he did not.

When the laws were rewritten, the new wording of the corner-kick and direct free-kick rules, which were suddenly relevant to each other, became clumsy and vague. 'It had always been understood that the corner-kick was a type of free-kick and that the player taking it could not play the ball a second time until it had been played by some other player,' wrote FA lawmaker Stanley Rous years later. 'In 1923 this condition was made specific, but by some mischance the words 'and corner-kick' were omitted.' A minute loophole admittedly, but one a ball could be dribbled through by a saucy chancer nonetheless.

Ernest Edwards, the sports editor of the *Echo*, was such a man. He pointed out the anomaly to Everton winger Sam Chedgzoy, suggesting the player should try it on in their upcoming match against Tottenham Hotspur at White Hart Lane. Chedgzoy did so, taking a first half corner and dribbling it into the area himself before slotting it into the net.

A sprawling argument ensued, with Spurs apoplectic and the referee initially in agreement with them. Chedgzoy had been well briefed by Edwards and made his case well. The goal stood. Within weeks the rule had been amended to close the loophole – though it was too late for Billy Smith to have a chance of claiming a place in history.

LUTON TOWN 12-0 BRISTOL ROVERS:
FIRST-TIME STRIKER SCORES TEN
(1936)

Over a four-month period between December 1935 and April 1936, goalscoring records went tumbling. On December 14, 1935, Ted Drake scored seven goals in a first division match for Arsenal against Aston Villa. Drake was thought at the time to have merely equalled the achievement of Preston's Jimmy Ross against Stoke in 1888, but Ross's record was later found to be bogus, so the top flight record was Drake's. Twelve days later, on Boxing Day, that record was smashed by the ludicrously-monikered Bunny Bell of Tranmere, who scored nine against Oldham in a 13-4 win. It was a record which looked set to stand for some time.

But Bell's record of nine goals lasted only 104 days. Joe Payne had only made six appearances for Luton in nearly two years before he faced Bristol Rovers on Easter Monday, all of them on the wing. Against Rovers he was thrust into the team as an emergency striker. He started well enough, scoring the opener in the 23rd minute. His team mate Fred Roberts made it 2-0 soon after, before Payne added a third just before half-time. Then in the second half, bedlam: Payne scored eight more goals to take the score to 11-0 before George Martin added the 12th in the final minute to put a tin lid on Rovers' nightmare afternoon. Payne finished with a record-breaking ten goals.

Payne's antics put 10,000 on Luton's next home gate, and though he was hardly able to repeat the feat against Coventry, he did score in a 1-1 draw. Having accidentally unearthed a goalscoring phenomenon, Luton were promoted to the Second Division the following season, where Payne scored 55 goals in 39 games. Payne won a sole cap for England, scoring twice in an 8-0 win in Helsinki against Finland in 1937. He eventually earned a move to Chelsea, having scored 83 in 72 for Luton, and found the net 21 times in 36 First Division games. War and injury blighted his career thereafter. His famous record, however, still stands today.

GLASGOW 1-0 SHEFFIELD: WATSON'S
FIRST REPRESENTATIVE HONOUR
(1880)

Preston goalkeeper Arthur Wharton is often credited as the first black footballer, signing for the Deepdale club in 1886, but Queen's Park and Scotland left-back Andrew Watson preceded him by several years.

Watson was born in British Guiana, the son of a Scottish sugar planter and a local woman. Sent to school in London at the age of fourteen, he enrolled at the University of Glasgow in 1875. Whether education was his main concern is uncertain, though his record in Natural Philosophy goes some way to explaining his priorities. During his time on the course, Watson didn't borrow a single book from the library, and achieved an overall mark of eight, the highest in class being 1,548. Meantime, he was making a name for himself at local club Maxwell FC, moving in 1876 to Parkgrove FC, where he was also secretary, organising the club's fixtures.

According to Scottish FA reports of the time, he was a 'powerful' and 'very fair back' who 'tackled well' – and by April 1880 Watson had been chosen to represent Glasgow in a representative fixture which, in those days, had almost the same status as a full international. His performance in the match led to a transfer to Queen's Park, the biggest club in the country, where by now he was receiving notices as 'one of the very best backs we have ... has great speed and tackles splendidly with a powerful and sure kick.' In 1881, he was given his first of three Scottish caps: Scotland won the games in which he played 6-1 (England), 5-1 (Wales) and 5-1 (England).

In 1882, Watson moved to London on business, much to Scotland's chagrin. He had been so popular with the Scottish selectors that, when he was unfit for an international in early 1882, one quipped that, should Watson somehow become available again, he would happily drug his replacement to ensure he played.

APRIL 15

THE HILLSBOROUGH DISASTER – AND THE REAL TRUTH
(1989)

At the 1981 FA Cup semi-final between Tottenham Hotspur and Wolverhampton Wanderers at Hillsborough, 38 Spurs fans required medical treatment for crush injuries suffered at the Leppings Lane end of the ground. Seven years later, during the next semi-final staged at the stadium, Liverpool fans complained of crushing on the same terrace during their team's tie with Nottingham Forest. In both instances, the club with the larger support had been given the smaller end of the ground. Neither incident received much media coverage at the time.

In 1989, Liverpool and Forest met in the semi-finals at Hillsborough for the second season running. Once more, the lack of organisation was asking for trouble – Liverpool's support again given the Leppings Lane terrace – but this time police incompetence was fatally added to the mix. Despite severe overpopulation in the terrace's central pens, incoming fans were not guided to the outer sections. To make matters worse, a gate was opened outside the ground to ease turnstile congestion. Fans walked into the end unaware of what was happening at the front of the pens, where fellow supporters were already being crushed against the fences. Disaster was no longer avoidable. At 3.06pm, just after Peter Beardsley had rattled the Forest crossbar, the game was stopped. Ninety-five fans had been crushed to death, another victim would die in hospital nearly two years later.

Untruths became commonplace. That day the BBC reported that the deaths had occurred after 'fans rushed through a broken turnstile', while several newspapers alleged fans had pickpocketed and urinated on the dead (though all bar the *Sun*, who sold the story as 'The Truth' and have never been forgiven, later recanted). The findings of the Taylor Report absolved Liverpool's support of all blame and pointed the finger at the South Yorkshire Police – although none of the force was prosecuted.

Four days later, as Milan played Real Madrid in a European Cup semi-final, the referee stopped play for a minute's silence. The San Siro could not stay quiet; instead the crowd sang an impromptu version of 'You'll Never Walk Alone'.

APRIL 16

BALTIMORE BAYS 1-0 ATLANTA CHIEFS: US SOCCER BEGINS WITH ACRONYMS
(1967)

North American football had flirted with professionalism since the 1920s, but in 1966, moves were made to finally give US soccer fans the settled professional league they had been longing for. There was only one problem: three separate leagues were preparing to launch at once. In a maelstrom of confusing acronyms, the North American Professional Soccer League (NAPSL), the North American Soccer League (NASL) and the National Soccer League (NSL) battled to get the nod from the United States Soccer Football Association (USSFA) to become the officially recognised FIFA league.

It was nip-and-tuck until NBC transmitted the 1966 World Cup final, when the penny dropped with the USSFA administrators that big bucks could be made from a game which was relatively cheap to run compared to other US sports. Demanding a share of the profits in return for a FIFA sanction, the USSFA gave their blessing to the only league prepared to pay, the NASL. At which point the NAPSL and NSL merged to become the National Professional Soccer League (NPSL) and announced they were launching anyway in April 1967 – two months ahead of the NASL. To confuse matters further the NASL renamed itself the United Soccer Association (USA).

The NPSL – a 'bandit' league of ten teams – launched with an off-key fanfare. The league's first game was a dour defensive battle between Baltimore and Atlanta. Baltimore won the fixture 1-0. CBS televised the game, but it was not a good advertisement for the sport, especially as co-commentator Danny Blanchflower spent the majority of the game spluttering incredulities at the standard of play he was witnessing.

At the end of May 1967, the officially sanctioned USA, which consisted of imported teams playing in their off-season, began. The season ended with two high-scoring finals in each league. Oakland beat Baltimore 4-2 in a two-legged NPSL final. Los Angeles Wolves (who were actually Wolverhampton Wanderers) beat the Washington Whips (Aberdeen) 6-5 in a one-off USA thriller. Sense prevailed the following season and the leagues merged to become the NASL – the USA's original name, of course. A glitzy era was about to begin: within eight years Pelé was in town.

CELTIC 1-1 RANGERS: THE HAMPDEN RIOT
(1909)

A week earlier, Celtic fans were hoping for their league-winning side to secure the double for a third year running, but the Scottish Cup Final had ended in a 2-2 draw, leaving them hanging. So 61,000 returned to Hampden Park to watch the 'Old Firm' battle it out again. When it ended in another draw, this time 1-1, many of the crowd assumed there would be extra-time. For a while, it looked likely – Celtic players were initially hesitant to leave the pitch – but when a linesman plucked a corner flag from its moorings, it was a sure sign proceedings were over for the day. A third replay was set.

The third replay did not happen. While the official Scottish FA (SFA) rulebook clearly stated that extra-time would only occur after 'a series of three draws', nobody in the crowd was interested. 'Of late, draws between Celtic and Rangers have occurred with monotous regulalrity and the ill-informed man in the street has been heard to hit off the situation by the explanation that these indecisive matches have been "arranged for a gate",' explained the *Guardian* of the crowd's thought processes. With no more football to watch, the throng turned nasty.

Amid chants of 'play the tie', the crowd invaded the pitch, uprooting goalposts and pulling down nets, throwing stones, planks and chunks of loose terracing, and ripping up the turf. Overwhelmed, the police retreated. Fans set light to pay boxes, fuelling the flames with whisky, reportedly shouting (though presumably edited): 'We can not get our money returned, but we will get our money's worth!' When the fire brigade arrived they too were attacked with bottles and sticks. It took over two hours to clear the 9,000 supporters who had remained to make their forceful point and 130 people ended up in hospital. Both Celtic and Rangers asked the SFA to cancel the third replay. The 1909 Cup was never awarded; Celtic would not have their double.

ARSENAL 1-2 SHEFFIELD WEDNESDAY:
THE SORROW OF MORROW
(1993)

Steve Morrow was a bit-part player at George Graham's Arsenal. He had made his debut for Northern Ireland in 1990, two years before his top-flight debut. Morrow was a late addition to the line-up for the 1993 League Cup final against Sheffield Wednesday. His task was a tough one: to keep Chris Waddle, a player who had been arguably the best winger in world football, under some sort of control.

The defensive midfielder played a blinder. Waddle, the 1993 Football Writers Player of the Season, had a quiet game. John Harkes and Paul Merson traded early long-range goals, before Morrow scored a 68th-minute winner. Merson broke down the left and cut a ball back from the byline into the centre; Wednesday midfielder Carlton Palmer attempted a clearance, but only succeeded in placing the ball on a tee, six yards out, for Morrow to drive home.

What looked like being remembered as Palmer's personal nightmare became Morrow's. When the final whistle blew, Arsenal captain Tony Adams ran over to the match-winner. In a moment of elation he hoisted Morrow onto his shoulders. Morrow lost his balance and fell to the ground using his right arm to break his fall. As he hit the ground, his arm snapped in two. Morrow also dislocated his shoulder and was stretchered off with an oxygen mask taped to his face. 'The only thing in my mind at the time was an acceptance that I was going to miss the FA Cup final,' reminisced Morrow years later. 'While most players who leave the pitch after scoring a winning goal are elated, I just felt a huge disappointment.'

Arsenal went on to win the FA Cup final, also against Wednesday, the first time a team had won both English cups in the same season. There was another first at that final: when Morrow collected his League Cup gong before the match, he became the first player to receive a medal at a final ahead of the game. Despite nerve damage to his wrist, he returned to Arsenal the following season and played in thirteen matches, including their famous victory over Parma in the final of the 1994 European Cup Winners Cup.

APRIL 19

SHEFFIELD UNITED 1-1 SOUTHAMPTON:
NUDE GOALKEEPER ATTACKS REFEREE
(1902)

The 1902 FA Cup final between Sheffield United and Southampton offered a chance at redemption for both clubs, as it featured the losing sides from the previous two finals. In 1900, Southampton had become the first non-league team since the inception of the Football League in 1888 to reach the cup final, though they were easily beaten 4-0 by Bury. A year later, Sheffield United were embarrassed in the final as Tottenham Hotspur became the first non-league team to win the FA Cup. Spurs won that tie 3-1 after a replay, which had only been necessary after falling foul of the worst refereeing decision in the history of FA Cup finals. When 2-1 up, Spurs hacked a United shot out of play; the referee gave a goal kick, the linesman flagged for a corner, then the ref changed his mind and gave United a goal. Spurs would see to it that justice prevailed.

In 1902 it was Sheffield United's turn to suffer from a controversial refereeing call. With three minutes to go, United were 1-0 up against non-league Southampton – whose side contained C.B. Fry, the England Test cricketer – when the ball reached the feet of Saints captain Harry Wood. There was more than a hint of offside, but referee Tom Kirkham waved play on. Wood tore clear of the chasing United defence, drew legendary goalkeeper William 'Fatty' Foulke off his line, and slipped the ball under the keeper's voluminous frame. A replay was required.

After the game, an incensed – and naked – Foulke was spotted chasing Kirkham with a view to discussing the matter in the physical style. Kirkham was no stranger to controversy – he once oversaw a game of three halves between Sunderland and Derby after turning up late, with the first 45 minutes already played – but Foulke need not have worried, as United won the replay 2-1.

BIG RON LEFT TO RUE HIS OPEN-MIC IMPROV
(2004)

After conceding two goals in the last twelve minutes to a Monaco team down to ten men, Chelsea had just been beaten 3-1 in the first leg of their Champions League semi-final. Normally that would have been the top-line story of the evening. However ITV's chief summariser Ron Atkinson was about to reduce one of the biggest matches of the European season, to all but a footnote. Having finished broadcasting to Britain, Atkinson was unaware the microphones were still switched on and transmitting over a feed to Middle Eastern countries including Egypt and Dubai. It was at this point that he decided to deliver his considered verdict on the poor performance of Chelsea central defender Marcel Desailly. 'He's what is known in some schools as a fucking lazy thick nigger,' opined Atkinson, proving he was none too smart himself.

A storm ensued, causing Atkinson to resign from his commentary job with ITV, then his column at the *Guardian* (which, unfortunately in the circumstances, went under the title of 'Big Ron's Chalkboard'). 'I made a stupid mistake which I regret,' said Ron after his outburst. 'It left me no option but to resign. At the moment I can't believe I did it.' Atkinson still couldn't believe he'd done it several months later, when he appeared in BBC fly-on-the-wall documentary 'What Ron Said', which examined his attitude to race. In it, a testy Atkinson claimed he had 'over-apologised' for making some 'alleged' remarks. 'I might be an idiot but I'm not a racist,' ran Atkinson's self-defence.

At a function at Hillsborough in January 2005, the 'non-racist' Atkinson had them rolling in the aisles. 'The Chinese people have the best contraception in the world,' he chortled, 'but I can't understand why there's so many of them, because their women are so ugly.' As ever, the joke was on 'Big Ron'.

APRIL 21

THE END OF BELFAST CELTIC
(1949)

On Boxing Day 1948, the reigning Irish League champions Belfast Celtic travelled to Windsor Park, home of their arch-rivals Linfield. Just like Celtic and Rangers in Glasgow, the sectarian enmity ran deep. In 1912, a game descended into a full-blown riot, after Linfield had taken an early lead and Celtic fans had brandished the Irish tricolour, resulting in 60 hospitalisations. 'The ground having recently been undergoing alterations,' the Press Association reported, 'stones, half-bricks and clinkers were lying about in abundance, and the temptation to use these as missiles proved irresistible'. One man was 'found to be suffering from a revolver shot to the right side of the head'. The Boxing Day game in 1948 also descended into bedlam, and while no gunshots were fired, the repercussions were somehow much worse.

Midway during the first half of a game that ended as a 1-1 draw, Linfield's Bob Bryson had his ankle broken by an innocuous challenge from Celtic's Jimmy Jones. After the final whistle, Linfield supporters raced onto the pitch and hared after the Celtic players, who, according to eye-witness reports, literally had to 'run for their lives'. Jones was caught by the mob and hauled onto the terracing, where he was kicked unconscious and had his leg broken. Defender Robin Lawlor and goalkeeper Kevin McAlinden were also given a severe beating.

Many Linfield supporters wrote to Belfast nationalist newspapers expressing shame at the behaviour of the minority mob. Questions were asked in the Northern Ireland House of Commons over the role of the police, who many thought did little to quell the riot, but Celtic directors decided to withdraw from the league at the end of the season anyway. On April 21, 1949, permission was granted for them to take their leave of Northern Irish football for good. Celtic enjoyed a final fling 38 days later, beating a full Scotland side 2-0 while on a farewell tour in the USA.

SHEFFIELD WEDNESDAY 1-2 EVERTON:
THE CATTERICK ERA BEGINS
(1961)

It was the denouement of Everton's most successful league campaign since winning the title in 1939, but a fifth-place finish was not considered enough for a club being bankrolled by Littlewoods Pools owner John Moores. With Everton the latest club to have the nickname 'The Bank of England' bestowed on them, their sights were now set higher. And so, infamously, on March 15, two games before the end of the season, Moores informed manager Johnny Carey of his sacking in the back of a taxi. (The phrase 'taxi!' would subsequently be shouted by fans countrywide at any manager they were thoroughly sick of, a historical footnote which may or may not be of interest to viewers of Sky's 'Soccer A.M.'.)

Four days earlier, Harry Catterick, manager of title challengers Sheffield Wednesday, walked out of his job. Earlier in the season he had tried to leave the club for Nottingham Forest, but his request to be released from his contract had been refused by the Wednesday board. Now, with mere months remaining on it, he had been allowed to leave. Not that he had lined up anywhere to go to, he insisted. 'I would like to stay in football,' was his modest response.

But three days after Carey's dismissal, Catterick was announced as the new manager at Goodison Park. A quirk of the fixture list meant his first game was at his old club. The 2-1 win was the beginning of a successful period for the club. Within two years Catterick had led Everton to their first title for 24 years with a team starring Alex Young, Roy Vernon, Fred Pickering and Ray Wilson. The FA Cup in 1966 and a further league title in 1970 would follow.

Meanwhile Carey would still have his day in the sun, post-taxi ride. He led Leyton Orient to their only ever season in the top flight in 1962, and came second behind Manchester United in the 1966/67 title race while in charge at Nottingham Forest.

APRIL 23

CARDIFF CITY 1 – 0 ARSENAL: TRIXIE THE LUCKY FA CUP FINAL CAT
(1927)

Few gave Cardiff City a chance in the 1927 FA Cup final. The Welsh club had spent the majority of the season fighting relegation, and were expected to be rolled over by Herbert Chapman's star-studded Arsenal.

Nevertheless the team took a relaxed approach to training, and during the build up to the final took in a game of golf at Royal Birkdale. As the round progressed, they realised that a small black cat was following them from hole to hole. Unable to shake it off, some players became convinced it was an omen, and would bring them the luck their season had so far been lacking. Team captain Hughie Ferguson persuaded the owner to let Cardiff keep the cat in exchange for a ticket for the final.

The cat, given the name Trixie, accompanied the players to the cup final. It was a dull affair until the 74th minute, when Ferguson shot towards the bottom-right corner of the Arsenal goal. Arsenal's Welsh goalkeeper Dan Lewis dived and appeared to collect the ball, but let it squirm through his grasp, before knocking it in with his elbow for the game's only goal. Ironically – for this was St George's Day – this would be the first and as yet only time the Cup would be won by a non-English side.

Cardiff put their win down to lucky charm Trixie, while Arsenal developed a superstition of their own. Lewis blamed his mistake on the 'slippy' new jumper he was wearing; for years afterwards, Arsenal would never wash their keeper's kit before the game.

FENERBAHÇE 1-1 GALATASARAY:
SOUNESS'S TERRITORIAL CLAIM
(1996)

After an early exit from the UEFA Cup and a poor performance in the league, Galatasaray needed to win the Turkish Cup final – and so did Graeme Souness. It was his only chance of survival at a club he'd taken over just twelve months previously.

Galatasaray were, however, up against bitter rivals Fenerbahçe, who were fighting for the double. In the first leg, Dean Saunders fired Galatasaray to a 1-0 home win from the penalty spot, but Fenerbahce were expected to win the return easily. It didn't pan out like that, though: Fenerbahce scored in the first half to level the tie, but Galatasaray held out and the game went to extra-time. Just when the final looked like it was going to penalties, Saunders – a rare successful signing for Souness, scoring 15 goals in 27 games – popped up to score the winner from a corner in the 116th minute.

The final whistle had barely been blown when Souness vaulted over the hoardings, grabbed a giant Galatasaray flag from a fan, waved it in front of them awhile, then proceeded to run to the centre circle and plant it slap bang in the middle of Fenerbahçe's patch. Cue minor uproar. The Galatasaray fans went crazy, as did the rest of the stadium, albeit in a different fashion. Fenerbahçe fans raced onto the pitch in order to kick the flag down, offering Souness advice on where he could put his newly-won cup while doing so.

The act did little for Souness's career. He was sacked three weeks later as a result of his poor league position; warned over his 'ungentlemanly conduct' by the Turkish FA; referred to as the 'Nasty Scot' as parallels were drawn with a flag-planting incident on an Aegean island which almost led to a war between Turkey and Greece and needed a 24-hour security guard for the remainder of his time in the country – but nonetheless it made him a hero to one half of Istanbul.

ANDERLECHT 3-0 NOTTINGHAM FOREST: GURUCETA'S GAME
(1984)

It was semi-final night in Europe and it had been a mixed one for the six British clubs competing. Fans of Liverpool and Tottenham Hotspur were happy enough – their teams had progressed to the European Cup and UEFA Cup finals, with wins over Dinamo Bucharest and Hajduk Split respectively. Others hadn't been so lucky. European Cup Winners Cup holders Aberdeen had crashed out to a late goal against Porto, while Manchester United lost in the last minute of their semi-final in the same competition to Juventus. For the two other unlucky British teams, the bittersweet sense of what might have been was even more acute.

In the other European Cup semi-final, Dundee United travelled to Roma with a 2-0 lead. They lost the return 3-0, though the referee's 'abhorrence of physical contact of even modest degree' was noted at the time by the *Guardian*. United found it hard to play their natural game, and while it has never been suggested the official was 'bent' – indeed he disallowed a Roma goal with the score 0-0 – Roma and their president were banned by UEFA in 1986 for trying to bribe him before the game.

Meanwhile a similar turnaround was being played out in the UEFA Cup in Brussels, where Anderlecht were overturning a 2-0 first leg loss at Nottingham Forest. The Belgian side too won 3-0, though in as close to blatantly corrupt circumstances imaginable. A non-existent foul gave Anderlecht a penalty in the last minute. After the penalty was converted, Paul Hart had a clearly legitimate header, which would have taken Forest to the final, chalked off. It later transpired referee Emilio Guruceta had been paid £18,000 by the Belgian club, who in 1997 were banned from Europe for a year. Justice was done, albeit not for Forest, when Spurs beat Anderlecht on penalties in the final.

ARSENAL 2-0 HUDDERSFIELD: THE GRAF ZEPPELIN FINAL
(1930)

The 1930 FA Cup final was destined to go down in history before it had even started. In honour of Herbert Chapman, who had set Huddersfield on their way to a hat-trick of title wins in the mid-1920s but was now manager of Arsenal, the two teams ran out side by side for the very first time, a tradition that continues to this day. It was not the only notable event the 93,000 inside Wembley saw that afternoon.

Huddersfield started the game hot favourites; they had been the team of the 1920s. In addition to their three championships, they had been runners up in the league twice and won the FA Cup once, reaching the final in another season. But this was not to be their day, and they would fall victim to a landmark piece of opportunism in the 17th minute of the match. In his days with Raith Rovers, Alex James had got used to taking quick free-kicks after being fouled; referees in Scotland usually allowed them. In England he rarely got away with the tactic, to the point that an exasperated Chapman had ordered him to desist. James refused to listen, and after being upended 40 yards from goal, he jumped up and passed the ball out to the left flank to Cliff Bastin, who returned the ball for James to pelt the opener into the net. The decision to allow the goal to stand proved controversial.

Huddersfield moods were not improved at the start of the second half, when the German airship Graf Zeppelin hovered in sinister fashion 200 feet above Wembley, dipping its nose to King George VI and casting a shadow over the entire pitch. 'The match was stopped and it was weird to see the tens of thousands of spectators all staring up into the air at us,' said pilot Captain Lehmann after the flight. Lehmann was perhaps fortunate he could not hear the jeers from Town's fans, who were convinced their team was being put off. It was unlikely to have been a major distraction, though Arsenal did go on to win 2-0.

APRIL 27

RANGERS 2-3 ABERDEEN: THE UNLUCKIEST MANAGER EVER?
(1968)

Davie White doesn't have much of a reputation at Ibrox. In his two years and 26 days as manager of Rangers from 1967 to 1969 he won nothing, the only Light Blues boss to fail to land a trophy until the truncated seven-month reign of Paul Le Guen in 2006/07. White was always battling against the odds. He had been appointed as assistant to Scot Symon in 1967 with a view to grooming him for the future, but when Symon was surprisingly sacked five months after White's arrival, the new man was given the top job earlier than planned. Not only had White been promoted unprepared, he'd landed the task when arch-rivals Celtic, the newly crowned European champions, were at the zenith of their talents. Talk about being thrown to the (Lisbon) lions.

White suffered astonishingly bad luck during his opening season. Rangers went the entire campaign undefeated right up until the final round of fixtures. Neck-and-neck with Celtic, but miles behind on goal average, they needed to beat Aberdeen at Ibrox and hope Jock Stein's side failed to win at Dunfermline. But White's hopes were be stymied by his club's intransigence. Celtic's fixture was to be played three days later, as Dunfermline were contesting the Scottish Cup final on the last Saturday of the season. Rangers refused to move their game – which meant not only did the final draw its lowest crowd since the war, Celtic would know exactly what they had to do on Tuesday. Had Rangers moved their game to the same day, Celtic would have had to face the newly crowned cup winners – Dunfermline beat Hearts in the final – with doubt in their minds. As it was, Rangers had lost their only game of the season, and all Celtic had to do was avoid a 16-goal defeat.

The year after, White took Rangers to the cup final – where they lost 4-0 to Celtic. He had been 90 minutes from the title, but before November was out, he was gone.

BOLTON WANDERERS 2-0 WEST HAM:
THE DARK GREY HORSE FINAL
(1923)

The Empire Stadium at Wembley was commissioned as part of a complex to house a 1924 fair promoting trade throughout the British Empire. Building began in January 1922 and only took 300 working days to complete. The FA, meanwhile, were looking for a prestigious venue to hold England internationals and the FA Cup final. An agreement between The British Empire Exhibition Inc. and the FA was soon reached: the 1923 FA Cup final would be Wembley's first event.

After two minutes David Jack put Bolton a goal up against West Ham. John Smith put the ball into the net half an hour later, but the effort was incorrectly ruled out for offside. It didn't matter though; Smith scored in the second half to secure the cup for Bolton. But what happened on the pitch – in football terms, at least – would not be the story that day.

The FA had assumed the cavernous Empire Stadium's capacity of 127,000 would be more than enough to house the crowd, so the match was not made all-ticket. In the event, between 200,000 and a quarter of a million people turned up – and with turnstiles, barricades and gates stormed, nearly all of them made their way into the stadium. At 3 p.m., when the match was due to kick off, the entire pitch was covered by a throng of fans spilled from the stands.

Constable George Scorey had been trotting down Oxford Street on his 13-year-old horse Billy, when he was ordered eight miles up the Edgware Road to sort out the mess at Wembley. After making their way onto the pitch, Scorey and Billy moved in ever-increasing circles to push the crowd back as far as they would go – to the touchlines. The game went ahead thanks to their efforts, though in somewhat farcical circumstances. Throw-ins were only given if the ball bounced over the fans' heads; if it bounced back off their bodies, play went on.

Billy – who was blamed by West Ham for digging up the pitch, thus hampering their play – was not white, despite the legend of 'The White Horse Final', but in fact dark grey. It had been an overcast day, and in order for the horse to be picked out in photos, the film had to be overexposed.

ENGLAND 1-3 WEST GERMANY: 1966, ROUND TWO
(1972)

One of the greatest ever performances by an international team took place between England and West Germany, at the old Empire Stadium, Wembley. Much as England supporters will find it difficult to admit, it did not come in the 1966 World Cup final.

In that famous game in June 1966, Alf Ramsey's side had been the better of the two sides. But since then, the fortunes of the two countries had taken different turns. In 1968, nearly two years after England won the World Cup, the two teams met again in Hanover where West Germany won. The victory had only been secured by a deflected Franz Beckenbauer shot, but it was the first ever German victory over England. 'We realised we could really beat the English and lost some of the respect we had,' explained the goalscorer. Another two years on, at the 1970 World Cup in Mexico, West Germany turned a 2-0 quarter-final deficit against England into a 3-2 win. It was another win that owed a great deal to luck – Uwe Seeler's equaliser, eight minutes from time, was a back header which could have gone anywhere. After that the Germans took control and scored a late winner.

Another two years passed, and when the teams contested the first leg of the 1972 European Championship quarter-final, luck played no part. 'Not for 20 years have England been so thoroughly chastened in their own back yard,' reported the *Guardian*, with a nod to the home side's 6-3 humiliation at the hands of Hungary in 1953. The scores were level at 1-1 until four minutes from time, but two late goals reflected German superiority. Rodney Marsh, who came on in the 61st minute, years later said that Gunter Netzer gave the greatest individual performance he had ever seen.

The teams continued on their particular trajectories. West Germany went on to win the 1972 European Championship, then the 1974 World Cup – for which England did not qualify. England finally beat Germany again in Euro 2000 (1-0), then a year later in Munich trounced them 5-1 in a 2002 World Cup qualifier. Germany, of course, went on to reach the final.

APRIL 30

CIGARETTES, BOOZE AND BAYER
LEVERKUSEN'S TREBLE HORROR
(2002)

After Klaus Toppmoller danced across the BayArena turf to celebrate his Bayer Leverkusen team beating Manchester United to the 2002 Champions League final, he famously announced that 'now is a time for cigarettes and drinking'. The assumption was that the fags and booze would be used as party accoutrements – but they could easily have been implemented as nerve-calmers, because Leverkusen's promising domestic season was beginning to fall apart at the seams.

Not for nothing were the club known as 'Neverkusen'. In their 98 years the club had only won the 1988 UEFA Cup and 1993 DFB-Pokal (the German cup). Famous for bridling at the final hurdle, since 1997 they'd finished second in the Bundesliga three times. The most painful defeat was in 2000. Needing a draw against mid-table Unterhaching to land the title, star man Michael Ballack's own goal set up a 2-0 defeat and gave the prize to Bayern Munich. But that was nothing compared to 2002.

On April 20, Leverkusen held a five-point lead in the Bundesliga over Borussia Dortmund with three games to go. Within a week, defeats to Werder Bremen and lowly Nuremberg had handed the lead to Dortmund. A final day win over Hertha Berlin wasn't enough; Dortmund beat Bremen and Leverkusen were runners-up again. They became runners-up again in the following weekend's cup final, going down 4-2 to Schalke. All that was left was the Champions League – and Real Madrid put paid to that with a 2-1 win. 'It hurts to end with nothing,' said Toppmoller. 'It is difficult and makes us feel bitter.'

The horror wasn't over for Ballack, though. He missed Germany's World Cup final appearance that summer through suspension – then endured another 'Treble Horror' at Chelsea in 2008, as they came second in league, Champions League and Carling Cup.

MAY

BARCELONA SUSPEND HELENIO HERRERA:
THEIR GREATEST FOLLY
(1960)

When the Argentinian coach Helenio Herrera left Portuguese club Os Belenenses to take over at Barcelona in April 1958, the Catalan club had not won *La Liga* for five years. In the interim, their great rivals Real Madrid had won three titles and two European Cups – and were about to add another league and European double to that tally. Under Herrera, the balance of power began to shift.

Herrera did not make any showpiece signings, preferring to work with what he called 'the most extraordinary group of players I have ever had to deal with in my career.' Sándor Kocsis, Zoltán Czibor, Luis Suárez, Eulogio Martínez, László Kubala were among them. Known as 'The Magician', Herrera's approach was as psychological as it was tactical. He knew, for example, that the superstitious Suárez was convinced he would score if wine had accidentally been spilt at a team meal prior to the game, so Herrera made sure he 'accidentally' tipped a glass over every time. He was no slouch tactically either – he experimented with an early version of overlapping full-backs before the term meant anything – but whatever he did, it worked. Almost his first act as manager was to lead Barça to a 6-0 win over a London XI in the 1958 Fairs Cup final; a trophy in his first full season. Barcelona won the league and cup double, beating Real Madrid 3-0 along the way. A second league title followed the year after.

All was not perfect, though. Herrera was reluctant to play fans' favourite Kubala, which put him at odds with half of the Barcelona board. He was backed by president Francesc Miró-Sans, but when he sided with his players in a dispute over bonus payments ahead of their 1959/60 European Cup semi-final against Real Madrid, he alienated his main boardroom ally. A 6-2 aggregate defeat was the final straw for Miro-Sans. Herrera was suspended, his contract not to be renewed.

Barça's decision didn't initially appear an act of folly. The following year they put Real out of the 1960/61 European Cup – the end of Madrid's imperious European reign. But Barça lost the final to Benfica – and did not win the *La Liga* for another thirteen years. Herrera meanwhile went to Internazionale, where during the mid-60s his '*La Grande Inter*' won three Serie A titles and two European Cups.

MAY 2

BLACKPOOL 4-3 BOLTON: THE MATTHEWS – AND MORTENSEN – FINAL
(1953)

When Stanley Matthews transferred from his hometown club Stoke City to Blackpool in 1947, most observers thought, at the age of 32, the great winger was going to quietly see out his playing days by the seaside, before retiring to the hotel he owned there. So when Blackpool reached the FA Cup final in his first season, it was assumed the match was the nation's favourite player's last chance of winning a medal.

Blackpool led that 1948 final 2-1 at half-time, but Matt Busby's first great Manchester United team came storming back in the second half to land the trophy with a 4-2 win. The nation quietly sighed. Amazingly, Matthews and Blackpool were back at Wembley three years later for another last chance. The 1951 final, however, saw Blackpool put to the sword by two goals from Newcastle United's Jackie Milburn. With Matthews now 36 years old, the fairytale was surely never to be told.

Or was it? A further two years down the line, Blackpool contested their third FA Cup final in six years. At 38, this really was the final shot. Opponents Bolton didn't seem to have read the script: Nat Lofthouse opened the scoring after two minutes, and though Stan Mortensen equalised after 35, Willie Moir restored Bolton's lead five minutes after. When Eric Bell made it 3-1 on 55 minutes, the jig looked up for Matthews.

But Bell had torn a hamstring, which allowed Matthews to attack down his flank. Stanley set up his namesake Mortensen for his second with 22 minutes to play, then with less than 60 seconds of normal time left, Mortensen completed his hat-trick with a peach of a free kick. With extra-time looming, Matthews crossed once again for Bill Perry to run in the winner.

'This final will go into history as the Matthews Match,' was the *Daily Express*'s on-the-button claim. Matthews was forever embarrassed at being solely associated with the final, believing Mortensen was the true hero of the hour. As a dark aside, when Mortensen died in 1991, the popular joke was that his wake would be known as 'The Matthews Funeral'.

MAY 3

DUNDEE 2-0 HEART OF MIDLOTHIAN:
DOUBLE HEARTBREAK
(1986)

'If a scriptwriter had come up with an end-of-the-season climax like this I think it would have been rejected as being too fanciful,' opined BBC commentator Archie McPherson, as Dundee and Heart of Midlothian kicked off at Dens Park on the final day of the 1985/86 Scottish Premier League campaign. For once, Archie had a point.

Hearts had been 200/1 outsiders to win the league at the start of the 1985/86 season, and began as though that was a generous price. They conceded a last-minute equaliser in their opening game at home to Celtic, lost 6-2 at St Mirren, then went on to taste defeat in four of their next six league fixtures. After that, though, things changed. The team went on a 27-match unbeaten run which took them to the brink of the title. In their final game of the season, they had only to avoid defeat to win their first championship since 1960.

The situation was precarious, though. Dundee needed a win to keep their hopes of a UEFA Cup place alive, while Celtic were only two points behind Hearts. Should Celtic win at St Mirren and Hearts lose, they could snatch the title, though there would have to be a five-goal swing. So when Hearts went in 0-0 at half-time to hear Celtic were 4-0 up, Jambo nerves began to jangle. They held onto a crucial point until, with eight minutes to go, Dundee's Albert Kidd scrambled home a corner, then added a second six minutes later after a glorious run down the right wing. Hearts' 2-0 defeat, coupled with Celtic's eventual 5-0 victory, meant they had lost the title on goal difference, having led for almost the entire season.

In a savage irony, the last time Hearts had been pipped on the final day, by Kilmarnock in 1965, saw them edged out on the old goal-average rule. Had the difference and average rules been applied the other way round, Hearts would have won both titles. And to ramp up the Heart-break, they were thrashed 3-0 by Aberdeen in the Scottish Cup final a week later. Dundee, despite Kidd's efforts, didn't make the UEFA Cup.

MAY 4

'IL GRANDE TORINO' WIPED OUT AT SUPERGA
(1949)

Football's first great post-war team was Torino. Built around the sensational goalscoring exploits of Valentino Mazzola, who scored 118 goals in 195 matches for the club, Torino won four *Scudetto*s in a row between 1945/46 and 1948/49 – or five if you count their Serie A victory in 1942/43 before the championship was suspended for World War II.

'*Il Grande Torino*' (The Great Torino) were so dominant that the club at one point supplied ten of the eleven players for the Italian national team. Goalkeeper Valerio Bacigalupo missed out as coach Vittorio Pozzo thought sending out the entire Torino team would be unrepresentative. Italy were one of the favourites for the 1950 World Cup in Brazil – but tragedy would rob Italy's 'Azzurri' of any chance of winning. Towards the end of the 1948/49 season, with Torino leading Serie A, the side were flying back from a friendly fixture against Benfica in Lisbon. On the approach to Turin, their Italian Airways plane encountered low cloud, and on its descent hit a wall by the Basilica of Superga. All 31 on board were killed, including Mazzola.

Torino went on to win the league that season. There were only four fixtures to complete and the club sent out its reserve side, their opponents also fielding their reserves as a mark of respect. But the club went into a steep decline thereafter and were relegated in 1958. They did not win another Italian title until 1976. Italy meanwhile did not get out of their group in the 1950 World Cup.

Mazzola left behind a son, Sandro, aged six. Mazzola Jr. went on to score the winning goals in the 1964 European Cup final for Inter, won the 1968 European Championship, and played in the 1970 World Cup final.

MAY 5

EVERTON 3-3 ARSENAL: BILL DEAN BREAKS
GOALSCORING RECORD
(1928)

In 1925, a change was made to the offside law. Instead of there needing to be three players between attacker and goal, the rule now required only two. Defences took a while to adjust tactically, and during this period strikers flourished. In the 1926/27 season, Swindon's Harry Morris scored 46 goals in the Third Division (South). The same year George Camsell broke the Football League scoring record in the Second Division, by scoring 59 of Middlesbrough's 122 goals. Camsell's haul included nine hat-tricks, a record for a single season which still stands today – but his overall record would only last a single season.

Bill Dean – he hated his nickname 'Dixie' – joined Everton from Tranmere Rovers in 1925. The club had been struggling in the lower reaches of the First Division when he joined, but his first-season tally of 32 goals helped propel Everton to mid-table safety. The team struggled the season after, but then Dean had missed four months after nearly killing himself in a motorbike crash. When he returned, the goals continued to flow, and in the 1927/28 season, Dean's efforts secured the First Division championship for Everton with a game to spare. He had up to that point scored a ludicrous 57 league goals – and so needed a hat-trick in the final game at home to Arsenal to beat Camsell's mark.

Dean scored two in the first half to draw neck-and-neck with Camsell, the first a header from a corner, the second a penalty. The third took its time in coming, however. Only eight minutes of the game remained when Dean claimed his hat-trick and the record by walloping in a towering header – the 40th of those 60 goals. He wandered off the pitch with a minute to play to avoid being mobbed by fans.

But was it just all down to the change in the offside law? That can be argued – he never scored 60 again – but Dean left Everton in 1937 for Notts County, having scored 349 goals in 399 appearances. Defenders weren't *that* confused, and anyway, they had a decade to work it out.

MAY 6

TOTTENHAM HOTSPUR 2-0 LEICESTER CITY:
THE FIRST 20TH-CENTURY DOUBLE
(1961)

Bill Nicholson's first match in charge of a struggling Tottenham Hotspur in 1958 was a ridiculous 10-4 victory over Everton, but there was no immediate sea-change as the club only narrowly avoided relegation that season. The new manager's first big decision that year was to drop half-back Danny Blanchflower. His second big decision was to reinstate Blanchflower and hand him the captain's armband when it became clear his experience was necessary to maintain Spurs' First Division status.

Nicholson's other major move that season had been to sign defender Dave Mackay from Hearts. Then in the 1959/60 season he plundered Scotland for two further important signings; right midfielder John White from Falkirk, and goalkeeper Bill Brown from Dundee. Along with the addition of goalscoring midfielder Cliff Jones, his team began to take shape. Spurs finished the season in third place, two points behind champions Burnley – but having lost four of their last eight games, there was a painful sense of what might have been.

They did not wait long to rectify matters, winning the opening ten games of the 1960/61 season, drawing the eleventh, then winning the next four, before finally losing the seventeenth at Sheffield Wednesday. It was a record-breaking start. By the turn of the year, Spurs were ten points ahead of their nearest rivals Wolves. Spurs concentrated on the FA Cup, though, and took their foot off the gas. Four more losses by the end of March meant Wolves were only four points behind. Shades of the previous campaign began to emerge. Nicholson berated his team in the press for being 'lazy' – and they responded with four wins on the spin. The decisive game on April 17 against Wednesday, the first team to beat them that season, landed Spurs the league.

Three Saturdays later they won the FA Cup final in a dour 2-0 win over Leicester City and became the first team since Aston Villa in 1897 to win the double. Characteristically, Nicholson was annoyed with his side for failing to put on a jazzy display in the Wembley showpiece.

CHAMPIONS – AND TOP SCORERS – MANCHESTER CITY RELEGATED
(1938)

'Typical City.' It's a refrain familiar to modern-day supporters of the perennially hapless Manchester club. But for all their recent travails, including playing out a draw in the last match of the 1995/96 season only to find out they'd needed a win to avoid relegation; dropping to the Third Division in 1998; losing 8-1 in 2007/08 on the same day neighbours United won the league – none of it was a patch on their slapstick inter-war years.

In 1925/26 City were relegated from the First Division with the highest goals total, 89, of any demoted team in history. They would have avoided the drop had they not missed a penalty in the last match. The year after, promotion was all but assured with a final-day 8-0 victory – but rivals Portsmouth won 5-1 to pip them by a goal average of 0.0041.

City went up as Second Division champions the following year, scoring 100 goals, and during the 1930s their commitment to all-out attack was both their greatest asset and their undoing. In 1936/37, crack striker Peter Doherty scored 30 goals as City rattled in 107 on the way to the club's first ever title. That landmark achievement was sullied the following season as City became England's only reigning champions to suffer relegation.

They managed this despite scoring more goals, 77, than anyone else in the division – Doherty netting 23, Eric Brook 16 and Alec Herd 12 – and ending the season with a positive goal difference. They had only failed to score in four league games all year, but two of those matches came in their final three fixtures (which naturally sandwiched a 6-2 win). 'The use of the word 'staggering' may be justified from different angles,' was the spluttering reaction in the *Observer* the day after history was made. Which was another way of saying: 'typical City.'

THE FIRST *SCUDETTO* – ALL IN ONE DAY
(1898)

At 9 a.m. on May 9, 1898, the first Italian Championship kicked off on a field – the Velodromo Umberto 1 – just outside Turin. Four teams: Genoa; Internazionale di Torino; Ginnastica di Torono and FC Torinese competed for the right to call themselves champions of Italy. These days such an accolade takes the best part of nine months and 34 matches. The very first title was done and dusted that very same day by tea-time.

Internazionale di Torino won the first ever game 1-0, beating local rivals FC Torinese. The third Turin side in the competition, Ginnastica, were beaten 2-1 by a Genoa side containing a British goalkeeper called James Richardson Spensley. Spensley was the man who had staged the first ever properly organised football match in the country five months earlier. On January 6, 1898, his Genoa side were beaten 1-0 by a representative Turin XI featuring players from both FC Torinese and Internazionale di Torino. Spensley and Genoa got their revenge for that friendly defeat in the Championship final, becoming the first Italian champions by beating Internazionale di Torino 2-1 after extra-time.

Genoa dominated the league for the next two decades. They won the title a further eight times, but in 1925 their run came to a messy end. The Fascists had recently taken power, and military presence increased at football matches. Unfortunately for Genoa, in a play-off for the league against Bologna in Milan, events were manipulated by Bolognese Fascist leader Leandro Arpinati. With his team 2-0 down, Arpinati's 'blackshirts' invaded the pitch, after which the pressurised referee claimed a 'goal' had been scored. Bologna went on to 'equalise'. After two replays, the second staged behind closed doors at 7 a.m., Genoa were defeated 2-0. The 1925 championship became known as 'The Great Theft', and would gain extra resonance for Genoa in 1958, when teams were allowed to wear a golden star in honour of every ten titles they had won. Thanks to Arpinati, Genoa never got to wear a golden star.

THE HEARTS OF OAK DISASTER
(2001)

In 2000, the Accra Hearts of Oak Sporting Club were enjoying their most successful season to date. They had won the Ghanaian league, the national cup and had beaten Esperance Sportive of Tunisia 2-1 away in the first leg of the Confederation of African Football (CAF) Champions League on December 2. They won the second leg 3-1 two weeks later to become African champions, but the dream started to turn sour for Hearts, even before it had been realised.

The second leg descended into surreal violence. Esperance were 1-0 up with 15 minutes to play and chasing the second goal they required when rioting broke out. Police fired tear gas into the stands and CAF president Issa Hayatou narrowly missed being hit by a stray canister. One fan ran onto the pitch to give Esperance goalkeeper Chokri El Ouaer a sharp object to cut himself with in order to get the match abandoned, but the referee was wise to his game and ordered the player to be substituted. When the match restarted after an 18-minute hiatus he was replaced by a striker, Esperance's reserve keeper left on the bench. Hearts rattled in three to secure a 5-2 win – but they were later banned for a year from playing on the continental stage within 200km of Accra, as a punishment for the riots.

Less than five months later, Hearts of Oak were involved in yet another incident involving tear gas, but this time the consequences were tragic. After Hearts scored two late goals against their great rivals Kotoko Asante in a league match on May 9, 2001, Asante fans starting ripping up seats. Police sprayed tear gas into the crowds, who then fled for the exit only to find the gates were locked. It was the biggest football disaster in African history as 126 people were killed in the stampede.

It was the fourth footballing tragedy to befall the continent in less than four weeks. Just three days earlier, fighting among fans at a match in Ivory Coast left one fan dead; while on April 29, fourteen were killed in a stampede at a match in Congo. On April 11 a crush at Ellis Park in Johannesburg in a match between Orlando Pirates and Kaiser Chiefs left 43 dead.

Although FIFA decided to go ahead with the first African World Cup in 2010, a shadow had been cast over a continent-wide safety record described as a 'culture of neglect'.

NAPOLI 1-1 FIORENTINA: MARADONA'S *SCUDETTO*
(1987)

What Maradona failed to do for Barcelona, he more than made up for at Napoli. At Barcelona he was just another player in the team; at Napoli he *was* the team and would live like a king. Until the arrival of Maradona, Napoli had never won much – a couple of Coppa Italias, and two Serie A runners-up slots in the 1970s – but from 1984 to 1991 Napoli won the championship twice, finished second twice, won another Coppa Italia and the UEFA Cup. So loved was Maradona, many Neapolitans even rejoiced when he led Argentina to the 1986 World Cup.

On the night Napoli won their first ever *Scudetto* – after a match in which future Italian legend Roberto Baggio announced himself to the country with a penalty for Fiorentina – the streets of Naples exploded in unprecedented euphoria. Maradona's image was immortalized across the city – on murals and walls, with statues and memorials.

But as in Spain, a cloud followed Maradona around, and he soon fell into a world of drugs, depression and womanising. During his time in Italy he became notorious for walking away from a woman he'd fathered a child with in 1985. And while he was not, of course, above the influence of local gangsters the Camorra, his relationship with them caused fewer raised eyebrows than not facing up to fatherhood in the strictly Catholic province.

Despite his ongoing personal traumas, Maradona continued to play sparkling football. In 1989 he led them to Championship victory once more – despite only turning up four games into the season after arguments with the manager. Maradona never experienced such highs again – on a football pitch anyway – and it is unlikely Napoli ever will either. In the 1990/91 season they dropped to eighth position in the league. Although the period of Maradona's departure in 1991 saw the rise of the superb Gianfranco Zola, the gap he left was bigger than anyone could ever have imagined. The decline was marked. In 2004 a bankrupt Napoli found itself in Serie C1 (the Italian third-tier), though by 2008 they were promoted back to Serie A.

MAY 11

THE BRADFORD FIRE KILLS 56
(1985)

A crowd of 11,076 gathered at Valley Parade to watch newly crowned Third Division champions Bradford City's final game of the season against mid-table Lincoln. Bradford were on a high after lifting the trophy and a lap of honour before the match; it was their first title since winning the Third Division (North) in 1929, and the crowd were in celebratory mood. The match also marked the end of an era as the Main Stand was about to get a major revamp in preparation for the Second Division, where stadium safety regulations were tighter.

The first half of a meaningless match was about to end goalless when, two minutes before half-time, rubbish which had accumulated for decades under the wooden Main Stand – litter was regularly swept there through holes – caught alight. The fire spread quickly. Within two minutes of flames being spotted licking out from under the stand in G Block, the entire section was on fire; within two more, the whole stand was engulfed. Fans spilled onto the pitch to escape, though 56 failed to make it. More than 200 others were injured. Most died from suffocation at the back of the stand, having tried to escape through padlocked exits. The cause of the fire is thought to have been from a cigarette or match dropped into a polystyrene cup.

Two days later it was reported that the club had received letters warning of the potential danger which had developed under the fated stand. 'The timber construction is a fire hazard and in particular there is a build-up of combustible materials in the voids beneath the seats,' a letter released by West Yorkshire County Council read. 'A careless discarded cigarette would give rise to a fire risk.' And so it came to pass, though the club insisted that they had never seen the letters.

Few blamed the club, though: it was felt a litany of entrenched regulatory failings – to be dealt with in the Popplewell Report – were ultimately to blame. Wooden football stands would never again be built.

MILAN 0-5 READING: BERKSHIRE'S
FINEST TROUNCE *ROSSONERI*
(1913)

During the 1905/06 season, Willy Garbutt – the Englishman who would come to be regarded as Italian football's first proper coach after taking over at Genoa in 1912 – played a few games for Southern League side Reading. As a result of Garbutt's link to the club, they were invited to tour Italy in the summer of 1913.

Having taken a couple of days to reach Italy by train via Paris – where they stopped to enjoy an evening of food and fine wine – Reading arrived in Genoa on May 10. The next afternoon they set about beating the local side 4-2, their manager Garbutt refereeing the game. After enjoying another banquet that evening, they travelled to Milan, where the next day they recorded what now appears an amazing result.

Milan were, of course, not the force they are now – although their striker Louis Van Hege later won gold for Belgium at the 1920 Olympic Games. The game, played at Milan's Civico Arena, was desperately one-sided. Reading scored four in the first half, before easing off in the second and adding only one more.

Two days later Reading suffered their only defeat on the tour, 2-1 at Casale, where they were billed as runners up of the First Division (in fact, they had come eighth in the Southern League). They bounced back the day after, and in style, beating Italian champions Pro Vercelli 6-0. The tour ended that Sunday with a 2-0 win over Italy – and of course another banquet.

A triumph, though times change. Milan have since won six European Cups; Italy four World Cups; Reading the 1988 Simod Cup.

DINAMO ZAGREB P-P RED STAR BELGRADE: BOBAN ATTACKS POLICEMAN
(1990)

Eric Cantona's infamous leap over the hoardings at Selhurst Park has a certain light balletic grace, but was nothing compared to the feet-first attack by Dinamo Zagreb midfielder Zvonimir Boban on a policeman during a game against Red Star Belgrade in 1990. Cantona's salvo handed a league title to Blackburn Rovers; Boban's has been credited in some quarters as literally kick-starting a civil war.

In 1990, Yugoslavia was a nation being held together by a thread. With Communism crumbling, nationalist tensions between its states were rising and independence was on the agenda. Matches between Red Star, from Yugoslav and Serbian capital Belgrade, and Dinamo, from the capital of Croatia, were fiery at the best of times, and often overshadowed by violence between groups of hardcore nationalist fans. This match was no different.

As the match started at Dinamo's Maksimir stadium, 3,000 Red Star fans had already started to rip up the stadium seats. The Yugoslavian – and in the eyes of the home crowd pro-Serbian – police stood by and watched. In retaliation, Dinamo fans jumped over the ground's barriers and headed for the Red Star end. What followed was a mass brawl so bad that some fans had to be airlifted from the stadium. In the midst of all this, one Dinamo fan lay stricken on the ground, having been beaten by a baton-wielding policeman. Boban intervened, high-kicking the officer in the face.

Within a year, Croatia declared independence from Yugoslavia. The kick was seen as symbolic of Croatia rising up against Serbian oppression, though a symbol is all it was – Boban's actions did not actually start the subsequent war. Not least because it was later found that the policeman Boban kicked was in fact not a Serb but a Bosnian Muslim.

GERMANY 3-6 ENGLAND: THE ENGLISH
GIVE THE NAZI SALUTE
(1938)

It is one of the most infamous images in English football history – but at the time, the England team's salute to the Nazi party at a friendly against Germany in Berlin was afforded little attention.

An article in the *Guardian* two days after the match noted how 'the stadium was dressed in swastikas flown from the poles around the ground' and that during the playing of 'Deutschland über Alles' the 'Englishmen gave the Nazi salute as it had previously been decided they should'. But most reports avoided mention of the political climate – the Nazis had annexed Austria two months previously – concentrating instead on the blistering heat and England's blistering football. Cliff Bastin of Arsenal had scored the first of six goals for the visitors, who were 4-1 up by half-time. One of Germany's consolation strikes was scored by Hans Pesser, the only former Austrian in the side. Relations on the field between the teams were friendly.

Who called for the salute and who opposed it is not completely clear. The Foreign Office wanted to keep in line with the government's policy of appeasement and deemed the salute necessary. FA secretary Stanley Rous claimed it was 'left to the players who all agreed they had no objection and no doubt saw it as a bit of fun rather than any political significance'. Defender Stan Cullis later insisted that an FA official visited the dressing room and instructed the players to give the salute. 'I along with the other England players objected to giving the Nazi salute, despite the FA informing us it was the only courteous salute to the German People. We were informed in a diplomatic way that if we didn't give the salute we wouldn't be selected for future England games.'

England did not play the Germans again until December 1954. The newly-crowned world champions, having beaten the hot favourites Hungary in the final in Switzerland, were themselves beaten 3-1 in a friendly at Wembley (though only three members of the team that performed the 'Miracle of Berne' played). Stanley Matthews, who had scored in Berlin and given the salute, was man of the match.

JINKY JOHNSTONE LARGES IT AT LARGS
(1974)

The Scotland squad were staying in a hotel in the Ayrshire town of Largs, preparing for that weekend's Home International against England at Hampden Park. How thorough that preparation was is a moot point, though on the Tuesday night several members of the team decided to go to a nearby pub for some cold drinks. Coming back along the pebbled beach well after midnight, winger Jimmy 'Jinky' Johnstone clambered into a rowing boat along the sea front. Defender Sandy Jardine decided it would be a good idea to give the boat a shove out into the water.

Johnstone stood up in the vessel to belt out a rendition of 'Bonnie Scotland'. The rest of the party joined in the chorus from the shore. It was at this point, with the boat quickly sailing out to sea, that Jinky realised that the boat had no oars. Other reports suggest the boat did have oars – but no oarlocks. Either way, while Johnstone's buddies were singing the praises of the Scottish nation, their star winger was sailing off towards Ireland. It was only after a few minutes that they realised Johnstone was in bother; the singing stopped and the coastguard was called. By the time help arrived, Johnstone was over half a mile out towards the Irish Sea. Johnstone was heavily criticised in the newspapers for the incident, but responded magnificently: first by setting up a goal in a 2-0 win for Scotland over the 'Auld Enemy' at the weekend, then by flicking an unambiguous V-sign at the press box by way of celebration.

It was not the only time Johnstone got in a spot of bother before the finals. On June 2, just before Scotland were due to play a friendly against Norway in Oslo, Johnstone and Billy Bremner were 'severely reprimanded' by the Scottish FA for 'a serious breach of discipline' in a student bar. The pair offered their 'profuse apologies' and were not omitted from Scotland's World Cup squad.

Still that was not the end of Johnstone's turbulent year. Upon returning from Scotland's decent showing in West Germany, he was found guilty of assault after a fracas in a Coatbridge pub car-park back in February. He had been called a 'dumpling' for blocking someone's view of that night's cabaret performance, and responded with a swift kick to the side of his critic's head.

MAY 16

MILAN 1-0 LEEDS: UNITED MUGGED IN EUROPE, PART ONE
(1973)

Don Revie's great Leeds United side spent eleven seasons at the top of the English game between 1964 and 1975. Their return of two league titles, two Fairs Cups, an FA Cup and a League Cup should not be sniffed at, but during this period Leeds turned falling at the last hurdle into an art form. Revie famously wore his lucky suit to every match, but much good it did him, as Leeds's litany of close shaves is second to none.

In their glorious decade, Leeds finished as league runners up five times. The 1965 FA Cup final was lost in extra-time to Liverpool. The team were four minutes from the 1970 FA Cup, but conceded a late equaliser to Chelsea. The replay was lost after conceding another equaliser when twelve minutes from victory. That 1969/70 season also saw Leeds, as well as finishing second in the league to Everton, lose a European Cup semi-final to Celtic.

In 1971, failure to play to the whistle at home to West Bromwich Albion allowed Jeff Astle to score an infamous (albeit comfortably offside) winning goal. The title was handed to Arsenal. In 1972, all Leeds needed was a point at mid-table Wolves on the final day of the season to complete the double. Never at the races, they lost 2-1, gifting the league to Derby. Then in 1973, Bob Stokoe's Second Division Sunderland beat Leeds 1-0 in one of the biggest FA Cup final shocks of all.

Worse was to come that season. In the 1973 European Cup Winners Cup final, Leeds had three legitimate penalty appeals turned down and Norman Hunter sent off. Milan scored the only goal of the match with a free-kick past a poorly marshalled Leeds wall. Referee Christos Michas was later found guilty of match fixing and banned for life by UEFA, though Milan were allowed to keep the trophy.

Leeds might have hoped for some karmic return in the 1975 European Cup final against Bayern Munich – but another two penalty claims were denied and Peter Lorimer had a goal chalked off for offside, before Bayern scored two late goals. By then Revie had left to let his lucky suit do its worst for England; the match marked the end of an ultimately unlucky era for the club.

BAYERN MUNICH 4-0 ATLÉTICO MADRID:
THE BAYERN ERA BEGINS
(1974)

Bayern Munich were not always the biggest club in Germany. When they became Bundesliga winners in 1969 it was only their second title, having previously won a sole German championship final in 1932. But having assembled a team featuring Franz Beckenbauer, Gerd Müller, Sepp Maier and Paul Breitner, all that was about to change.

In 1972 they won their second Bundesliga, pipping Schalke on the last day of the season – if thrashing them 5-1 can be classed as 'pipping'. It was the first in an unprecedented title hat-trick in Germany. Bayern won the league the following season by a record-breaking eleven points, then beat their closest rivals of the era, Borussia Monchengladbach, to the 1973/74 title. However, it was in Europe they would really make their mark: they were about to follow Ajax's three European Cups in a row with a hat-trick of their own.

Their reign owed a little to luck. In the first round of the 1974 European Cup, Bayern were 15 minutes from going out against Swedish minnows Atvidabergs, having thrown away a 3-1 first leg lead. An Uli Hoeness goal took the game to penalties, which they scraped 4-3. Bayern then struggled to beat opponents from the other side of the Berlin Wall, edging past Dynamo Dresden 7-6 on aggregate having at one point been 6-3 up in the tie. And in the final against Atlético Madrid, having gone behind to a goal from a young Luis Aragonés, a last-minute 30-yard daisycutter from defender Georg Schwarzenbeck earnt them a replay, which they won gloriously, 4-0. Bayern's luck continued in the 1975 final, Leeds United being denied two good penalty shouts and an onside goal before Bayern scored twice late on to win the cup. In the 1976 final, St Etienne hit the post twice before conceding the only goal of a scrappy match.

Bayern's luck in European Cup finals eventually ran out. In 1987 they were 13 minutes from victory before conceding two late goals to Porto – one an outrageous backheel by Rabah Madjer. Then in 1999, one up against Manchester United having hit post and bar, with a minute to go…

MAY 18

REAL MADRID 7-3 EINTRACHT FRANKFURT:
THE GREATEST GAME?
(1960)

Eintracht Frankfurt had enjoyed their last visit to Glasgow, beating Rangers over two legs, 6-3 and 6-1, in the semi-final of the 1960 European Cup. Returning to Scotland for the Hampden Park final, the Germans faced Real Madrid – who were about to deliver their signature performance.

Within eleven seconds of the kick off, the crowd of 135,000 collectively gasped as Ferenc Puskás, with a flick of his left boot, rolled the ball into the Eintracht area and nearly set Canario free on goal. The crowd spent the following 90 minutes of action sighing and cooing at Real's display, at times sounding more like an appreciative theatre audience than a football crowd. Puskás's shimmies brought warm applause, Francesco Gento's bursts of speed down the left drew cheers, Alfredo di Stéfano's mesmerising stepovers actually caused laughter.

Eintracht opened the scoring through Richard Kress on 18 minutes, but by the half-hour Real were ahead, di Stéfano guiding home a low cross, then ramming home a fumble by Frankfurt keeper Egon Loy. Over to Puskás, who made it three just before half-time by roofing a shot from a tight angle on the left. Puskás added a calm penalty after the restart, bundled home Gento's fizzing cross, then turned and swept an effort into the top-left corner. Erwin Stein pulled one back for Eintracht, but straight from the resulting kick-off, five Real passes set di Stéfano free to score. Stein added another consolation, and that was that: 7-3.

The whistle blew with the ball at Puskás's feet. He picked it up: he'd earned the right to keep it. He didn't, though, shoving it in Stein's chest with the German striker pestering him for it. Puskás didn't need trinkets; Real had just won their fifth cup, after the greatest final, and maybe the greatest game, ever.

RENTON 4-1 WBA: THE FIRST 'WORLD CUP' IS LIFTED
(1888)

In August 1887, Scottish Cup holders Hibernian took on FA Cup winners Preston North End in a friendly at Hibs' Easter Road ground. Posters appeared all over Edinburgh billing the encounter as 'The Association Football Championship of the World'. Hibernian won the match 2-1 and therefore had the right (whichever way you look at it, as nobody else had bothered to stage such an event) to call themselves the first world champions, beating Uruguay to it by 43 years.

The world championship billing was, however, very much an afterthought. It was a last-minute piece of opportune marketing on behalf of the English and Scottish FAs. Hibernian, it should be noted, had no trophy to hoist. A similar mistake was avoided the following year, when Scottish Cup winners Renton – fresh from thrashing Cambuslang a record-breaking 6-1 in the final – met FA Cup holders West Bromwich Albion in May 1888 for the 'Official World Championship of the United Kingdom and the World'.

In torrential rain at Cathkin Park, Renton ripped West Brom to pieces. The English team had not wanted to play the tie, understandably so since the adverse weather had claimed four lives in Glasgow that week. The Scottish side won 4-1 – and lifted a foot-high pewter trophy which proved they were 'Champions of the United Kingdom and the World'. Less than a month later, Renton further proved their worth by going down to Preston and beating a side who were about to go through the entire first season of the Football League unbeaten, 4-2.

However someone, somewhere obviously decided that claiming world bragging rights was a ludicrous concept. The world championship, such as it was, was quietly dropped by both FAs the following year, never to be spoken of again (outside Edinburgh and Renton, at least).

BARCELONA 1-0 SAMPDORIA: BARÇA WIN THE EUROPEAN CUP IN COLOUR
(1992)

The early years of the European Cup were not kind to Barcelona. The great Real Madrid teams featuring di Stéfano, Gento, Puskás et al had won the first five stagings of the trophy. Even when Barcelona became the team to end their imperious reign, knocking them out in the semi-finals of the 1960/61 tournament, they were beaten 3-2 by Benfica in the final. Real Madrid made two more European finals in the next three years, then added a sixth trophy with their 'ye-ye' team in 1966. When it came to the biggest prize of all, Barça's cupboard remained steadfastly bare.

By the 1980s their record in the tournament was still awful. One of the biggest clubs in the world had competed in the same number of European Cup finals as Partizan Belgrade, Panathinaikos, Leeds United, St Etienne, Brugge and Malmo. And when they did reach their second final in 1986, they quickly wished they hadn't, losing a penalty shootout to Steaua Bucharest, having failed to convert a single spot-kick.

The monkey was shaken off their back in style in 1992, when Johan Cruyff's 'Dream Team' beat Sampdoria 1-0 at Wembley. Ronald Koeman's blistering free-kick from 25 yards with eight minutes of extra-time to play was the only goal of the evening. Barça's fans taunted Real, who had last won the trophy 26 years ago: 'You've never won the cup in colour.' Cruyff, already a Barcelona hero, became a fully-fledged legend.

MAY 21

FIFA FORMED – BUT THE BRITS DON'T PLAY BALL
(1904)

Trust the British to have a sniffy attitude to international relations. In a three-day meeting in Paris which began on May 21, 1904, Robert Guérin, the treasurer of a French national sports federation, brought together the football associations of France, Belgium, Denmark, Holland, Spain, Sweden and Switzerland under the banner Fédération Internationale de Football Association: FIFA. The international governing body of football was born – although as the Brits had little interest in international competition, their response was lukewarm to say the least.

Their attitude betrayed itself in the run-up to FIFA's formation. The Dutch football association had written to the FA to sound them out in 1902, only for the FA to take over a year to reply to their letter. FIFA pressed on anyway. By the end of 1905 Czechoslovakia, Hungary and Italy had joined up – along with England, who decided to use the organisation to impose their rulebook as the worldwide standard.

There were manifest teething troubles. Scotland and Ireland's applications were initially rejected – as they were part of the United Kingdom it was felt their membership would open the floodgates to all number of regional states. A fair point, though not one which couldn't be circumvented: the dominance of the British game at the time meant Scotland, Ireland and Wales were admitted despite their presence contravening the statutes.

By 1914 FIFA had cast its net wide. Non-European nations such as Argentina, Chile, South Africa and the USA became members. But World War I broke up the happy home: in its wake the British associations refused to play former enemies and resigned from FIFA. They soon returned – only to leave again over the issue of 'broken-time' payments, which compensated amateur players for missing work, a practice abhorrent to the FA. The row meant the home nations missed the first three World Cups, as they only returned to the fold in 1946.

GLASSMANN BLOWS WHISTLE ON MARSEILLE
BRIBING SCANDAL
(1993)

It should have been the greatest week in Olympique Marseille's history, but it proved to be their most shameful. On March 26, 1993, Marseille became the first French side to win the European Cup, upsetting the odds to beat Fabio Capello's Milan in the final with a Basile Boli header (in what proved to be Marco van Basten's last match). The following weekend, they pipped Paris Saint Germain to the Ligue 1 title back home, their fifth consecutive championship. Marseille had reached the pinnacle.

It didn't take long for them to fall off their pedestal. On May 20, during the French title run-in, Marseille had won a crucial game 1-0 at relegation-haunted Valenciennes. It transpired that Marseille defender Jean-Jacques Eyedelie had given Valenciennes striker Christophe Robert's wife an envelope containing £30,000 in used Francs to 'take their foot off the gas and let the match go'. She buried the money in her mother's garden, with the intention of later divvying it up between Robert and his team mate Jorge Burruchaga (scorer of the winning goal for Argentina in the 1986 World Cup final), who, along with Robert, had agreed to accept the bribe.

Valenciennes midfielder Jacques Glassmann had also been approached but had refused to accept the bribe. Meanwhile some of his team mates heard a rumour that Marseille had been offering bribes, and informed the referee at half-time during the fateful match. Robert panicked and tried to implicate several members of the squad, and so two days after the game, Glassmann approached his coach Boro Primorac and blew the whistle. The French league stripped Marseille of their title – second-placed Paris St Germain were offered it but refused – while UEFA banned Marseille from European competition, though their 1993 Champions League win was allowed to stand. Robert, Burruchaga and Eydelie were all slapped with indefinite bans.

Marseille owner Bernard Tapie was later jailed for a systematic sequence of match fixing. Glassmann won a FIFA Fair Play award for his actions, but was treated as a pariah in France and was eventually forced to retire.

KEANE, MCCARTHY AND THE SAIPAN INCIDENT
(2002)

Roy Keane had long been unimpressed with the way the Republic of Ireland prepared for matches. The players flew cramped-up in economy class, while the FAI suits reclined in business. Instead of pasta, fruit and cereals, there were cheese sandwiches and pizza. Instead of energy drinks, there was booze. Keane was also unhappy with the just-along-for-the-ride attitude which pervaded the squad, an attitude he felt went all the way up to manager Mick McCarthy. After letting slip a 2-0 lead in a World Cup qualifier away to Holland, McCarthy was 'pleased as punch' with the resulting 2-2 draw. Keane was livid. For him, the diet symbolised everything that was wrong with the preparation: 'In my book we'd failed Mick's Challenge – cheese sandwiches.'

Ireland qualified for the 2002 World Cup in Korea-Japan. But upon arriving at their training camp in Saipan, Keane discovered that the training equipment had not yet arrived: no tracksuits, no medical equipment, no footballs. Worse still, Ireland's training pitch was rock hard and full of potholes. Steve Finnan turned his ankle while jogging and admitted that had he been going at full pelt, he would have broken it. McCarthy had assured Keane that preparations would be up to scratch. In Keane's view, that promise had not been kept.

When a training match had to be curtailed because the goalkeepers were 'tired', Keane decided to go home. He was talked out of it, though the story leaked. He gave an interview to the *Irish Times* explaining why he had threatened to go: 'Enough is enough. Training pitch, travel arrangements … this trip is the tip of the iceberg.' On May 23 the interview was published, causing McCarthy to confront Keane in front of the squad. Keane's response was straight to the point: 'I didn't rate you as a player, I don't rate you as a manager, and I don't rate you as a person. You're a fucking wanker and you can stick your World Cup up your arse.' Keane was sent packing on the next plane home.

Keane had believed Ireland had a chance of winning the weakest World Cup in living memory. They went out on penalties in the second round, to Spain, McCarthy unaware Ireland's opponents had been down to ten men in extra-time.

PERU 0-1 ARGENTINA: OLYMPIC CRUSH KILLS 328
(1964)

The Pre-Olimpico, the South American qualifying tournament for the Olympic Games, was particularly tight ahead of the 1964 Tokyo event. With the round-robin league reaching its denouement, neither Argentina, Brazil nor Peru had lost a game in the group; the top two would qualify, so it was nip-and-tuck. Despite playing hot favourites Argentina – who had just thrashed Chile 4-0 – Pre-Olimpico host nation Peru were determined to hold on to their unbeaten record in front of their own fans at Lima's Estadio Nacional.

Throughout the first half the game remained goalless. Fifteen minutes into the second, Néstor Manfredi scored for Argentina. The Peruvians kept up the pressure and six minutes before the final whistle they scored in front of the 50,000 strong crowd, who exploded in celebration, believing they were in touching distance of a place in the competition. But the Uruguayan referee, Ángel Pazos, disallowed the goal for a foul. A fan leapt over the nine-foot barrier and threatened the referee. Within seconds a shower of bottles, bricks and stones flooded onto the pitch. Fearing for his life, Pazos left the pitch, abandoning the game and declaring the Argentinians 1-0 winners.

Outraged fans rushed the pitch. Police unleashed dogs and tear gas into the closed south end of the stadium. More than 2,000 spectators tried to flee the stadium, but with the gates locked in a stadium packed to the brim, disaster was inevitable. 'A few of the victims were fatally wounded by police, but most of the scores of police shots were in the air,' reported the British United Press. 'Instead of restoring order, they contributed to the panic.' The resulting crush killed 328. 'The pitch looked like a battlefield with missiles strewn everywhere,' reported Reuters of the aftermath.

On the streets outside, fans set fire to cars and buses and threw paper bombs into garages. One hospital alone reported receiving 140 dead bodies. A seven day period of mourning was declared and the following qualifiers cancelled. Argentina were awarded first place, while a broken Peru lost 4-0 to Brazil in a play-off for second. Neither South American qualifier progressed further than the group stages in Tokyo.

INTERNAZIONALE 1-2 CELTIC: THE LISBON
LIONS DEFEAT *CATENACCIO*
(1967)

The continental reign of Helenio Herrera's Internazionale began against a British team: in the first round of the 1963/64 European Cup, they shut up shop against Everton at Goodison Park for a goalless draw, then took the Merseysiders back to the San Siro, picking them off with a single goal by Jair. Four seasons later it was comprehensively ended by one.

Inter's win over Everton had been Europe's first exposure to Herrera's top-notch brand of *catenaccio*: the infamous 'bolt defence' using a sweeper, relentless man-for-man marking – and the occasional break up-field to counter-attack through the powerful genius of Sandro Mazzola. Herrera had attempted to play an attacking game in Europe while Barcelona manager, but had been picked off in the 1960 European Cup semi-finals by Real Madrid. With Inter he was taking no chances. The tactic worked. After beating Everton, Inter went on to the final, where they stifled an ageing Real Madrid and picked them off on the break to win 3-1. They retained their cup the year after with an even more tedious display, grinding out a one-goal victory in the final against Benfica.

Inter lost a tight 1966 semi-final to Real Madrid, but were back in the final the year after – where they faced Celtic, whose philosophy was diametrically opposed to Herrera's stifling catenaccio. 'I am going to tell him how Celtic will win,' said Celtic manager Jock Stein before the game, 'but it will not help him in any manner, shape or form: we are going to attack as we have never attacked before.' Which is exactly what happened. Ironically, Inter's early push, which led to Mazzola converting a penalty after just six minutes, hindered them. Their natural instinct was to sit back and soak up pressure, which played into Celtic's hands. The Scottish team – famously all born within a 30-mile radius of Parkhead – had 39 attempts at goal during the next 84 minutes, while Inter offered only two. Just after the hour, Tommy Gemmell hit a 25-yard screamer with two players offside, then with seven minutes to go, Steve Chalmers hammered the final nail in catenaccio's coffin.

TOULOUSE 6-3 ANGERS: ASSASSINATION AT
THE FRENCH CUP FINAL
(1957)

On the day of the 1957 Coupe de France final, the Guerre d'Algerie (the Algerian War of Independence) was in full swing. Ali Chekkal, the former vice-president of the Algerian Assembly, and a man opposed to independence from France, was in the VIP box at the Colombes Stadium in Paris alongside French president René Coty. Chekkal was there to watch two of the 76 Algerians who plied their trade in French football contest the cup final.

Three months earlier, Chekkal had been part of a delegation to the United Nations which attempted to justify a continued French presence in Algeria. He was a marked man in the eyes of radical Algerian activists, who distributed pamphlets ordering him to be shot on sight. Having witnessed Said Brahimi and Ahmed Bouchouk help their Toulouse side to a 6-3 win over Angers and pick up the trophy from Coty, Chekkal left the stadium and was waiting for a car to whisk him back to the safety of his guarded hotel room. Then unemployed plumber Mohammed bin Sadok approached Chekkal and fired a bullet into his back. As bin Sadok was 'severely beaten by police', according to reports, Chekkal was whisked to hospital, but within hours he was dead, victim of the only political assassination at a major football final. 'I chose Chekkal because he was the last Muslim friend of the French,' explained his assassin later.

The assassination represented – literally – one of the first major warning shots in Algeria's battle for independence. Football was seen as crucial in the battle. In April 1958, eight French-based Algerians – including Toulouse duo Brahimi and Bouchouk – defected to play for an Algerian Independence Movement team. According to *Le Monde*, the French public was 'more sensitive to Algerian footballers than Algerian politicians'. Ironically, many of the players who defected returned to France post-independence – as they were seen as Francophiles in their homeland.

STRELTSOV, THE 'RUSSIAN PELÉ', GIVEN LIFE
BAN FOR ALLEGED RAPE
(1958)

It didn't take long for Eduard Streltsov to make a name for himself. In 1954, while playing for Torpedo Moscow, he became the youngest player to score a goal in Soviet football aged just 16. A year later, he was crowned the league's top scorer. When called upon to make his debut for the USSR in a friendly against Sweden in 1955, he scored a hat-trick by the 42nd minute of the match. His second cap brought a second hat-trick, this time against India. It was a whirlwind start to what looked like becoming a stellar career.

At the 1956 Olympics Streltsov played a crucial role in getting USSR to the final. In the semi-final against Bulgaria, with his side a goal down and down to ten men with eight minutes of extra-time to play, he scored an equalizer, then set up the winner. Although he was rewarded for his efforts by being dropped for the final – the Soviets won gold – Streltsov was expected to be a major player for the Russians in the World Cup in Sweden two years later.

He did not make it to the tournament. On May 25, 1958, the last night of training before the World Cup, Streltsov and two team mates were invited to a party by a Russian general who was holidaying near the team's camp. What exactly happened there is unclear to this day, but the consequences were devastating. Streltsov was accused of raping a woman he had been introduced to at the party. He confessed to the crime, although it was rumoured he had only done so as a bargaining chip for his place at the World Cup. On May 27, he was banned from football for life and on July 24 sent to a gulag.

Conspiracy theories abound about Streltsov. He had reportedly turned down an order to move from Torpedo to join either CKSA or Dynamo Moscow, teams favoured by the Communist establishment. He was also rumoured to have spurned the advances of – and insulted – a powerful Politburo member's daughter.

Or he could simply have been guilty of the crime. Whatever the truth, Leonid Brezhnev eventually sanctioned his release in 1964, and Streltsov rejoined Torpedo a year later, where he enjoyed an Indian summer, winning Soviet Footballer of the Year in 1967 and 1968.

SWINDON 3-0 NAPOLI: TOWN BECOME
ANGLO-ITALIAN KINGS
(1970)

In 1969, Swindon Town became the second Third Division team to land the League Cup in three seasons. Swindon's midfield star Don Rogers stunned Arsenal by sashaying through a quagmire – the Wembley pitch had been churned up before the big occasion by the Horse of the Year show – to score one of the great Wembley solo efforts in extra-time to secure a seismic 3-1 shock victory. The trophy should have allowed them to enter the following year's Fairs Cup, but like Rodney Marsh's QPR before them in 1967, their lowly league status forbade it.

Unlike QPR, Swindon got their day in the sun. By way of compensation they were given a place in a new competition primarily set up for the purpose of rewarding them: the Anglo-Italian League Cup. They were to play Coppa Italia winners AS Roma – a team featuring midfielder Fabio Capello – and after losing 2-1 in Rome, won 4-0 at the County Ground to lift the cup 5-2 on aggregate. The experiment was so successful it was decided more Anglo-Italian trophies should be set up.

So the following year, in 1970, Swindon entered the first Anglo-Italian Cup. Six teams competed from each country in two groups: Sheffield Wednesday, Middlesbrough, West Bromwich Albion, Sunderland and Wolves made up the English group; while Napoli, Juventus, Roma, Fiorentina, Lazio and Vicenza (then temporarily known as Lanerossi) battled away in Italy. Swindon topped the English table, earning the right to take on Italian victors Napoli in their Sao Paolo stadium, where they would run riot – as would the local fans.

After Arthur Horsfield put Swindon 3-0 up on 63 minutes, the home crowd erupted and began lobbing bottles and stones. After 79 minutes, with hundreds of benches having been torn up and dispatched onto the pitch, the match was abandoned and the trophy awarded to Swindon. More than 100 people were injured and £20,000 of damage was caused. Don Rogers didn't seem to mind though: 'I have got a nice medal for it and my wife's got a bracelet.'

MANCHESTER UNITED 4-1 BENFICA: THE END
OF BUSBY'S QUEST
(1968)

'This is United's finest hour and mine too,' Matt Busby told the world's press after George Best's famous 'El Beatle' performance had set Manchester United on their way to a 5-1 European Cup quarter-final victory over Benfica in March 1966. Then in private he told his wife, with reference to the continental quest he had embarked upon a decade earlier in 1956: 'I've a feeling this is it.'

He was wrong on both counts. It took another two years, and another match against Benfica, before Busby achieved his dream. In the wake of the 5-1 win in 1966, United expressed hopes of drawing an 'ageing' Real Madrid in the semi-final, who they expected to beat easily. But the wish proved an act of hubris: while the supposedly decrepit Madrid side went on to win the trophy, United crashed out in the semi-finals at the hands of unfancied Partizan Belgrade. 'I'm sick of the thought we've lost our greatest chance,' said a distraught Busby after the tie.

Wrong again. Redemption arrived in the 1968 European Cup. This time United did draw Real Madrid in the semi-finals. After winning 1-0 at Old Trafford, they were 3-1 down at the Bernabéu and seventeen minutes away from elimination when David Sadler scored. United were going through on away goals; seven minutes later Munich survivor Bill Foulkes made sure they'd reach the Wembley final, where they'd face Benfica again.

United won the final 4-1 after extra-time thanks to a Bobby Charlton double, Alex Stepney's late smothering save from Eusébio, a Best solo effort and Brian Kidd header on his 19th birthday. This time Busby's words, ten years after Munich, would ring true for ever: 'This is the greatest night of my life, the fulfilment of my dearest wish. I'm proud of the team, proud for Bobby Charlton and Bill Foulkes, who have travelled the long road with me.'

MAY 30

DI BARTOLOMEI COMMITS SUICIDE, 10 YEARS AFTER ROMA'S LOSS
(1994)

On May 30, 1984, AS Roma met Liverpool in the European Cup final at their own ground, the Stadio Olimpico. The Roman side narrowly missed being crowned champions after losing on penalties. History being written by the victors, the shoot-out is remembered for Bruce Grobbelaar's 'spaghetti legs' and Alan Kennedy's ice-cool winning kick. 'I was always confident, you know,' said Kennedy after the match. 'I just plonked it down and said to myself 'I know where I'm going to put this'. I took a penalty on Monday morning in training and put it in exactly the same spot, just like that.' Few recall Roma initially having the upper hand during the penalties, Steve Nicol missing Liverpool's first, Roma going ahead with an exquisite two-step kick by captain Agostino di Bartoloemi.

The year before, Roma had won their second *Scudetto*, thanks in no small part to the deep-lying playmaking of di Bartolomei. He scored 66 goals in 308 games for the club, seven of them coming in Roma's championship season. But having come so close to lifting the European Cup for his club, he was soon deemed dispensable along with title-winning manager Nils Liedholm, and both were sent on their way to a struggling Milan. Di Bartolomei didn't enjoy his time at the San Siro and, after Silvio Burlusconi and Arrigo Sacchi arrived, he was on his way down the leagues to see out an almost-great career.

After leaving the game he tried but failed to set up a football school but found himself struggling with debts and depression. A decade to the day of the devastating defeat against Liverpool, Di Bartolomei shot himself through the heart with a pistol. His suicide came as a complete shock to his family and friends. 'I can't see a way out,' he wrote in his suicide note. Thousands of fans attended his funeral, along with the bulk of the 1980s Roma side.

YELLOW AND RED CARDS ARE INTRODUCED
(1970)

Referee Ken Aston was the man in charge of the infamous 'Battle of Santiago' between Chile and Italy at the 1962 World Cup, but the match that led to him leaving a lasting legacy in football was another tempestuous World Cup fixture.

Aston, who retired in 1963 after adjudicating that year's FA Cup final, was put in charge of refereeing by FIFA at the 1966 World Cup. During the quarter-final between England and Argentina, Antonio Rattin was sent off for 'violence of the tongue', even though the German referee could speak no Spanish, and Rattin no German. It was down to Aston to come down from the stands and persuade Rattin to leave the pitch after an eight-minute protest. The morning after the match, Bobby and Jack Charlton were surprised to read in the papers that they both had also fallen foul of the referee during the game, picking up a caution apiece. Alf Ramsey had to double check with FIFA to clarify the situation; it was clear that something needed to be done to improve the lines of communication between referee and player.

Driving home from work one day down Kensington High Street, Aston was repeatedly stopped by traffic lights – at which point a bulb flashed above his head: 'Yellow, take it easy; red, finished. I thought, well, this is the way to overcome the language problem in international matches. And so I sat on this until 1970 and launched the red and yellow cards in the World Cup Finals in Mexico.' In the opening match on May 31, Evgeny Lovchev of USSR was the first man to be cautioned with a yellow card. The calming effect must have worked, because no reds were shown during the entire tournament.

Aston was once asked if any other events stood out in his long life. The former World War II soldier replied: 'I would suppose hanging some senior Japanese officers stands out most in my mind.'

JUNE 1

LAWRIE MCMENEMY LEAVES SOUTHAMPTON FOR SUNDERLAND
(1985)

When fans invaded the pitch after Grimsby Town won the Fourth Division championship in 1972, manager Lawrie McMenemy addressed the crowd to restore order. The minute McMenemy finished his oration, a young lad on crutches threw away his props and cried: 'It's all right, Lawrie! I can walk now!' Bystanders stood open-mouthed as the boy strutted off, McMenemy suddenly enveloped by a God-like aura.

'Big Lawrie' might not have performed a miracle that day – it transpired he knew the young man, who had been on the mend for weeks – but Southampton fans will argue that he managed a few during his time on the south coast. He moved to The Dell from Grimsby in the summer of 1973. Within three years he had guided the Saints to the FA Cup as a Second Division side, Bobby Stokes scoring a late winner against Manchester United. Saints continued to over-achieve under McMenemy: they were promoted the season after their cup win, were runners-up in the 1979 League Cup, signed Kevin Keegan from Hamburg in 1980, and came second in the league behind Liverpool in 1983/84.

By 1985, McMenemy decided he had taken the club as far as he could, and jumped ship for Sunderland. As the old joke goes, like the *Titanic*, he should never have left Southampton. Despite spending big money on Eric Gates, George Burley and Alan Kennedy, he could not get Sunderland promoted, and after his gold Mercedes was vandalised by fans in March 1987, with the team one point from the relegation zone, he resigned.

A month later, Sunderland lost their final game of the season 3-2 at home to Barnsley after being 2-0 up, then missing a penalty at 2-1. A win would have kept them up but, as it was, they lost a relegation play-off against Gillingham to drop into the Third Division for the first time in their history.

THE BATTLE OF SANTIAGO: CHILE 2–0 ITALY
(1962)

The 1962 World Cup was hosted by Chile in exacting circumstances. Far from affluent in the first place, Chile was still recovering from the 1960 Valdivia earthquake which killed nearly 6,000 people. So when Italian journalists Antonio Ghirelli and Corrado Pizzinelli sent reports back home painting a picture of Santiago as a poverty-stricken slum full of loose women, feelings ran understandably high – especially as the reports were distorted in the Chilean press to whip up local support ahead of the group game between Chile and Italy.

Ghiredelli and Pizzinelli fled the country before the tournament started for their own safety – an Argentinian journalist, mistaken for one of them, was badly beaten in a bar – but the situation snowballed at the match itself. The first foul came within 12 seconds, the first red card after eight minutes, Italy's Giorgio Ferrini refusing to walk and being dragged off by the police. After an eight-minute delay, Chile's Leonel Sánchez, the son of a professional boxer, responded to niggly fouls from Mario David by flattening him. Referee Ken Aston did not punish Sánchez, so David kicked Sánchez in the neck and was sent off.

David Coleman's BBC commentary paints a picture of its own: 'There's trouble already, with a fight going on in the middle there! ... This is absolutely ridiculous! Ferrini took an open kick at a player who was nowhere near the ball ... And he's off! ... The police are being called on, or is it the army? ... There we go again, that was one of the neatest left hooks I've ever seen! ... Ooh, that was one of the worst tackles I've ever seen, he's bought it right in the face! ... And he's off! ... Now we've got a rugby match and a fight.' At the end of the game, after Chile beat nine-man Italy with two late goals, Aston admitted: 'I wasn't reffing a football match. I was acting as an umpire in military manoeuvres.'

JUNE 3

BRAZIL 1-1 SWEDEN: THE DISGRACEFUL REFEREEING OF ARGENTINA '78
(1978)

The 1978 World Cup was only into its third day when the most ridiculous refereeing decision in the competition's entire history was made. In the final minute of Brazil's opening group game against Sweden, the Brazilians won a corner. An inviting ball was swung in from the right for Zico to head home. However, in between the ball leaving the Brazilian midfielder's forehead and hitting the back of the net, Welsh referee Clive Thomas blew the final whistle – after a whole eight seconds of injury time. Ben Nasser may have missed Maradona's Hand of God in 1986 and Graham Poll may have booked Croatia's Josip Šimunić three times against Australia in 2006, but those decisions were simply inept; this one was wanton.

Thomas's pompous decree would normally be the sort of decision to be described, in football parlance, as scandalous, but in the context of the 1978 World Cup that would be a contextual mistake. Truly scandalous decisions were being made elsewhere. Home nation Argentina – the country under the yoke of a despotic military junta – benefited from some dubiously friendly decisions during the tournament. The day before Brazil played Sweden, Argentina spent a whole 90 minutes kicking Hungary off the park – yet it was the Hungarians who had two men sent off when they finally retaliated. A similar story unfolded against France, which saw the home side benefit from a penalty given for a ludicrous non-existent handball.

In Argentina's third match, against Italy, Israeli referee Avraham Klein was having none of it and Argentina lost 1-0. Klein had been pencilled in for the final, so when Argentina made it (thanks to an extremely suspect 6-0 win over Peru which knocked Brazil out of the semi-final group) the junta put pressure on FIFA to change their choice of referee. The new man allowed the home side to keep opponents Holland waiting for ten minutes before kick off, then complained about René van de Kerkhof's protective arm bandage. The gamesmanship – along with a fiercely partisan atmosphere in El Monumental – unsettled the Dutch. Argentina won 3-1, but never has a World Cup victory been viewed with so much suspicion. Thomas's misdemeanor was suddenly seen in the pathetically petty light it deserved.

ENGLAND 1-2 SCOTLAND: THE CROSSBAR BREAKS
(1977)

If there is one image over all others which defines old-school Scottish football, it's not Billy McNeill and the Lisbon Lions lifting the European Cup, nor Archie Gemmill dancing through the Dutch defence. It's not Willie Miller holding the Cup Winners Cup aloft, nor Jim Baxter playing keepie-uppie against the champions of the world. It is of thousands of long-haired tartan-clad goons in bad trousers ripping up the Wembley turf and tearing down the goalposts.

Scotland were fast gaining a reputation as a very good team indeed – this was before the humiliation of Córdoba a year later – and after beating England away for the first time in ten years had just won the British Championship for their new manager Ally MacLeod (who had been in the job for less than a month). They had done so with goals from Gordon McQueen and Kenny Dalglish, and an imperial display down the right flank by Danny McGrain who, according to the great sportswriter Hugh McIlvanney, was at the time 'surely the finest right-back in the world'. (McGrain would miss the 1978 World Cup, a critical blow for the Scots.)

At the final whistle, as Don Revie's flaccid England side skulked off the pitch, thousands of celebrating Scotland's supporters – they had taken 40,000 down to London for the game – flooded onto it. Fans clambered onto the crossbars of the goals, causing them to snap in two; the frames would soon be completely dismantled. Meanwhile others began to lift chunks of turf as souvenirs. Eventually the mounted police arrived and – with shades of the 1923 final – slowly cleared the pitch. 'This is the most disgusting thing we have ever seen at Wembley,' seethed stadium spokesperson Len Went after the game. 'It will take between £5,000 and £10,000 just to put the playing field right.'

There would later be 41 arrests outside the stadium immediately after the game, most of them Scottish; the total over the weekend was 289. The events dampened English enthusiasm for the Home Internationals; within seven years the tournament had been disbanded. The final annual England-Scotland fixture was played in 1989, a 2-0 win for the English at Hampden Park.

JUNE 5

BRAZIL 6-5 POLAND: FOUR INTERNATIONAL GOALS – YET WILIMOWSKI LOSES
(1938)

It is never a good sign when your goalkeeper goes by the name of 'Potatoes', but that was the fate of the Brazil side which lined up for their first-round match against Poland in the 1938 World Cup. Algisto Lorenzato went by the name of Batatais and played with the agility of a sack of them. Luckily for Brazil, that did not matter.

Brazil were 3-1 up at half-time, but Polish striker Ernest Wilimowski scored twice in six second half minutes to draw his team level by the hour. Brazil took a 4-3 lead with 19 minutes to go, but Wilimowski completed his hat-trick a minute before the end to force extra-time. Before the first half of the extra period was up, Brazil had found a hat-trick hero of their own. Leônidas (who had blasted home his team's opener in regular time) scored twice. Wilimowski's fourth came in the 118th minute, too late to stop Brazil making it to the quarter-finals with a 6-5 win. But Wilimowski's goal did give him a little slice of history: as far as records show, he is the only player to ever score four goals in an international yet still lose the game. Meanwhile Potatoes, having let in five, was dropped for Brazil's quarter-final and semi-final matches, though he did play in the third-place play-off against Sweden (where he let in two, his team mates scoring four).

Brazil and Poland's 11-goal romp is not, however, the highest-scoring World Cup finals match of all time. That honour goes to Austria and Switzerland who, under an intense 95-degree Fahrenheit sun during the 1954 World Cup, shared 12 goals in what came to be known as the 'Heat Battle of Lausanne'. Austria won 7-5, thanks partly to Swiss captain and left-back Roger Bocquet being treated for sunstroke at half-time, a condition not helped by the fact he was at the time suffering from a tumour.

JUNE 6

THE 'BUNDESLIGASKANDAL': HORST'S UNHAPPY BIRTHDAY
(1971)

When the Bundesliga was formed in 1963, strict regulations had been put in place regarding maximum salaries. Players could only earn DM500 a year plus win bonuses, unless they were in the West German national side or transfer targets for foreign clubs, in which case they could double their money. With sixteen newly professionalised top-flight teams all clambering over each other to win the national championship, the system was wide open for creative accountants and loophole merchants.

On the final day of the 1970/71 season, three teams were competing to avoid the last relegation slot: Kickers Offenbach, and two teams who had lately been enjoying good runs of form, Arminia Bielefeld and Rot-Weiss Oberhausen. Bielefeld won at Hertha Berlin, Oberhausen drew at Branschweig, and Offenbach were thrashed 4-2 at Cologne: the Kickers were down. It would soon transpire, however, that simple form was not the sole reason for this.

On June 6, Kickers president Horst Canellas held a party to celebrate his 50th birthday. Having invited most of the country's top football names, he flicked the switch of a tape recorder. It was a recording of two Hertha Berlin players asking for DM140,000 to beat Bielefeld – who had offered them DM220,000 to throw the match. The tape also featured Cologne keeper Manfred Manglitz asking for DM100,000 to lie down against Kickers on the final day. Canellas did not pay. The whistle blown, the DFB banned the players – but upheld Kickers' relegation. Canellas went on to unearth more evidence, this time proving Oberhausen had indeed paid Branschweig players, but still it did not save his club. Bielefeld, considered the chief offenders, were eventually demoted – but not until the following year, too late to save the Kickers.

JUNE 7

BRAZIL 1-0 ENGLAND: PELÉ, MOORE, BANKS AND A 'GREAT GAME'
(1970)

The 1970 World Cup *was* Brazil: Pelé's attempt from inside his own half against Czechoslovakia, his dummy round the Uruguayan keeper in the semifinal, Clodoaldo's meandering run then Carlos Alberto's lash for the pièce de resistance last goal in Brazil's 4-1 rout of Italy in the final. Because of all that, it's easy to forget that at the start of the tournament, England were co-favourites to lift the trophy.

The two teams met in the group stages, with the common consensus being it was a dry run for the final. England were arguably stronger than the side which had won the 1966 World Cup, having lost only four times since winning their trophy. Brazil had won every single one of their six qualifying matches, scoring 23 goals in the process. The champions and the former champions did not disappoint: the match, packed with iconic moments, was a classic.

Pelé's early towering header into the bottom-left corner would have been one of the great goals – had Gordon Banks not pulled off an even better save, arcing back to spin the ball up and over the bar from what looked like an impossible angle. According to David Coleman on the BBC, Banks had 'picked the ball out of the net'; he practically had. Bobby Moore, considered to have kept Pelé quiet (in fact, he was marked by Alan Müllery), slid in on Jairzinho with perfect timing; anything else would have given away a penalty. Instead, Moore sauntered off with the ball. In the second half, Brazil's great moment was the goal. Pelé trapped the ball in the area, drew three defenders to him and swatted them all out of the game with one pinged pass out right to Jairzinho, who lashed home.

England would have come away with a draw had Jeff Astle not missed a sitter when he found himself clear on goal, but Brazil held out for their win – though referee Avraham Klein 'let it continue for a few minutes' because he felt it was 'such a great game'. When the whistle finally blew, Pelé and Moore embraced. Surely they would do so again in the final? West Germany had other ideas.

BENFICA 4-0 OS BELENESES: EUSÉBIO'S DEBUT
(1961)

It was the haircut that changed the direction of Portuguese football. In 1961, balding Benfica manager Béla Guttman popped into a Lisbon barbershop for a shave and a polish. By chance, also getting his hair cropped that day was José Carlos Bauer, the manager of Guttman's former club São Paulo, who were on tour in Portugal at the time. The two got chatting about football, at which point Bauer casually mentioned a young player he was scouting in Mozambique: Eusébio da Silva Ferreira, the 19-year-old Sporting Lourenco Marques striker.

Freshly buffed, Guttman left the hairdresser and hopped on the first plane to Mozambique. Well aware that São Paulo were waiting to pounce – and that Sporting Lourenco Marques had an informal arrangement with Benfica's rivals Sporting Lisbon – Guttman wasted no time in convincing Eusébio to sign a contract with his club. Guttman was in a strong bargaining position: Benfica were doing well in that season's European Cup and could promise Eusébio top-level football. By the end of May, Eusébio was sitting in the stands at the Wankdorf stadium in Berne as his new club beat Barcelona and became the first side other than Real Madrid to be crowned champions of Europe.

A week later, Eusébio made a scoring debut for his club against another of Benfica's local rivals, Os Beleneses. It was the start of an outstanding career in Europe. Eusébio scored twice as Benfica retained their European Cup in 1962 against Real Madrid, and won 11 Portuguese championships at the club. Benfica reached three more European Cup finals in his time at the club, though they lost them all. Eusébio also scored 41 goals in 64 appearances for his adopted country Portugal – including four in the famous 5-3 win over North Korea at the 1966 World Cup.

USA 2-0 ENGLAND: ENGLAND'S FIRST BLACK CAPTAIN
(1993)

'The black revolution in English football is not coming,' wrote the *Observer*'s Hugh McIlvanney in November 1978, 'it's here.' At the end of that month, in a match against Czechoslovakia, Nottingham Forest full-back Viv Anderson became the first black player to represent England in a full international. Leading up to the game, Anderson had been quizzed about his experiences as a high-profile black footballer. 'I expect to get some stick at the away matches,' he said. 'They were mad up in Newcastle. I was scared to go onto the pitch.' How the attitudes of English crowds have changed over time; Anderson's selection was a big step in changing them.

Another star of the moment was Laurie Cunningham, who McIlvanney had described as 'the most thrilling black performer in the Football League'. He had beaten Anderson to the punch, if not the full team, by debuting for the England under-21s in April 1977. Cunningham was signed for West Bromwich Albion the same year – by Johnny Giles, not Ron Atkinson, a common misconception – and the club would soon become England's first to field three black players in the same team. (Giles's short-lived successor Ronnie Allen added Cyrille Regis, before Ron Atkinson took Brendon Batson to the club and started referring to his black contingent as 'The Three Degrees'.) Times were indeed changing.

It was not until December 1982 that a black player would get his name on the England scoresheet, when Luther Blissett scored a hat-trick on his second cap against Luxembourg in a European Championship qualifier. And a full fifteen years had elapsed since Anderson's debut when Manchester United's Paul Ince became the first black captain of England in a friendly against the USA.

When Ince took charge of Macclesfield in 2006, he said: 'My main intention now is to keep the club in the division, but I was the first black man to captain England and I want to be the first black English Premiership manager.' He achieved his goal in June 2008, taking over from Mark Hughes at Blackburn Rovers.

BRAZIL 3-1 ENGLAND: A DOG URINATES
ON JIMMY GREAVES MID-MATCH
(1962)

Jimmy Greaves has had many lows in his life. If being dropped from England's 1966 World Cup final team and descending into raging alcoholism was not bad enough, finding himself presenting a mid-80s chat show with a theme tune containing the lyric 'If you want a laugh / Call at Greavsie's Gaff' was much, much worse.

Greaves's nadir came in Chile in 1962, when England's World Cup quarter-final against Brazil was invaded by a stray dog. After several players made failed attempts to catch the canine, 'Greavsie' finally succeeded where others had failed by getting down on all fours and barking, in order to coax it into his arms. But as he carried the mutt off, he was covered with a tepid jet of soupy canine urine for his trouble. 'I smelt so bad,' said Greaves, 'but at least it meant the Brazilian defenders stayed clear of me.'

It has been claimed that a highly amused Garrincha – who scored twice and set up another as Brazil beat England 3-1 to advance to the quarter-finals – thought the affair so hilarious that he took the stray dog home and kept it. But in fact the dog – who was given the name Bi – was raffled off to the Brazilian squad after the match. It was Garrincha who had won the raffle.

SCOTLAND 3-2 HOLLAND: GEMMILL'S
FUTILE WONDER-GOAL
(1978)

Scotland boss Ally MacLeod had insisted before the 1978 World Cup that he was a 'born winner'. He was certainly good at winning sponsorship contracts: ahead of the tournament Scotland put their name to Chrysler Avenger cars and Deep Heat muscle rub – 'Scotland's warm-up for the World Cup' – while Mrs MacLeod peddled Oxo. Unfortunately, MacLeod was not so schooled in the winning of football matches.

The Scottish squad certainly looked good enough to go some distance in Argentina: it included Kenny Dalglish and Graeme Souness of European champions Liverpool; John Robertson, Archie Gemmill and Kenny Burns of English champions Nottingham Forest; Sandy Jardine and Derek Johnstone of Scottish champions Rangers; as well as Martin Buchan, Lou Macari, Gordon McQueen and Joe Jordan of a revitalised Manchester United. But there were two notable omissions: injured defender Danny McGrain and in-form striker Andy Gray. MacLeod compounded his error in not picking Gray for his squad by not picking Souness for his teams to face Peru and Iran: Teófilo Cubillas put the Scots to the sword in the opener with a sweetly struck free-kick in a 3-1 win for the Peruvians, while Iraj Danaifar's equaliser for the Iranians turned MacLeod's team into a laughing stock.

Typically, Scotland then produced the single best performance of the entire tournament. Needing to beat 1974 finalists Holland by a three-goal margin, MacLeod finally picked Souness – though they went a goal down before Dalglish and Gemmill turned it round. Then Gemmill scored the greatest British goal in any World Cup, beating three men with a meandering solo run from the right-wing before spooning the ball over the keeper. Scotland needed only one more goal – but a Johnny Rep piledriver soon put a stop to their gallop. They were going home.

The Scottish FA – who in retrospect could have asked Jock Stein to manage the team – let the inept MacLeod keep his job.

FRANCE 1-0 DENMARK : PLATINI BEGINS
NINE-GOAL EURO '84 RUN
(1984)

There are plenty of World Cup campaigns which have been effectively driven by one player – Maradona in 1986, Garrincha 1962 and Cruyff in 1974. Only one European Championship has become synonymous with the efforts of one man. Host nation France were the favourites to win Euro '84, boasting the 'Magic Square' midfield quartet of Michel Platini, Alain Giresse, Jean Tigana and Luis Fernández. But Platini's utter domination of the tournament was still remarkable: he scored nine goals in five matches, an all-time European Championship record.

That he did so from midfield made the feat even more outstanding, even if he was given licence to push forward by manager Michel Hidalgo. Having qualified automatically as hosts, France hadn't played a competitive game since losing the 1982 World Cup semi-final against West Germany. They started shakily against an up-and-coming Denmark side – but Platini settled their nerves late on with a 78th-minute winner from the edge of the area. Against Belgium he cut inside from the left to dink over the keeper, before completing a hat-trick in a 5-0 rout with a penalty and a crashing header into the top left. He followed that display with an even-better hat-trick, scoring three in 18 minutes to beat Yugoslavia 3-2: another dink from the left, a diving header and a free-kick with no discernable backlift. It was a textbook hat-trick: a header and a shot with either foot.

In the semi-final against Portugal, Platini again took centre stage. With six minutes of extra-time to go, France trailed 2-1 but his quick feet in the box set up Jean-François Domergue to equalise, then he slammed home the winner with virtually the final kick of the game. In the final, albeit assisted by Luis Arkonada's fumble, he opened the scoring, then as captain lifted the trophy after a 2-0 win. Euro '84 was Platini's tournament.

REAL MADRID 11-1 BARCELONA: THE REGIME TEAM
(1943)

Matches between Spain's most bitter rivals Real Madrid and Barcelona gained a particularly political edge during the 1940s. General Francisco Franco had just come to power, and under his reign Barça underwent a forced process of de-Catalanisation. The regional flag was removed from their crest, their name changed to the more Spanish sounding Club de Futebol Barcelona, and the speaking of Catalan was limited to their Les Corts stadium. Real Madrid, however, enjoyed the regime's full support.

To what extent the politics affected games is debatable, but during the summer of 1943, Barça experienced one of their worst defeats ever at the hands of Real Madrid in the semi-final of the Copa del Rey – renamed, after Franco himself, the Generalissmo Cup.

Barcelona weren't in great shape in 1943. They'd only just avoided relegation in 1942, though had gone on to win the cup that season. Real were determined not to let them do so again. In the first leg, Barça won 3-0 at home – where their fans were criticised for jeering the away support. Former Real goalkeeper Eduardo Teus, in an infamous article in Madrid's *Ya* newspaper, opined: 'The crowd at Les Corts had whistled the Madrid players with the clear intention of attacking the representatives of Spain.' It would not be forgotten.

Just before the return leg in Madrid, Barça players were given an unscheduled teamtalk by Spain's Director of State Security. 'Do not forget that some of you are only playing because of the generosity of the regime that has forgiven you for your lack of patriotism,' he said. It was not the pep talk they needed.

By half-time Madrid were 8-0 up. 'Barça simply ended up by not playing, fearful of making the most innocent of tackles,' wrote Catalan-born writer Juan Samaranch after the eventual 11-1 hammering. Barcelona, he said, were reduced to 'impotence' by the 'coercion of the crowd.'

Exactly what effect the pre-match threat had is lost in the mists of time. Opinions are divided, and not just along tribal lines: while many Real fans like to remind Barça of the 11-1 scoreline, some are embarrassed about it and wonder if the club should strike it from their official records.

Madrid lost the 1943 cup final 1-0 to the Basque club Atlético Bilbao.

WEST GERMANY 3-2 ENGLAND: THE REVENGE FOR '66
(1970)

In retrospect, you could argue that England's visit to Mexico to defend their world crown at the 1970 World Cup was fated to fail. Pretty much everything that could go wrong did. Some of their travails were self-inflicted – the hostile reception from local crowds and the constant beeping of car horns outside the England hotel every night, for example, had resulted from a press conference Alf Ramsey had given after a friendly in Mexico a year earlier. The England manager had ludicrously complained that the Mexican crowd had 'abused and jeered' his team. 'I would have thought they would have been delighted to welcome England,' he moaned.

Other misfortunes were less of their own making. The most sinister was the arrest of Bobby Moore in Bogota a week before the beginning of the tournament, as England went on tour to acclimatise. Held under house arrest at the home of the president of Millonários, Moore had been accused of stealing a bracelet. It was a trumped-up charge, but not one that would be officially dropped until 1975 – three years after the accusers had themselves been charged for conspiracy to defraud! Still, after three days Moore was released and allowed to return to Mexico.

England also ran out of luck on the morning of their quarter-final with West Germany; Gordon Banks had fallen ill after catching a bug from a bottle of beer and would be replaced by Peter Bonetti. The change would be fateful: with 23 minutes to go, England were coasting 2-0 up when Bonetti allowed a speculative Franz Beckenbauer shot under his body. Bobby Charlton was replaced two minutes later – another self-inflicted wound, as it allowed Beckenbauer to romp forward – and soon enough the jig was up, the Germans equalising with a fortuitous backwards header by Uwe Seeler, then winning in extra-time after Gerd Müller slammed home a volley. The thought England had used up all their luck when Geoff Hurst's shot came crashing down off the Wembley crossbar in 1966 couldn't be escaped.

ITALY 3-1 HAITI: ZOFF – AND JEAN-JOSEPH – BEATEN
(1974)

Italian goalkeeper Dino Zoff had gone 1,143 minutes without conceding a goal before the start of the second half of Italy's 1974 World Cup opener against African minnows Haiti. Once the game restarted, his world record only lasted another 60 seconds. With the Italians caught up-field attacking, Philippe Vorbe broke into the centre circle, walloped a hopeful long ball up to Emmanuel Sanon, who rounded the advancing Zoff to his left, and rolled the ball into the centre of the goal. It was an embarrassing moment for Italy, though within 18 minutes they were ahead and finished the game 3-1 winners. Zoff can take solace in the fact that his record stands to this day.

The game, however, would have an unpleasant postscript. Haitian central defender Ernst Jean-Joseph became the first player in World Cup history to fail a drug test. The player tearfully protested his innocence, saying he had taken nothing stronger than a cure for his asthma, but that didn't stop Haitian goons dragging him from the team hotel two days later, bundling him into a car – beating him as they did so – and driving off.

It was a worrying incident. The Haitian president Papa Doc Duvalier's police brutes, the Tontons Macoutes, had form with footballers. The infamous secret police, named after a voodoo spirit, kidnapped and killed Joe Gaetjens, the scorer of the USA's winning goal against England in the 1950 World Cup, and an outspoken critic of the Duvalier regime. There was no reason to think their approach under Papa Doc's successor, his son 'Baby Doc', would be any different. But there would be good news (although it only came after the finals had ended): Jean-Joseph had not been killed, or even arrested. He went on to play for Haiti in the 1978 and 1982 World Cup qualifiers.

JUNE 16

RIO DE JANEIRO ALL-STARS 3-1 SÃO PAULO ALL-STARS: MARACANÃ OPENS
(1950)

In 1946, Brazil were awarded the right to host the 1950 World Cup and decided a new showpiece stadium would be required. Up until that point, Hampden Park in Glasgow was the biggest football ground in the world – it drew 149,415 people to the 1937 Home Championship match between Scotland and England, the official world record attendance at the time. (Wembley had hosted approximately 200,000 fans at the chaotic 1923 FA Cup final, but nobody was counting that day to know for sure, and anyway the ground's official capacity was only 100,000.) But with the building of the Maracanã in Rio de Janeiro, which would be capable of holding 200,000 fans, Hampden would soon lose its special status.

Construction started in 1948 but took longer than planned; the stadium wasn't ready for the start of the 1950 World Cup. As building work went on around them, a Rio representative team beat a selection from São Paulo in the official curtain-raiser on June 16, 1950; Fluminese striker Didi scoring the first ever goal at the ground for Rio. Eight days later, Brazil beat Mexico 4-0 there in the opening game of the World Cup. Pieces of barely-set concrete, dislodged after a ceremonial pre-match cannon salute, rained on the 81,649 crowd. The capacity had been halved that day for reasons of safety, and no wonder.

One month to the day after its official opening – and with the fixtures and fittings now firmly in place – came the match the Maracanã will forever be associated with: the 1950 'Fateful Final' between Brazil and Uruguay, the latter's triumph breaking the hearts of the crowd, estimated to be an above-capacity 210,000. The official attendance for the game was a mere 173,850.

The Maracanã is no longer what it was. In 1992 a stand collapsed, killing three fans, and the ground was converted into an all-seater. It now only holds 95,000 spectators, 55,000 fewer than the current world number one, the May Day Stadium in Pyongyang, North Korea.

JUNE 17

DIANA ROSS MISSES PENALTY: USA '94
BEGINS AS IT WILL END
(1994)

When the USA were awarded the right to host the 1994 World Cup finals in 1988, it didn't take long for the scare stories to start doing the rounds. To keep America interested, there would be bigger goals, the game would be split into quarters, there would be regular stoppages for advertising. Of course America left well alone, as they were always going to do. However, they weren't going to let the opening ceremony go by without an extra sprinkle of showbiz glamour. The star turn was to be Diana Ross, belting out a couple of numbers then shanking a penalty hopelessly off target.

Ross's bungle provided a memorable start to the tournament, and one which would give it a perfect symmetry. The star turn on the football field in USA '94 was Roberto Baggio. Baggio was anonymous in Italy's shock opening defeat to the Republic of Ireland, then was substituted against Norway after goalkeeper Gianluca Pagliuca was sent off. Baggio sleepwalked his way through a further 178 minutes of football until, two minutes from the end of Italy's game with Nigeria, and with his country facing a second-round exit, Baggio passed the ball into the bottom-left corner of the net from the edge of the area. His precision goal set Italy on their way. A penalty against the Nigerians in extra-time was followed by a late quarter-final winner against Spain, then both of Italy's goals in their semi-final win over Bulgaria.

His first in the semi-final had rivalled Diego Maradona's slalom effort against Belgium at the same stage in 1986. Baggio, as Italy's one-man show, drew comparisons with Maradona's overall contribution that year as well. But Baggio was carrying an injury in the final and couldn't deliver the knockout blow. Fate cruelly decreed that in the final's penalty shootout against Brazil, he would bring an end to the tournament just as Ross had opened it. Like Cruyff before him, Baggio had defined a World Cup without actually winning it, a small consolation.

REAL MADRID 2-1 BARCELONA: ZAMORA'S GREATEST SAVE
(1936)

Ricardo Zamora was a brilliant but controversial figure in Spanish football history. Born in Barcelona, he rejected Catalan nationalism, seeing himself first and foremost a Spaniard. With a taste for cognac, an eye for the ladies and a heavy addiction to cigarettes, his stories off the pitch were almost as remarkable as his saves he made on it – placing him in history as one of the best goalkeepers of all time.

He began playing for RCD Español in 1916, but after a row with the manager in 1919 was transferred to Barcelona. Within three years at the club he'd won the Catalan Cup three times and the Copa del Rey twice. But his time at the club ended in 1922 when he was suspended for lying to the taxman about his signing-on fee.

It wasn't his first, or last, brush with the law. After the 1920 Olympics (where he was sent off for slapping an Italian) Zamora was arrested for smuggling an absurd amount of Havana cigars back into Spain under a train seat. Had he only been able to resist leaning out of the window and lighting one of the contraband cigars, he'd have probably got away with it.

Zamora rejoined Español from 1923 to 1930, at which point he signed to Real Madrid for a hefty fee. His signing to a second anti-Catalan club was something Barça fans would never forgive him for. At Madrid, he added two league victories and two cups to his personal roll of honour, the last coming in one of two matches which would define his career. The first had been in 1929, when Spain became the first non-British side to defeat England, beating them 4-3. The second was the 1936 Spanish cup final. Real Madrid were 2-1 up against Barcelona but a man down. With seconds remaining, Escola hit a pearler. Just as the crowd jumped to their feet to celebrate, Zamora made one of the most spectacular dives of his career to turn the ball away.

A month after that match, with the Spanish Civil War gathering momentum, Zamora was reported as having been killed by Republicans. Thousands mourned and cursed the 'reds', but it soon became clear the news was a ruse by Fascist troops to gain support. To quash the rumours, the Republicans arrested Zamora and sent him to prison. Within months he'd escaped with the help of the Argentinian Embassy and was later found on the streets of Nice sipping his cognac. According to Zamora, his tales of football heroics had even spared him an execution.

ITALY 4-2 HUNGARY: THE MUSSOLINI 'WIN OR DIE' MYTH
(1938)

The stench of Fascism pervaded the 1938 World Cup. There was no Austria as Germany had swallowed the country up in the Anschluss. Eight former Austrians would play for a 'Greater' Germany during the tournament, but that wouldn't stop them going out after a 4-2 first-round replay defeat by the Swiss. With the Spanish embroiled in a civil war, it was left to Italy to keep up a presence for the blackshirts.

In the quarter-final, they did so literally. Against hosts France in Paris, Italy had lost the toss for the right to wear their first-choice 'Azzurri' strip. Instead of turning out in their usual white change tops, the team were ordered to wear black shirts. (They had never done so before, nor have they since.) Whether this provocative gesture contributed to France's subsequent 3-1 defeat is moot. If anything the chief culprit was their goalkeeper Laurent Di Lorto, the only one not in black. Di Lorto attempted to catch Gino Colaussi's aimless up-and-under, but only succeeded in spiking it volleyball-style into his own net, before crashing into his post face-first. It was the only light moment in a dark tournament.

Italy made it through to a final against Hungary – before which they received a telegram from Mussolini. On it was the phrase 'Vincere o morire!' Loosely translated, this was taken by the outside world to mean 'win or die.' After Italy won 4-2, the Hungarian keeper quipped dryly: 'I may have let in four goals but at least I saved their lives.' A nice sentiment, were it not for the fact that the telegram was merely a rallying cry along the lines of 'do or die'.

Italy's coach Vittorio Pozzo, meanwhile, became the only man to win the World Cup twice as a manager, having already led his country to victory in the 1934 finals.

In 1936, team members Enrique Guaita and Raimundo Orsi had fled Italy in the wake of their adopted country's invasion of Ethiopia, embarrassing the Fascist regime. What Mussolini might have said to them in a telegram had he been given the chance can only be guessed at.

JUNE 20

CZECHOSLOVAKIA 2-2 WEST GERMANY: THE PANENKA
(1976)

The 1976 European Championship was the first time a major trophy was decided by a penalty shoot-out, so how fitting that it would be settled by the greatest – and most famous – penalty kick of all time. Even so, it's a shame that Euro '76 is ultimately only remembered for one kick, because it was one of the great tournaments.

Unlike today, where 16 countries take part in the Euros, only four teams contested the finals. The tournament began at the semi-final stage, and both games were dramatic. Reigning world and European champions West Germany faced hosts Yugoslavia, and went two down after half an hour through goals from Danilo Popivoda and Dragan Džajić, before Heinz Flohe and Dieter Müller levelled things. Müller went on to complete a hat-trick in extra-time, his two last goals coming in the last five minutes as the Germans secured a 4-2 win.

The other semi-final was even better, and saw Anton Ondrus give Czechoslovakia an early lead against Holland before the same player put through his own net with 13 minutes to play. But the Czechs were always in charge, despite Pollák being sent off on the hour and won 3-1 with two goals in the last six minutes of extra-time from Zdeněk Nehoda and František Veselý. Holland's Wim van Hanegen was sent off for refusing to restart the match after Nehoda's goal.

The third-place play-off having also been a minor classic – Holland losing a two-goal lead before beating the Yugoslavs 3-2 in extra-time – the pressure was on the final to deliver. No problem: for the third match out of four, a two-goal lead was shed, West Germany finally equalising through goals from Müller and Bernd Hölzenbein. The game went to penalties. After Uli Hoeness missed, it was down to Antonín Panenka – who chipped the ball gracefully down the middle leaving Sepp Maier, who had dived to his left, desperately clawing thin air with his right hand as he fell.

The 'Panenka', as it is now known, is not as easy as it looks (which is not very easy at all). Zinedine Zidane, one of the greatest players of all time, nearly made a total pig's ear of it in the 2006 World Cup final between France and Italy (though he got away with it thanks to some friendly forward spin off the crossbar). And the less said about Gary Lineker's attempt to equal Bobby Charlton's England goalscoring record against Brazil in 1992 the better.

JUNE 21

SPAIN 2-1 USSR: FRANCO 2-1 KHRUSHCHEV
(1964)

Spain had withdrawn from the first ever European Championship in 1960 after dictator General Francisco Franco forbade them to play their quarter-final against USSR. The Soviets went on to win the title, beating fellow iron-curtain state Yugoslavia 2-1.

The 1964 tournament was again marred by political tension, Greece withdrawing without playing a single match after refusing to play Albania. But this time Spain, as hosts of the tournament, would not back out. They reached the final – where their opponents were none other than the USSR. And this time Franco was there to witness the clash.

Spain could no longer boast their naturalised Hungarians László Kubala and Ferenc Puskás, but they did have midfielder Luis Suárez, who in 1960 was the first (and to this day only) Spanish-born player to win the European Footballer of the Year award. In the quarter-finals Spain beat the Republic of Ireland 7-1 on aggregate, then won the semi-final with an extra-time goal from Amancio Amaro against a talented Hungary side, which would later shine in the 1966 World Cup.

A crowd of 75,000 gathered in the pouring rain at the Santiago Bernabéu Stadium for the match they might have played four years previously. And despite their relatively inexperienced squad Spain went on to beat the Russians 2-1 to win their first international trophy. A magnificent goal from Jesús Mariá Pereda put them up 1-0 after just six minutes, though the Russians were quick to equalise with a goal from Galimzyan Khusainov. Spain hung on until the 83rd minute when Marcelino Martinez, who had netted several throughout the competition, headed the ball past Lev Yashin. The greatest goalkeeper of the era was powerless to respond.

It was a glorious victory for the Spanish – though Franco used it as a symbol of his Fascist regime's superiority over Communism.

BRAZIL 3-0 ZAIRE: MWEPU'S RUSH OF BLOOD
(1974)

In the early seventies, Zaire were one of the strongest sides in African football. The team had won the African Nations Cup in 1968 as the Democratic Republic of Congo and then again, as the renamed Zaire, in 1974 – the same year they became the first black African nation to qualify for the World Cup.

On paper, Zaire's record in West Germany that summer is appalling. They lost 2-0 to Scotland, 3-0 to Brazil and 9-0 to Yugoslavia. But their efforts merit closer analysis. They held a side containing Billy Bremner, Denis Law, Peter Lorimer, Kenny Dalglish and Joe Jordan to a respectable 2-0. Next came Yugoslavia on June 18, and while it's hard to explain away a nine-goal defeat, there were extraneous circumstances. Officials from the Zairean Football Federation had pocketed the players' wages and allowances for the Scotland match, and when the team heard they would again not be paid, they refused to play. They backed down at the last minute but did not put in the effort they did against the Scots.

Zaire were out, but there was still pride to play for. Hours after the Yugoslavia match finished, enraged dictator Mobutu Sese Seko sent guards to visit the team, promising dire reprisals should they lose their final group game to Brazil by more than three goals. And it was in this game one of the most iconic, infamous moments in the history of sport would be played out, as with Brazil preparing to take a free-kick just outside the Zairean box, Mwepu Ilunga roared out of a defensive wall and hoofed the ball miles up the pitch. The incident is widely considered to be a hilarious one, though some say he merely ran out of the wall because he'd seen countless European players do it and thought it was legal. But consider what went through Mwepu's mind: the free-kick was awarded with eight minutes of the match to play – and Zaire were 3-0 down. What would *you* have done?

MITTEN LEAVES MANCHESTER UNITED FOR 'ELDORADO'
(1950)

Charlie Mitten, Manchester United's left-winger, who had outshone Stanley Matthews in the 1948 FA Cup final, was on an end-of-season tour in New York with his club in 1950 when the phone in his hotel room rang. It was the president of Santa Fe: the Colombian club had just signed Neil Franklin and George Mountford from Stoke City, and both players had recommended Mitten. Would he be interested in signing?

The answer seemed obvious: the maximum wage was still in effect in England, and Mitten was on £8 a week, yet Santa Fe were offering £10,000 just as a signing-on fee. However there was a catch: the Colombian DiMayor league was not recognized by FIFA, and should he join Santa Fe he would be castigated as a football outlaw. In order to make a decision, on June 23 Mitten left United's tour and flew down to Bogota to see what was on offer. When he got there, he was shown his prospective house, maid, chauffeur and car. His yearly salary of £5,000 plus bonuses of £35 per win were laid out. Passage for his wife and children was included. It was a no-brainer. When he returned to Manchester, he informed Matt Busby of his decision. 'Good God, do they want a manager?!' joked Busby, who understood Mitten's choice.

Mitten enjoyed a productive first season in Colombia – 'I must have scored about 24 or 25 goals. Uruguay had just won the World Cup and a Colombia selection played them three weeks after … I played with Alfredo di Stéfano and Héctor Rial and we beat them 3-1' – but it would be his only one. FIFA readmitted the DiMayor league with the proviso the 'outlaws' would be sent back to the clubs they came from. Mitten was suspended by United on his return and sold. Real Madrid showed an interest, but Mitten's wife was homesick. Instead he joined Fulham.

THE 1950 WORLD CUP STARTS – WITHOUT INDIA
(1950)

After last-minute complications, FIFA found themselves practically begging for teams to come and fill the last three places at the 1950 World Cup finals. Keen to get the British teams on board – they had been absent from international tournaments since the 1920s – FIFA offered places to the winners and runners-up of the Home Championship.

Although England and Scotland qualified, the Scottish FA decided not to take part – because they hadn't won the tournament! Scotland captain George Young, encouraged by England's Billy Wright, pleaded with the SFA's George Graham to change his mind, but despite this show of British solidarity it made no difference. Scotland stayed at home. England would lose to the USA and wish they'd done the same.

FIFA had other problems. Argentina pulled out having fallen out with Brazil after some rough matches in the mid-1940s. Czechoslovakia declined their place too. France wanted the programme of events changed when they saw that their matches were held 2,000 miles apart; Brazil refused, so they were out too. Post-war, Germany were banned. With only 13 teams competing, the draw ended up being hilariously skew-whiff: there were two groups of four, one of three – and one of two.

All this must have really wound India up. For the first time in the country's history, they had qualified for a place in the finals – several other Asians teams had dropped out and they'd proved themselves competent in a 2-1 defeat against France in the 1948 Olympics – but suddenly, with bags already packed, FIFA dropped a bombshell. The Indians couldn't come, because they didn't wear football boots.

'We were all very excited about going to the 1950 World Cup,' said Indian midfielder Venkatesh Shanmugham. 'Sadly, we did not know then that barefoot play was not allowed in the World Cup. We got to know it very late. We went to Singapore, Malaysia, Sri Lanka and even played an all-Chinese team in Hong Kong as part of our World Cup warm-up tour. But in the end, there was disappointment.' India, having invested in some boots, went on to win the first Asian Games in 1951 and finished fourth in the 1956 Olympics.

WEST GERMANY 1-0 AUSTRIA: 'EL ANSCHLUSS'
(1982)

Algeria were one of the strongest teams in Africa. They had been runners-up in the 1980 African Cup of Nations, fourth two years later, and boasted two dangerous attackers in Rabah Madjer and African footballer of the year Lakhdar Belloumi. But few expected them to beat the reigning champions of Europe in their opening game at the 1982 World Cup finals. Which is exactly what they did, Belloumi setting up Madjer for the opening goal, then scoring the winner in a 2-1 win over West Germany – a team boasting European footballer of the year Karl-Heinz Rummenigge. It was one of the biggest shocks in World Cup history.

The subsequent set of results in the group set up an intriguing climax: Austria beat Chile 1-0, then Algeria 2-0; West Germany regrouped by thrashing the abject Chileans 4-1, who were in turn defeated 3-2 by Algeria. That result meant Algeria had become the first African side to win two matches at a World Cup, but they weren't through yet. Algeria had been leading 3-0 at half-time, but the two goals conceded in the second half left the door ajar for West Germany, who would have otherwise been as good as out. Now all the Germans needed was a narrow win against Austria and Algeria would be out.

After 11 minutes, Horst Hrubesch bundled in the goal West Germany needed – and that, pretty much, was that. Both teams passed the ball around the back for 80 minutes, happy to keep what they had. The Algerians, homeward bound, condemned the charade as a 'sinister plot' and demanded both teams be disqualified under the terms of 'the principle of sportsmanship'. Austria manager Georg Schmidt confessed that the action was 'shameful', but German coach Jupp Derwall had no such qualms: 'We came to progress, not play football,' he revealed. The match did provide one service to football: FIFA abandoned staggered final group games, which had allowed some teams the advantage of knowing what they had to do.

JESUS GIL PRESENTS FUTRE AT ATLETICO ELECTIONS
(1987)

Gregorio Jesus Gil y Gil was president of Atlético Madrid from 1987 until just before his death in 2004. A preposterous man, it is fitting that he presided over one of the most preposterous reigns in history.

Gil made his millions in the late 1960s through property development, for which he became infamous. In 1969 he built an apartment complex in Segovia, north of Madrid, but did so without bothering to employ an architect or surveyor; or waiting for the concrete to set properly before he ushered paying punters in. As 700 people sat eating in a newly-opened restaurant, the roof caved in, killing 58 diners. He was sent to jail, though later pardoned by Spain's dictator, Franco.

Eighteen years later, having made further millions in the construction industry, Gil decided to run for the presidency of Atlético. The carrot he dangled in front of the voting members in the presidential election was the promise of signing Portuguese winger Paulo Futre, who had just won the European Cup with Porto. Gil was elected by a landslide.

Over the next 17 years, Gil and Atletico appointed 39 managers. During one particularly fraught three-season spell the club went through 15. On the plus side, Atlético won the 1996 league and cup double; it was their first league title since 1977. On the minus, the club were relegated in 2000 and spent two seasons in the Segunda Division. Gil abolished the youth team which contained boyhood fan Raúl, who went on to become a Real Madrid legend. Gil also expressed a wish that the team plane would crash and kill the squad after a defeat in Las Palmas.

Gil died in 2004 awaiting verdicts of two trials: he had been accused of 'misappropriating' 390m euros while mayor of Marbella (including money used to sponsor Atlético), as well as fraudulently acquiring his majority shareholding in the club.

Atletico have won nothing since 1996.

HUNGARY 4-2 BRAZIL: THE BATTLE OF BERNE
(1954)

Hungary were odds-on favourites to win the 1954 World Cup, but Brazil were still smarting from the 'Fateful Final' of 1950 and weren't going to go down lightly in this quarter-final. The football on display by the two teams would arguably be the greatest in a World Cup fixture to date. The violence they showcased certainly was. And that's not counting what went on away from the world's gaze, in the dark of the Hungary dressing room afterwards. Hungary raced into a two-goal lead within seven minutes, Nándor Hidegkuti and Sándor Kocsis the scorers. Brazil came back with an 18th-minute Djalma Santos penalty. Brazil were then further boosted when a midfield brawl midway through the first half saw József Toth go off injured.

The score stayed 2-1 until just after the hour, when Brandaozinho was harshly penalised for handball in the box; Lantos skelped the ball into the net. Brazil were livid and stepped up their fight-back. Julinho lashed the ball into the Hungarian net to make it 3-2. From that point on, according to the injured Ferenc Puskás, watching from the stands, the match degenerated into 'a desperate tussle of ruthless brutality'. Brazil's José Carlos Bauer clattered Bozsik who, after receiving lengthy treatment, came back incensed and was soon sent off for tussling with Nilton Santos, who also walked. Hidegkuti trampled across a prostrate Indio's shins. Humberto became the third man to be sent off for whacking Koscis, who survived the assault to score a late fourth and seal victory for Hungary.

As Hungary celebrated noisily afterwards, a soda siphon suddenly flew into their dressing room and the lights went out. Details are sketchy: according to Puskás, during a ten-minute fracas the Hungarians were 'confused and bewildered amidst the grunts, blows and cries from those who were hurt'. Other reports have Puskás taking a broken bottle to Pinheiro's head. 'Who had come best out of the extra-time in the dressing room it was impossible to decide,' was Puskás's only later admission. 'There had been no referee.'

JUNE 28

FRANCE 6-3 WEST GERMANY: JUST FONTAINE'S 13 IN ONE WORLD CUP
(1958)

At the 1954 World Cup finals in Switzerland, Hungarian forward Sándor Kocsis, the 'Golden Head', scored eleven goals as his country reached the final. He'd failed to score in the last game, Hungary losing the final 3-2 to West Germany in the 'Miracle of Berne'. But with the heartbreak came a small consolation: nobody thought his Swiss goalscoring spree, a World Cup record, would be bettered any time soon.

Sure enough, it was lost in the very next tournament – to a man who wasn't even expecting to play in it. Just Fontaine had just helped his club, Stade de Reims, to the league and cup double in France, but he wasn't necessarily first choice to lead the line of the national side. When team mate Rene Bliard turned his ankle during pre-tournament training, however, Fontaine was in – and grabbed his chance with both hands.

In the group games, Fontaine rattled in a hat-trick as France turned over Paraguay 7-3; scored twice as his team went down to a late winner in a 3-2 defeat by Yugoslavia; then scored the winner in a 2-1 win over Scotland. Another two goals came in a 4-0 quarter-final win over Northern Ireland, before his ninth of the tournament came in the semi-final – but it wasn't enough to stop Brazil winning 5-2. It was a case of what might have been for France, a feeling exacerbated in the third-place final, where Fontaine scored four in a 6-3 win over 1954 champions West Germany. 'I still have regrets of that match,' said Fontaine of the Brazil semi-final years later. But he could at least take succour in his surely unbeatable record.

Fontaine's Reims lost the 1959 European Cup final to Kopa's Real Madrid. A year later his career was effectively over after suffering a second broken leg. He had scored 30 goals in 21 matches for France.

USA 1-0 ENGLAND: GAETJENS STUNS THE WORLD
(1950)

USA coach Bill Jeffrey knew his team hardly had a hope in hell. England were one of the World Cup favourites and had just won their first group match against Chile 2-0, albeit unconvincingly. The Americans had lost their opening fixture, 3-1 to Spain.

The English had been troubled by the heat, however, and were finding it hard to acclimatise. Stanley Matthews was left on the bench for the game, behind Jimmy Mullen and Tom Finney in the pecking order. The decision was met with disbelief, but team selector Arthur Drewry was confident a line-up featuring Finney, Billy Wright, Stan Mortensen, Alf Ramsey and Wilf Mannion would be more than good enough in Belo Horizonte.

In the 38th minute the USA's Haiti-born striker Joe Gaetjens headed home into the bottom-right corner of England's net for the game's only goal. A huge shock, but one which did not register much back home. How much attention was afforded the World Cup by the English at the time can be measured by the following description of the goal in the *Guardian* (hidden away on page 10): 'An Argentine-born player called Gaetjens scored with a good shot from twenty yards.'

Another British paper published the result as 10-1 to England, assuming the score had been a misprint. But England were also beaten in their following game, by Spain, and were sent home. Having played in blue shirts, they vowed to never wear the colour again.

GERMANY 2-1 CZECH REPUBLIC:
GOLDEN GOAL, TINPOT CLIMAX
(1996)

The extra-time 'golden goal' was introduced by FIFA in March 1993, but it was not a new idea. The world's second ever football tournament – the Cromwell Cup, played in Sheffield under the ersatz football-rugby-Eton Wall Game-Aussie Rules mishmash known as 'Sheffield Rules' – was decided by such a method. The final between Garrick and the Wednesday Club had ended goalless after 90 minutes, and so both captains agreed that the first to score would win.

The report from the *Sheffield and Rotherham Independent* of February 17, 1868 suggests the denouement was something of a farcical anti-climax. 'After playing ten minutes, the Wednesday Club got the ball to the low end, and one of the other side, in making a lick, got too much under. The ball went up almost perpendicular, and in dropping cannoned off someone through the goal. The Wednesday men and their friends, who had assembled in great force, gave vent to their voices, and we have not heard such a shout since the memorable county match versus Surrey, so unexpectedly won.' Hurrah!

The first golden goal to settle a major tournament was equally farcical. An absorbing Euro '96 final was abruptly truncated when Czech Republic goalkeeper Petr Kouba's weak hands hinged back to let a weak Oliver Bierhoff shot spin apologetically into the net. With the Czechs given no chance to bounce back, most neutrals felt a sense of injustice. The same sense of injustice was again felt when France applied a similar juddering halt to Italy's gallop in Euro 2000, and Liverpool nixed Alavés 5-4 in an otherwise wondrous 2001 UEFA Cup final. After tinkering with a 'silver goal' format, which at least allowed teams some scope to bounce back, FIFA dispensed with the idea altogether in 2004.

JULY 1

AFTER SIMEONE, BECKHAM SAYS SORRY
(1998)

'I want every England supporter to know how deeply sorry I am.' England supporters always need a scapegoat for World Cup failure, and David Beckham knew it. The night before he had been sent off as England played Argentina in the second round of the 1998 World Cup, kicking out and giving Diego Simeone the opportunity to fall limply over his outstretched leg. 'I will always regret my actions during last night's game,' he added. 'I only hope that I will have the opportunity in the future to be part of a successful England team in the European Championships and World Cup.'

It had been an up-and-down campaign for Beckham, who played in all the qualifying games but was dropped at the start of the tournament. Coach Glenn Hoddle suggested he had become distracted by his relationship with Victoria Adams from the Spice Girls. Beckham denied this, and took his chance when finally selected against Colombia, scoring with a spectacular 25-yard free-kick. It was his first goal for England and he had waited 17 internationals for it.

The next game ended in personal disaster with the Simeone incident, though few now remember Beckham was the player to pick out Michael Owen for his spectacular solo goal. England lost on penalties, but Hoddle stood by his man. Sort of. 'It was a mistake. It was a foolish thing to do, and he has got to realise he can't do that sort of thing at this level. It was a mistake but we can't go overboard about it and I'm not looking for someone to blame.' Nobody listened much. The *Mirror* roused the angry mob by printing a dartboard with the 23-year-old's face on it. An effigy of Beckham hung from a noose outside the Pleasant Pheasant pub in South London. Death threats were received. Possibly most hurtful of all, some sponsorship deals were frozen.

The one man who didn't get seem to understand what all the fuss was about was Kim Milton Nielsen, the Danish referee who had sent Beckham off. 'It is only football,' he wrote, 'it is a nice thing, but it is not the whole world. There are wars and places where people do not have enough food. These are far more important.' He also had some advice for the player. 'I hope he can learn from this. He needs to be more relaxed. People like Maradona and Pelé had to put up with some very bad fouls throughout their career, far worse than what happened to Beckham.'

Beckham had the last laugh. The following season, with crowds baying for his blood, he was a highly influential figure as Manchester United won the Treble.

ANDRÉS ESCOBAR SHOT DEAD
(1994)

Looking back on their dismal performance in the 1994 World Cup finals, it is easy to forget that, going into the tournament, Colombia were one of the favourites to win the trophy. Their stunning qualification campaign was the reason behind the optimism. The team, built around the languid skills of midfielder Carlos Valderrama, had become the first team to beat Argentina in 30 matches, winning 2-0 at home. Then on September 5, 1993, they dramatically announced themselves to the world. In order to qualify automatically, they needed to avoid defeat in Buenos Aires against the same opposition. Not only did they avoid defeat, they trounced Argentina 5-0.

Pelé tipped them to become world champions. But the best player the game has ever seen is arguably its worst ever pundit. Colombia arrived in the USA a shadow of the team they had been just eight months earlier. Their preparation had been questionable, playing an unlucky thirteen sponsor-driven friendlies in the six months preceding the tournament. They spent the opening 15 minutes of their first game against Romania pinging the ball about, until Florin Raducioiu scored against the run of play. Gheorghe Hagi's long-range goal 19 minutes later took the wind out of Colombia's sails and the game ended 3-1 to the Romanians.

Colombia's campaign was over after their second match, a 2-1 defeat by hosts USA. The game featured an own goal by Colombian central defender Andrés Escobar, sliding in to cut out John Harkes's cross, but succeeding only in turning it into his own net. Back home, Escobar paid a heavy price for his botched clearance. In the car park of a Medellin nightclub, he got involved in an argument with a man over bets lost by the own goal. Escobar was shot six times in the chest. 120,000 people lined the streets for his funeral.

ITALY 1-1 ARGENTINA: ITALY VS MARADONA...
AND NAPLES
(1990)

While Diego Maradona's presence at Napoli made him a hero in the southern city, his achievements and transformation of a hitherto unspectacular club agitated the rest of Italy – a country renowned for its stark north-south divide. Not only had Maradona just led Napoli to their second *Scudetto* in four seasons, pipping Milan from the industrial north, he was about to play for his country in Italy's World Cup. Diego and Argentina were not going to get much love from the home crowds.

During the group stages, the Napoli captain was whistled and booed by the Italians in almost every match. The holders' opening-game defeat by Cameroon was met with nationwide hilarity. Argentina were lucky to escape from their group as one of the tournament's best third-placed teams – especially as Maradona had got away with an outrageous handball on the line against USSR to deny his opponents a goal.

Argentina improved, albeit to a cacophony of abuse. In the second round they beat Brazil. Maradona, carrying an injury, set up the winner, amid suggestions that a spiked water bottle had been thrown on and doped Brazilian captain Ricardo Gomes. Then in the quarter-finals they edged past a decent Yugoslavia side on penalties, to set up a semi-final against... Italy. In Naples.

Maradona was not going to let the opportunity to cause mayhem slip, and in the build up to the match spoke to his club fans. 'The Italians are asking Neapolitans to be Italian for a day, yet for the other 364 days of the year they forget all about Naples. The people do not forget this.' On the day of the match the Italian fans unveiled a banner, which read: 'Maradona, Naples loves you, but Italy is our homeland.' It was not an unequivocal shunning, and the crowd were notably less noisy than they had been at Italy's other games. A nervous Italy failed to put away their opponents, and the match went to a penalty shoot-out which Argentina won, the scorer of their decisive penalty being, of course, Maradona.

Italy still rejoiced in the final, though not as they would have wished at the start of their tournament. Argentina lost to West Germany, Maradona's every touch jeered. The feeling was mutual. During the Argentine national anthem before kick off, as the cameras rolled by, Maradona could be seen clearly mouthing '*hijos de puta*': sons of whores.

WEST GERMANY 3–2 HUNGARY: THE MIRACLE OF BERNE
(1954)

Nobody expected West Germany to have a chance in hell against Hungary in the 1954 World Cup final. The 'Magical Magyars' – built around the legendary attacking force of Ferenc Puskás, Sándor Kocsis, József Bozsik and Nándor Hidegkuti – were unbeaten in two years and had set about proving their majesty en route to the final. They beat Korea 9-0; previous World Cup finalists Brazil 4-2; reigning World Cup champions Uruguay 4-2 and West Germany 8-3. The Germans had since regrouped to reach the final themselves, but after their earlier humiliation their only hope was to keep the score down.

Within eight minutes, Hungary were 2-0 up. But West Germany were a decent team themselves – that 8-3 defeat was suffered by a second-string selection – and had dispatched Austria 6-1 in the semi-final. Not only that, Hungarian talisman Puskás was carrying an injury (ironically picked up during that 8-3 win). After 18 minutes, the Germans had drawn level through Max Morlock and Helmut Rahn.

The Germans also had a trump card: screw-in boot studs, an innovation by Adidas founder Adi Dassler. With the pitch becoming wet and muddy, the Germans changed to long studs and became surer of foot. Six minutes from time, Rahn took a pop from the edge of the area. 'Rahn shoots, goal! Goal for Germany!' cried radio commentator Herbert Zimmermann, who then did something that turned him into an instant legend: he said absolutely nothing for eight seconds, a lifetime in radio. Then finally, he added: 'Germany lead 3-2! Call me mad! Call me crazy!' Puskás did put the ball into the net late in the game – but it was ruled out for offside. The game was over. Between June 15, 1952 and February 18, 1956, Hungary played 51 matches, winning 43 and drawing seven; the final was their only defeat.

ITALY 3-2 BRAZIL: ROSSI'S GAME
(1982)

Italy did not start the 1982 World Cup well. They drew all three of their group games, against Poland, Peru and Cameroon, scoring just two goals, though that was still enough to qualify them for the next round – on goals scored! Their malaise was summed up by the dreadful play of one man: star striker Paolo Rossi.

Rossi was banned from football for two years for his part in the 1980 'Totonero' betting scandal, and had only played three Serie A games since the ban had been lifted. The three matches he had played for Juventus were enough to win him a championship medal, but he was clearly not up to speed and in the group games his passing and positional play was woefully bad. The crowd booed, while the Italian press made it clear they wanted Rossi dropped.

But the team were certainly in no mood to listen to the press, who had among other things printed unsubstantiated rumours that Rossi was having an affair with his team mate Antonio Cabrini. 'They were also saying we had been seen in bars, that we were shooting up drugs,' said midfielder Bruno Conti, 'so we got together and called a news blackout.' Subsequently the under-fire squad became a close-knit unit.

In the second-phase mini-group with Argentina and Brazil, things got worse for Rossi. He missed a glorious one-on-one chance against Argentina, though the team won 2-1. But then it all came right against Brazil, in a game Italy needed to win. After just five minutes Rossi planted a low header past Walter Peres. Though Sócrates was quick to equalise, beating Dino Zoff at his near post, Rossi pounced on a terrible square-ball from Cerezo – an almost identical mistake to the one Clodoaldo made in the 1970 final to allow Roberto Boninsegna to equalise – and put Italy 2-1 up on 25 minutes. Falcão levelled the scores again in the second half, but six minutes later Rossi turned in Marco Tardelli's mishit shot to complete his hat-trick. Zoff's iconic 88th-minute save on the line from Oscar sealed one of the World Cup's most famous victories, but it was Rossi's match.

Italy – and Rossi – were on their way. Rossi went on to score both goals in his side's 2-0 semi-final win over Poland, then the opener in the final as they beat West Germany 3-1. Favourites Brazil, meanwhile, were going home, their 1982 vintage of Zico, Sócrates and Falcão destined to be remembered alongside Hungary '54 and Holland '74 as one of the greatest sides never to win the World Cup.

JULY 6

FAROE ISLANDS 6-0 YNYS MON: THE FIRST ISLAND GAMES MATCH
(1989)

The Island Games was intended to be a one-off bit of light amusement between British islands, as part of a 1985 Isle of Man sporting jamboree. But when organisers casually asked Greenland, the Faroe Islands and Saint Helena from the South Pacific if they'd also be interested in taking part, a proper tournament was organised. Fifteen islands took part in an event with the emphasis firmly on athletics. A roaring success, it was decided the Island Games should become a biennial event.

The third staging of the games saw football added to the roster. The opening game saw the only FIFA-affiliated country to take part in the event – hosts, the Faroes – beat a team from Anglesey 6-0. The Faroes went on to win all four of their matches to take gold, Anglesey took silver and Aland bronze. Faroes apart, the Games represented an opportunity for teams who had no chance of ever being involved in FIFA tournaments to engage in a meaningful competition.

The Faroes held onto their title in 1991, but that was to be the last time they competed. By then, they had bigger fish to fry. Having gained full membership of FIFA and UEFA in 1988, they competed in their first ever competitive international on September 12, 1990. The result sent shockwaves through Europe. In front of a crowd of 1,544 they beat Toni Polster's Austria – who had just played in the 1990 World Cup – thanks to a 61st-minute goal from timber shop worker Torkil Nielsen. Austria manager Josef Hickersberger handed in his resignation.

Since then the Faroe Islands – population 47,000 – have struggled, though they have occasionally turned in magnificent results in qualifying campaigns. Two draws with Scotland, draws with Lithuania, Slovenia and Bosnia, and in 2007 a loss to world champions Italy of only 2-1. Meanwhile at the Island Games, both Guernsey and Jersey have since equalled the Faroes' record of two golds, while a special mention must go to tiny Sark. They ended the 2003 tournament having lost 19-0, 20-0, 16-0 and 15-0 – 70 goals in five days – though their keeper, Leon Burletson, did save two penalties in the 20-0 defeat...

JULY 7

WEST GERMANY 2-1 NETHERLANDS: TOTAL
FOOTBALLERS BEAT THEMSELVES
(1974)

The contrast between the West German and Dutch teams during the opening couple of weeks of the 1974 World Cup was stark. The Germans had been arguing about cash bonuses should they win the tournament, then lost a politically sensitive group game to East Germany. The result caused their manager Helmut Schön – who had defected from the east before the Berlin Wall went up – to suffer a minor meltdown. Team captain Franz Beckenbauer was forced to prop his manager up, whilst trying to calm an agitated squad.

The Dutch were swanning around like rock stars. Their 'Total Football' philosophy – where every outfield player interchanged positions as and when play dictated – was the talk of the tournament. Their captain Johan Cruyff's backheel turn against Sweden was its defining image. Holland's iconoclastic approach was such that Cruyff, who had a personal boot deal with Puma, refused to go to the World Cup at all unless his shirt was shorn of all its Adidas branding. While the rest of the team played with Adidas's trademark three stripes on their shirts, Cruyff had a bespoke version with two.

But their super-cool attitude was to be their undoing. Having qualified for the final, they decided to kick back in their hotel one night. 'Cruyff, Champagne, Naked Women and a pool!' announced German tabloid *Bild*. The Dutch wives were not pleased with the news. Danny Cruyff in particular was constantly on the phone home, upsetting preparations.

Then came the final. Having taken an outrageous first-minute lead, scoring a penalty before West Germany had even touched the ball, they decided to showboat. It was to prove a mistake. An irate German side pushed forward, scoring a penalty themselves. They then snatched the lead just before half-time through a typical piece of opportunism from Gerd Müller, scoring his 68th international goal in his 62nd – and final – match for his country. Berti Vogts shackled Cruyff, and despite a second half of constant Dutch pressure, the kings of Total Football had been beaten. Partly by a determined West Germany; partly by themselves.

JULY 8

WEST GERMANY 3-3 FRANCE: SCHUMACHER'S ASSAULT ON BATTISTON
(1982)

The 1982 World Cup semi-final between France and West Germany was one of the all-time classics. An end-to-end 120 minutes saw France go 3-1 up in extra-time, thanks in part to a spectacular close-range volley from Marius Trésor. France were denied what looked a certain place in the final, first being pegged back by Karl-Heinz Rummenigge and Klaus Fischer, then losing the World Cup's first penalty shootout. But all that was destined to become a historical footnote, because on 57 minutes, Michel Platini had sprung the West German backline with a wonderful angled through ball. The substitute Patrick Battiston, who had been on the pitch for seven minutes, ran onto it as German keeper Harald Schumacher raced out of his area. It wasn't quite a 50-50 ball as Battiston had a marginal advantage. But who would get there first?

Earlier in the match there had been signs of Schumacher's state of mind that evening. In the first half, with France striker Didier Six sliding in to try to meet a low cross, Schumacher claimed the ball. As the goalkeeper got up, he slyly dug his knee into Six's back. A couple of minutes before Battiston raced towards his area, the German keeper had threatened to fling a ball at some spectators in the crowd. He was in a determined mood. So it proved when Battiston poked the ball past him. The French midfielder's effort bounced wide right of goal, but that didn't stop Schumacher leaping into a late challenge, clattering the onrushing Battiston's head with his forearm and torso.

As Battiston lay prone, spark out, his team mates frantically waving for medical assistance, Schumacher was waving too – insisting that he should be allowed to restart the game immediately with a goal kick, as no foul was given and no card shown. An unconscious Battiston – Platini later said his team mate looked so pale he thought he had died – was carted off by stretcher to be given oxygen in the dressing room. He also required dental treatment for his two broken teeth, which Schumacher offered to pay for, arguing his actions had merely been 'professional'. Some profession.

JULY 9

ITALY 1-1 FRANCE: THE MATERAZZI FINAL
(2006)

After seven minutes of the 2006 World Cup final between France and Italy, Zinedine Zidane, in his final match before retirement, converted a Panenka-style penalty – just. Zidane became only the fourth man to score in two World Cup Finals; Vavá, Pelé and Paul Breitner being the others. With ten minutes remaining, he looked like joining the select band to have won the trophy twice, France looking much the stronger side in extra-time. But it was not to be his day. It would not be Zidane's final.

Instead it was Marco Materazzi's. The Italian defender was involved in all three of the game's major incidents. He was judged to have brought down Florent Malouda to concede the early penalty from which Zidane scored. He levelled the game twelve minutes later with a towering header. Then, with ten minutes of Zidane's career left, Materazzi said something to the French midfielder. Zidane promptly stuck his head into Materazzi's chest and was sent off in disgrace. The wind taken out of French sails, Italy held out and won the penalty shoot-out 5-3. Both returned home as national heroes. Zidane still won the Golden Ball as the tournament's best player.

What had been said? Lip readers were hired the world over, but no conclusive evidence was gleaned. All Zidane would admit to was that 'something personal' about his mother and sister had been mentioned. 'I'm sorry,' apologised Zizou, 'but I can't regret what I did because he should have not said that.' Two months later, Materazzi broke the silence. 'I was tugging his shirt,' Materazzi explained. 'He said to me "if you want my shirt so much I'll give it to you afterwards," I answered that I'd prefer his sister.'

The world had been shocked at Zidane's action, though in truth the only surprise had been the surprise. In all, Zidane was shown red fourteen times in his career. In the 1998 World Cup against Saudi Arabia, he was sent off for stamping on Saudi defender Fuad Amin. Along with Cameroon's Rigobert Song, he is one of only two men to have been sent packing in two separate World Cups.

JULY 10

RANGERS SIGN MO JOHNSON
(1989)

When Graeme Souness took over as manager of Rangers in 1986, he was asked if he would ever break the most infamous unwritten tradition in Scottish football. 'How could I take the job if I was told I could not sign a Catholic?' he responded. 'I'm married to one!' The family of Mrs Danielle Souness, in a delicious comic flourish, had built a business organising pilgrimages to Rome. It was inevitable that at some point Souness, never a man to shirk a challenge, would sign Rangers' first Catholic star. Not many would have guessed the identity of who that player would turn out to be.

Since 1986 Souness had sounded out several high-profile Catholics but none of the deals had come to fruition. He attempted to lure Ian Rush back to Britain from Juventus, but the striker returned to Liverpool instead. Oxford United's Ray Houghton also preferred a move to Anfield, while Liam Brady chose to spend his dotage at West Ham rather than Ibrox. Breaking with tradition was proving harder than Souness had anticipated, and when it happened it came with a touch of the surreal.

On May 12, 1989, Celtic paraded their former player Maurice Johnson, who had moved to Nantes in 1987, in one of their shirts, claiming they had re-signed him. 'It is a dream come true for me to be back at Parkhead,' said the player. Johnson then had a change of heart 'for personal and tax reasons', claiming he had not signed a legally binding contract. FIFA ruled that the £1.25m deal was binding as of July 1, but Celtic pulled out, at which point Souness made his move. 'I am absolutely thrilled to be joining one of the biggest clubs in Europe,' simpered Johnson, who went on to score 46 goals in 100 games for the club. Some Rangers 'fans' will never recognise them.

ENGLAND 0-0 URUGUAY: AN AWFUL START
TO ENGLAND'S WORLD CUP
(1966)

With the benefit of hindsight it's easy to forget that, before the 1966 World Cup began, Alf Ramsey's claim that 'England will win the World Cup' was considered by many observers to be wishful thinking. Holders Brazil, West Germany and Italy went into the tournament as favourites, and though England were a strong side and had won their last seven games, many thought that Ramsey's 'wingless wonders' would not be wonderful enough to break down stubborn continental defences when the pressure was on.

That feeling increased after the opening match of the tournament as the hosts took on a packed Uruguay defence and made no impression whatsoever. 'Let's not talk too much about England winning the World Cup,' wrote former England international Billy Liddell after a dour 0-0 draw, the first time the home side had failed to score in 52 post-war games at Wembley. 'We ought to be more worried about whether they are going to qualify from their group. More use should have been made of the wings. How England could have done with a Tom Finney out there to take that ball round the back and get it over.'

England now had to win their final two group games against Mexico and France in order to be sure of qualification for the quarter-finals. The pressure appeared to be telling on Ramsey, who refused to give the BBC a post-match interview. 'I was available before and no-one wanted me,' he snapped. 'Now it is too late.' He then turned down a request from the president of Uruguay's FA to visit the England team in the dressing room. England's odds to win the World Cup drifted out to 6-1.

The hosts stuttered past Mexico and France, then struggled to break down ten-man Argentina in the quarter-finals. The team may have been misfiring, but at least they had made it to the semi-finals. It was only then the wingless wonders would show what they were really capable of.

JULY 12

DON REVIE RESIGNS AS ENGLAND MANAGER
(1977)

England were extremely unlikely to qualify for the 1978 World Cup finals in Argentina. They needed to beat Italy in their last group game by four goals and hope the Italians would score no more than one at home to Luxembourg. After a 1977 Home Championship campaign which saw them lose to both Scotland and Wales at Wembley, rumours were suggesting manager Don Revie's three-year reign was over. Revie himself, though, was having none of it. 'Everyone seems to be forecasting that I will go if we don't qualify,' he said on June 25, 'but I'll make up my mind about that when it happens.'

Revie's stubborn stance didn't stop the gossip. It even intensified when, on July 4, Tommy Docherty was sacked by Manchester United. For the following seven days Revie was hotly tipped to leave his England post and take the vacant Old Trafford job. Then, on July 11, the gossip stopped as he announced his plan to quit as England manager – in the pages of the *Daily Mail*. 'Nearly everyone seems to want me out so I am giving them what they want,' he said. 'The situation has become impossible.' FA secretary Ted Croker responded by saying the news 'was a complete shock' and 'came right out of the blue'. The morning after, Revie's letter of resignation arrived at the FA. At which point it became clear he would not be going to take over Manchester United.

During March, Revie had been approached to become head of soccer development of the United Arab Emirates. In June, he had made a clandestine visit to Dubai, and soon after agreed a £60,000-a-year tax-free deal with a £100,000 bonus. 'This is an offer I cannot refuse,' he said. 'If everything goes through OK it is an unbelievable opportunity to secure my family's future. I had many offers to stay in England but the tax structure, let alone the salaries available, makes it impossible to earn this kind of money at home.'

History has been unkind to Revie, who was treated as a pariah ever after. The FA tried to ban him from football for ten years on a charge of 'bringing the game into disrepute' and though that was overturned in court, he was never likely to gain work again in England. But he was only earning £25,000-a-year with the FA – who were odds-on to sack him soon in any case. As he said, it really was an offer he could not refuse.

FRANCE 4-1 MEXICO; USA 3-0 BELGIUM:
THE FIRST WORLD CUP BEGINS
(1930)

The 1930 World Cup was the only one to be held in a single city. Sweden, Italy, Spain and Holland had all applied to be host nation, but FIFA chose Uruguay, and the first tournament was played out solely in Montevideo. The Uruguayan capital was more than big enough to accommodate the 13 teams who would compete for the trophy – there were three stadiums, Peñarol's Estadio Pocitos, Nacional's Gran Parque Central, and the spanking-new Estadio Centenario. But it wasn't quite able to generate sizable interest for every single match.

The opening Group Three game between Romania and Peru drew the smallest crowd that would ever be seen at a World Cup. Only 300 people turned up to Estadio Pocitos (though the official number was a whopping 2,549), which was a shame as the match was well worth a look. Adalbert Desu opened the scoring for Romania after 50 seconds with a 30-yard shot, Peru equalised midway through the second half through Luis Souza Ferreira, only for the Romanians to score twice in the last 16 minutes to seal a 3-1 win. The stormy match also saw Peruvian captain Plácido Galindo become the World Cup's first ever sending off.

At the same stadium the day before, only 4,444 had witnessed a slice of history: the first World Cup goal. Played concurrently with USA vs Belgium at Parque Central, France's game against Mexico saw Lucien Laurent open the scoring on 19 minutes. Only four games in World Cup history were watched by a smaller crowd. But Uruguay eventually proved itself the right choice as host as 221,099 people went through the turnstiles during the semi-finals and final.

JULY 14

HONDURAS AND EL SALVADOR'S 'FOOTBALL WAR' BEGINS
(1969)

World Cup qualifiers can get heated at the best of times. But when the competing countries are neighbours with complex political, racial and socio-economic tensions, all bets are off. So when El Salvador met Honduras – a country home to more than a quarter of a million Salvadoran immigrants fleeing their overcrowded, impoverished and oppressive state – in a 1969 CONCACAF qualifier for Mexico '70, there was more than a place at the finals on the agenda.

In the first meeting of the two-legged semi-final on June 8, Honduras beat El Salvador 1-0 helped by a home crowd in the capital Tegucigalpa.

When Honduras made the journey to El Salvador for the return leg on June 15, things took a turn for the worse. The Hondurans were greeted with rotten eggs, dead rats and bricks through their hotel windows. At the match, the stadium was surrounded by Salvadoran soldiers. As home fans booed the national anthem of Honduras, a dirty cloth was raised instead of the Honduran flag. El Salvador went on to win 3-0. The match was followed by riots. Back in Honduras, the troubles escalated as Salvadorian immigrants were attacked, causing them to flee back across the border.

With a win apiece, and aggregate goals not counting, a third and final play-off was required on June 27. The day before the match, El Salvador severed all diplomatic ties with Honduras while border skirmishes continued. The game went ahead anyway, played on neutral territory in Mexico, both sets of fans separated by 5,000 Mexican police. After ninety minutes the scoreline was 2-2, but El Salvador scored in extra-time to secure their berth in a play-off with Haiti for the right to go to the World Cup.

Just over two weeks later, El Salvador invaded Honduras in what would become known as the 'Football War'. By the time a ceasefire was called six days later, more than 3,000 people had died and more than 100,000 were homeless. As for the football, El Salvador beat Haiti over three matches, making it to a World Cup for the first time in their history. They lost all their games at Mexico 1970.

It was eleven years before the two countries finally signed a peace treaty. A year after that, in 1982, both countries qualified for Spain '82. Both finished bottom of their group, but while Honduras escaped with an honourable draw against hosts Spain, El Salvador suffered a record 10-1 defeat by Hungary.

HUNGARY 3-1 BRAZIL: BRAZIL'S ENGLISH NIGHTMARE
(1966)

Brazil were favourites to triumph at the 1966 World Cup and retain the trophy they had won in 1958 and 1962, but their star player wasn't so sure. According to Pelé, Brazil's preparation for the tournament had been 'a total and unmitigated disaster'. Aymore Moreira, coach in 1962, had been replaced with Vicente Feola, who had presided over the 1958 win. Feola, under pressure from Brazil's top clubs, all of whom wanted representation at the upcoming World Cup, toyed with a squad of 46 players in the months before the event. He eventually travelled to England with an unsatisfying mishmash of veteran players from the 1958 and 1962 campaigns.

Brazil still had Pelé and Garrincha, and while the latter was past his best in the wake of a knee operation, they had never lost a match when both players were in the team. The pair were too strong for Bulgaria in the opening match as that run continued. Both scored in a 2-0 win, Garrincha's free-kick a thing of violent beauty. But Pelé had been kicked around like an old sock and was rested for the following match against Hungary.

The match was one of the all-time classics. Brazil nearly went ahead after 23 seconds, when Lima's shot from nearly 40 yards was tipped round the post. Hungary did go ahead after three minutes, Ferenc Bene cutting inside from the right to stroke home. After that it was all Hungary, though it took another hour for them to go ahead again through a magnificent first-time volley from János Farkas. Kálmán Mészöly made it 3-1 with a penalty and Brazil's first World Cup loss for 12 years was sealed. It was Garrincha's last cap – and the only time he ever lost in a Brazil shirt. In the next game against Portugal, Pelé came back but was kicked off the park. Brazil lost 3-1; the shambles of 1966 was over.

BRAZIL 1-2 URUGUAY: THE FATEFUL FINAL
(1950)

The 1950 World Cup was the only edition with no planned final match – the outcome would instead be decided by a final pool of four teams – but the fates conspired to produce the most dramatic ending anyway. Results between hosts Brazil, Uruguay, Sweden and Spain meant that the last tie of the tournament, featuring the two South American sides, would decide the outcome. Brazil needed only to avoid defeat at the Maracanã to be crowned champions of the world.

Everyone in the world-record 210,000 crowd expected Brazil to win. They had beaten Sweden 7-1 and Spain 6-1, while Uruguay could only draw 2-2 with the Spanish and scraped a 3-2 victory over Sweden. The mayor of Rio took to the pitch and gave an address: 'You who in less than a few hours will be hailed as champions by millions of compatriots! You who will overcome any other competitor! You, who I already salute as victors!' A fateful speech before what would go down in history as the 'Fateful Final'.

The sale of oranges and soft drinks had been banned: according to Reuters they were 'handy weapons for anyone who disagrees with the referee'. None were thrown. Brazil went one up after 46 minutes through Friaca, but 20 minutes later Uruguay winger Alcide Ghiggia skated past Brazilian left-back Bigode and crossed for Juan Schiaffino to equalise. It was still enough for Brazil, but with 11 minutes to go, Uruguay's Ghiggia skinned Bigode again and beat goalkeeper Moacyr Barbosa. After the final whistle blew, according to FIFA's Jules Rimet, the silence of 205,000 people was 'morbid, sometimes too difficult to bear.' The British United Press reported 'women prostrate with grief ... the announcer thunderstruck'.

A heavy load was borne by Barbosa, who became the scapegoat for the loss. 'The maximum punishment in Brazil is 30 years imprisonment,' he said just before his death in 2000, 'but I have been paying, for something I am not even responsible for, for 50 years.'

ARGENTINA 0-0 URUGUAY: URUGUAY WIN FIRST OFFICIAL
SOUTH AMERICAN CHAMPIONSHIP
(1916)

The South American Championship of Nations is the oldest surviving international tournament in the world. The first event was held in 1910 in Buenos Aires, but is not regarded as an official championship. Only Brazil, Uruguay and Chile were invited to take part, and Brazil backed out before a game was played. Argentina won the last match in the group – a game that had been initially postponed after crowds burned down a stand at the ground of Racing Club – beating Uruguay 4-1.

The majority of historians consider the second staging of the tournament, in 1916, to be the first official South American Championship. Again it was held in Buenos Aires – to celebrate the centenary of Argentinian independence – but this time the result was reversed. Uruguay held Argentina to a goalless draw in the final match of a four-team league (Brazil had deigned to turn up this time).

The rest of South America soon joined in, but it was fitting that Argentina and Uruguay had shared those first two tournaments. Both teams have won the competition fourteen times (not counting, as they do everywhere outside Buenos Aires, that 1910 result). Brazil have surprisingly only won the event eight times; half of those wins since 1997. Their failure to match their world dominance in South America can partly be put down to the staging of only two tournaments between 1959 and 1975, the period Brazil were at their very strongest. Prior to that they often sent weakened sides to compete.

Frequent on-pitch brawls were a major factor in the irregular staging of the event. After a game in 1959 between Brazil and Uruguay ended up with ten players in hospital, many countries lost interest and the tournament nearly died out. After two low-key tournaments in the 1960s – one of them won at ridiculously high altitude by hosts Bolivia – the tournament was rebranded in 1975 as the Copa America. Since then it has become a regular fixture on the calendar, adding a new dimension in 1993 with 'foreign' guest invitations such as Mexico, USA, South Korea and Japan.

LEVANTE 1-0 VALENCIA: GRANOTES WAIT 70 YEARS
FOR CUP RECOGNITION
(1937)

With a civil war raging in Spain and the country split between Nationalist and Republican rule, both *La Liga* and the Copa del Rey had been suspended. In Republican Spain, however, the game went on. Regional leagues around Barcelona and Valencia were organised, and in 1937 it was agreed to merge the two, creating the *La Liga del Mediterraneo*. Madrid was also still under Republican rule, and so Real and Atlético had asked to join the fun, but with Barcelona running the show, the clubs were unsurprisingly turned down.

The round-robin Mediterraneo was contested by eight teams – and by way of a climax to the season, the top four would then compete in a cup competition, La Copa de Espana Libre (the Free Spain Cup). A triumphant Barcelona won the right to be joined by Espanyol, Girona and Valencia. But Barça decided their time would be better spent far away from the war, touring the USA and Mexico. Their place in La Copa was taken by the fifth-placed team, Levante, the second team from the city of Valencia, who had never won a major trophy in their existence.

The form and history books were turned upside down. The first round of La Copa was another round-robin table, the top two from four facing off in a grand final. Levante amazingly topped the league, beating Valencia 4-0 and 5-2 along the way, before subjecting their city rivals to a third defeat, 1-0, in the final. To this day the 1937 Copa de Espana Libre – the competition's one and only staging – remains Levante's sole trophy success. Yet it would be a bittersweet success: only in 2007 did the Spanish FA recognise the achievement as an official cup win. Still, better late than never.

NORTH KOREA 1-0 ITALY: AZZURRI HUMILIATED
(1966)

With a squad containing five members of the Internazionale side who had won the 1964 and 1965 European Cups, Italy were one of the teams strongly fancied to win the 1966 World Cup. During the qualifiers they beat Finland and Poland 6-1 and Scotland 3-0. They then saw off Bulgaria 6-1, Argentina 3-0 and Mexico 5-0 in friendlies. 'I've stayed in Italy with Inter, Torino and Bergamo and reckon I know more than most about foreign form,' said England's 1962 World Cup striker Gerry Hitchens on the eve of the event, 'and it's Italy to win the World Cup outright!'

All of those good results had, however, been at home. Since the start of 1965 they had only won once away, losing two of their last three to Hungary and Scotland. They started the World Cup solidly, if unspectacularly, by beating a poor Chile side 2-0. Italy then lost by a single goal to the USSR. Still, even a draw against North Korea, would be enough for the 'Azzurri' to progress. North Korea had essentially qualified by default, after African and Asian countries had boycotted the tournament en masse in protest at the single finals place available to both continents.

What Italy would have given for an embarrassing draw. The loss they suffered was up there with the World Cup's biggest humiliations to date. It was partly self-inflicted. Captain Giacomo Bulgarelli injured himself while attempting to scythe through the back of Park Seung-Jin, reducing Italy to ten men for an hour. Then just before half-time Park Do-Ik shot across a slothful Enrico Albertosi into the bottom-left corner. Italy couldn't respond. Rotten tomatoes awaited them on their return.

JULY 20

FA CUP INAUGURATED
(1871)

The Football Association had been founded in 1863, but the world's first association did not inaugurate the world's first tournament. In 1867 the Sheffield FA was formed, and in that year they held the Youdan Cup. Sponsored by local theatre owner Tommy Youdan, it saw 12 local teams compete for the chance to lift football's first ever trophy. Hallam were the winners, beating Norfolk after an anti-climatic 0-0 draw on 'rouges'. Rouges were a 'minor point' scored by shooting through additional posts on the outside of either goalpost, and only counting in the event of a goalless draw.

The following year, the Sheffield FA held the world's second tournament. The Cromwell Cup was named after another local benefactor, Oliver Cromwell, no relation. It too provided an anti-climax for a final. Wednesday beat Garrick 1-0 in sudden-death extra-time after a hopeless up-and-under was spilled by a Garrick player into his own goal.

The FA were taking note. On July 20, 1871 secretary Charlie Alcock made the following proposal: 'It is desirable that a Challenge Cup should be established in connection with the Association, for which all clubs belonging to the Association should be invited to compete.' Fifty FA clubs were eligible to enter the first tournament, which began later that year on November 11. The results that day included a 0-0 draw between Crystal Palace and Hitchin. Both teams qualified for the next round!

Scottish amateur giants Queen's Park were given a bye to the semi-final stage. The Scots drew 0-0 with Battersea-based Wanderers, but they could not afford to come back south for the replay and so their opponents made the final – where they beat Royal Engineers 1-0. The trophy stayed in the hands of public-school southerners until 1883, when Blackburn Olympic became both the first northern *and* working-class club to win the cup. It had become a national obsession.

DEATH OF THE GHOST: WHITE KILLED BY LIGHTNING ON GOLF COURSE
(1964)

Bill Nicholson's famous Tottenham Hotspur team of the early 1960s is these days synonymous with Danny Blanchflower, Dave Mackay and Jimmy Greaves. But arguably the most influential player of that era is one rarely mentioned these days: John White.

A Scottish international, the slight White was known as 'the Ghost' for his unerring habit of finding space all over the pitch while going unnoticed by opposing defenders. White's small frame meant he was nearly left unsigned by Nicholson, who wondered if the Falkirk player could cut it in the English First Division. Mackay (who knew him from the Scotland squad) and Blanchflower both petitioned for his purchase. When Nicholson found out White had been a cross-country runner during his time in the Army, the deal was done in 1959.

White, who could play on either wing, helped Tottenham to unprecedented levels of achievement. Spurs won the 1961 league and cup double, the 1962 FA Cup, and the 1963 Cup Winners Cup, becoming the first British club to win a European trophy. Along with Terry Dyson, who bagged a brace, White was the star of that 5-1 trouncing of Atlético Madrid, scoring with an exquisite drag-back and shot with no discernable backlift. In his time at Tottenham, the team finished no lower than fourth in the league. Of the 15 matches he missed while at the club, Spurs only won one.

In July 1964, White was staying with his friend Mackay in Middlesex. During a round of golf at the Crews Hill Club in Enfield, a thunderstorm broke out and he took shelter under a tree. At 4 p.m. he was struck down by a single bolt of lightning. Nicholson's Spurs would no longer be the force they once were.

JULY 22

AJAX REFUSE TO PLAY IN THE INTERCONTINENTAL CUP
(1971)

The Intercontinental Club Cup was inaugurated in 1960, the brainchild of UEFA general secretary Henri Delaunay. A two-legged contest between the winners of the European Cup and the Copa Libertadores, it initially served up some star-studded spectaculars.

In 1960, after Peñarol and Real Madrid drew in Montevideo in the first leg, Ferenc Puskás and Alfredo di Stéfano shared three goals in the first eight minutes of the return as the Spanish side won 5-1. A year later Peñarol bounced back to thrash Eusébio's Benfica 5-0 on their way to the prize. In 1962 Pelé trounced the Portuguese almost single-handedly, scoring five of the eight goals Santos scored over two legs.

But in 1963 the tournament began to turn sour. In that year's final, both Santos and Milan had a man sent off. Milan's goalkeeper Balzarini required stitches in his head and hand. Six players were sent off in an ill-tempered play-off between Racing Club and Celtic in 1967. In 1968 Manchester United had two players dismissed in two ties against Estudiantes. Estudiantes then excelled themselves in 1969 against Milan in a maelstrom of kicking and gouging, three members of their team being jailed for the evening by an embarrassed Argentinian president. In 1970 Feyenoord's Joop van Daele had his glasses whipped off his nose by Estudiantes defender Oscar Malbernat, who duly passed the spectacles to his team mate Pachame – who stomped on them.

The relentless 'antifutbol' convinced 1971 European champions Ajax to withdraw from the tournament when their chance to compete came around. Nacional of Uruguay, in the poor house and desperate for the revenue, begged UEFA to put pressure on the Dutch club to compete, but they would not be moved. European Cup runners-up Panathinaikos contested the final instead.

Ajax played the following year, but when Johan Cruyff had his ankle damaged by rough Independiente play, Europe decided enough was enough. For the next few years, the European champions – Ajax, Bayern Munich, Liverpool and Nottingham Forest – declined to enter.

ENGLAND 1-0 ARGENTINA: RATTIN SENT OFF FOR 'VIOLENCE OF THE TONGUE'
(1966)

Argentina had already picked up one warning from FIFA over their conduct in the 1966 World Cup before they reached the quarter-finals. Rafael Albrecht was sent packing in a group game against West Germany for kneeing Wolfgang Weber in the swingers. Another dismissal was soon to follow. Argentina had enjoyed the better of their early quarter-final exchanges against England, but then captain Antonio Rattin, already booked for an innocuous trip on Bobby Charlton, questioned the booking of a team mate. He was shown a second yellow for the 'look on his face' and 'violence of the tongue' – even though the German referee spoke no Spanish and Rattin no German. Ordered to leave the field, Rattin initially refused and took ten minutes to do so.

Alf Ramsey referred to Argentina as 'animals' after the match and attempted to stop the players exchanging shirts, though England actually committed more fouls in the game and had both Bobby and Jack Charlton booked. The Argentinian FA was fined a whopping £85 by FIFA and Rattin was banned for four matches.

It was one of the World Cup's most controversial moments, and one which has always polarised opinion. Argentina were afforded a heroes' welcome on their return to Buenos Aires. Rattin was mobbed by women who 'kissed him ecstatically on both cheeks and tried to wrap him up in an Argentine flag', reported Reuters. 'The crowd cheered a group carrying a plastic globe, symbolizing the world championship Argentina claims morally to have won.'

The English view was very different. 'There is little question that Argentina deserve their sentences,' began a front page report in *The Times*, which today reads like a satire on Little England mentality. 'It is true that Rattin was dismissed from the field not for any physical infringement but for the unruly use of his tongue … that is the way in Latin America, where there is little respect for authority on the field of play. The fact is Rattin set a bad example to the rest of his men, which led to other incidents and tested to the full the self-control of the England players. Jack Charlton has on occasion in the past been quick to retaliate, but to find his brother also guilty on this occasion underlines the provocation.'

The report concluded by castigating the Argentinians for turning up at a Government reception in London on the evening of the match one hour late – after their coach got lost on the way from the team hotel in Welwyn Garden City.

FIGO JOINS REAL MADRID: THE FIRST
OF 'LOS GALÁCTICOS'
(2000)

Real Madrid had just won their second European Cup in three seasons under incumbent club president Lorenzo Sanz, but that wasn't good enough for the Real membership as they voted in the presidential elections. Up against Sanz in the election was Florentino Perez, who hadn't looked likely to trouble his opponent until he produced a piece of paper with Figo's name on it. 'Vote for me and I will deliver you Figo,' said Perez, claiming he had a watertight contract with Figo ensuring the Barcelona winger would sign if he won the election. If either party backed out, they would owe the other £18m.

This was denied by Figo. 'I have made an irrevocable decision,' he said on July 14. 'I will not be a Real Madrid player. If any of the fans have felt upset or disappointed about what has happened I would like them to forgive me, but they should only believe what I say.' However, a week later Perez was elected, and it soon became clear a deal had been struck. Figo had never really wanted to join Real, but had decided along with his agent, Jose Veiga, that Perez was unlikely to win the election. The pair felt the contract would strengthen Figo's hand while renegotiating his contract at Barcelona. Now he was committed to leave for Real.

And so, on July 24, Figo was paraded at the Bernabéu in a Real Madrid shirt claiming that he was 'happy to be here'. Of one of the most bizarre transfers in history, Figo said: 'It was a difficult and important decision, but on top of everything, at this moment, I had to think only of myself and for that reason I made this decision. Now I'm here with Real. I want to win as much as possible with Real Madrid.'

Figo was to be the first stage in Perez's new policy of signing one big-name star each summer: 'los Galácticos'. Zinedine Zidane followed in 2001, and the pair won the European Cup in 2002. But from then on in the policy began to go wrong. Ronaldo rolled into town in the summer of 2002, just as level-headed boss Vicente del Bosque was shipped out. As Michael Owen then David Beckham arrived, the team became increasingly lop-sided; after winning *La Liga* in 2002/03, the club did not win anything for four years.

THE BRITS RETURN TO THE FIFA FOLD
(1946)

The British associations had been playing silly beggars with FIFA ever since the international federation was founded in 1904. Initially taking over a year to reply to an invitation to join – and then turning it down – they eventually deigned to sign up, only to continually find themselves at loggerheads with the rest of the world. Having already demanded the right for England, Scotland, Wales and Ireland to be counted as separate nations as opposed to the United Kingdom (an argument they won), they then refused to co-operate with their Great War enemies after the hostilities ended (an argument they lost). They finally flounced off in 1928 over the issue of broken-time payments.

Broken-time payments were a means of compensating amateur players who represented their countries in Olympic competition. FIFA agreed to them, but the British associations dug their heels in. Players were either amateur or paid professionals; there was no middle ground. The decision to leave FIFA was costly. It meant the countries would not be able to compete in the first three stagings of the World Cup. Attitudes were so entrenched that England even turned down an invitation to play as a non-FIFA member in the 1938 tournament to replace Austria, the country having just been swallowed up by Nazi Germany.

After the war relations thawed. With the British realising that the world was happy to move on without them, they returned to the fold, a decision aided by FIFA's promise to allow each United Kingdom country a separate vote. The move was celebrated by the staging of a Great Britain versus Rest of Europe match at Hampden Park in May 1947, which raised £35,000 for a struggling post-war FIFA and saw Britain win 6-1. It would, however, be the last time the British celebrated on the world stage for a while. Their isolationist policy soon came home to roost, with both England and Scotland humiliated in their first World Cup outings (the English beaten by USA in 1950, the Scots tonked 7-0 by Uruguay in 1954).

STEAUA BUCHAREST 2-1 DINAMO BUCHAREST: CEAUSESCU'S CUP
(1988)

Romania's Communist dictator Nicolae Ceausescu was not much of a football fan. This did not, however, stop his party using the sport as a political tool. During the 1970s and 1980s, many of the state organisations were directly linked to the country's top clubs. Dinamo Bucharest was run by the Securitate, the secret police, and their rivals Steaua Bucharest by the state army. Needless to say Dinamo were the more feared team, and flourished with police support, whereas rivals Steaua would often fall victim to unfair refereeing and blocked transfers. By 1984, Dinamo had won their 12th national title, while Steaua could only boast three.

In 1983, Ceausescu's son Valentin, who followed football religiously, was made president of Steaua. From that point on, decisions would start to magically go Steaua's way, almost to the point of farce. Between June 1986 and December 1989, the team went 104 games unbeaten in the league.

In 1988, with the cup final between Steaua and Dinamo balanced precariously at 1-1, Gavrila Balint scored in injury time for Steaua, who celebrated a certain win. But then the referee called Balint's goal offside. Under Valentin's order – although Balint would later disagree with this version of events – Steaua walked off the pitch. The Cup was awarded to Dinamo, but amazingly the goal was later retrospectively awarded, with the trophy awarded to Steaua!

After the 1989 revolution and the fall of the Ceausescus, Steaua decided to hand the trophy back to Dinamo, who declined the offer. The Romanian FA still considers the victory to be Steaua's. Looking back, it seems the best way to view that match is from Dinamo defender Ioan Andone's point of view. At the end of the game, Andone dropped his shorts and waved his penis at those looking on from the VIP box.

But it would be unfair to say that Steaua's successful run was solely down to biased decisions. During that period the club reached two European Cup finals, losing to Milan in 1989 but becoming the first from an Eastern Bloc country to win the trophy in 1986. A team starring the legendary Marius Lăcătuș beat Barcelona on penalties after a dour goalless draw. Goalkeeper Helmuth Duckadam dropped out of football for three years soon after. He was rumoured to have had his arms broken by Ceausescu's hoodlums after complaining about the scant financial rewards for the victory, but this was apocryphal: he had merely suffered from a serious blood disorder.

BLACKBURN ROVERS SIGN ALAN SHEARER
(1992)

In 1990, Blackburn steel magnate Jack Walker sold his family business to British Steel for £360m and used some of the money to fund a takeover of his boyhood heroes, Blackburn Rovers. The deal didn't create much of a stir nationally at the time – except from some patronising amusement when the Second Division club offered to buy Gary Lineker from Tottenham Hotspur – but it was one which would soon change the face of football in the 1990s.

Walker decided one of the reasons the Lineker bid had failed to be taken seriously was Blackburn's lack of a high-profile manager. Don Mackay had been relatively successful at Rovers – he had won the 1988 Full Members Cup and taken Rovers to the promotion play-offs two seasons in a row – but the team had narrowly avoided relegation to the Third Division in 1990. Mackay's days were numbered. In October 1991, Kenny Dalglish, who had resigned from the Liverpool job eight months earlier, took over.

Dalglish got Blackburn promoted in his first season, though it was a struggle. Three points clear at the top in mid-March, they lost six on the spin to fall out of the play-off places and required a final-day win at Plymouth to scrape back into them. They went two goals down at home to Derby in the play-off semi-final, before recovering to win the tie 5-4 on aggregate, going on to scrape past Leicester in the final.

Now a Premier League club and with Dalglish in charge, Blackburn could make a splash in the transfer market. They did so by breaking the British record with a £3.3m deal for Southampton striker Alan Shearer. It would prove to be a signing worth every penny, as his 34 goals in 42 games took Rovers to the title three seasons later. But it is worth remembering Dalglish was seen to be taking one hell of a gamble at the time. Shearer's subsequent career tends to obscure the fact he had only scored 23 goals in 118 league appearances while at The Dell.

GERMAN FA AGREES TO FORM BUNDESLIGA
(1962)

For a country with no professional players or a national league, a haul of one World Cup was not bad going. But West Germany's 1954 world championship aside, the country was not punching its weight on the international stage. By 1962, European competition was seven seasons old, and only Eintracht Frankfurt had reached a final – where they were soundly thrashed, 7-3 by Real Madrid in the 1960 European Cup. Things didn't look like changing any time soon. Nuremberg had just been beaten 6-0 by Eusébio's Benfica in that year's European Cup, Werder Bremen had been beaten 4-2 in the Cup Winners Cup by Atlético Madrid, Cologne had crashed out in the first round of the UEFA Cup at the hands of Internazionale, and the national team had been beaten by Yugoslavia in the quarter-final of the World Cup. Something had to give.

So on July 28, the DFB agreed to launch a new national league to replace its regional Oberliga set-up (in which the championship was decided in a final after a series of inter-region play-offs). The new Bundesliga wouldn't be *quite* professional – players would be 'licensed' which effectively meant they could earn a capped salary – but it was a major step in the right direction. Most of the big clubs made-up the first 16-team league (although Bayern Munich didn't make the cut, and unsuccessfully protested against the decision) and on August 24, 1963 a new era in German football began.

It had been feared bigger clubs like Schalke, Borussia Dortmund and Nuremburg would dominate, but the first eight championships were shared between eight different clubs. Although by the 1970s, Bayern and Borussia Monchengladbach were carving it up between them. On the international stage, though, dividends in the new quasi-professional era were soon being reaped. Borussia Dortmund won the 1966 Cup Winners Cup, a trophy taken off them a year later by Bayern Munich. Bayern, in 1974, became the first German European Champions. During that period, West Germany reached two World Cup finals, winning one, plus a semi-final.

IRAQ 1-0 SAUDI ARABIA: WAR-TORN IRAQ
WIN ASIAN CUP
(2007)

During the 1970s and 1980s Iraq qualified for three Olympic tournaments, won gold in the Asian Games in 1982, and qualified for the 1986 Mexico World Cup. By this point, Saddam Hussein's son Uday was in charge of Iraq's International Olympic Committee. Under his yoke, the national football team would often be subjected to horrific punishments for failure to perform during the 1990s and early 2000s, when the nation was affected by two gulf wars.

'A missed penalty or other poor play entailed a ritual head-shaving at the Stadium of the People or being spat on by Uday's bodyguards,' reported the *New York Times* in 2003, after speaking to former Iraqi midfielder Habib Jaafer. 'Some players endured long periods in a military prison, beaten on their backs with electric cables until blood flowed. Other punishments included matches kicking concrete balls around the prison yard in 130-degree heat.'

After the fall of Saddam's regime, the team began to build on their pre-war successes. In 2004 they reached the quarter finals of the AFC Asian Cup. The same year their Olympic team qualified and reached the semi-finals of the 2004 Athens Olympics, where they won the fair-play award. To the protest of some players, president Bush's election campaign featured a clip of the Iraqi and Afghanistan flags flying at the Greek Games. 'At this Olympics there will be two more free nations and two fewer terror regimes,' ran the Bush mantra. 'He can find another way to advertise himself,' retorted Iraq midfielder Salih Sadir.

The team's momentum would not be stopped by political point-scoring. A year after their Olympic showing, Iraq won gold at the West Asian Games and then in 2006 they won silver at the Asian Games. In 2007 Iraq won their first Asian Cup, defeating South Korea in the semi-finals 4-3 on penalties – fifty were killed by terrorist bombs as victory was celebrated on the streets of Baghdad – then Saudi Arabia 1-0 in the final through top scorer and captain Younis Mahmoud. Iraq won the 2007 FIFA National Team of the Year award for their effort, and the right to play in the 2009 FIFA Confederations Cup – competing alongside the USA.

THE 1966 WORLD CUP FINAL: ENGLAND 4-2
WEST GERMANY
(1966)

Everyone knows the story of the greatest day in English sporting history. Ray Wilson's poor clearing header which allowed Helmut Haller to score the opener on 12 minutes; Geoff Hurst's equaliser seven minutes later; Martin Peters scoring what looked like being the winner on 77 minutes, only for Wolfgang Weber to scramble home in injury time; *that* Hurst shot which didn't cross the line but counted nonetheless; Hurst latching onto a majestic Bobby Moore pass to set the seal on things with the last kick of the game.

And of course everyone knows the famous piece of commentary which accompanied Hurst's hat-trick goal. 1966 had been an up-and-down year for BBC commentator Kenneth Wolstenholme. The FA Cup final hadn't been kind to him. 'It's Wednesday's Cup!' he screamed as the Sheffield side went two up, only for Everton to launch a three-goal salvo to prove that was palpably not the case. So Wolstenholme needed to raise his game significantly with the World Cup coming to town. And so he did with this mix of linguistic genius and serendipity: 'Some people, some people are on the pitch! They think it's all over. It is now!' But here's how ITV's Hugh Johns recorded it: 'Here's Hurst. He might make it three. He has! He has! So that's it! That's it!' 'I wish I had been able to find a line,' sighed Johns years later, 'but by that time I was pretty darn tired. That is awfully flat when you think about it.'

Meanwhile Scotland striker Denis Law had called in the promise of a round of golf from an English friend who really wanted to watch the game, simply to annoy him. Upon hearing the score at the end of the round, Law threw his set of clubs into a bush in a wild rage.

CLYDEBANK 1-2 EAST STIRLING: BRITAIN'S RECORD LOW CROWD OF 29

(1999)

In 1964, the owners of East Stirlingshire merged their club with Clydebank Juniors. The arrangement only lasted for one season before the clubs divorced, but during it the newly formed East Stirlingshire Clydebank FC drew 14,900 spectators for a Scottish Cup first-round replay. It was the highest attendance a team under the Clydebank banner would ever entertain.

Just over 34 years later, Clydebank drew their lowest crowd ever for their first game of the 1999/2000 campaign – and with a pleasing symmetry the visitors were East Stirlingshire. The official reason given by the club for a preposterously low turnout of 29 paying customers was that the fixture clashed with the tall ships race starting that day in Greenock. The real reason? Spectators were boycotting the fixture in protest at the club's new groundsharing arrangement, having moved to Greenock Morton's Cappielow ground that season. For the record, that day's bumper crowd witnessed David Muirhead put East Stirling ahead on 33 minutes, David Stewart levelling things up 11 minutes after the break, and Gary Higgins converting a winning penalty for the visitors – no doubt to wild cheers – with 17 minutes to play.

That figure of 29 does not *officially* constitute the all-time lowest attendance in Britain. That record is held by Stockport County, for whom 13 people paid on the door to witness their game against Leicester City on May 7, 1921. But Stockport's ground had been temporarily shut due to crowd trouble, and the match had been played at Old Trafford after Manchester United's home game with Derby. Only 13 paid to watch the second game that day – but nearly 2,000 are said to have remained from the United-Derby tie. Which makes Cappielow's crowd of 29 the smallest ever to witness a league game in Britain.

AUGUST 1

ASK VORWÄRTS 2-1 RED STAR BRNO:
THE CUP WINNERS CUP BEGINS
(1960)

The first edition of the European Cup Winners Cup wasn't taken particularly seriously by the continent as a whole. Belgium, France and Spain were three of the ten federations involved in setting up the competition in February 1960, yet none of them even bothered to enter a team to contest the inaugural trophy. There were still ten entrants, though. Vorwärts of East Germany set the ball rolling against Czech side Red Star Brno in the preliminary round, scoring the historic first goal and winning the first game, though they lost 2-0 in the second leg and failed to make the competition proper.

In the other preliminary tie were Jim Baxter's Rangers, who scraped through 5-4 on aggregate against Ferencvaros. In the first round proper they trounced Borussia Monchengladbach 11-0, then in the semi-final knocked out FA Cup winners Wolves, only to lose the final 4-1 on aggregate to Fiorentina. Their good run was a harbinger of things to come for British clubs, who would go on to dominate a tournament quickly gaining in stature.

Tottenham Hotspur won Britain's first European trophy in 1963, with Jimmy Greaves and Terry Dyson scoring two apiece in a 5-1 rout of Atlético Madrid. West Ham added to the English tally in 1965 against 1860 Munich. Liverpool should have made it three the following year, but lost a tense match against Borussia Dortmund to a freakish long-range lob. Arsenal fans felt Liverpool's pain in 1995, losing to Nayim from the halfway line against Real Zaragoza.

In addition to Spurs and West Ham, ten British teams have lifted the trophy. Manchester City (1970), Chelsea (1971, 1998), Rangers (1972), Everton (1985), Manchester United (1991) and Arsenal (1994) all won the Cup, but the most famous victory has to be Aberdeen's 2-1 win over Real Madrid in 1983. 'A great night for Britain,' suggested an on-pitch reporter immediately after the match. 'It's a great night for Scotland,' deadpanned Alex Ferguson.

AUGUST 2

SANTOS 2-3 PEÑAROL: THE THREE-AND-A-HALF HOUR GAME
(1962)

The Copa Libertadores, the South American equivalent of the European Cup, didn't start with an immediate bang. The straight knockout format of the tournament, which began in 1960, didn't appeal to South American audiences. When a rethink in 1962 led to the competition being organised in a more popular league-based structure up until the final, fans started taking it more seriously. Just how much more seriously quickly became apparent.

Peñarol of Uruguay had won the first two Copa Libertadores and, thanks to the free-scoring antics of Alberto Spencer, were hotly expected to make it three titles in a row. Their opponents in the two-legged final were Santos of Brazil, who would normally have been considered a greater threat, but star man Pelé had picked up a groin injury two months previously at the World Cup and was out.

Against the odds, Santos registered a shock 2-1 first leg win in Montevideo. The return in Brazil was tumultuous. With the sides tied at 2-2 after 51 minutes, referee Carlos Robles was knocked out by a rock thrown from the crowd. Upon regaining consciousness, Robles suspended the game for an hour before deciding to play out the final 39 minutes. When Spencer put Peñarol 3-2 up, a play-off seemed on the cards, but then Pagão scored from a blatantly offside position. Robles let the goal stand. He feared for his life, and no wonder. The linesman, who had flagged to disallow Pagão's strike, had been whacked with a bottle from the Brazilian crowd. After three-and-a-half hours the match ended 3-3, and Santos assumed they'd won on aggregate. Conmebol had other ideas, chalking off Pagão's goal retrospectively and ordering a play-off. Even then, justice was not fully meted out: by the time the replay came round 28 days later, Pelé was up on his feet again, and scored twice in a 3-0 romp for Santos.

NIGERIA 3-2 ARGENTINA: AFRICA'S FIRST WORLD TITLE
(1996)

Pelé and former England coach Walter Winterbottom both famously predicted that an African nation would win the World Cup before the year 2000. That never came to pass, though one major world title did go to Africa before the millennium was out.

Since World War II, the Olympic Games football tournament had been dominated by countries from the Eastern Bloc. Competitors had to be technically amateur to compete in the Olympics, which suited communist countries as their players all held nominal state positions and were full-time professional players in all but name. From 1948 to 1980, only four out of 27 medals went to countries outside the Eastern Bloc, the sole gold going to Sweden in 1948. (The rule wasn't all bad, as it allowed two Hungarian legends to get some tangible reward. Ferenc Puskás's Aranycsapat won gold in 1952, as did Ferenc Bene's superb mid-60s side in 1964.)

FIFA and the Olympic committee changed the rules in 1984, banning players who had competed in the World Cup at any stage. In 1992 they went further and turned the tournament into an under-23s competition. By 1996 three over-age players were allowed, meaning the event was not far off the World Cup in terms of quality. Argentina and Brazil were expected to contest the final that year, with teams boasting players such as Hernán Crespo, Claudio Lopez, Diego Simeone, Roberto Carlos, Bebeto and Ronaldo. The South Americans met their match against a Nigeria side determined to break Africa's duck.

Nigeria did so in some style. In the semi-finals they faced reigning world champions Brazil. With 12 minutes to go they were 3-1 down. First Victor Ikpeba and then, in the last minute, Kanu took the match to extra-time, where Kanu's golden goal sent Nigeria into the final. Again Nigeria upset the odds. 2-1 down against Argentina with 16 minutes remaining, Daniel Amokachi equalised before Emanuel Amunike scored the winner with the final kick of the game. Africa finally had its world title – though not the one Pelé or Winterbottom were talking about.

AUGUST 4

BILLY MEREDITH SUSPENDED BY FA FOR BRIBE
(1905)

Billy Meredith didn't take long to become a Manchester City hero. On his second game for the club, Meredith scored two goals in an 1894 derby against Newton Heath, soon to become Manchester United. He scored a further ten goals in 17 matches from the right wing that season, an amazing feat considering he worked down the pit as a pony driver during the week. By the end of the campaign, City had convinced him to become a full-time professional. It was the start of a career which would define Mancunian football for the best part of three decades.

Meredith's goals helped to establish City as a major force in English football. He scored 29 in 33 as City won the Second Division title in 1899, the club's first major honour. In 1904 the club nearly won the double, coming second to The Wednesday in the league, but winning the FA Cup final against Bolton, Meredith scoring the winning goal. Famous for running about with a toothpick poking out from under his tache – his first choice was chewing tobacco, but City's laundry lady complained that he was leaving brown saliva patches on his shirt – Meredith had become the game's first superstar.

City challenged for the title again in 1904/05, and on the last day of the season needed to win at Aston Villa to become champions. They lost 3-2, but worse news was to come. Meredith had offered Villa's Alec Leake £10 to throw the game, and in August was suspended for 18 months. While waiting for his ban to be lifted, Meredith was signed by Manchester United and became the first chairman of the Players' Union. On New Year's Day 1907, Meredith was allowed to take to the pitch again, beginning a 15-year career at United which saw him win two league titles and an FA Cup.

He returned to City in 1921. Three years later, aged 49, he scored his 151st and final goal for City against Brighton & Hove Albion in an FA Cup tie; his final game was that season's 2-0 semi-final loss to Newcastle.

Meredith died aged 83 in 1958, soon after the Munich air disaster. That overshadowed the news, though a *Times* obituary called Meredith 'a genius', adding 'no other man has ever played football chewing a quill toothpick'.

HULL 1-1 MAN UNITED: THE FIRST ENGLISH PENALTY SHOOT-OUT
(1970)

The Watney Mann Invitation Cup was British football's first competition to carry a sponsor's name. Running for four seasons in the early 1970s – later becoming football's chief contribution to the tired 'Does-anyone-remember-spangles?' nostalgia industry – it was a pre-season invitational tournament contested by the two top-scoring teams from each of the Football League's four divisions (who hadn't qualified for Europe).

Manchester United's speedy descent from the pinnacle of European football, which ended in their relegation from the top-flight in 1974, can first be charted here. Just over two years previously they had beaten Eusébio's Benfica in the final of the European Cup, and now here they were struggling to beat mid-table Second Division side Hull City in a pot paid for by a brewer. Having won 3-2 at Third Division Reading on the very first day of the tournament, they travelled to Hull for the semi-final and after only 11 minutes found themselves 1-0 down after Hull's all-time leading goalscorer Chris Chilton finished off a flowing move. Hull were unlucky not to make it 2-0 late in the second half, Butler hitting the post with 12 minutes to go, and paid for it as Denis Law headed home soon after to force a draw.

The game, for the first time in English football, was settled by what was referred to then as the 'Settling' rule: a penalty shoot-out. George Best took the very first kick and converted. The first player to miss was, of all people, Denis Law, whose penalty was saved by Hull keeper Ian McKechnie. United prevailed 4-3 – the deciding kick being blazed over Chris Waddle-style by... Hull keeper McKechnie. United booked a place against Derby in the final three days later, when Brian Clough's side thrashed them 4-1.

The tournament is much derided now, but did give two smaller clubs their day in the sun. In 1971 Colchester beat West Brom on penalties in the final after a 4-4 draw. The year after, Bristol Rovers triumphed against Sheffield United on spot kicks after a goalless match. Stoke won the final staging of the cup in 1973, beating Hull 2-0 in the final.

AUGUST 6

BARCELONA'S 'MARTYR PRESIDENT' JOSEP SUNYOL EXECUTED
(1936)

In the mid-1920s, Barcelona began suffering from the military dictatorship's campaign to stamp out Catalanism. They were banned from flying the Catalan flag at their stadium, forced to use Spanish in all official documentation, and ordered to supply the police with details of all their members. The club quickly became a potent symbol of Catalan identity, a way of sticking two fingers up to the country's rulers in Madrid. When Barça pipped Real Madrid on the last day of the very first Spanish league championship in 1928/29, their fans celebrated more than just a footballing victory.

Josep Sunyol, a politician campaigning for Catalan independence, recognised this. In 1928, he joined Barcelona's board with the intention of using their ever-growing fanbase to rouse support for his left-wing political ideals. Football offered Sunyol a big platform. In 1930, he set up his own weekly paper *La Rambla*, which opposed the military dictatorship in the region, and of course gave all the latest insider news from FC Barcelona. Fans also gathered outside the paper's headquarters for away matches – these were the days before television – and cheered as Sunyol put up the team's latest scores on a giant board.

By the time he took up presidency of the club in 1935, Sunyol had cemented his role as a deputy for the left-wing Esquerra party. But the club's first and only cup final under his yoke would be a symbolic failure. Against bitter rivals Real Madrid, Barça lost 2-1 to a team of ten men, being denied a late equaliser after a spectacular save from ex-Barça keeper Ricardo Zamora.

In July 1936, civil war broke out. Before Sunyol had time to lead Barça to any more finals he was dead. With fighting raging between nationalists and republicans, Sunyol strangely decided to make a trip into the countryside, which was littered by troops loyal to General Franco and the Spanish nationalist party. En route, he was gunned down by a firing squad in the Guardarrama Hills to the south of Madrid.

When troops discovered who had been shot they immediately tried to cover up the death. Some reports claimed he had fled the country, others said he was being held prisoner by the Fascists. Officially, Sunyol had 'disappeared'. It was not until the fall of the Franco regime in 1975 that full details began to emerge and even then Barça seemed reluctant to talk about Sunyol's murder. Eventually, in 1996, a monolith was erected in the hills where he died, his name spelt Josep Suñol – in Castilian, not Catalan.

GERMANY 0-2 NORWAY: HITLER SUFFERS
AT THE FOOTBALL
(1936)

It was surely the most hilarious double sporting whammy of all time. On August 3, at the 1936 Berlin Olympics, Adolf Hitler attended the final of the 100 metres. With steam parping from every facial aperture, Hitler looked on in impotent rage as Jesse Owens stormed to victory. The furious Führer did some storming of his own – straight out of the stadium, refusing to bestow the gold medal on the black sprinter.

Four days later, Hitler attended Berlin's Poststadion, along with Joseph Goebbels and Rudolf Hess, to watch Germany's second round match in the Olympic football tournament. They had easily beaten Luxembourg 9-0 in the first round, and Hitler arrived expecting the team to easily dispatch Norway. 'The Führer is very excited, I can barely contain myself, a real bath of nerves,' wrote Goebbels in his diary ahead of the match. But the Norwegians were a decent side, and went ahead after six minutes. There was more fury: 'The Führer is very agitated, I'm almost unable to control myself,' wrote Goebbels, continuing the incontinence riff. With seven minutes to go, Norway scored their second, at which point Hitler got up and, like he did after the Owens race, left the arena in a funk.

Hitler never watched a match again, so he missed the next public relations disaster for the Nazis. At the 1938 World Cup, in the wake of the Anschluss, Sepp Herberger picked a Greater Germany side containing an almost equal number of Germans and Austrians. But the policy benefited nobody: while Austria had been one of the teams of the 1930s, they were on their way down, while the Germans, ironically, had been improving. Switzerland sent the shambolic amalgam of a side packing, 4-2 in the very first round.

AUGUST 8

CHELSEA 1-2 EVERTON: ALAN BALL DEBUTS HIS WHITE 'HUMMEL' BOOTS
(1970)

Alan Ball gave a man-of-the-match performance in the 1970 Charity Shield at Stamford Bridge. FA Cup holders Chelsea shot out of the blocks in the season's opening fixture and did everything but score. Ball took over and set up a first goal for Everton which utterly disrupted their opponents' rhythm, then dictated the flow of the rest of the game. Despite his efforts, all anyone could talk about after the game was the fact he was sporting a pair of shiny white Hummel boots.

However while the boots were indeed white, they were not made by Hummel. Ball had been paid £2,000 to publicise the flashy footwear, but upon wearing them came to the conclusion that they were 'crap, like cardboard', painted his old Adidas boots white, and ran out in those instead. 'I got the young apprentices to paint them,' he admitted years later. 'It was great, until one day it rained and the black came through. A not-too-happy Hummel rep saw what I'd done so I said goodbye to the two grand.'

It wouldn't be the last time a player would chance his arm with a boot deal. Stan Bowles was offered £200 to wear Gola boots during England's international with the Netherlands on February 7, 1977. He accepted – only to have £300 dangled in front of him later in the day by Adidas. His solution was simple: to wear a Gola boot on one foot, an Adidas boot on the other. 'Nobody knew what I had done 'til a few days later,' he said, 'but obviously it didn't go down too well when they found out.' Was it any wonder England lost 2-0 that evening, played off the park by the Dutch to such an extent that Johnny Rep sidled up to Kevin Keegan after only ten minutes and whispered in his ear: 'This is the worst England team I have ever seen. You have problems here.'

THE DEATH MATCH: FC START 5–3 FLAKELF
(1942)

In the World War II film *Escape to Victory*, prisoners of war Pelé, Bobby Moore, Ossie Ardiles and, er, Russell Osman defeat a team of Nazis in a propaganda tournament and make as the title suggests. The film was loosely based on the legend of occupied Ukraine's FC Start, who were said to have taken on a team of German all-stars in 1942 and told, after leading at half-time: 'Well done, you've played good soccer and we appreciate it. But now in the second half, take it easy; because as you yourselves must realise, you have to lose. You must. This is an order. If you don't lose, you'll be shot.' Start ignored the diktat, scored three more after the break, and were sent to a mass grave at Baby Yar.

The truth was slightly more complicated. During 1942, Start consisted mainly of former Soviet professionals from the temporarily disbanded Dynamo Kiev. They played several matches against occupying soldiers and won them all convincingly, once thrashing their opponents 11-0. It was at this point the Nazi administration ordered a high-profile match against a German team, Flakelf, appointed an SS officer as ref, and intimated that there would be severe repercussions should Start win.

Nevertheless, Start won 5-3, the final indignity for the Nazis coming when defender Klimenko rounded the German keeper in the dying seconds but, instead of rolling the ball into the net for a sixth goal, contemptuously kicked it back up the pitch. A week later, after Start had won another match 8-0, the team were rounded up and sent to Siretz labour camp, where five of the team were tortured then shot.

Some historians question the accuracy of the match reporting, suggesting a romanticised myth, but one thing is certain: for Start, unlike Pelé and his mates, there would be no Hollywood ending.

AUGUST 10

LIVERPOOL 1-1 LEEDS: NO CHARITY BETWEEN BREMNER AND KEEGAN
(1974)

Poor Kevin Keegan had already been roughed up once in the summer of 1974. On a post-season tour of Eastern Europe with England, he was seized by Yugoslav officials in Belgrade after larking around in passport control. Grabbed round the neck, pinned against a wall, and punched on the nose and in the stomach, he was dragged into a side room and detained until FA officials negotiated his release. In the melee, it was reported that 'an earthenware coffee set' he had just purchased in the airport shop had also been smashed.

So the last thing Keegan needed was to be involved in one of English football's most notorious brouhahas on the opening day of the new season. In the curtain-raising Charity Shield, Liverpool faced a Leeds side wound up beyond all reason by their new boss Brian Clough, who had immediately alienated half of his squad by telling them they had 'cheated' for years under the managerial auspices of Don Revie. Leeds captain Billy Bremner and midfielder Johnny Giles had walked out onto the pitch with faces like thunder, and their moods didn't change when the match started. First Giles was booked for fouling Keegan, then Bremner got stuck into the striker, who retaliated. Bremner and Keegan squared up to each other, continued to row in front of the referee, and were both sent off. They became the first British players ever to be given their marching orders at Wembley. Both men tore off their shirts and stomped off to the dressing rooms in a huff. Liverpool won the game on penalties after a 1-1 draw.

Bremner and Keegan were handed 11-game bans by the FA; three for their dismissals, eight for flinging off their tops. Bremner spent his time off getting involved in the political machinations behind the scenes at Elland Road, where Clough was forced out of office after 44 days. Keegan used his to play golf and get married.

FOOTBALL LEAGUE LAUNCH NOT-SO-SUPER SUPER CUP
(1985)

The Football League had to react quickly to English teams being banned from competing in Europe by UEFA in the wake of the Heysel tragedy. They inaugurated the Super Cup, a tournament designed to fill the calendars and coffers of the clubs who would normally have qualified for European competition. In principle it was an admirable idea to solve a real problem; in practice it was a shambolic failure that achieved nothing.

Six clubs were invited to participate: Everton, who as champions would have been in the European Cup; Manchester United, the FA Cup winners denied a Cup Winners Cup jaunt; Norwich City, the (relegated) League Cup winners, who had earned a place in the UEFA Cup; and Liverpool, Tottenham Hotspur and Southampton, whose league positions had also earned UEFA Cup places.

To ensure there would be enough fixtures, the six teams were placed in two groups of three in order to eliminate one team per group. The remaining four teams would go on to knockout semi-final ties. However, all this resulted in was farcical fixture congestion. Liverpool and Everton both reached the FA Cup final and the semi-finals of the League Cup, and had to postpone and rearrange several fixtures. As the Merseysiders would be the two teams to eventually reach the final, the denouement to the Super Cup had to be held over until the following season – as the 1985/86 campaign could not be extended due to the upcoming World Cup in Mexico.

By the time Liverpool won the two-legged final 7-2 on aggregate in September 1986, the tournament had already been shelved, destined to be a one-off. Everton's supine display in the final ties may be put down to the (possibly apocryphal) story which has manager Howard Kendall sending his team out for one Super Cup match having told them the whole thing was a 'waste of time'.

AUGUST 12

FA CALL IN KEANE BIOGRAPHY OVER HAALAND RETRIBUTION
(2002)

Manchester United were trailing 1-0 in a 1997 Premiership match at Leeds when, with five minutes remaining on the clock, their captain Roy Keane let his frustrations get the better of him. Chasing a ball with Alf Inge Haaland, who had been man-marking him all day in a niggly duel, he stretched out to trip the Leeds midfielder up. 'As I slid in to make the challenge my studs caught the turf,' Keane remembered five years later in his autobiography. 'I actually heard my cruciate ligament snap.'

Keane's honest autobiographical account of that moment and its aftermath got him into serious trouble. According to him, Haaland had accused Keane of 'faking' injury. It was a slight he would not forget. In April 2001, United hosted Manchester City, for whom Haaland was now playing, and Keane decided to wreak his revenge. 'I fucking hit him hard,' recalled Keane in his book, of a hideous knee-high lunge on the player. 'The ball was there (I think). Take that, you c*nt. And don't ever stand over me again sneering about fake injuries ... I didn't wait for [the referee] to show the card. I turned and walked to the dressing room.'

Keane's book, and his admission of premeditation, was serialised in the *News of the World* and *The Times* in August 2002, just before its publication. The FA did not wait for it to hit the shelves, calling in the manuscript on August 12. Keane's ghost biographer Eamon Dunphy claimed he had used some 'artistic licence', but that made no difference. Keane, who had been banned for three games for his 2001 sending off at the time, was hit with a further disrepute charge which led to a £150,000 fine and a five match ban. There was little regret. 'I had no remorse,' Keane told *Observer Sport Monthly*. 'What goes around comes around. He got his just rewards. My attitude is an eye for an eye ... [but] I never went after a player to injure him in my life. Not even Haaland.'

Haaland retired in 2002 with a serious knee injury. He briefly considered suing Keane, before admitting it was his other knee that was causing him trouble.

AUGUST 13

HARDAKER STOPS UNITED'S POST-MUNICH EUROPEAN CUP RETURN
(1958)

In the immediate wake of the Munich air disaster in February 1958 which killed eight Manchester United players, Red Star Belgrade suggested UEFA should postpone that season's European Cup and posthumously anoint the stricken team 'honorary champions of Europe'. UEFA did not agree to the request and the tournament went on, but Europe's governing body were not totally without sentiment. Recognising the terrible price United had paid in pursuit of European glory, they offered the club a place in the following season's competition – even though they had not won the league.

Matt Busby accepted, though was immediately informed by the Football League that, as they were not champions, his team could not compete. Alan Hardaker, secretary of the League, who had two years previously attempted unsuccessfully to persuade the United manager to shun European competition, gleefully delivered the news. Hardaker had managed to convince Chelsea to bale out the year before. His opinion of the new competition could be gleaned from an 'unguarded aside' he gave to the renowned football writer Brian Glanville. 'He confided to me with a grin,' recalled Glanville, 'that he didn't much enjoy dealing with football on the continent: 'Too many wogs and dagoes!''

Busby appealed against the diktat to the FA, who came to the conclusion the League had no power to stop United competing and gave them the go-ahead. Then, on August 13, Hardaker went to war. He demanded a meeting with the FA in order to argue his position, and after a fortnight of having their own rulebook waved in their face behind closed doors, the FA caved in. On August 31, United were banned from entering the tournament.

Hardaker later argued that he was simply protecting the Football League from fixture congestion, but most interpreted his motives the way Bobby Charlton did: 'He was making it as difficult as possible for the man who had defied him with his insistence that United would fight on this new frontier of football.' United did not compete in the European Cup again until 1965.

AUGUST 14

TASMANIA BERLIN 2-0 KARLSRUHER: A FALSE DAWN
(1965)

Tasmania Berlin started their first season in the Bundesliga with a solid win. Two second half goals from Wulf-Ingo Usbeck secured a 2-0 victory over Karlsruher that sent them to joint second in the nascent 1965/66 table. If there was ever such a thing as 'antifutbol', then this result was an 'anti-harbinger'.

Tasmania should arguably have been awarded a place in the inaugural Bundesliga in 1963, being the most successful team in the local Oberliga Berlin in the five years before the inception of the new league. Their place was awarded to Hertha Berlin instead. Soon after, in the 1964/65 season, Hertha were demoted for breaching transfer-limit rules. The DFB insisted that Berlin should be represented in the top flight, so went on a search for the next-best-placed club from the capital.

That was Tennis Borussia, but as they'd finished behind Saarbrucken and Aachen in the promotion play-offs, the DFB felt they could not be promoted ahead of teams they'd failed against. Down the tables the administrators went. Spandauer were next, but noting there were only two weeks to go until the start of the new season, decided the prize on offer was fool's gold. Tasmania, the next on the list, had no such qualms.

More fool them. After their opening victory, Tasmania went on a record-breaking 31-game winless streak which only ended on May 21, 1966, the penultimate day of the season. Wolfgang Neumann's 83rd-minute goal beat Borussia Neunkirchen – who were also relegated. Their record was appalling. They had lost 28 of their 34 games, garnered only eight points, and boasted a goals for-and-against record of 15-108. Their first home game drew 81,500 fans; against Borussia Monchengladbach in January they had pulled in 827. Spandauer meanwhile finished a comfortable third in the Regionalliga Berlin, feeling quite pleased with themselves.

ATLÉTICO MUNICIPAL 2-0 UNIVERSIDAD DE PEREIRA:
THE DIMAYOR BEGINS
(1948)

When Argentinian club Vélez Sarsfield toured Colombia in January 1948, 12,000 came to see them play in Bogota. Such a crowd was unheard of in the country, and it gave impetus to the idea of a professional league. The DiMayor league began in August that year. Colombia was in political turmoil – liberal president elect Jorge Eliecer Gaitán had been assassinated in April, sparking a decade-long civil war known as 'La Violencia' – and football became a welcome distraction. The DiMayor was a stunning success, and club owners decided to strengthen the league by signing as many overseas stars as possible.

This proved easier than it sounded, as in Argentina and Uruguay players had gone on strike demanding better pay and conditions. In the summer of 1949, Millonários de Bogota president Adolfo Pedernera popped down to Argentina to see who he could prise away. He came back with 'El Maestro': Adolfo Pedernera, who had helped River Plate to six Argentinian titles. Within months, more than 50 Argentinian players were playing for various clubs in the DiMayor. The problem was, none of the clubs paid a penny in transfer fees, simply luring the players to Colombia with sky-high wages. The Colombian FA, worried about their international status, asked FIFA to suspend the league to restore order. They did so, but order did not follow.

Free from FIFA's red tape, the rebel DiMayor clubs simply took their blackballing as a chance to cherry-pick whoever took their fancy from around the globe. This gave rise to the 'Eldorado' era. Some of the best players in the world descended on Colombia, including eight members of the Uruguay team who won the 1950 World Cup. The Millonários side of Padernera, Alfredo di Stéfano and Nestor Rossi – known as 'Ballet Azul' (The Blue Ballet) – became famous worldwide.

But it could not last. The Colombian economy was soon in crisis due to the turmoil in the country, while FIFA were desirous of an amicable solution. A truce was called and in 1953 the DiMayor returned to the international fold.

AUGUST 16

NOTTINGHAM FOREST 1-0 LIVERPOOL:
A WHOLE NEW BALL GAME
(1992)

The first live Football League match was transmitted by ITV in September 1960, but the programme was not a success. *The Big Game* between Blackpool and Bolton was appalling. The cameras were positioned behind the goals and ITV only showed it from the last five minutes of the first half. To make things worse, star man Stanley Matthews was out injured. The viewing figures were low, and within weeks the contract between broadcaster and league had been scrapped.

It took another 23 years before a league match would be shown live on television in its entirety, when ITV showed Tottenham Hotspur vs Nottingham Forest in October 1983. ITV and the BBC showed regular live matches during the mid-1980s, but football hardly benefited financially by the arrangement as the broadcasters operated as a cartel, keeping the price low. When administrators tried to hold out for more money, in 1986, the game was taken off the screens for six months before the League returned cap in hand to take the £4.5m on offer.

But the climate was changing. The introduction of satellite technology meant the BBC and ITV were no longer the only players. British Sky Broadcasting made a £99m ten-year bid for league rights in 1988, which led to ITV breaking from the BBC and offering £44m for four years. ITV won the bid – partly because the big clubs would pocket the majority of a prize which had been previously split equally between all the league's 92 members. With this deal, the seeds of a breakaway 'super league' had been sown. In 1991 the FA Premier League was born, to be launched in the summer of 1992, after ITV's TV deal ran out.

ITV bid £262m for the new Premier League TV contract, and looked to have won it. At this point, Spurs chairman (and Amstrad satellite dish manufacturer) Alan Sugar was screaming 'You've got to blow them out of the water!' down a phone. But to whom? Hours later Sky tabled a £304m bid and won the contract.

That August, Teddy Sheringham fired past David James to score Sky's first live goal: a 'whole new ball game', as the adverts had it, was born.

WIMBLEDON 0-3 MANCHESTER UNITED: BECKHAM SCORES FROM HIS OWN HALF
(1996)

It was always Pelé's ambition to score a goal from inside his own half. He was destined never to achieve that particular dream, though he nearly managed it on the greatest stage of all. Coming up to half-time in Brazil's opening 1970 World Cup match against Czechoslovakia, he took possession of the ball inside his own half. Glancing up, he spotted keeper Ivo Viktor stationed on the edge of his area – and from beyond the halfway line pinged a snapshot in the direction of the empty net. The effort had Viktor beaten all ends up, but the ball moved slightly in the thin air and veered right, just wide of goal.

What Pelé failed to do in a 21-year professional career, 21-year-old David Beckham managed right at the start of his second full season for Manchester United. On the opening day of the 1996/97 Premiership season, United were playing out time against Wimbledon at Selhurst Park, already two goals ahead. Just before the final whistle, Beckham spotted Wimbledon goalkeeper Neil Sullivan out of his goal, and with an almighty swing of his right boot, sent the ball sailing over the head of the backtracking keeper and into the net.

With a huge smile on his face, Beckham spread his arms out wide to receive the acclaim; he knew this was going to turn him into a major superstar. Which it did. Sullivan was left sprawling in the net with a red face – and it wouldn't get any better as he would be lobbed from 40 yards in Wimbledon's very next game by Newcastle midfielder David Batty.

Sullivan had been asking for trouble that day. While Beckham's goal is rightly remembered, what's often forgot is that Jordi Cruyff, on his United debut, had tried exactly the same thing ten minutes before Beckham's effort, Sullivan again having gone walkabout. How differently two careers might have panned out if that had gone in.

AUGUST 18

HAITI 0-6 BRAZIL: O JOGO DA PAZ
(2004)

In February 2004, a bloody rebellion in Haiti left 300 dead and president Jean-Bertrand Aristide running for his life. With the country in deep turmoil, the United Nations stepped in to try and take control. Their peacekeeping troops contained a significant number of Brazilians – which gave the UN an idea.

The Brazilian football team was incredibly popular in Haiti. When the South Americans won the World Cup in 2002, a two-day national holiday was declared. So the UN proposed that a friendly between Brazil and Haiti – o jogo da paz (a 'Match for Peace') – might help the process of unification between the warring factions. Brazil agreed and waived their normal $1,000,000 fee. The island's interim prime minister Gerard Latortue offered $1,000 to the first home player to score in the game. O jogo da paz would quickly become Haiti's most talked about game since Emmanuel Sanon scored against Italy in the 1974 World Cup finals.

The issue of ticket allocation proved somewhat tricky. At first organisers came up with the idea of exchanging tickets for guns. But it was decided the 'Match for Peace' might turn into bloody carnage if thousands of armed gangs turned up and were unable to gain admission. Tickets were given out to students and families instead.

Tens of thousands lined the streets of Haiti's capital, Port-au-Prince, to watch as the world champions landed and made their way in armoured tank to a freshly painted and fumigated Silvio Cator Stadium. Brazil's line-up included Ronaldo, Kaká and Roberto Carlos, but it was Ronaldinho who stole the show, weaving past five defenders to score one of his three goals. He had clearly paid no attention to Brazilian president Luiz Inacio Lula da Silva's pre-match teamtalk, when he jokingly asked the team not to score too many goals since they were on a goodwill mission. The Haitian crowd didn't seem to mind, though, happy to have any excuse for a party.

Unfortunately, the political situation did not improve and many of the national team soon defected to America. But for 90 minutes Haiti forgot its woes and was given something to celebrate for years to come.

MANCHESTER UNITED 4-1 ARSENAL:
THE KNIGHTON ERA BEGINS
(1989)

Old Trafford was not a happy place in the summer of 1989. The club were still searching for their first championship since 1967 and were stuttering under Alex Ferguson. They looked as far away from a title as they ever had been. In May, Arsenal had won the title with the last kick of the season at Liverpool. The two clubs, finishing first and second, were 25 points ahead of United, who languished in 11th place.

But then, a day before the start of the new season, the biggest takeover deal in the history of British football was announced. Property magnate Michael Knighton had bought out unpopular chairman Martin Edwards in a £10m deal, and had guaranteed a further £10m to complete the 'Theatre of Dreams' stadium plan Edwards's father Louis had set out in the mid-1960s.

A new era was dawning, and it began spectacularly. Minutes before the first game of the season against Arsenal, Knighton ran out onto the Old Trafford pitch in a United tracksuit top and shorts and juggled a ball with his head before slamming it into an empty net. The crowd went wild. Two minutes into the game, Steve Bruce had headed United in front. The home side routed the new champions 4-1.

But after the showboating, the deal fell through, as Knighton's two main financial backers pulled out. Knighton was forced to withdraw from the deal. Two years later, United floated on the Stock Exchange, the club valued at £18m. Ferguson turned things around on the pitch and the club would become one of the richest in the world. Knighton later took some credit, insisting it was his idea to treat the club as a global brand.

In 1992, Knighton bought Carlisle United with the intention of making them a force in English football. After a series of disastrous decisions, including overstretching finances by building an unnecessarily large stand and making himself manager, Carlisle were stuck battling against relegation from the Football League. He was eventually bought out in 2002 after the club had been put into voluntary administration, as the Manchester United fans who cheered his juggling act thirteen years earlier thanked their lucky stars.

AUGUST 20

BOSMAN WINS HIS LEGAL BATTLE
(1995)

In 1990, FC Liege midfielder Jean-Marc Bosman's contract was nearly up. He had his eyes on French team Dunkerque, but the Belgian First Division club were not going to let him go without a substantial offer. Bosman was held in limbo, but unlike so many players before him, he protested, arguing that he should be able to move freely within the European Union without a transfer fee agreement.

Five years of legal wrangling later, the European Court of Justice ruled in favour of Bosman. In December 1995 it concluded that football transfer laws did not comply with the EU freedom-of-movement laws for workers. FIFA changed their policy accordingly. From then on, players would be able to change clubs within the EU whether or not a transfer fee was paid.

Ultimately this gave players more control than their clubs, particularly among those most in demand. The first high-profile British player to benefit was Liverpool winger Steve McManaman. When his Anfield contract expired in 1999, he was able to negotiate his own deal with Real Madrid. The club received nothing for a player who would go on to score in the European Cup final the following season.

But while the Bosman effect has benefited many of the game's stars, the greater freedom of movement afforded across the continent has also had negative effects for lesser players. In 2003, a report was published by Swansea University which stated that 'the post-Bosman influx of overseas-born players – especially in the higher divisions – has had a marked effect on the career prospects of UK-born youngsters, many of whom have had to accept a move to a lower division in order to extend their careers beyond their early-20s.' Smaller clubs have suffered too, with predatory big clubs now able to entice away their big names. One man thinks some legislation needs to be put in place to readdress the balance. 'I think we should have a system where players have to stay at their first professional club for a certain amount of time,' argues… Jean-Marc Bosman.

BOLTON WANDERERS 4-2 CHARLTON ATHLETIC:
THE FIRST SUBSTITUTE
(1965)

Substitutes had been a long time coming in English football. Just about every FA Cup final in the 1950s had been blighted by injury, and with no replacements allowed, this ruined most of the games as a spectacle. Arsenal's Walley Barnes suffered a split cartilage in 1952, and his team lost to Newcastle. Jimmy Meadows suffered a broken leg in 1955 as his Manchester City team lost to Newcastle. Manchester United goalkeeper Ray Wood broke his jaw in 1957 and was forced to hobble around on the wing, while Luton's Roy Dwight (cousin of Elton John) broke his leg as Luton went down to Nottingham Forest in 1959. Even the classic Matthews Final of 1953 was marred by injury, Stan only able to wreak havoc down the right wing after Eric Bell pulled up lame.

The cup final jinx continued into the 1960s. Future Wigan chairman Dave Whelan broke a leg as Blackburn went down to Wolves in 1960, then Leicester defender Len Chalmers picked up an injury early in the 1961 final, allowing Tottenham to complete the double with ease. Something had to be done. Finally, at the start of the 1965/66 season, substitutes were allowed in league and cup for the first time.

Clubs were initially not allowed to make tactical substitutions – a player had to be injured before he could be replaced. The very first change was made eleven minutes into the new season, as Charlton goalkeeper Mike Rose took a knock and midfielder Keith Peacock came on. All in all thirteen players were replaced on that opening day, though much good it did the teams, as eight of them lost their matches. The new rule was also seen to be unsporting. There were several recorded instances of crowds booing as the substitutions were made, displeasure made particularly loudly at Highbury, that bastion of old-school tradition.

LIVERPOOL 3-2 ARSENAL: THE FIRST EVER
MATCH OF THE DAY
(1964)

The first live league football on television was an unmitigated disaster. In 1960 ITV had shown *The Big Game*, the second half of a match between Blackpool and Bolton. The action was shot from behind one of the goals as opposed to from the side, it ended 0-0, and the attendance was 10,000 less than it had been the previous season. The programme was soon pulled. Football on television was restricted to the FA Cup final plus the odd England international thrown in.

Four years later, the BBC launched BBC2, and needed programmes to fill its new channel. The corporation offered the Football League £3,000 to divvy up between 92 clubs for the right to show a highlights programme (it now being possible to use videotape rather than film, allowing quick editing). With assurances that attendances would not suffer – the identity of the match would remain secret, and the programme would not go out before 9.30 p.m. at the very earliest – the clubs agreed. *Match of the Day* was born.

On the first day of the 1964/65 season, the programme was launched by Kenneth Wolstenholme, standing pitchside at Anfield, where the reigning champions were about to host Arsenal. 'Welcome to *Match of the Day*,' smiled the commentator, 'the first of a weekly series on BBC2. This afternoon we are in Beatleville.' Liverpool won 3-2, though few of their fans were able to watch a replay of the game that night, as the new BBC channel had yet to reach the north.

Despite some resistance within the game – Burnley tried to sue the FA and the BBC when they attempted to film highlights of an FA Cup tie against Bournemouth in 1966 – most welcomed the development. In any case, the genie was out of the bottle. While viewing figures were not exceptionally high to start with, the programme quickly gained in popularity. In the wake of England's 1966 World Cup win, the programme moved to BBC1. In 1968 ITV countered with *The Big Match*. By 1969 *Match of the Day* was being transmitted in colour (the curtain raiser again featuring Liverpool, this time against West Ham).

MANCHESTER CITY 3-1 WIMBLEDON:
DONS' FIRST DIVISION DEBUT
(1986)

In the mid-1970s, Wimbledon were a club in a hurry. Between 1975 and 1977 they won a hat-trick of Southern League titles, a period during which they further proved their credentials by beating First Division Burnley in the FA Cup in 1975 then holding reigning champions Leeds to a draw at Elland Road. In 1977 they were granted admission to the Football League. Within nine seasons, they had won promotion to the First Division, the most amazing ascension in League history.

Not everyone was enamoured with their feat. FA secretary Ted Croker questioned whether it was a good idea letting such a small club, with their rickety Plough Lane ground, into the top flight of English football.

After an opening day defeat at Manchester City one of the players had their bag stolen in the car park after the match, causing manager Dave Bassett to observe that 'it's still much better than playing at Rochdale'. The team then won three games on the spin and went top of the First Division.

'My mum will want this season to finish tomorrow,' smiled Bassett after a late Dennis Wise goal at Charlton put the Dons ahead of reigning champions Everton on goal difference. 'I'm not saying this is two fingers up to Ted Croker, but we have shown football does need clubs like us.' Wimbledon finished the season in sixth place. A year later they beat champions Liverpool to win the FA Cup.

Wimbledon spent fourteen seasons in the top flight, but the dream turned sour. In 2002, new owner Pete Winkleman requested to relocate the club and set up what was effectively a franchise in Milton Keynes. Under his proposal the club would move more than 70 miles and change its name, but keep its league place.

A three-man FA commission made up of a commercial lawyer, a former referee who had once been punched during a match by a fan, and the operations manager of Aston Villa was set up. During the hearings, Kris Stewart, chairman of the club's independent supporters group was asked if he could 'choose between life for the club in Milton Keynes or death in Merton.' He replied that he regarded both as death. Instead he hoped to resurrect the club and start at the bottom of the pyramid. Unable to comprehend the sentiment, the commission outrageously gave Winkleman's scheme the go-ahead. The spirit of the club lives on today in AFC Wimbledon.

TOTTENHAM 1-1 CHELSEA: GREAVES INTRODUCES HIMSELF
(1957)

On the opening day of the 1957/58 season, Jimmy Greaves made his debut for Chelsea. His overall game did not impress the man from the *Observer* much – 'Greaves, a newcomer of 17, hits the ball hard with his right foot but has no left foot at all' – but he did make one telling contribution: 'Greaves trapped an innocent-looking forward lob and pushed it home from short range.' It would prove to be a fairly typical display. Greaves made a career out of doing nothing for 89 minutes, yet popping up during the other one to score a goal.

He also made a habit out of scoring on every major debut. In 1959 he was called up to play for England and scored the goal in a 4-1 defeat by Peru in Lima. Two years later, after scoring 41 goals in the 1960/61 season for Chelsea, he moved to AC Milan for £80,000 and again scored on his debut. His goalscoring ratio in the notoriously parsimonious Serie A was nearly a goal a game – but his time in Italy was brief, and not a success. After three months and ten matches which brought nine goals, he was dropped from the team, manager Nereo Rocco deciding his insouciant style unbalanced the team. Rocco may have had a point as Milan were seventh when Greaves left for Tottenham in a £99,999 deal, but went on to win the *Scudetto*.

Spurs boss Bill Nicholson had deliberately ensured Greaves would not be burdened with the pressure of being Britain's first £100,000 player, and it worked. On his debut he scored a hat-trick against Blackpool, and finished the season with 21 goals from 22 starts. Up until the time he left for West Ham in 1970, Greaves scored 220 goals in 321 matches for Spurs, winning two FA Cup medals and a Cup Winners Cup. Upon arrival at West Ham, he scored twice on his debut against Manchester City, and retired the year after having claimed 357 goals (still an English record) in 516 top-flight games. The less said about his 1978 comeback for Barnet, and indeed England's 1966 World Cup campaign, the better.

AUGUST 25

SHEFFIELD WEDNESDAY 3-2 ARSENAL:
SHIRT NUMBERS 1–22
(1928)

Numbers on shirts seem obvious and logical today, but it took the Football League Management Committee a long time to become convinced they were a good idea. On the opening day of the 1928/29 season, Sheffield Wednesday and Arsenal ran out at Hillsborough with their players numbered 1-22, while Chelsea and Swansea Town did likewise in a game at Stamford Bridge. The experiment brought Chelsea, who won 4-0, more luck than Arsenal who lost 3-2. All clubs were told to stop the practice with immediate effect, both FA and League being of the opinion that club colours were being desecrated. In a fit of pique, Arsenal manager Herbert Chapman ordered the reserve team to continue wearing the numbered shirts.

Shirt numbers were not to be the only link Chapman and his counterpart at Chelsea, David Calderhead, had regarding apparel. In 1933 Calderhead dismissed a suggestion by the *Daily Mail* cartoonist that Chelsea should wear white sleeves on their blue shirts. Within weeks Chapman had taken up the idea for Arsenal.

Numbering crept into the game, though. In the 1933 FA Cup final, players were assigned numbers for the first time in order to assist radio commentary, Everton wearing 1 to 11, Manchester City 12 to 22. Everton wore their numbered shirts again the week later against Wolves, but it would not be until 1939 that the League Management Committee took a decisive vote on the matter. Cost was a concern to some clubs, but the motion was passed, 24 panel members voting for numbers and 20 voting against.

The new system did not debut until after the war, however. Numbered shirts were introduced as standard for the first time at the start of the 1946/47 campaign. FIFA did not insist on squad numbers in the World Cup until 1954.

AUGUST 26

ALFREDO DI STÉFANO RELEASED
AFTER CARACAS KIDNAPPING
(1963)

The Argentinian superstar Alfredo di Stéfano had not expected to be woken at the crack of dawn while on a pre-season tour with Real Madrid in Venezuela. But on the morning of August 24, minutes after being summoned down to the lobby of his Caracas hotel, he was ordered into a car by a group of masked strangers at gunpoint. He was being taken hostage by a group of rebels from the National Liberation Army Front headed by the young revolutionary Commander Maximo Canales, also known as Paul Del Rio.

Back at the gang's headquarters, Del Rio explained to di Stéfano that they had kidnapped him for publicity purposes, in order to highlight the corruption he argued was rife in the Venezuelan government. Sure enough, Di Stéfano and his captors made front pages the next day, although the stunt did not precipitate change.

Two days after his kidnapping, Di Stéfano was bundled back into a car, dropped off in the capital's Liberation Avenue, and made his way back though the city streets to the Spanish Embassy. Questioned as to why he was kidnapped at a press conference that evening, he said: 'I am not a politician so I'd prefer not to try to explain. All I know is that they never mistreated me.' He then went on to say his captors had 'apologised a thousand times for the inconvenience'.

'We wanted to do a propaganda operation so the world would hear our demands,' Del Rio later explained, 'and to that end we used the most famous player in the world at that time. It was an act of romanticism, of mutual solidarity between the hostage and the kidnappers. He was our guest. We wanted him to understand what we were doing and why.'

Bizarrely, as Di Stéfano's career was coming to an end, Del Rio's was on the way up. Within years he had established himself as one of the country's leading artists. In August 2005, the two were reunited at a premiere of a film about Real Madrid, the imaginatively titled '*Real: The Movie*'. It was another shameless publicity stunt.

AUGUST 27

NEWCASTLE UNITED REPLACE DALGLISH WITH GULLIT
(1998)

Kenny Dalglish did not perform particularly poorly as manager of Newcastle United. Dalglish, one of only three men to win an English league title with more than one club, took Newcastle to second in the 1996/97 Premiership, and led them to the club's first FA Cup final in 24 years in 1998. But coming after the fast-and-loose Kevin Keegan, his more pragmatic style of football was never going to be a hit at St James' Park, whose crowd he never won over.

Dalglish didn't enjoy much luck before the start of his first full season in charge. Immediately after Newcastle had sold Les Ferdinand to Tottenham in the summer of 1997, Alan Shearer seriously injured ankle ligaments in a pre-season friendly at Everton. New signing Jon Dahl Tomasson was suddenly forced to lead the front line. It was too much responsibility for the 22-year-old in his first season in England; he only scored four goals in 34 appearances. He left at the end of the season for Feyenoord, where he won the 2002 UEFA Cup, before a successful move to Milan. Dalglish's ability to spot talent was vindicated too late for Newcastle. The side finished the season four points off the relegation places.

Dalglish was given money to strengthen his team and spent £9m on Dietmar Hamann and Nolberto Solano. But after drawing the first two games of the following season Dalglish was sacked. In came former Chelsea manager Ruud Gullit, who promised 'sexy football' but did not deliver, Newcastle finishing thirteenth. Again the board gave their manager money to spend in the close season – over £15m was spent on Kieron Dyer, Alain Goma and Marcelino – and again they wielded the axe just after the start of the season. A year and a day after taking over from Dalglish, Gullit was out. His successor Bobby Robson delivered five steady seasons, but he too was booted out just after the start of a campaign. None of the six Newcastle managers since have matched Dalglish's record between 1996 and 1998.

AUGUST 28

SEVILLA'S ANTONIO PUERTA DIES
(2007)

By the beginning of the 2007/08 season, Juande Ramos's Sevilla had become one of the top teams in Spain. After achieving nothing for 58 years, they had won a remarkable five trophies including two UEFA Cups and the Copa del Rey in the previous 18 months. They were hoping to continue their run by defeating AC Milan in the UEFA Super Cup – but then a terrible tragedy stopped them in their tracks.

Thirty minutes into the first half of Sevilla's first league match of the season against Getafe, 22-year-old defender Antonio Puerta, one of the players who had brought them such recent success, collapsed just outside the goalmouth at his home ground, the Estadio Ramon Sánchez Pizjuan. As Puerta lay face down on the ground, his team mates rushed to his aid and prevented him from swallowing his tongue. Puerta got up, and for a moment it looked as if he might not need serious medical attention. But within minutes Sevilla's number 16 was led off the pitch and rushed to the Virgen del Rocio hospital. En route, Puerta suffered two heart attacks. Three days later he died from multiple organ failures resulting from a weak heart.

Sevilla president Jose Maria del Nido described it as 'one of the saddest days in the history of Sevilla FC. The diamond left-footed player has left us, a player that changed our lives now leaves us.' Thousands of fans and players attended the funeral held at the club's ground and more than 20,000 lined the streets outside. Fernando Torres described his death as a void, 'impossible to fill'.

Despite dying so young, Puerta had left fans plenty to remember him by. In April 2006, Puerta scored a spectacular winner in extra-time against Schalke to put Sevilla through to their first UEFA Cup final. Sevilla went on to win the trophy, beating Middlesbrough 4-0 in the final. The following year they defended their title, Puerta scoring the winning penalty against Espanyol.

Three days after his death, Sevilla lost to AC Milan in the Super Cup. The team wore shirts bearing Puerta's name on the front and back. Six weeks later, Puerta's girlfriend gave birth to their son Aitor Antonio. It was decided that the number 16 shirt would be retired, unless it was reinstated by Aitor.

AUGUST 29

ARSENAL 0-1 TOTTENHAM: CHAPMAN AND BUCHAN'S FIRST MATCH
(1925)

When the 1925/26 season kicked off, Arsenal welcomed two new men who would have a profound effect on the team: the revolutionary manager Herbert Chapman, who had led Huddersfield to two consecutive titles, and Sunderland's top scorer Charles Buchan.

Even aged 33, Buchan was hot property. Sunderland manager Bob Kyle had wanted £4,000 for the all-rounder, claiming he was still a 20-goals-a-season prospect. But Arsenal chairman Henry Norris brokered a bet instead. He gave Sunderland £2,000 and promised to pay £100 for every goal Buchan scored in his debut season. As it turned out, Buchan scored 21 goals as Arsenal finished second, five points behind Chapman's old club Huddersfield, so Arsenal ended up paying Sunderland an extra £100.

Like Norris, Chapman also had transfer tricks up his sleeve. On signing Bolton's David Jack in 1928, Chapman made sure the Bolton bigwigs were given double measures of alcohol while his own 'whisky and ginger' drinks would remain free from any of the hard stuff. The sober Chapman knocked more than £2,000 off Jack's fee.

Buchan and Chapman did not enjoy a good start to their Arsenal careers. Having lost the first game of the season to rivals Spurs, Arsenal were belaboured 7-0 at Newcastle a month later. But the result had positive effects in the long-term. Buchan demanded the team play an extra central defender to counter the new offside law which was helping forwards score more goals. Chapman acquiesced, and although the team took five years to win their first trophy under the new man, the new tactic – known as WM – proved crucial to Arsenal's dominance in the 1930s.

Buchan by then had retired, having scored 56 goals in 112 games. After his last match at Everton in 1928, the *Guardian* reported that he was presented with a 'token of esteem and of good wishes, a portfolio and gold mounted fountain pen and pencil on behalf of the players and the club'. The pen became useful as in 1933 he became a journalist for the *Daily News* and in 1951 gave his name to the world's first football magazine: *Charles Buchan's Football Monthly*.

AUGUST 30

ARSENAL BACK IN THE FIRST DIVISION –
THANKS TO NORRIS
(1919)

Arsenal found themselves remarkably better placed when football resumed after World War I. At the end of the 1914/15 season they had finished fifth in the Second Division, but four years later, with the help of their very persuasive chairman – the recently knighted 'friend to everyone', Tory MP Sir Henry Norris – they were up.

Norris had taken advantage of the division's expansion from 20 to 22 clubs. It had been expected, as in the expansions of 1898 and 1905, that the bottom two clubs in the First (in this case Chelsea and Tottenham) would stay up while the top two clubs in the Second (Derby and Preston) would be promoted. Derby and Preston's promotions were assured, but the other two places were up for grabs. Norris argued that Spurs deserved to be relegated on account of their league position. Chelsea, however, did not, as Manchester United would have been in their relegation position in 1915 had they not gained two points from a fixed match against Liverpool.

By arguing for Chelsea – but not calling for the demotion of United and Liverpool – Norris was winning Brownie points for Arsenal. Other clubs were impressed with his powerful contacts. Among others, Norris was close friends with Liverpool chairman 'Honest' John McKenna, president of the Football League. So when it came for the League committee to decide who would get the final First Division place, Arsenal won more votes than Spurs, Wolves and Barnsley, who had all finished the 1914/15 campaign in higher positions. There were dark accusations of bribes having been offered, but nothing was ever proven.

Spurs resolved to 'obtain by the verdict of the ball what they had been denied by the vote'. And that's what they did. By 1920, Spurs were back in the top flight. One of their first clashes with Arsenal at White Hart Lane in 1922 was far from amicable. Unusually for that time, two players were sent off, while several sustained injuries. When Spurs scored, the Arsenal crowd got rowdy. Fighting continued outside the stadium. Both clubs were given warnings by the FA, though a report in *The Times* claimed the 'spectators were almost entirely to blame' for the trouble. A fierce rivalry was born. Arsenal have never been relegated since.

AUGUST 31

THAILAND 3-2 INDONESIA: MURSYID EFFENDI BANNED FOR LIFE
(1998)

The 1998 Tiger Cup should be remembered for providing the biggest shock in the event's history. Hosts Vietnam were expected to win, but unfancied Singapore made off with the spoils, thanks to Sasi Kumar's 71st-minute winner in the final against the hosts. But the rest of the world only recalls the tournament for some outrageous gamesmanship in the opening round.

Before they met in their final Group A match, both Thailand and Indonesia had already qualified for the semi-finals. A win or draw would see Indonesia top the group – but with Group B already completed, they knew the section winners would take on the strong hosts Vietnam in the semi-finals. The losers would face the weaker Singapore, who had surprisingly pipped Vietnam to their group on goal difference.

With Indonesia hoping to lose and Thailand trying not to win, neither team took the match particularly seriously – at one point Indonesian goalkeeper Hendro Kartiko could be found in the opposing half taking potshots from open play – so while four goals were shared, none were celebrated with gusto. Then, with a minute to go, Indonesian defender Mursyid Effendi, under no pressure, whacked the ball into his own gaping net. He clapped himself as he ran back up the pitch.

The applause rang hollow. After the tournament, both teams were fined $40,000 for 'violating the spirit of the game', while Effendi was banned for life.

SEPTEMBER

SUNDERLAND 8-0 DERBY COUNTY: THE GAME
OF THREE HALVES
(1894)

Derby County suffered many an embarrassment during their risible eleven point season in the 2007/08 Premier League, but modern-day Rams fans can take consolation – albeit scant – that nothing was quite as bad, or as downright farcical, as this. It was the first day of the 1894/85 season, and Derby had travelled to Sunderland's Newcastle Road ground for the opening fixture. The only problem was that the official referee, Frederick Kirkham, had not arrived in time for kick off. The decision was made to start the match with a deputy official. At half-time, Derby were losing 3-0 – at which point Kirkham arrived and offered them the option of starting the match again. Unsurprisingly, they accepted.

Much good it did them. The second first-half ended exactly as the original one did. Sunderland went on to add five more in the second half, ending the day 8-0 winners after 135 minutes of football which had seen them score 11 goals without reply. The score was instructive, as Sunderland ended the season as champions. Derby finished second from bottom, only avoiding the drop by winning a relegation 'Test match' play-off 2-1 against Notts County.

It would not be the last time a Kirkham's decision making would come into serious question. At the 1902 FA Cup final, referee Tom Kirkham was forced to lock himself in a cupboard to avoid livid Sheffield United goalkeeper 'Fatty' Foulke, after allowing non-league Southampton a contentious goal. He then became manager of Tottenham Hotspur. Not much is known of his time at the club, but when a club-sanctioned official history describes one of their former charges as 'unpopular with players and fans alike', it can be safely deduced that it was not a roaring success.

SEPTEMBER 2

BELGIUM 2-0 CZECHOSLOVAKIA: THE ABANDONED
INTERNATIONAL FINAL
(1920)

It looked for a while like the big story of the 1920 Olympic football tournament would be a first round shock. Great Britain had won the first two stagings of the event at London 1908 and Stockholm 1912, and were expected to triumph in Antwerp in 1920. But Britain were dumped out in the first round 3-1 by Norway, and went home complaining that other countries were paying their players 'broken-time' compensation for missing work, circumventing the Olympic amateur ideal. The fact that Britain had circumvented it themselves when picking up golds, by playing amateurs who turned out for professional outfits like Chelsea and Derby, appeared to pass them by.

A bigger shock occurred in the final between the home nation Belgium and Czechoslovakia. Robert Coppée and Henri Larnoe had put the Belgians 2-0 up after 30 minutes. When Czech defender Karel Steiner was sent off in the 39th minute, Czechoslovakia walked off the field refusing to continue, and the match became the first – and only – major international final to be abandoned. The Czechs filed a complaint to the Olympic committee, claiming intimidation by pitchside Belgian soldiers and accusing British referee John Lewis of being biased in favour of the home side. The appeal was turned down flat, but the Czechs may have been right about Lewis; he was known for struggling to keep up with play – hardly surprising, given that he was in his seventies at the time.

Belgium were awarded the gold medal, but with the Czechs disqualified, a consolation tournament was staged to decide silver and bronze. Even that would prove to be controversial as losing semi-finalists France had already gone home and could not compete, so their place was taken by Spain – who ended up taking silver.

SEPTEMBER 3

BRAZIL 2-0 CHILE: ROJAS FAKES INJURY
(1989)

Brazil had competed in every single World Cup finals since the tournament's inception in 1930 – the only country to have done so – but their presence at Italy '90 wasn't a given. The *Seleção* vintage of the late 1980s wasn't the best. Only Romário, Careca and Bebeto, their trio of strikers, were thought of as world class. When the side conceded a last-minute equaliser in their qualifying group match in Chile, elimination became a very real threat. Brazil enjoyed a superior goal difference to their opponents, but it meant that if the Chileans won the final group game in Rio between the two sides, they would go through at Brazil's expense. It would be tense.

With the match goalless at half-time, the huge crowd at the Maracanã were on tenterhooks. But there was relief four minutes into the second period, Careca scoring the opening goal. Chile needed to score at least twice to reach the finals. The crowd celebrated by throwing coins and batteries onto the pitch. With time fast running out for Chile, their goalkeeper Roberto Rojas saw a way out. In the 67th minute, a flare landed within striking distance of Rojas. He fell to the ground, and after a stoppage of five minutes, was stretchered off the pitch clutching a bloody head. Chile captain Fernando Astengo led his team off the pitch, declaring the situation 'unsafe'. The match was abandoned. The next day papers in Chile spoke of 'war'; rocks were thrown at the Brazilian Embassy in Santiago.

However upon studying video footage, it became clear Rojas hadn't been hit by a flare at all. In a desperate attempt to get the match awarded to Chile, Rojas had deliberately cut himself with a blade kept inside his glove. Coach Orlando Aravena ordered him via walkie-talkie to stay down and allow himself to be carried off. Astengo and the team doctor later helped to conceal the blade. Rojas and Aravena received life bans, and Chile were eliminated from the 1990 World Cup and the following tournament. Brazil were awarded a 2-0 walkover and went through to the finals.

In 2001, Rojas's ban was lifted by FIFA. Contrite and apologetic, he returned to his old club Colo Colo and set up a goalkeeping school.

SPORTING 3-3 PARTIZAN: THE FIRST EVER
EUROPEAN CUP MATCH
(1955)

Having won the English championship in 1955, Chelsea had been invited by UEFA to play in the following season's inaugural European Cup. The London club were interested in competing in the new competition, but there was a problem: their chairman Joe Mears was also president of the Football League. As president Mears was heavily influenced by the League's chairman, the notoriously forceful Alan Hardaker. Chelsea bowed out and the tournament went on without them.

The week the European Cup got under way, Chelsea lost 2-1 at Blackpool. Sporting Lisbon of Portugal, meanwhile, were hosting the first ever match in the new continental jamboree. Their star João Martins scored European football's first goal after 14 minutes. Martins also scored the last of the match to force a 3-3 draw with Partizan Belgrade of Yugoslavia.

Fourteen other clubs contested the trophy: Aarhus (Denmark), Anderlecht (Belgium), Djurgarden (Sweden), Gwardia Warsaw (Poland), Hibernian (Scotland), Milan (Italy), PSV Eindhoven (Holland), Rapid Vienna (Austria), Real Madrid (Spain), Reims (France), Rot-Weiss Essen (West Germany), Saarbrucken (East Germany), Servette (Switzerland) and Vörös Lobogó (Hungary). Most, but not all, of the clubs were their country's reigning champions. Hibernian, for example, had come sixth behind Aberdeen, but their chairman was also running the Scottish FA, whose shame was avoided as the Edinburgh club reached the semi-finals.

Alfredo di Stéfano's Real Madrid, of course, went on to win a classic 1956 final, beating Reims 4-3 after falling 2-0 behind. Chelsea were left to think of what might have been. 'The club probably just chickened out of something few people knew enough about,' said Mears's son Brian years later. The year after, Manchester United would be bolder.

SEPTEMBER 5

CELTIC GOALKEEPER JOHN THOMSON
KILLED AGAINST RANGERS
(1931)

'For it's a grand old team to play for / For it's a grand old team to see / And if you know your history / It's enough to make your heart go sad.' When Celtic supporters sing this portion of 'The Celtic Song', the theme their team runs out to at Parkhead, they replace the final word with a heartfelt 'oh-oh-oh-oh'. But the sentiments are the same, as the song refers to John Thomson, the 22-year-old Celtic and Scotland goalkeeper who was killed in an accidental collision during the 'Old Firm' derby at Ibrox in 1931.

In the second half in that fateful match, Rangers forward Sam English went in at speed to challenge for a 50-50 ball in the Celtic area with the advancing Thomson. The keeper went down in an attempt to smother the ball, but English's knee hit Thomson's head and fractured his skull. As Thomson lay prone, one arm sticking up in the air, players on both sides rallied round and English immediately calling for assistance. Thomson was stretchered off, with most in the crowd assuming he had merely been concussed. The rest of the match passed without incident, ending goalless. However later that night in Glasgow's Victoria Infirmary, Thomson died. He had won the Scottish Cup with Celtic twice in 1927 and 1931, and had been capped four times for his country.

English, an Ireland international, was cleared of any blame for the tragedy in an inquiry. He had the support of John Thomson's family and all Celtic and Rangers players on the field at the time, but crowds in Scotland would not let him forget the incident and the deeply traumatised player left for Liverpool. He was a success at Anfield, scoring 24 goals in 47 games, but crowds continued to bait him and he eventually retired at 28, seven years after Thomson's death.

SEPTEMBER 6

ENGLAND 0-0 COLOMBIA: HIGUITA KICKS CLEAR, BARNES BOWS OUT
(1995)

Eccentric footballers are ten a penny, but Colombian goalkeeper René Higuita's life has been more colourful than most. Known as 'El Loco' (the crazy one), Higuita has spent time in prison after profiteering from a kidnapping deal involving drug baron Pablo Escobar, been banned from playing for taking cocaine, had extensive cosmetic surgery after being voted Colombia's 'ugliest icon', and single-handedly got his country knocked out of the 1990 World Cup while attempting a dragback near the centre circle. Cameroon's Roger Milla whipped the ball off his toe and rushed off to pop it into an empty net.

Despite it all, though, Higuita is destined to be remembered for one thing: the most outrageous save of all time. In the 21st minute of a friendly match against England at Wembley, Jamie Redknapp shanked an aimless cross into the box. The ball headed goalwards and was surely an easy take for Higuita – but the keeper dived forward, arched his back, flicked up his heels and, while still in mid air, backheeled the ball off the line and over his head to safety. The save came to be known as the 'Scorpion Kick', Higuita's legs having curled over his back like an arthropod's tail. Some naysayers point out that the linesman had put his flag up for offside – but the referee never blew his whistle and the game continued without stoppage. Had the ball gone in, the goal would have stood.

The game was also notable for the last appearance in an England shirt of John Barnes, who came on for the last 16 minutes in place of Redknapp. Barnes's inconsistent contributions in an England shirt left him underappreciated by many, but it's worth remembering that had he been given more than 16 minutes to run riot down the left wing against Argentina in the 1986 World Cup quarter-final, England may well have won that match and perhaps even the cup. It was fitting that one of the greats bowed out after a match featuring one of the great saves.

SEPTEMBER 7

NORTHERN IRELAND 1-0 ENGLAND:
HEALY ENDS 33 YEARS OF HURT
(2005)

With the 1958 World Cup quarter-finals too distant a memory for most, the 1980s represent the high-water mark for the Northern Ireland football team. In 1982, they reached the second round of the World Cup in Spain with a famous 1-0 victory over the hosts in Valencia. Gerry Armstrong fired the ball underneath the sprawling Luis Arkonada and ten men held out for half an hour. In 1984, they won the last-ever Home International tournament, and proclaim themselves to be British champions to this day. They reached the World Cup finals again in 1986, where there was no shame in Pat Jennings letting in that screamer from Brazil right-back Josimar, especially as he was picking up a European-record 119th cap on the day.

But the team went into steady decline after that. After a non-descript 1990s, the nadir was reached between March 2002 and February 2004, when Northern Ireland embarked on a 13-game run without scoring a single goal. Those 1,298 scoreless minutes represent another European record, a run which did for manager Sammy McIlroy. It was ended in his successor Lawrie Sánchez's very first game, David Healy scoring in the 56th minute of a Windsor Park friendly against Norway. And having waited 1,298 minutes to score, Northern Ireland took exactly one more minute to score again – albeit at the wrong end, Keith Gillespie's own goal sealing a 4-1 defeat.

The goal drought ended, the team began to play again. In the 2006 World Cup qualifiers they had drawn England, and lost 4-0 away. More of the same was expected in the return, but with a 74th-minute goal, Healy became the first Northern Irishman to score against the English since Terry Cochrane in 1980. It gave Northern Ireland a 1-0 win, their first against England since 1972 and the first at home against them since 1927.

The barren patch now firmly in the past, Northern Ireland had one last European record to claim. In the Euro 2008 qualifiers Healy scored thirteen goals, including a hat-trick in a 3-2 home win over Spain, breaking Croatian striker Davor Suker's previous mark of twelve.

SEPTEMBER 8

THE FIRST DAY OF THE FOOTBALL LEAGUE
(1888)

Six months and six days after Aston Villa director William McGregor first mooted the idea of the Football League to Blackburn, Bolton, Preston and West Bromwich Albion, the first league season in football history got underway. A classified check from that debut afternoon:

Bolton 3-6 Derby
Everton 2-1 Accrington
Preston 5-2 Burnley
Stoke 0-2 West Bromwich Albion
Woverhampton 1-1 Aston Villa.

The first goal of the nascent Football League was scored by Aston Villa defender Gershom Cox. Its founding father McGregor was unlikely to have been taken with this chain of events, however. Cox's goal, scored on the half-hour, was put through his own net. There were earlier goals in the games at Preston – where Fred Dewhurst opened the scoring on two minutes – and at Bolton, but both of those matches kicked off at 3.45 p.m., while Villa's game at Wolves began at the more familiar 3 p.m.

Two founder members didn't play on the opening day. Blackburn took their bow the week after in a 5-5 draw at home to Accrington, while Notts County lost 2-1 at Everton the same afternoon. The first round of results meant the League's first table-toppers were West Brom, who, by dint of having not conceded a goal, were ahead of Preston on goal average. Preston overhauled them after their second match and never relinquished first place, ending the season unbeaten as 'The Invincibles'.

Stoke finished bottom, though with only one division they did not have to concern themselves with relegation. Notts County and Accrington would be the first founder members to lose their top-flight status four years later under the new two-division system.

SEPTEMBER 9

RIMINI 1-1 JUVENTUS: POST CALCIOPOLI, JUVE'S FIRST SERIE B GAME
(2006)

The 2006 'calicopoli' scandal was orchestrated not by amateur businessmen, as the 'Totonero' scandal was, but by a man at the very top of the game: Luciano Moggi, general manager of Juventus, the biggest club in the country.

Juventus were being investigated by Turin prosecutors as part of doping allegations against their club doctor (who would later be found guilty of giving players drugs in the mid-1990s, a period which coincided with the club reaching three European Cup finals in a row). Moggi was unaware that the prosecutors had ordered Juve's phones to be tapped. The recordings showed Moggi attempting to strike deals with referees' representatives both at home and in Europe. Moggi was even taped attempting to convince a government minister to give the go-ahead to fixtures likely to be postponed out of respect to Pope John Paul II, whose death at the time was imminent – because the team Juve were to face Fiorentina, were struggling with injuries and suspensions.

The investigations also fingered officials from Milan, Lazio, Fiorentina and Reggina. While initially all clubs bar Reggina were demoted to Serie B, nothing concrete in terms of match-fixing stuck to any club except Juventus. Complaining bitterly about seemingly arbitrary punishments – although bang to rights themselves – Juve ended up being the only team sent down a division. They were also stripped of the two titles they had won while Moggi's influence on referees was being brought to bear.

And so it was, on September 9, 2006, Juve played their first league game outside Serie A in their history – at lowly Rimini. The 'Old Lady' could only manage a draw against a ten-man team. Despite having also had nine points deducted, Juve went on to finish the season as Serie B champions. Milan, meanwhile, won the 2007 European Cup.

WALES 1-1 SCOTLAND: JOCK STEIN DIES AT NINIAN PARK
(1985)

Jock Stein's last managerial decision was, typically, a telling one. With just over half an hour to go of Scotland's World Cup qualifier at Cardiff's Ninian Park, his team were trailing to a Mark Hughes goal and looking to be heading out of the competition. It was at this point that, to the raising of many an eyebrow, he decided to replace Gordon Strachan of table-topping Manchester United, with Davie Cooper of struggling Rangers. Sure enough, with nine minutes to go, Scotland won a penalty – and it was Cooper who coolly slotted home. Stein's decision, like so many in his career before it, had been vindicated.

With time running out, and Scotland on the front foot, photographers crowded round the benches to take a shot of Stein's reaction to probable qualification for Mexico '86. Stein became agitated. 'I saw Jock collapse,' said Wales manager Mike England. 'The whistle went for a free-kick and I thought it was full-time. I saw photographers bothering him and he put out a hand to try and move one of them away. As soon as Jock turned round I knew something was wrong. I thought he had a heart attack.'

The whistle went. The Scots had held on for the draw which took them to a play-off against Australia for a place in the 1986 finals, one they were destined to win. But it would be Alex Ferguson who would lead the side to Mexico. Stein had been carried from the dugout into the treatment room underneath the stands. He died on the physio's table a few minutes later, in spite of the efforts from the Scotland and Wales team doctors. Above on the terraces, Scotland's fans celebrated wildly, unaware their country's greatest manager of all time was gone at the age of 62.

SEPTEMBER 11

VILLA'S FA CUP STOLEN FROM SHOP WINDOW
(1895)

The FA Cup has been flung around in post-match celebrations for over 100 years, so it should come as no surprise that the current trophy is in fact the fourth edition of the famous pot. Though only one replacement has come about as a result of wear and tear.

The first – the 18-inch 'Little Tin Idol', as it was affectionately called – was bought for £20 in 1872 by FA chairman Charles Alcock. Like many a present, he ended up taking receipt of it himself. The team he captained, The Wanderers, won the first two FA Cups. Wanderers also won it three years consecutively from 1886 to 1888, which technically meant they could keep the cup in perpetuity, but the fashionable Corinthian spirit of the time prevailed, and they passed it on to the next winners, the Old Etonians, instead.

The Little Tin Idol kept doing the rounds until 1895, when Aston Villa won the trophy. They would be the last club to lift it. After agreeing to let their prize be displayed in the window of Birmingham cobbler William Shillcock's shop, the 23-year-old cup was stolen and never seen again. Villa were fined £25 by the FA, quite a result as they were rumoured to have insured the trophy for £2,000. In 1958, an 83-year-old man admitted to having melted down the cup in order to make counterfeit coins; the money, of course, was long spent.

A replica trophy was minted and stayed in use until 1910, when the FA discovered they did not have the patent on the design and that several replicas (of the replica!) had been made. The cup was withdrawn and awarded to five-time cup winner and FA president Lord Arthur Kinnaird.

A third cup – the design we know today – was knocked up in time for Bradford City to lift it in 1911, and replaced 80 years later with an exact replica. Kinnaird's trophy was auctioned in 2005 and was bought by the owner of the Football Museum in Preston for £478,000, breaking a sports memorabilia record.

SEPTEMBER 12

ARBROATH 36–0 BON ACCORD;
DUNDEE HARP 35–0 ABERDEEN ROVERS
(1885)

In the 1885/86 Scottish Cup, Dundee Harp recorded quite a victory in their first-round tie against Aberdeen Rovers: an amazing 35-0. The match referee had thought Harp had scored 37 goals, but the club secretary was convinced there had only been 35, and so that score was lodged with the Scottish FA, and the celebration of a world-record win began.

Harp full-back Tom O'Kane was feeling particularly pleased with himself, as it was his first match for the club since transferring from Arbroath. He decided to send a telegram to his former club to boast of Harp's amazing feat. O'Kane considered the immediate reply he received – that Arbroath had gone one better in their tie that very same day against another hapless Aberdonian side, Bon Accord – to be a great joke. But upon returning to his home in Arbroath later that evening, O'Kane was informed by the locals that Arbroath's win was no joke. They had indeed thrashed Bon Accord, a cricket team, by a cricket score: 36-0. It is a record for a senior match which stands to this day (as does 18-year-old John Petrie's tally of 13 goals, which has been equalled but not beaten).

Harp learned of their bad luck the morning after, when O'Kane ran the 18 miles back to Dundee to inform club officials. The club regretted their decision to doctor their goal tally downwards. But perhaps justice was done: the referee in Arbroath's game later talked of his 'regret' at 'chalking off seven goals... so rapid was Arbroath's passing that it was very doubtful they could be offside'. Arbroath went on to beat Forfar 9-1 in the second round and Dundee East End 7-1 in the third, before losing to Hibernian 5-3 in the fourth. Queen's Park went on to win the trophy that year... but who remembers that?

FIFA INVESTIGATE 20-MATCH BAN FOR REFEREE MORENO
(2002)

When Italy were sent crashing out of the 2002 World Cup by hosts South Korea, the country went looking for a scapegoat. It wasn't a long search. Instead of homing in on their own man Christian Vieri, who had missed an open goal from two yards with a minute of normal time to play, the first target was Korean striker Ahn Jung-Hwan, scorer of the winning golden goal and employee of Italian side Perugia. Though not for very much longer. 'I am a nationalist and I regard such behaviour not only as an affront to Italian pride but also an offence to a country which two years ago opened its doors to him,' said Perugia owner Luciano Gaucci. 'I have no intention of paying a salary to someone who has ruined Italian soccer.'

That, however, turned out to be a bit of a joke by Perugia. They were getting shot of Ahn, who wasn't considered good enough, anyway. Focus instead shifted onto Ecuadorian referee Byron Moreno, who had sent off Italian playmaker Francesco Totti in extra-time. Moreno had judged – somewhat harshly, though not outrageously so – that Totti had dived. As a result, councillors of Sicilian holiday resort Santa Teresa Riva decided to name a brand new set of public toilets after him. 'I'm sure Moreno will be happy to know that it will be his name everyone will be cursing at when a bad batch of tomato sauce comes back to bite them,' said mayor Nino Bartolotta.

IFA president Sepp Blatter admitted Moreno had made a mistake but that it was a 'human' and not a 'premeditated error'. Eyebrows, as well as loo seats, were raised three months later when a match refereed by Moreno back home in Ecuador degenerated into farce and an inquiry was ordered.

Ecuador's top team, Liga Deportiva Universitaria de Quito, were at home to Barcelona de Guayquil and 3-2 down at the end of 90 minutes. Moreno signalled for six minutes of stoppage time, then played on until LDU equalised after eleven added minutes, and only blew his whistle when they had scored a winner after thirteen. The Ecuadorian FA banned Moreno for 20 matches, though the result stood.

FIFA soon discovered that Moreno was standing as a candidate in upcoming local elections in Quito, and upheld the ban. A predictable postscript came in May 2003: after three games back from his ban, Moreno was suspended again after dismissing three players from LDU's rivals Deportivo Quito in a league game.

SEPTEMBER 14

BURNLEY 2-1 LEEDS: CLOUGH PLAYER-POWER
RIFT REFUTED
(1974)

As manager of Derby County, Brian Clough would often chide Don Revie's Leeds United for their poor disciplinary record. But in a *Sunday Express* column in 1973, he went too far. 'Revie should have been personally fined and Leeds United instantly demoted to the Second Division after being branded the dirtiest club in Britain,' wrote Clough after Leeds were fined by the Football League for persistent misconduct. His strident words brought Clough a disrepute charge of his own and led to his eventual sacking by an embarrassed Derby board.

Out of work, Clough and his sidekick Peter Taylor went to Third Division Brighton & Hove Albion, where they struggled disastrously. In two thunderingly embarrassing home games, Brighton lost 4-0 in the FA Cup to non-league Walton & Hersham and 8-2 in a league match against Bristol Rovers. Then, in the summer of 1974, Revie took the England job – at which point Leeds asked Clough and Taylor if they would like to take over at Elland Road. It was an unthinkable offer and one which, even more unthinkably, Clough accepted. Taylor stayed put at Brighton, perhaps anticipating the train-wreck everyone but Clough and the Leeds board could see coming.

Clough's first act at Elland Road was to call a player meeting and inform the Leeds squad that they had only won their medals by 'cheating' and they might as well throw them in a 'bloody great bin.' As rallying cries go there have been better. Clough immediately alienated a close-knit squad mourning the loss of their father figure Revie, and when early results failed to go his way – Leeds were fourth from bottom after losing three of their first six games – the players called a meeting of their own to tell the board they had lost confidence in him. Leeds sacked Clough 44 days into his reign, sending him on his way with a huge payoff which would make him financially secure for life.

Remarkably, on the evening of his sacking, Clough and Revie picked the bones over the matter on local television, both men referring to the players' meeting. Two days later, the Leeds squad released an official statement insisting they had given 'the same support to Mr Clough as we did to Don Revie.' That evening, club captain Billy Bremner helped to pick the Leeds team at Burnley. None of Clough's new signings were selected.

Clough arrived at Nottingham Forest in 1975, where he went on to win the league and two European Cups within five years. Leeds did not win a trophy again until 1992.

SEPTEMBER 15

BALDERSTONE PLAYS FOR DONCASTER –
AND LEICESTERSHIRE
(1975)

As cricketer-footballers go, Chris Balderstone of Carlisle United and Leicestershire might not have been quite in the class as Denis Compton. Compton won the league and FA Cup with Arsenal and is one of only eight men to boast a Test batting average for England of over 50. But then Compton never played a football match in the evening after helping his county win the championship that same afternoon. Apart from Balderstone, nobody has.

Balderstone was the last man to play both football and cricket at the top level in England, though he very nearly never made it to the First Division at all. Before the start of the 1973/74 season, Balderstone was stripped of the captaincy by Second Division Carlisle United and suspended for deciding to finish the cricket season first with Leicestershire. But the club softened their stance and Balderstone was recalled, helping Carlisle win promotion. Balderstone scored a decisive penalty against Spurs to send Carlisle top of the first published table of the new season – although it was all downhill from there, as Carlisle were relegated in last place. Balderstone was transferred to Fourth Division Doncaster, but his greatest achievement was yet to come.

At stumps at Chesterfield on the day Leicestershire won the 1975 County Championship, Balderstone was 51 not out. He was then whisked 30 miles up the road to Belle Vue where Doncaster ground out a 1-1 draw with Brentford. He was back at Chesterfield the next morning to complete his century and take three wickets as Leicestershire wrapped up the game. His innings of 116 is the only century to have been built round a Football League match.

SEPTEMBER 16

THE WORLD'S FIRST EVER LIVE FOOTBALL ON TV: TRAINING AT ARSENAL
(1937)

Just as the British Broadcasting Corporation gave a test run to football's first radio commentary at Highbury, so the first live televised game came from Arsenal's ground. This was mainly down to the proximity of the stadium to the BBC's home at Alexandra Palace. But Arsenal had also gambled on televised football becoming the next big thing, and when building their new East Stand the year before, had ensured there was a bespoke gantry for cameras.

The match – as much as it can be called that – was a training run-out between Arsenal and their reserve team. Nevertheless, the prospect was enough for that morning's *Guardian* to work itself up into a breathless tizzy. 'The players will be introduced by Mr George F Allison, manager of the club,' began the preview. 'The television demonstrations will show tactics on the field, shooting in goal, dribbling and goalkeeping. Three cameras will be used, one being on the stands to give a comprehensive view of the ground, and two others near the goalmouth to give close-ups of the play and players and visual interviews. No film will be used, transmission being by radio direct to Alexandra Palace which can actually be seen from the ground.'

The listings – on channel 'Television' – ran thus: 3.00 'Fancy that!'; 3.30 British Movietonews; 3.40 Football at the Arsenal; 3.55 Cartoon; 4.00 Close. Only 15 minutes of the training were shown, but the experiment was considered a success. 'The football demonstrations from the Arsenal ground showed that even on the small screen television can give something worth seeing from a game covering so great an amount of ground,' was the *Observer*'s verdict. That year's FA Cup final between Sunderland and Preston was shown in part. The first full match was the England-Scotland international the following April. Live football had arrived and few would have guessed how omnipresent it would become in later years. We can only wonder what sort of programme 'Fancy that!' was.

SEPTEMBER 17

ARSENAL 5-0 NEWCASTLE UNITED: NOT QUITE A 'SATURDAY SPECTACULAR'
(1960)

For the club that pioneered live televised football, Arsenal did their level best to ruin the practice at birth (give or take 23 years). After Arsenal's first and reserve teams featured in the world's first live transmission, in 1937, live football became a fixture on British television screens, albeit an infrequent one. FA Cup finals were shown on the BBC from 1938 onwards, as were some England-Scotland internationals. Everyone in football seemed happy enough with that.

Then in the mid-1950s along came ITV and the European Cup. The new broadcaster featured the groundbreaking continental midweek games live. Having garnered impressive viewing figures for Manchester United's forays into Europe, ITV decided to pitch for Football League games. Despite opposition to the move – many club chairmen thought it would erode attendances – ITV struck a £150,000 ten-year deal with the Football League in 1960. A compromise was struck. The chosen game wouldn't kick off until 6.50 p.m., and ITV wouldn't join the action until the last few minutes of the first half at 7.30 p.m., allowing fans at other games plenty of time to get back home. On September 10, the First Division match between Blackpool and Bolton became ITV's first edition of '*The Big Game*'.

The Big Game planned for the following week was a goalfest, as Arsenal routed Newcastle 5-0. Unfortunately viewers were treated to 'Saturday Spectacular' instead – the Arsenal board had banned ITV. Blackpool's crowd against Bolton of 17,166 had been down 12,050 on the corresponding fixture from the previous season, while viewing figures had been poor. A drab game ended 1-0 to Bolton, while star turn Stanley Matthews was out injured. Tottenham Hotspur were up next for The Big Game – and followed Arsenal's lead in turning the cameras away. Live football would not become a regular fixture on television screens until October 1983, Spurs hosting Nottingham Forest in England's first full televised live League game.

SEPTEMBER 18

AJAX 8-2 FEYENOORD – CRUYFF'S
FINAL ACT OF DEFIANCE
(1983)

He led Barcelona to the 1974 *La Liga*, then a month later took Holland to the World Cup final. After that, Johan Cruyff's career seemed to be that of a man slowly, prematurely winding down. His last three years at Barça were pretty much a non-event, with only the 1978 Copa del Rey to show for them. He helped the Dutch team reach the World Cup in Argentina, but then retired from all football before the tournament began, aged only 31.

A year later he came out of retirement and went to America, with the hope of becoming the Pacific coast's answer to Pelé. While the Brazilian became an icon in New York with the Cosmos, few cared what Cruyff was doing in Los Angeles with the Aztecs. He won the US Player of the Year title two years in a row, the second after a move to the Washington Diplomats, but by 1981 he had left an indifferent nation to return to Spain. Cruyff was to sign for Levante of the Segunda Division.

Then out of nowhere came an Indian summer. Cruyff's deal with Levante fell through, and Ajax offered him a route back into top-class football. He seized the chance with both hands, scoring on his debut in December 1981 against Haarlem and helping his old club to the title. As part of the side that retained the title the season after, Cruyff expected an extension to his contract. It was not forthcoming. So in a wild fit of Cruyffian pique, he responded by signing for Ajax's bitter rivals, Feyenoord.

The move initially appeared rash. Early in the 1983/84 season, Feyenoord went to Ajax and suffered a club-record 8-2 humiliation. 'We are still going to win the league,' Cruyff told team mates – including young free-scoring midfielder Ruud Gullit – afterwards. Which they did, remaining unbeaten at home and adding the Dutch Cup for good measure. At which point Cruyff finally took his leave of the stage, his job done.

SEPTEMBER 19

MANCHESTER UNITED 2-0 PECSI MUNKAS: ENGLAND'S POST-HEYSEL RETURN
(1990)

English clubs had been banned indefinitely after the Heysel disaster at the 1985 European Cup final, but in the 1990/91 season UEFA allowed them to return. There would be no representation in the European Cup – champions Liverpool had been given an additional two-year ban, later reduced to one, for their involvement in the tragedy – but runners up Aston Villa competed in the UEFA Cup, while Manchester United took their place in the Cup Winners Cup.

It was a successful return for the English from the very first night: Villa beat Czech side Banik Ostrava 3-1 at Villa Park, while United beat Hungarians Pesci Munkas 2-0 at Old Trafford. Clayton Blackmore's goal after 10 minutes was the first English club goal in European competition since Kevin Sheedy made it 3-1 for Everton in the 1985 Cup Winners Cup final.

Both teams won their ties, but Villa only made it as far as the next round after a difficult draw against Internazionale. United, however, enjoyed the luck of the draw in their campaign: avoiding the likes of Juventus, Sampdoria, Dynamo Kiev and Steaua Bucharest, they merely had to beat Wrexham, Montpellier and Legia Warsaw to reach the final.

They couldn't avoid all the big teams, though. Nobody expected Alex Ferguson's side, still very much a work in progress, to beat Johan Cruyff's Barcelona side built round Ronald Koeman and Michael Laudrup in the final. But they won the Cup Winners Cup 2-1, the winner a wonderfully taken goal from an acute angle by Mark Hughes. There was a long reality check to follow, though. Barça won the European Cup the following year and it would take United seven years, and several embarrassing defeats along the way, before they took English football back to the very top level it occupied before Heysel.

EMPOLI 1-0 JUVENTUS: RUSH'S ITALIAN NIGHTMARE BEGINS
(1987)

Ian Rush had scored 139 goals in 224 league games for Liverpool, so it was little surprise when Serie A – at that time the richest league in the world by a long chalk – came calling for his services. Juventus paid £3.2m for their man, and expected the goals to come as quickly as they had done in the English First Division. They were to be sorely disappointed.

Rush made his debut at Empoli and barely got a touch. 'It was very tight and very warm out there,' puffed Rush after the game. 'I didn't really get one good ball all match but you expect it to be difficult here.' His remarks didn't go down well with Juve manager Rino Marchesi, who responded dryly: 'If he wants more passes then he should go looking for more of them.'

So the new boy knuckled down and in his next match, at home to Pescara, Rush scored twice in a 3-1 win. But he only scored one more goal before the end of January, amid rumours that he was homesick and failing to integrate with Italian society. Rush ended the season with 13 league and cup goals, making him the club's top scorer, but the return was below expectations. Despite the team being in transition after the retirement of Michel Platini, Rush took the blame for Juventus's poor sixth-place finish, though he did end his horror season on a high note by scoring the only goal of a game in Brescia – for Wales, vs Italy…

By August 1988 Rush had re-signed for Liverpool. He was infamously reported as saying his time in Italy had been 'like living in a foreign country', but it transpired one of his Anfield team mates had fed the line to the press as a joke. While he'd been away, Liverpool had played the most celebrated football in the club's history. When Aldridge heard the news of Rush's return, he rang up the local *Liverpool Echo* to check it was true. Rush never quite hit the heights of his previous spell at the club, while Aldridge left the club against his will for Real Sociedad in 1990.

ENGLAND 0-2 IRELAND: THE IRISH BEAT HUNGARY TO IT
(1949)

When Alf Ramsey saved England from defeat at Wembley in October 1953 by converting a late penalty against a Rest of Europe team, he became, not for the last time, a national hero. His kick, the equaliser in a 4-4 draw, meant the nation had yet to be beaten by a foreign team on home soil. Ramsey's deeds had merely postponed the inevitable, though. Just over a month later Ferenc Puskás and Hungary rolled into town and trounced England 6-3. A nation faced up to the fact that England's proud record was gone. 'England were at last beaten by the foreign invader on solid English soil,' noted a mournful *Times*.

The strange thing was that the record had ended four years earlier. In September 1949, Ireland played England in a friendly at Goodison Park and came away 2-0 winners. Con Martin of Aston Villa scored a first-half penalty. England threw the kitchen sink at the Irish only for their star man, Tom Finney, to be repeatedly thwarted down the left wing by Manchester United's Johnny Carey. Ireland delivered a sucker punch late on when Peter Farrell broke through the English back line and lobbed Bert Williams as he came off his line.

'It was England's first home defeat by a side other than from one of the home countries,' reported the *Manchester Guardian* the morning after, a subtle shifting of the goalposts. *The Times* would prefer to note that England were 'unbeaten on British soil by a side outside these islands'. But whichever way it was spun, the fact remained the same: the partition of Ireland in 1920 had set up the Irish Free State and latterly the Republic of Ireland, so this was not a British team and by definition foreign. England's record was gone.

But if you really want to clutch at straws – and let's face it, the Hungarian humiliation is a much better story – a small anomaly allows England to claim Ireland's team that day was partially British anyway. Thanks to FIFA's confusing laws, three of their side – Martin, Tom Aherne and Davy Walsh – were also able to turn out for Northern Ireland, and had played for both Irish sides during the 1950 World Cup qualifiers. Although that really is getting desperate.

SEPTEMBER 22

WOODGATE'S HAPLESS REAL MADRID DEBUT
(2005)

'Fuck me! What a debut!' Statements don't come much pithier – or more accurate – than Jonathan Woodgate's trenchant analysis of his first match as a Real Madrid player. The Spanish club had signed him in August 2004 from Newcastle United for £13.4m, but had to wait 516 days to get the first glimpse of their new player, a recurring thigh injury keeping him out for the entirety of his first season. Finally he made his debut in a *La Liga* game against Athletic Bilbao.

On purely comedic terms, the wait was worth it. After 20 minutes he was lucky to escape a booking for a tackle on Joseba Etxeberriá. After 25 minutes, Woodgate attempted to clear the same player's shot but only succeeded in sending a header bulleting into his own net. Just before half-time he was booked, for a crude challenge on Carlos Gurpegi. Then on 66 minutes he was shown a second yellow for a shove on his nemesis Etxeberriá. 'I just can't believe I got sent off,' said Woodgate afterwards. 'I want to thank the public, who were brilliant when I was walking off. They were all clapping and cheering.'

It was generous of them. Woodgate's Real Madrid debut made for an interesting comparison with those of two of his team mates that day. David Beckham had scored within three minutes of his, while Ronaldo took all of 58 seconds to endear himself to his new fans with a goal. Woodgate's European bow for the club was more pleasant, scoring in a 4-1 win over Rosenborg, but by the time he left Madrid he had been voted the worst signing of the 21st century by readers of *Marca*.

Woodgate could, however, take solace in the fact that there have been worse debuts. Arsenal substitute Jason Crowe lasted 33 seconds of a 1997 League Cup tie against Birmingham before being sent packing for a high tackle.

SEPTEMBER 23

ALFREDO DI STÉFANO SIGNS FOR REAL MADRID – NOT BARCELONA
(1953)

In March 1952, Millonários of Bogota took part in a friendly triangular tournament at Real Madrid's Chamartin stadium to celebrate the Spanish club's 50th anniversary. In Millonários' first match, against Sweden's Norkoeping, little-known Argentinian midfielder Alfredo di Stéfano scored twice. In their second, playing the birthday boys, di Stéfano bagged another two. Scouts representing both Real and Barcelona decided there and then that di Stéfano must be their man.

The problem was, nobody was quite sure who di Stéfano belonged to. He had walked out on Argentinian side River Plate to join Millonários in 1949. With the Colombian league unrecognised by FIFA at the time, this left a tangle of red tape. In the summer of 1953, Barcelona made their move, agreeing in principle a deal with River Plate, who were happy to sell providing Millonários agreed. Which they didn't. Not that it stopped di Stéfano, who left for Barcelona anyway, playing for the Catalans in a couple of friendlies. The deal seemed done. Then Real got involved, paying Millonários 1.5m pesetas for di Stéfano. Barça responded by giving River Plate 4m pesetas. Which is when things became both farcical and complicated. The Spanish federation passed a law banning the purchase of foreign stars, so Barcelona president Marti Carreto and his Real counterpart Santiago Bernabéu agreed to jointly sell the player to Juventus. At which point the Spanish federation lifted the ban on foreigners and suggested both teams share di Stéfano, season by season. An exasperated Barça pulled out, Real giving them the 4m pesetas they had paid to River Plate.

Conspiracy theories abounded. Josep Samitier, who had been conducting the negotiations for Barça, was a good friend of Bernabéu; Carreto was rumoured to be a Francoist. Two weeks after signing for Real, di Stéfano scored four goals in a 5-0 win over Barcelona.

BARCELONA 4-0 ATLETICO BILBAO: THE BUTCHER OF BILBAO BREAKS MARADONA'S ANKLE
(1983)

Diego Maradona's stint at Barcelona was far from a happy one. He joined the club for a world-record £5m from Boca Juniors after the 1982 World Cup and quickly fell out with coach Udo Lattek. Lattek's authoritarian approach and intense training methods went against Maradona's grain. He contracted hepatitis. He started taking cocaine. Even when Lattek was replaced by the laid-back César Luis Menotti, his former coach with Argentina who didn't begin training until three in the afternoon, things didn't improve. Maradona was expected to bring the *La Liga* title back to the Camp Nou for the first time since 1974, but he wasn't delivering.

The 1983/84 title race was a tight one. Reigning champions Atletico Bilbao kept their crown on head-to-head results with Real Madrid, both teams finishing a point ahead of Barcelona. Many thought the title was effectively decided in early September, when Bilbao came to the Camp Nou. Menotti had accused Xavier Clemente's side of 'defensive and destructive' play – and he was proved right. Barça won 4-0 that day, but Maradona's ankle tendons were cut to ribbons by a brutal challenge from behind by Andoni Goikoetxea, who earned the nickname 'The Butcher of Bilbao' for that very tackle. After the game, Menotti said Goikoetxea was part of a 'race of anti-footballers'. Maradona missed over three months of the season.

Maradona managed to get some sort of revenge. First in the league in the new year, when he scored both Barcelona's goals in Bilbao in a match littered with more than fifty fouls, then in the final of the Copa del Rey. Barça lost the final 1-0, but on his way from the pitch Maradona responded to a V-sign by delivering a series of high-kicks at four Bilbao players, including Goikoetxea. It would be his last act for the club, as he left in the summer, heading towards glory in Naples.

SEPTEMBER 25

FULHAM 4-1 HEREFORD UNITED: BEST AND MARSH TACKLE EACH OTHER
(1976)

Tommy Trinder had been a comedian for the best part of six decades, so he knew a thing or two about showbusiness. Which is what he must have had in mind when, as chairman of Second Division Fulham, he signed George Best and Rodney Marsh in August 1976. Best and Marsh had both been lost to English football, the former walking out of Manchester United in 1974, the latter of neighbours City a year later. The pair had ended up in the United States, playing for Los Angeles Aztecs and the Tampa Bay Rowdies respectively. Trinder had got them to agree to play for Fulham in the NASL off-season.

Their signature performance for Fulham came in the first month of the season. A joyous riot at Craven Cottage against Hereford saw Best hit the post from 30 yards and Marsh score twice, one an absolute belter cutting in from the left and curling the ball into the top right corner. But the abiding memory of the match is Best accidentally taking the ball off Marsh – and then Marsh deliberately going back to tackle his own team mate. If anyone ever needed the 1970s maverick phenomenon explaining to them, pointing them this way would do the job.

As the season wore on, Best mainly hit the headlines for the wrong reasons. In October he became one of the first players to receive one of the new red cards introduced in English football that season, being sent off at Southampton. In December he was fined £75 for making an obscene gesture in the direction of the referee at Chelsea. In February he drove his car into a lamppost in front of Harrods at 4 a.m., explaining: 'I had been out to dinner and called in at Tramps discotheque. I wasn't given a breath test and even if I had it would have been negative. I had three drinks all evening.' Fulham ended the season escaping relegation by the skin of their teeth; Best and Marsh went back to the US in the summer.

Best came back at the start of the 1977/78 season and lasted one more game before a payment dispute put an end to his dalliance with the Cottagers, the showbusiness having long since turned into a soap opera.

SEPTEMBER 26

SK BRANN, THE MOST ERRATIC CLUB IN THE WORLD, FOUNDED
(1908)

Newcastle United, Tottenham Hotspur, Hearts, Hibernian, Fiorentina, Bayer Leverkusen… leagues the world over are packed with teams whose level of support is in inverse proportion to the amount of success they enjoy. But few of them can hold a candle to Brann of Norway.

Sportsklubben Brann (never Brann Bergen) were formed in 1908 and are one of the most popular clubs in the country. This popularity is not influenced by success. They took a while to get going. Despite winning two Norwegian Cupen, in 1923 and 1925, they failed to make an impact in the league until the 1960s. When they did, it was to prove surreal.

Brann were relegated from what was then known as the Hovedserien ('The Main League') in 1959/60. They bounced back the season after, then in the following two seasons landed their first two titles with a team built around winger Roald Jensen (who would later leave for Hearts). After the two championship wins, they were dispatched back down to the lower league from whence they came. It was a lunatic five-season run.

Brann didn't leave it there. They later embarked on a manic period as the ultimate yo-yo club, hovering between what had then become the 1.divisjon ('1st Division') and the second eight years in a row, going down and up between 1979 and 1986, since when they have remained in the top flight ever since. For the best part of two decades this was a world record, until Aris in Cyprus managed to bounce up and down ten years in a row between 1997 and 2006. Brann won their third championship, now the Eliteserien ('The Elite Series') in 2007, a record which palled when juxtaposed with that of Rosenborg, who have 20 titles to their name. But then that is not really the point of Brann.

LIVERPOOL 0-0 NOTTINGHAM FOREST:
THE PRE-MATCH BOOZE UP
(1978)

It was a first round tie in the 1978/79 European Cup, though in one of the weaker line-ups in the tournament's history – Juventus would be beaten by Rangers, Real Madrid by Grasshoppers Zurich – in retrospect it could have been the final. Liverpool were the reigning European champions and hadn't been knocked out of Europe for four years, having won the UEFA Cup in 1976, then the European Cup in 1977. But they had been drawn against Nottingham Forest, who had their number domestically, having beaten them to the English title and the League Cup the previous season. Liverpool were still favourites to progress – but would come unstuck thanks to a typical Brian Clough management masterclass.

In the first leg on September 13, Forest had beaten Liverpool 2-0 at the City Ground. The goalscoring hero of the hour was a 22-year-old Garry Birtles, thrown in at the deep end by Clough for only his third Forest game. 'Birtles did well,' said his manager. 'Two years ago he was laying tiles and if he doesn't score again on Saturday he could be back there.' Birtles didn't, but was in the team for the return anyway.

With such a big prize at stake, Forest were understandably nervous on the way up to Anfield two weeks later. Clough knew the perfect relaxant. 'We travelled up by coach and the boss said to one of the young lads in the party, right, get the players a drink,' remembered midfielder Tony Woodcock. 'We each had a bottle of beer, and the boss also encouraged us to have a couple of glasses of wine with our meal at the hotel. A couple of hours' sleep and we were on our way to Anfield.' Forest held out for a 0-0 draw in which Liverpool never threatened to score. 'They threw everything at us except the docks,' smiled Clough, 'but we didn't really panic.' Forest went on to win the European Cup.

Clough also pulled the same stunt before that season's League Cup final against Southampton, producing a crate of beer and ordering everyone to tuck in. The result: 3-2 to Forest.

SEPTEMBER 28

USSR 3-1 HUNGARY: THE FIRST EUROPEAN CHAMPIONSHIP BEGINS
(1958)

The idea of a European Championship was mooted not long after Jules Rimet got the wheels in motion for his World Cup in the mid-1920s. Like the World Cup, it was the brainchild of an administrator at the French Football Federation. Henri Delaunay proposed the cup in 1927, but with organisation for the World Cup taking precedence, the idea was put on the back-burner. Political events made any pan-European agreement impossible during the 1930s and 1940s, but the idea was back on the cards in the mid-1950s. UEFA had recently been founded, and with European club competitions about to take off, it was only a matter of time before an international tournament was up and running as well.

At a UEFA congress in 1957, a motion to set up a European Championship was finally put to the floor. It wasn't a wholly popular idea. The British associations, just as they had done with the World Cup, dragged their feet, abstaining through fear the tournament would interfere with the Home Internationals. Seven other countries voted against, including West Germany, Italy and Holland. But the majority of UEFA's 29 members carried the motion, and the ball was set rolling. Delaunay had died in 1955, so didn't get to see his idea put into practice. But the trophy would bear his name. The final stages of the first knock-out cup – from the semi-finals on – were to be held in France in the summer of 1960, though the tournament started well before then.

The first match was played between the USSR and Hungary in September 1958. Anatoly Ilyin scored the first goal of the competition after four minutes, his country winning the two-legged tie 4-1 on aggregate. The first championship was mainly notable for General Franco's refusal to let the Soviets enter Spain to contest a quarter-final. The Russians were given a walkover to the semi-finals. They eventually won the tournament, beating Yugoslavia 2-1 in the final. The format of the European Championships remained unchanged until 1980, when eight teams contested in the first proper finals.

BILL SHANKLY DIES
(1981)

In February 1974, with their manager Bill Shankly's contract due to run out at the end of May, Liverpool Football Club issued a public plea for the man who rescued the club from Second Division oblivion in 1959 to stay. 'I have told Mr Shankly that he can decide the terms of the new contract and he can decide whatever length of contract he wants,' said club chairman John Smith. 'My sincere hope is that it will be for life. Mr Shankly assures me that he will be delighted to stay with the club for which he has brought so much success.'

Five months later, on July 12, Shankly stunned the world by retiring out of the blue. 'It is time for a rest,' he explained. 'I feel, as does my wife, that the pressures have been building up so much over my 40 years in football … I want to have some time off to pursue my hobbies.'

The problem was, Shankly's only hobby was football. He soon regretted his decision to quit, but by then it was too late as Bob Paisley had been appointed as his successor. Shankly made himself available to give the new man the benefit of his experience, but he soon found his advice was not required. 'There were problems I would have liked to talk over with him but I didn't,' admitted Paisley years later. 'I had to stand on my own two feet.' Eventually Shankly had to be told to stay away from the training ground, as his old players were unsure who to refer to as 'boss'. Despite a public clamour for Shankly to be rewarded with a seat on the Liverpool board, no such offer was forthcoming. The club always pointed to the travails of several Manchester United managers with Matt Busby looming over them. 'Bill was the type that, if he offered advice, you'd have to take it,' explained Paisley, who reluctantly agreed with the club's decision.

Shankly spent much of his remaining years chatting to players at a training ground where he was welcome – Everton. He died of a heart attack in September 1981. The more romantically inclined always argue that it was a heart that was broken.

SEPTEMBER 30

BLACKPOOL 4-0 CHELSEA: DOCHERTY TAKES OVER FROM DRAKE
(1961)

Chelsea were something of a music-hall joke before Ted Drake arrived as manager in 1952. Drake had been a famous striker with Arsenal and England during the 1930s. He won two league titles and an FA Cup while at Highbury. He was top-scorer for the team twice (once with 42 goals), netted the winner in the 1936 FA Cup final, and memorably scored seven in one match against Aston Villa in 1935, still a top-flight record. As a manager, he had a similar disinclination to hang about.

Chelsea having won nothing whatsoever, the first thing Drake did was to rid the club of its homely image. The club crest at the time of his arrival featured a cartoon of a smiling Chelsea Pensioner. That was immediately jettisoned for a Rangers-style CFC logo, then soon after the rampant lion still in use today. The club would no longer be known as 'The Pensioners' but 'The Blues'. Minor details perhaps, but ones which instilled a winning mentality.

In 1954/55 the title was expected to be contested between Manchester United and Wolverhampton Wanderers. Chelsea were certainly not expected to feature in the race, especially after losing their first four games. But Drake's side – built around defenders Peter Sillett and Ron Greenwood and striker Roy Bentley – had gained a reputation as battlers. They only lost another three of their next 25 matches to take the title from Wolves. But the style of play was much criticised – as it would be the next time they won the title, under Jose Mourinho – and despite the emergence of Jimmy Greaves the following seasons proved disappointing.

After several mid-table finishes, and a slow start in 1961/62, Drake was sacked having 'discussed our lack of success since we won the championship' with his board. He was replaced by eager player-coach Tommy Docherty, who couldn't turn things round immediately. Docherty's inauspicious start against Blackpool set the trend as the club were relegated. But just as Drake had modernised in the 1950s, so Docherty would in the new decade. The new side, promoted from the Second Division, featured Ron Harris, Terry Venables and Bobby Tambling and came to epitomise the 1960s.

OCTOBER

OCTOBER 1

NEW YORK COSMOS 2-1 SANTOS: PELÉ'S LAST GAME
(1977)

The first season of the North American Soccer League (NASL) in 1968 was a huge success on the pitch. The Atlanta Chiefs became the champions, beating San Diego Toros 3-0 in a two-legged final. The Chiefs then proved their pedigree by beating Manchester City, fresh from winning the league in England, 3-2. City coach Malcolm Allison suggested the result was a fluke. Challenged by Atlanta to a rematch, Allison could only watch with queasy shame as City went down again, this time 2-1.

Off the pitch, interest dwindled. Attendances were low, the majority of American spectators unwilling to sit through 90 minutes which could easily end up goalless. Live television audiences were hardly much higher – arguably not helped by CBS's insistence on making referees pause the game after blowing-up for fouls so the broadcaster could go to an advert – and the plug was soon pulled. By the end of 1969 most franchises had folded and the NASL consisted of four clubs.

The league struggled on, however, and was given a boost in 1971 when Warner Bros. decided to put money into a revived New York franchise. The new team, called the Cosmos, harboured showbusiness-sized ambitions. In June 1975 they coaxed Pelé out of retirement with a $7m offer. Henry Kissinger also helped, smoothing things over with the Brazilian government, who had named Pelé an 'official national treasure' in order to prevent him leaving to work in other countries. The move was an off-pitch success, sparking a surge of interest in the game. 'My contract is not just to play for the Cosmos, it is to promote soccer in the US,' insisted Pelé. However it only came to life on the pitch during Pelé's final season, after Lazio striker Giorgio Chinaglia had signed to take advantage of the Brazilian's work in midfield. Chinaglia having scored the goal which sealed the 1977 title for the Cosmos, the stage was set for Pelé's farewell two months later. He was chaired off after a friendly against his old side Santos in front of 75,000, having played a half for both sides and scored. The rain lashing down, it was said that 'even God cried'. The NASL moneymen certainly did; it was all downhill from there.

OCTOBER 2

GIGI RIVA BREAKS SPECTATOR'S ARM WITH SHOT
(1970)

Gigi Riva is not the only player in history to break someone's arm with a powerful shot. Lily Parr, the legendary striker from the Dick, Kerr Ladies team of the early 1920s, was once challenged by a male goalkeeper to take some penalties against him. 'Bloody hell, get me to the hospital as quick as you can,' the keeper is reported to have said after Parr hit one with venom, 'she's broken me bloody arm!' – but he is undoubtedly the most famous player to do so.

Riva was coming to the end of a spectacular calendar year. He had scored 21 goals in 30 Serie A games to help his team, Cagliari, to the 1969/70 league title. Never before had a team from one of Italy's islands won the *Scudetto* – and it has never happened since. The Sardinian side were deeply unfashionable. They had only joined Serie A for the first time in 1964. On arriving at the club, both Riva and Italian national goalkeeper Enrico Albertosi commented how they had previously thought Sardinia was a 'penal colony'. But Riva and Albertosi – along with former Inter winger Angelo Domenghini – transformed Cagliari into Italy's best side. It wasn't *all* down to Riva – along their way to the title they let in only 11 goals, still a European league record – but his outrageous strike rate in parsimonious Serie A meant the big striker was the team's figurehead.

Riva scored an extra-time goal in Italy's classic 4-3 semi-final win over West Germany in the Mexico World Cup, but the year was all downhill from there. He had a poor final and, having done so well in Serie A, was criticised for his display back home.

Then the moment for which he is arguably most famous: a 120kph shot at a Cagliari training session which flew wide and broke nine-year-old Danilo Piroddi's arm. It was a complete accident, and one for which there would be a terrible karmic payback. In a Euro '72 qualifier against Austria 29 days later, Riva broke his right leg in an accidental challenge with Ronald Hof. Riva was never quite the same player again. He retired in 1976 and within months, Cagliari were relegated.

OCTOBER 3

LEN SHACKLETON ARRIVES AT NEWCASTLE
(1946)

Len Shackleton had scored 160 goals during the war for Bradford Park Avenue. Once hostilities were over, and with League football about to restart in August 1946, the striker decided that, at 23, his exploits should be rewarded with a move to a big club. It was not initially forthcoming until, on the morning of October 2, 1946, he was summoned to a hotel in Bradford by his manager Fred Emery.

Left sitting around most of the day, he was occasionally introduced by Emery to various club managers, although the chats never lasted very long. It was clear he was being touted around for a transfer, but the details were not quick in coming. This rankled with Shackleton, a born agitator. He was eventually told he would be joining Newcastle, although he would only find out the details the day after while reading a newspaper on the journey up to the north east, the fee had been £13,000. He would not forget the slight.

Shackleton was introduced to his new team mates and told he would be going straight in the team that weekend. His subsequent debut was the most spectacular in the history of the Football League. Newcastle beat hapless Newport County 13-0, equalling a record that still stands. Shackleton scored six, including a first half hat-trick in 155 seconds, another record at the time.

Things were fine on the pitch, but off it Shackleton embarked on a series of arguments with the Newcastle board, who he decided had shown him no respect. The rows covered team selection, living arrangements, training methods and money. Eventually, after refusing to watch a game with the rest of the team over the Christmas holidays in 1947, a parting of the ways was inevitable. Two months later he was sold to Sunderland for a British record £20,000. Shacketon later wrote an autobiography containing a blank page headed 'the average director's knowledge of football', though maybe the ones at Newcastle had a point. The wildly talented but disruptive Shackleton won nothing at Sunderland. Without him, Newcastle won three FA Cups in the 1950s.

OCTOBER 4

ENGLAND 2-0 SCOTLAND: CHURCHILL TURNS UP IN WEMBLEY WAR BOOST
(1941)

The outbreak of World War II on September 1, 1939 had brought the Football League to a standstill – much to the chagrin of Blackpool, who had won the first three games of the season. It took less than a fortnight for friendlies to be given the go-ahead, however, providing crowd numbers were kept between 8,000 – 15,000. With a restriction on the distance clubs could travel of fifty miles, the country spilt itself into seven mini-leagues. Soon the Government relaxed the ban on professional games, with air attacks on Britain looking unlikely at the time, so a new competition was formed: the Football League War Cup.

West Ham won the first final the following June, beating Blackburn Rovers 1-0 at Wembley. By then the 42,000-plus crowd was taking a gamble in attending the match: Hitler had recently invaded France, and the war was getting closer. Just over a month later, Luftwaffe bombs started raining down on London.

But the Blitz did not stop the War Cup. Despite continued attacks for the best part of the following year, more than 60,000 came to Wembley in 1941 to see the second staging of the final, Tom Finney's Preston drawing 1-1 with Denis and Leslie Compton's Arsenal. Preston went on to win a replay staged at Ewood Park to lift the trophy. The War Cup continued throughout hostilities. It was won by Wolves, Aston Villa, Charlton, Bolton and – some recompense for missing out on their 1939/40 title tilt – Blackpool.

Internationals did not stop either, and England vs Scotland matches were a regular occurrence. The most famous occurred in October 1941 when, in what was described as a 'well-kept secret' and a 'morale boost', prime minister Winston Churchill turned up to greet the teams before England's 2-0 win over Scotland. 'A terrific welcome was roared as he shook hands with the players,' ran a report at the time. Scotland had their revenge a year later, Bill Shankly scoring the winner as the Scots won 5-4 at Hampden.

JACK CHARLTON DEFENDS HIS 'LITTLE BOOK'
(1970)

Regional ITV station Tyne Tees had asked Jack Charlton for an in-depth interview, and the Leeds defender and World Cup winner was giving them one. Charlton was renowned for being a straight-talker, but as a veteran of 35 he was also an avuncular figure, so nobody expected the controversy to follow when he was innocently asked whether vendettas are sometimes pursued in football.

Charlton was quick to confirm that yes, of course they are. 'I cannot mention any names,' he began by way of illustration, 'but I have a little book with two names in it. And if I get the chance to do them, I will. I will make them suffer before I pack it in. If I can kick them four yards over the touchline I will.' The programme was only going out in the north of England, but soon enough the national press had picked up on Charlton's (albeit metaphorical) admission and the FA charged him with bringing the game into disrepute. Meanwhile columnists across the board from the *Express* ('These sickening comments!') to the usually measured John Arlott in the *Guardian* ('The menace of condoned thuggery!') queued up to give Charlton an (albeit metaphorical) shoeing. Even brother Bobby joined in: 'Jack must know what effect this is having, that it is not doing the game any good.'

Jack's response was calm and considered. 'I don't know what all the fuss is about,' he shrugged. 'I think some of the words have been taken out of context but I will stand by what I said. I am not a dirty player but what I referred to does happen. I was asked a question and I answered it honestly.' By the end of the month the matter had been quietly dropped by FA and newspaper columnists alike.

In some respects, the fuss seems a sign of more innocent times. Then again, in 2002, when Roy Keane admitted to lying in wait for Alf-Inge Haaland, the FA were equally quick to pounce.

OCTOBER 6

PRESTON 7-0 STOKE: ROSS SCORES
SEVEN... OR DOES HE?
(1888)

On December 14, 1935, reigning champions Arsenal travelled to Aston Villa more in hope than expectation. Villa were bottom of the league, having let in 52 goals over their 18 matches played, but the Gunners weren't in the best shape either. They were already six points off Sunderland's place at the top of the table, had star man Alex James missing through injury, and striker Ted Drake was forced to play with a heavily strapped knee. Arsenal needn't have worried, though. Drake scored a hat-trick by half-time, and within 15 minutes of the second had bagged himself another. Villa pulled one back through Jack Palethorpe, but it was hardly going to make much difference, a fact hammered home when Drake added his and Arsenal's seventh in the final minute.

Drake's last goal equalled a Football League record which had stood since the Football League was a mere five weeks old, when Preston North End striker Jimmy Ross had scored all his side's goals in a thrashing of Stoke City on October 6, 1888. Or so everyone thought. It was only ascertained years later that Ross in fact had only scored four in that game. (He had scored eight against Hyde in Preston's FA Cup record 26-0 win over Hyde, which may be where the apocryphal confusion arose.) Although Drake lost his Football League record 12 days later, when Tranmere's Harold 'Bunny' Bell scored nine against Oldham in a Division Three (North) Boxing Day fixture, he remains the only man to score seven in the top-flight of English football.

Drake's record did little for Arsenal that season. They ended in sixth place, nine points behind eventual winners Sunderland. Ross's four was more significant, as his Preston team ended their campaign unbeaten in the league as champions – and he scored in their 1889 FA Cup final win over Wolves. Who needs records?

OCTOBER 7

ENGLAND 0-1 GERMANY: THE FINAL GAME
AT OLD WEMBLEY
(2000)

The first game at the Empire Stadium, Wembley, was the 1923 FA Cup final between Bolton Wanderers and West Ham United. Had Dean Holdsworth not missed an open goal from six yards during extra-time in one of the 2000 FA Cup semi-finals, his Bolton side would have beaten Aston Villa to claim a place in the final and complete a pleasing symmetry. Having played in the Empire Stadium's first cup final, Wanderers would have played in the last.

As it was, Villa lost to Chelsea in the 2000 final, just months before the old stadium was due for demolition. There was one big match left to play, however. In their qualification group for the 2002 World Cup, Kevin Keegan's England faced the poorest Germany side in living memory. After 14 minutes, a poor tackle by Paul Scholes floored Michael Ballack. Dietmar Hamann sent a low 25-yard free-kick through David Seaman's hands and into the net. It was the last goal ever scored at the old Wembley.

England having lost in the famous old stadium's swansong, and with the rain tipping down on a dark afternoon, the cheap symbolism became too much for manager Kevin Keegan, who resigned after the game in the toilets. 'I have just not been good enough,' admitted the man who had just played Gareth Southgate in central midfield. And so the curtain came down on the Empire Stadium.

The demolition balls moved in. While it took 300 working days to build the stadium between 1922 and 1923, it would take over two years to knock it down again – then another five to get a new Wembley up in its place. The first big game in the grand new ground was the 2007 FA Cup final. Unlike Bolton, Chelsea delivered on the symmetry, winning the first in the new stadium as they had the last in the old, beating Manchester United 1-0 through a late Didier Drogba goal. Meanwhile England's first competitive fixture was a 3-0 Euro 2008 qualifying win over Israel. Steve McClaren did not resign.

OCTOBER 8

SUDAN 1-3 IVORY COAST: DROGBA'S
IMPROMPTU PLEA FOR PEACE
(2005)

The Ivory Coast was a country in desperate need of something to cheer. Since 2002, it had been embroiled in a bloody civil war between the rebel-held north and the government-controlled south. So when the national football team qualified for the 2006 World Cup finals – a first in the country's history – the players seized a chance to call for unity.

Theirs had been a remarkable achievement. The qualifying group had included five-time World Cup veterans Cameroon and reigning African champions Egypt. With emotions running high in the dressing room after the decisive 3-1 win in Sudan, Didier Drogba fell to his knees and made an address on live television to his countrymen: 'Ivorians, we beg your forgiveness. Let us come together and put this war behind us.'

The plea was – at least symbolically – met. When the team had crashed out of the 2000 African Nations Cup, they were sentenced to a three-day detainment at a military camp on the orders of erstwhile despot General Robert Guei. This time state reaction to their World Cup heroics was far more palatable. The players, whether they hailed from north or south, were rewarded by president Laurent Gbagbo. They were flown home on a private jet, named 'Knights of the Order of Merit', and promised a million-pound villa in Abidjan.

'All the players hated what was happening to our country and reaching the World Cup was the perfect emotional wave on which to ride,' Drogba later explained. Ivorian coach Henri Michel added: 'The players feel morally obligated to win. Victory calms the nerves at home, while defeat makes the fury fester. They want to be the knights in shining armour.'

Though Ivory Coast did not make it through a group containing Argentina, Holland and Serbia and Montenegro at the World Cup, their campaign was seen as a success. In June 2007, at an African Nations qualifier against Madagascar, leaders from both north and south stood together for the national anthem. 'I felt then,' said Drogba, 'that the Ivory Coast was born again.'

OCTOBER 9

ESTONIA 0-0 SCOTLAND: THE THREE-SECOND GAME
(1996)

In advance of their World Cup qualifier in Estonia, Scotland complained to FIFA that the floodlights at the Kadriorg Stadium in Tallinn just weren't up to scratch. An extra set of lights were ordered in, but it was a rushed job. So, instead of risking a potential lighting catastophe, FIFA announced, on the morning of the game, that kick-off would be brought forward from the scheduled 6.45 p.m. to three in the afternoon.

This caused a number of problems for the home side. While the majority of the Tartan Army would already be on their umpteenth pint in the local bars, most of the home side's fans would still be stuck at work. There was also the issue of the television broadcast, and the fact that a team lunch had been planned as well. So Estonia decided to ignore the change of plan and carry on regardless. When the referee blew his whistle to start the game at 3 p.m., it was clear Estonia weren't going to show. The only players on the pitch were Scottish. After one complete roll of the ball, the game was called off and Scotland celebrated their victory and an easy three points with a new chant, 'There's only one team in Tallinn'.

Several hours later, Estonia rocked up, hung around for a bit and left. What followed was an organisational farce orchestrated by FIFA. Under normal rules, Scotland should have been awarded the win, but a month later it was decided that a replay would take place on neutral ground in Monaco. And so, on February 11, 1997, the teams finally got the ball rolling properly. Scotland, of course, could only draw 0-0, effectively dropping two points they already had. But they went on to qualify anyway.

However it wasn't all bad news for Scottish-Estonian relations. In 2005, the BBC reported that 'Scottish business interests in the Baltic republic' were booming and 'already included an electronics factory, several bars and a Chinese restaurant. Many of them involve Tartan Army foot soldiers who stayed on after two World Cup qualifying matches, one of them the notorious game that never was.'

OCTOBER 10

MOROCCO 1-0 ZAMBIA: NO WORLD CUP REDEMPTION FOR COPPER BULLETS
(1993)

Zambia had just beaten Mauritus 3-0 in a qualifier for the 1994 African Nations Cup, and were en route to Senegal to play their first match in their attempt to get to the World Cup finals in America. The side, built around PSV Eindhoven winger Kalusha Bwalya, was the best in Zambia's history, and the 'Chipolopolo' (the Copper Bullets) were hopeful of reaching the finals of both tournaments. But their plane did not make it to Senegal.

On the morning of April 28, 1993, it was confirmed that their military jet, which had stopped in Gabon to refuel, had crashed just off the coast a few minutes after taking off. One of the engines on the plane had caught fire, and the pilot, who had already flown the leg from Mauritius to Gabon, had shut down the wrong engine in a tired panic. The plane plummeted into the sea, killing all thirty passengers. In total 19 players were killed, wiping out the entire squad apart from Zambia's five overseas-based players, who had separate arrangements made for them. A week later the bodies were flown back to Zambia and thousands lined the streets outside the Stadium of Independence.

Bwalya helped to quickly assemble a new team of untested players, but World Cup redemption was beyond them. In their final match in Morocco, Zambia needed only a point to qualify for the 1994 World Cup. They were 40 minutes away from realising their dream when Moroccan striker Abdeslam Laghrissi scored to secure a 1-0 victory. 'We were so close yet so far away,' said Bwalya. 'I think about the people at home and our friends who died. We are all very disappointed. After five months of hard work, we didn't deserve to go out like this.' Zambia would, however, take some solace from the African Nations Cup. Bwalya led them to the final which they lost 2-1 to Nigeria. The team were hailed as national heroes on their return.

TOTTENHAM HOTSPUR 10-4 EVERTON:
BILL NICHOLSON'S AMAZING DEBUT
(1958)

In 1951, Tottenham Hotspur became the first side to win the title having won the Second Division the year before. The mastermind behind the feat was Arthur Rowe, who developed a system known as push-and-run, a simple tactic which involved passing the ball quickly to a nearby team mate, then sprinting into space to offer the option of a return ball. Rowe's innovative management would rub off on two members of his team: Alf Ramsey repeated his feat of winning Second then First Division titles in 1962 using deep-lying forward Jimmy Leadbetter at Ipswich, while Bill Nicholson honed Rowe's push-and-run tactic to lead Spurs to a league and cup double in 1961.

Rowe's success brought heightened expectation at White Hart Lane. He suffered a breakdown in 1954, to be replaced by Jimmy Anderson. Spurs by now were mid-table stragglers, their existence only enlivened by occasional flirtations with relegation. After starting the 1958/59 season dismally – they lost their first three games 2-3, 2-4 and 0-5 – Anderson was 'retired' due to 'ill health'. Nicholson, by now assisting as coach, was given the job.

On his debut as a player for England, Nicholson had scored 19 seconds into the game against Portugal, so he knew how to make an instant impression. His first game as a manager was no less dramatic. Spurs scored after three minutes, were 6-1 up at half-time and finished the game winning 10-4, equalling a record for an aggregate score. As epoch-defining results go, like Everton it took some beating, but Nicholson couldn't turn Spurs round immediately. They continued to take regular pummellings in the league that season and only just finished above the relegation places. Their survival was mainly due to the efforts of Danny Blanchflower and new defensive signing Dave Mackay from Hearts. Within two years, though, Nicholson, Blanchflower and Mackay led Spurs to the century's first double.

OCTOBER 12

GAZZA NOT FAMOUS ENOUGH, ACCORDING TO JUDGE
(1990)

The 1990 World Cup was one of the poorest on record, but it did give the game one of its most enduring images: Paul Gasgoine's tears in the immediate aftermath of his booking in the semi-final between England and West Germany. 'Keep an eye on him,' mouthed Gary Lineker, apparently communicating with coach Bobby Robson on the bench.

That picture of 'Gazza' – with his England shirt covering half of his pink, puffed-up face – was reproduced everywhere, in papers, on mugs and t-shirts. Suddenly a player who had only secured his place in England's World Cup squad less than two months before with a late solo goal against Czechoslovakia had been catapulted to celebrity status

After the World Cup, Gazza and Lindesfarne got to number two in the charts with a cover of 'Fog On The Tyne'. Gazza – who had taken to occasionally sporting a pair of plastic breasts – followed this up with the number 31 smash 'Geordie Boys (Gazza Rap)'. He endorsed everything from aftershave to football boots, via salt-and-vinegar crisps. It wasn't long before he had a book in production, but when his publisher realised an unofficial biography called *Gazza* was on its way, Gascoigne sought an injunction from the high court, claiming the nickname was so well-known it suggested the tome was authorised.

This cut no ice with Mr Justice Harman, however, who upon being told Gazza was a 'very well-known footballer', replied: 'Rugby or Association football?' He then went on to point out that the Duke of Wellington had not liked being written about either, but had not been able to take action against biographers in his time. 'Do you think Mr Gascoigne is more famous than the Duke of Wellington in 1815?' asked the judge. The injunction was not granted.

Mr Justice Harman – also famous for kicking a taxi driver and suggesting there are 'only three kinds of women: wives, whores and mistresses' – eventually resigned in 1998 after being accused of weakening the public's confidence in the judicial system. He is not as famous as Gazza.

OCTOBER 13

GEORGE EASTHAM 1-0 NEWCASTLE UNITED FOOTBALL CLUB, LTD
(1960)

At the end of the 1958/59 season, George Eastham's contract with Newcastle United ran out. Unhappy with the house the club had provided him with, as well as the secondary job they had arranged for him – at the time players needed to supplement their income as the maximum wage of £20 a week was still in force – he refused to sign the new contract put in front of him and requested a transfer.

The club refused to let him go. They argued that his house 'was once occupied by the famous Jackie Milburn', and that his additional job at a glass manufacturer was perfectly acceptable. In any case, for Newcastle that was beside the point. Under Football League retain-and-transfer rules, if he did not sign the new contract offered him, the club could refuse his transfer request and place him in unpaid limbo. In protest, Eastham left Newcastle – the city, if not the club – to work outside the game as a cork salesman in Guildford. He had effectively gone on strike.

Newcastle cut their losses in October 1960, selling the player to Arsenal for £47,500 – although it was indicative of the attitudes of the time that the player only heard about it himself on the radio. Newcastle probably thought that would be the end of that, but the Professional Footballers Association encouraged Eastham to pursue the retain-and-transfer system through the courts, and put up his legal costs.

The trial began in June 1963. 'I regard this as a system from the Middle Ages,' argued Eastman's QC, Gerald Gardiner, in the High Court. 'It is really treating men like cattle, and really the position is that they are paid slaves.' Despite League secretary Alan Hardaker's contention that 'football anarchy' would result, on July 4, 1963 the judge declared the system an 'unreasonable restraint of trade'.

OCTOBER 14

BRAMALL LANE STAGES THE FIRST FLOODLIT MATCH
(1878)

With football gaining in popularity at a rapid rate during the late 19th century, experiments were made with methods which allowed more people to see more games. Which really meant, of course, ways the game's early entrepreneurs could make more money. And so it was that in 1878 fans turned up to Bramall Lane to watch a match between two Sheffield representative sides played out under a blue haze of four 8,000-candlepower lights balanced precariously on nine-metre poles. The money-making venture was not a total success, as approximately 6,000 of the 20,000 crowd managed to evade the turnstiles under the cover of darkness. Even so, it was an unusually large attendance and other clubs soon tried to follow suit. The Football League, though, were cautious after various hitches and floodlights were banned when competition began in 1888.

That didn't stop further experimentation. At a ladies match at Deepdale between Dick, Kerr and a Rest of England team in 1920 to raise money for ex-servicemen, two anti-aircraft searchlights illuminated the event. More than 12,000 people watched Dick, Kerr win 4-0. A decade later, Herbert Chapman attempted to convince the FA to allow Arsenal to play night matches after witnessing such a game in Belgium – he even installed lights at Highbury – but the authorities would not budge on the matter until 1951, far too late for Chapman to see his dream realised.

But Highbury was in the vanguard of floodlights nonetheless. The first FA-approved floodlit match was on September 19, 1951, Arsenal hammering Hapoel Tel-Aviv 6-1. In 1954, Wolves hosted their legendary 'floodlit friendlies' which captured the imagination of Europe and inadvertently brought about the creation of the European Cup. In February 1956, the Football League finally relented. The first league match played under lights, between Portsmouth and Newcastle, kicked off late due to technical problems. The players had to change beforehand by candlelight.

OCTOBER 15

GIGI MERONI KILLED – BY ONE OF HIS FANS
(1967)

Gigi Meroni was Italian football's answer to George Best. The most exciting winger in the country – he scored a goal every five games for Torino, many of them spectacular – Meroni was also a style icon, a poet, a painter, a lover of the Beatles and jazz, and a rebel. Wearing a mop of hair too long for conservative 1960s Italian society, he was ordered by national coach Edmondo Fabbri to get it cut if he wanted to play for the 'Azzurri'. Meroni refused. Fabbri picked him anyway.

The 1967/68 season was in its infancy, and Torino had just beaten Sampdoria 4-2. It looked like, for the first time since the Superga tragedy in 1949, the Turin club would seriously compete for the *Scudetto*. That evening, Meroni and his team mate Fabrizio Poletti crossed a busy boulevard in the centre of Turin, well away from a crossing and in the dark. An oncoming Fiat flipped Meroni into the air and across the carriageway, where a motorbike hit him and dragged him down the street. He died less than two hours later in hospital. The distraught Fiat driver, a 19-year-old called Attilio Romero, said he was one of Meroni's greatest fans.

The next weekend was the Turin derby against Juventus, a match which has gone down in legend. In eerie silence, Meroni's good friend, the striker Néstor Combin, scored a long-range free kick into the bottom left after four minutes, hit an outrageous 30-yard looping strike into the top left two minutes later which Meroni would have been proud of, and completed a hat-trick in the second half. He was wearing Meroni's number seven shirt. Torino's 4-0 win was, and still is, their biggest ever win over Juventus. Without Meroni, their title challenge did not last the pace; Torino would not win a post-Superga *Scudetto* until 1976.

Meroni's story took one last – and incredibly strange – turn. In 2000 Torino announced the identity of their new club president. It was Attilio Romero.

OCTOBER 16

DERBY 'REGRETFULLY' ACCEPT RESIGNATIONS OF CLOUGH AND TAYLOR
(1973)

Derby County were a struggling Second Division side when Brian Clough and his assistant Peter Taylor took over at the Baseball Ground in 1967. Within two years they had signed hard-tackling midfielders Dave Mackay and Willie Carlin and bustled their way into the First Divison. Within another three, they had beaten Don Revie's Leeds and Bill Shankly's Liverpool to the 1971/72 First Division title.

The following season, Derby were only a missed Alan Hinton penalty away from putting real pressure on Juventus in the second leg of the semi-final of the European Cup. That was in April; six months later Clough and Taylor were gone. County's 73-year-old chairman Sam Longson had grown exasperated at Clough's high-profile media work – he wrote a regular newspaper column and appeared on television panels as a pundit – and the manager's habit of regularly criticising the FA and the Football League in trenchant terms. Having repeatedly asked Clough to desist – and been signally ignored – Longson decreed that 'each and every newspaper article and television appearance must be approved by the board', otherwise Clough would face the sack. On the evening of October 15, Clough and Taylor resigned, in the hope of getting rid of Longson. But in an extraordinary meeting the following afternoon, the board backed their chairman.

'Do not portray me as a happy, laughing chairman,' Longson told a press conference in the Baseball Ground car park, 'I feel more like tears.' Clough responded by explaining that 'there are a million reasons why I have resigned, and you have just been talking to one of them – which is more than I have, because he slammed the phone down on me twice last week. My feeling now is one of nausea. I'm embarrassed and deeply ashamed for Derby County.'

In the immediate aftermath, there were talks of player strikes in support of Clough, but eventually the squad rallied round new manager Dave Mackay. Derby won another title in 1975 and appeared vindicated, especially in the light of Clough's subsequent failures at Brighton and Leeds. But then Clough went to Derby's bitter rivals Nottingham Forest. At Forest, in 1980, 'Old Big Ead' lifted his second European Cup, while Derby were relegated to the Second Division.

ENGLAND 1-1 POLAND: RAMSEY'S MEN FAIL
TO REACH WORLD CUP
(1973)

England had not deigned to enter the first three World Cups, but since falling in line with the rest of the world in 1950, had featured in every tournament since. They were expected to do so in 1974 from a three-team group including Wales and Poland, though manager Alf Ramsey had never guided England through qualification before. England were hosts in 1966 and champions in 1970. Their efforts to reach the finals in West Germany were unconvincing. England scraped a 1-0 win in Wales, then were lucky to escape with a 1-1 draw at Wembley in the return fixture. Then they lost to Poland, 2-0 in Chorzów. Still, a win in the last group game against the Poles at Wembley would see them through.

It was not to be. In the 57th minute, Grzegorz Lato robbed Norman Hunter down the left and slipped the ball inside to Jan Domarski, whose tame shot squirmed home. Hunter took all the flak for missing his tackle, but Peter Shilton let Domarski's effort slip through his hands. Allan Clarke equalised from the penalty spot six minutes later, but after that there was no way past inspired Polish goalkeeper Jan Tomaszewski, who had been dismissed before the match as a 'clown' by Brian Clough. At 1-1, it was not enough to see England through and Poland took the place instead.

Clough's was not the only pre-match quote which would look faintly ridiculous when the dust had settled. Ramsey had asked for league games to be postponed the weekend before in order to help his team prepare, but the Football League turned down his request. 'It is a football match, not a war,' said League chairman Alan Hardaker. 'If we do lose, the game is not going to die. It will be a terrible thing for six weeks and then everybody will forget about it.' Some hope. The pain didn't subside. Ramsey was sacked for his failure the following May, FA mandarin Sir Harold Thompson – who had supposedly detested Ramsey ever since 1964, when the England boss ordered him to put his cigar out if he wanted to dine with the team – gleefully wielding the knife.

OCTOBER 18

THE END OF SUNDERLAND'S STOKOE ERA
(1976)

Sunderland were, along with Arsenal and Aston Villa, the biggest and most successful club in England up until World War II, at which point their fortunes took a notable turn for the worse. Despite flinging millions at building the team – not always legally – in the 1950s, Sunderland were relegated for the first time in 1958. They regained their top-flight status in 1964, but they would never be the same. After six years struggling in the bottom half of the table, they were relegated again. By the time Bob Stokoe took over as manager in December 1972, the club were fourth from bottom of the Second Division and facing relegation to the third tier, an unthinkable ignominy for so grand a club.

Stokoe wasted no time in coaxing the best out of star players such as striker Dennis Tueart and defender Dave Watson, and by the end of the season Sunderland were up to sixth in the table. More amazingly – for they had been 250/1 to lift the FA Cup at the start of the season – they reached Wembley and beat holders Leeds United. Their win came thanks to an Ian Porterfield goal and Jim Montgomery's famous point-blank double save from Trevor Cherry and Peter Lorimer. 'When I saved that one from Lorimer I knew the cup was ours,' said Montgomery. 'I just couldn't see Leeds getting a better chance.' Cue the defining image of Stokoe at the final whistle, as he cavorted across the pitch in flasher's mac and trilby.

But the club's inability to build immediately on their cup win and get themselves out of the Second Division saw the departure of both Tueart and Watson to Manchester City. Sunderland eventually went up as champions in 1976 but Stokoe, having never properly replaced his star men, wasted nearly £300,000 on second-rate panic buys when back in the top flight. A day after a home defeat by Aston Villa, his resignation was announced and an era which, for a while looked like reviving a sleeping giant, was over.

In 1987, Stokoe took temporary control of the team after Lawrie McMenemy's departure, with Sunderland once again under threat of relegation to the Third Division. He was unable to save them a second time. Nobody blamed him.

OCTOBER 19

CELTIC 7-1 RANGERS: HAMPDEN IN THE SUN
(1957)

The two most jaw-dropping Scottish League Cup finals ever played both featured Celtic. One was in 1971, when Jock Stein's all-conquering side, who the previous season had wrapped up a sixth league title in a row, played newly promoted Partick Thistle. By the time 37 minutes had been played, Thistle were 4-0 up (they eventually won the tie 4-1). 'The year before most of us had been playing for Thistle reserves against Glasgow Police and Glasgow Transport,' said Thistle right-back John Hansen. The year before, Celtic had been playing Feyenoord in the European Cup final.

Celtic have better memories of the other jaw-dropper. In 1957 Rangers were reigning league champions, while Celtic were suffering the leanest spell in their history. They were League Cup holders, but had only won three other trophies since 1938 and were not fancied to triumph. But with the help of a Billy McPhail hat-trick, Celtic recorded the biggest winning margin in any British cup final, and inflicted a club-record defeat on Rangers. The result would be immortalised in song: 'Oh Hampden in the sun / Celtic 7 Rangers 1.'

After the game, Celtic midfielder Bobby Collins reported the shambles in the centre of the Rangers defence: 'I don't know if John Valentine had no faith in George Niven or Niven had no faith in Valentine, but ultimately they had no faith in themselves, something you can sense very quickly on a football field, and inevitably the game became a rout.' The *Sunday Mail* opined that 'Rangers were lucky not to lose ten', while the *Post* claimed it was football's 'October Revolution.'

Thirty-one years later, a shredded Celtic trailed Graeme Souness's Rangers 5-1 at Ibrox in a league game with half an hour still to play. Ibrox screamed for more, but Souness's side took his foot off the gas. 'Hampden In The Sun' would not be avenged; some have never forgiven them.

OCTOBER 20

SPARTAK MOSCOW 2-0 HAARLEM: THE BIGGEST DISASTER, THE BIGGEST COVER-UP
(1982)

Spartak Moscow's Sergei Shvetsov has always regretted scoring his side's second goal right at the end of their second round, first leg UEFA Cup match against Dutch side Haarlem in 1982. 'It would have been better if I had not scored it,' he reflected sadly, years later, of a goal which inadvertently led to the deaths of at least 340 spectators.

Low attendance figures for the match had meant fans were crammed into a single section of the Lutinki Stadium, Moscow, that fateful night. With their side a goal up with a couple of minutes remaining, Spartak fans began to make their way home on a bitterly cold evening. Then they heard a huge roar from the home fans; Shvetsov had just made it 2-0. Ecstatic with the injury-time goal, fans rushed back through a single exit tunnel to the icy stands, slipping on their way. They were confronted with a surge of supporters leaving the stadium. The next day Reuters quoted 'Soviet sources' who reported: 'Several spectators were injured in a crowd accident. Moscow's ambulance service said casualties had been taken to at least two hospitals but they would not say whether there were any deaths.' The reality was far worse.

Although the exact death toll may never be known, at least 340 people were trampled to death. Witnesses told of how they were trapped in the exit tunnel unable to get in or out of the stadium. Relatives of the dead were given minutes to say goodbye before bodies were buried en masse, and the next few matches at the stadium were cancelled to avoid any display of public sympathy.

It wasn't until after Mikhail Gorbachev's Glasnost reforms that the Soviet press shed some light on the incident. Until then the official death toll was 66; but in 1989, *Soviet Sport* newspaper confirmed the number was much higher and that 'the authorities staged a cover up'. The release of information came when the world was grieving the Hillsborough disaster.

OCTOBER 21

ENGLAND 4-4 FIFA: KUBALA'S RARE
INTERNATIONAL CHANCE
(1953)

Towards the end of 1953, England played a FIFA all-star XI in order to celebrate the 90th anniversary of the Football Association. Little did anybody realise it, but what they were really witnessing was the death throes of complacent English superiority. Having clearly underestimated the power of the Europeans, England needed a dubious last-minute penalty to scramble a draw at Wembley and maintain their proud record of having never been beaten on home turf by a non-British or Irish side. Whether it was worth all the effort and angst was a moot point. Just over a month later Hungary would head over and belabour England 6-3, laying waste to any delusions of grandeur.

The FIFA XI was made up of Europeans from six different countries and was described the following day in the *Manchester Guardian* as 'a team who blended together like good tobacco'. One of the stars of the match was László Kubala, whose second goal was, according to a correspondent betraying the attitudes of the time, 'a model shot. Who said the Europeans can't shoot!'

Kubala certainly could. Unknown to English audiences, the Hungarian had spent much of his early life on the run, temporarily fleeing to Czechoslovakia to avoid military service. After winning 6 Czech caps, he returned to Hungary to play for his national team, but in 1949 defected to escape Communism. The Hungarian FA banned him from international football for life. In response Kubala set up his own team of exiles called Hungária, for whom he was spotted playing by Barcelona. He debuted for the club in 1950, leading them to two *La Liga* titles and three Copa del Reys in three years.

Kubala went on to play for Spain, though FIFA's stance on the Hungarian FA's ban was altogether confusing. In 1954, having played in a World Cup qualification defeat in Turkey, he was ordered to step down in the resulting play-off. The teams drew and Turkey went through on the toss of a coin. So, despite being the only player ever to be capped for *three* countries, Kubala never got to play in a World Cup. The Wembley crowd may not have known it, but they were the lucky ones.

OCTOBER 22

HANS KAMPER PLACES AN ADVERT: FC BARCELONA IS BORN
(1899)

Hans Kamper's emigration from Switzerland to Barcelona was something of an accident. The 22-year-old had stopped off in the city in 1899 to visit an uncle while en route to West Africa to help his father set up a trading business. But he allowed himself to be waylaid – and within months had founded FC Barcelona.

On October 22, Kamper placed an ad in the *Los Desportes* sports paper for 'enthusiastic footballers' to come and play with a 'former Swiss champion'. (The young Kamper had already captained FC Basel and helped set up FC Zurich, and was keen to make his mark in Catalunya.) By November 29, he had enough players to officially form a club. Englishman William Wild was made their first president.

Kamper had fully embraced the Catalan spirit, changing his name to Joan Gamper and learning the language fluently. So from the beginning, Barça established themselves as a team for Catalan nationalists, with regional icon St Jordi on their crest. The blue-and-maroon strip was a nod to Kamper's Basel. Kamper served as president from 1910 to 1925, a period which saw the signings legends such as record goalscorer Paulino Alcántara and midfielder Josep Samitier. Barça won eleven Catalan titles and six Copa del Reys under Kamper.

But his association with the club came to an end in June 1925. Barcelona fans had booed the Spanish national anthem at a charity match in response to a government diktat prohibiting the proceeds to be spent on Catalan causes. Barça's Les Corts stadium was shut for six months and Kamper was asked to leave the country. He returned to Switzerland but on July 30, 1930 committed suicide having lost his assets in the 1929 Wall Street Crash.

ANTIFUTBOL: ESTUDIANTES DE LA PLATA 2–1 AC MILAN
(1969)

South American champions Estudiantes de La Plata were infamous for their cynical approach to the game: their style of play was known as 'el antifútbol'. How cynical were they? Pretty damn cynical: one of their tactics was known as 'pincharratas', and involved players carrying pins which they would jab into opponents at corners and free-kicks.

This win-at-all-costs approach reached its apogee in the second leg of their Intercontinental Cup final against European champions Milan in 1969. After 18 minutes, the Italian striker Pierino Prati was flattened by the elbow of Alberto Suárez (a player who had once served a 30-day jail sentence for twice stamping on the head of an opponent in a league match). While Prati was receiving treatment, Estudiantes goalkeeper Alberto Poletti sidled up behind the player and, as he tried to get up, kicked him in the back.

Minutes later, as Milan went 1-0 up, Poletti set about half the Milanese by himself as they celebrated their goal. Suárez then punched Néstor Combin in the face and was sent off. Combin, who was lucky not to lose an eye, was stretchered off. Immediately afterwards he was arrested by police who falsely claimed that the player, born in Argentina, had evaded national service. He was later released after frantic diplomatic efforts.

Estudiantes went on to win the game but, having lost the first tie by three goals, did not take the cup. Suárez quickly got his comeuppance. The Argentine president, watching from the stands, ordered his arrest, along with that of Poletti and midfielder Madero. Cue another 30-day stretch inside, along with a 30-game domestic ban.

OCTOBER 24

ENGLAND 2-0 DENMARK – GOLD AT THE OLYMPIC TOURNAMENT
(1908)

The 1908 Olympics were due to be held in Rome, but when Naples was covered in lava from the volcanic eruption of Mount Vesuvius in 1906, Italy could no longer afford to host the event. London stepped in at the last minute to hold what proved to be a rain-soaked event at the 70,000 capacity White City stadium (which years later would make way for BBC Television Centre).

Eight teams were in the hat to begin with: the Netherlands, Denmark, Sweden, Hungary, Bohemia, Great Britain (selected by the FA and purely English) and France (who entered two teams). But due to political problems in the Balkans, Hungary and Bohemia were forced to withdraw so the Netherlands and France A sailed through to the semi-finals without playing a single game.

That would be about the sum total of good news for the French. Their B team was beaten 9-0 in the first round by Denmark, while France A were then trounced 17-1 by the same opposition in the semi-final. The French A team were too proud to play for bronze, so Sweden were given their place and lost to the Dutch.

Britain/England did not score quite as many as Denmark en route to the final, though they did beat Sweden 12-1 and Holland 4-0. The showdown with the Danes was played in front of an 8,000 crowd and was won by the English 2-0, the goals coming from Frederick Chapman and captain Vivian Woodward. The Official Olympic Report however notes the scoreline 'rather flattered the winners who did not show real international form. Denmark, on the other hand, displayed the greatest vigour and determination with far more pace and dash than against France.' Britain met Denmark again in the 1912 Olympics in Sweden and beat them more comfortably, 4-2.

OCTOBER 25

OXFORD UNITED'S LAWRENSON SACKED BY MAXWELL
(1988)

Media mogul Robert Maxwell saved Oxford United from going bust in 1982, but the long-term cost would be high for the club. As was his way, the bumptious Maxwell wasted little time in getting on the wrong side of Oxford fans, as he tried to push through a merger with Reading to form the 'Thames Valley Royals'. Fans of both clubs – and luckily the board at Reading – were up in arms and the deal was never done. Maxwell threatened to close Oxford in a fit of pique, but never carried out his threat, partly because the team were going through a period of unprecedented success at the time.

Oxford won successive promotions in the mid-1980s, winning the Third and Second Division titles to reach the top-flight for the first time in their history in 1985. Three seasons of First Division football followed, plus the stunning addition of the 1986 League Cup. A team including John Aldridge, Ray Houghton and Kevin Brock stormed to a shock 3-0 win over QPR in the final. The League Cup was to be the high point. Aldridge and Houghton were sold to Liverpool, and although the former was replaced by Dean Saunders, the former Brighton striker couldn't stop Oxford finally succumbing to the inevitable and suffering relegation in 1988.

On the face of it, things still looked up. Oxford had recently installed Mark Lawrenson as manager, and with Saunders scoring freely the team had started their campaign to bounce straight back well. But there was a problem. Maxwell had loftier ambitions than Oxford could provide, and after an attempt to buy into Manchester United, purchased Derby County. To circumvent ownership rules, he had resigned as Oxford chairman in May and taken over at Derby, putting his son Kevin Maxwell in his place. Five months later, Oxford's star man Saunders was sold – to Derby. Lawrenson was sacked for complaining.

It was the thin end of the wedge. After Maxwell's large frame tipped off the side of his yacht in November 1991 and his pensions scam was revealed, Oxford – owned by the crook's estate – became insolvent. The splash sunk Oxford into nearly two decades of financial woe. In 2006 manager Jim Smith could not prevent them being relegated out of the League, after a 2-3 defeat against Leyton Orient on the final day of the season. They were replaced by Accrington Stanley – the club whose place they took when entering the League themselves in 1962. They are the only current non-league team to have won a major honour; no thanks are due to Maxwell.

OCTOBER 26

FA FOUNDED IN FREEMASONS TAVERN, COVENT GARDEN
(1863)

Football has been played in some form or other for centuries – there are records of the Chinese hoofing a ball around over two thousand years ago – but it was during the 19th century in Britain that the game really took off. Impromptu matches in fields and streets had been taking place since the 1200s, but by the 1820s students at public schools and universities across the country began to think about setting down some rules.

Their approaches varied wildly. Some rulebooks favoured a catch-and-run game, while some preferred dribbling with the ball at feet. Just about everyone had a differing opinion on where to draw the line regarding foul play. The Cambridge Rules of 1848 and the Sheffield Rules, set down ten years later, attempted to mould the game in a more refined dribbling style. Although both rulebooks forbade running while holding the ball, catching was still permitted; the game was closer to the tone of Australian Rules than Association. Meanwhile the Blackheath and (surprise) Rugby codes preferred a full-on handling and hacking game.

With schools, universities and clubs across the country sticking to their local codes, JC Thring, a master at Uppingham, drew up a mishmash of various rulebooks in 1862 to create what he called 'Simplest Game'. It did not catch on, but the idea of homogenisation did. In October 1963, representatives of Kilburn, Barnes, War Office, Crusaders, Perceval House, Crystal Palace, Blackheath School, Kensington School, Surbiton and Blackheath met in central London to agree new rules and form the Football Association. There were further rifts. In December Blackheath withdrew to pursue a handling version of the game which would become Rugby Union in 1871. The William Webb Ellis myth of picking up the ball during a football game at Rugby in 1823 is just that. When catching was finally outlawed in 1866, the ball was finally, literally, rolling.

OCTOBER 27

BRIAN CLOUGH GIVEN HIS FIRST MANAGERIAL JOB
(1965)

Tucked away in the Sport In Brief column of the *Manchester Guardian*, alongside the news that Everton's Colin Harvey had requested a personal hearing at the FA after being sent off against Fulham, was another seemingly insignificant snippet: 'B. Clough, a former Middlesbrough, Sunderland and England centre forward, has been appointed manager of Hartlepools United.' Nobody knew it yet, but in the years to come Clough would generate quite a bit more newsprint than that.

'B. Clough' never had the chance to truly realise his potential as a player. In a Second Division match on Boxing Day 1962, the 27-year-old Sunderland striker slid across a frozen penalty area to challenge for a ball with Bury goalkeeper Chris Harker. In a terrible collision he tore the cruciate ligament in his right knee. Clough returned to the first team two years later after Sunderland had been promoted, but his top-flight career was restricted to three matches before he was forced to retire. He had scored 267 goals in 296 games.

Clough was put in charge of the youth team at Sunderland and soon got a taste for management, developing players such as Colin Todd and John O'Hare. Both players later helped Clough win the First Division at Derby. But changes in management at Sunderland meant he lost his youth team job. Not for the last time in his life, Clough hit the bottle. But then came a call from Hartlepools chairman Ernest Ord, who had spotted something in Clough. He offered him the chance to become, at 30, the youngest manager in the league. 'The job saved his life,' said Peter Taylor, Clough's former team mate at Middlesbrough who became his right-hand man. 'He was a no-hoper, jobless, boozing heavily and on his way out.' Instead, Clough threw himself into work, and in his first full season Hartlepools, who usually had to apply for re-election to the league, finished eighth in the league.

Ord soon got fed up with Clough's penchant for publicity and threatened his manager with the sack, but was ousted by his own board, who preferred to keep hold of Clough. They couldn't do so for ever, though, and in 1967 Second Division Derby came calling.

OCTOBER 28

ARTHUR WHARTON, THE WORLD'S FIRST BLACK PROFESSIONAL, IS BORN
(1865)

Arthur Wharton was born in Jamestown (now Accra) in Ghana to a wealthy family with Scottish ancestors, and at the age of 17 moved to England for good in order to train as a Methodist missionary. Instead he quickly made his name in the country as a crack sportsman. Cycling, cricket, athletics, football: Wharton excelled in every sport he took up.

In 1886, he became the fastest man in the world, running the 100 yards in a record-equalling 10 seconds at the Amateur Athletic Association Championships. A year later he played in goal for Preston North End in all their FA Cup ties. The team were expected to win the trophy, but were stymied in the semi-final, losing 3-1 to West Bromwich Albion. Wharton played twice more for the club, but had moved on before the famous 1888/89 'Invincibles' season.

Wharton signed for Rotherham in 1889, becoming the first black professional football player in Britain (Andrew Watson of Scotland had been the first black amateur). After five years in the town – which also saw him run two pubs and squire two children – he moved to Sheffield United, but played only three games before the arrival of the legendary goalkeeper William 'Fatty' Foulkes. Soon after he returned to Rotherham. All the while he was coaching Stalybridge Rovers, where his signature signing was future Huddersfield and Arsenal boss Herbert Chapman. Wharton's professional career ended in 1901 at Stockport County.

Wharton's days ended sadly: his love of cigars, woman and booze saw him spend his dotage in alcoholic penury. He would be remembered, though. A letter published in the *Sheffield Telegraph and Independent* in 1942 told a (possibly apocryphal) tale of Wharton's goalkeeping prowess: 'I saw him jump, take hold of the cross bar, catch the ball between his legs, and cause three onrushing forwards to fall into the net. I have never seen a similar save since and I have been watching football for over fifty years.'

PUSKÁS – THOUGHT KILLED IN HUNGARIAN REVOLT – REPORTED ALIVE
(1956)

On October 23, 1956, the Hungarian revolution began. Five days later, rebel radio reported that Ferenc Puskás, the world's greatest footballer, had been killed fighting in the uprising. In a front-page obituary headed 'Puskás: Footballer and Idealist', the *Manchester Guardian* noted 'with an infinite sadness yet a strange sense of pride and thankfulness in the heart' that Puskás had died 'as most sportstmen would like to think they would have the courage to die – manning the barricades in the fight for freedom against tyranny'.

Happily, 24 hours later, Hungarian state radio announced that the superstar had not been killed. Puskás was, in fact, alive and well. 'All the players are safe and sound and preparing for their future work as a team,' added the report. However, given Hungary's state, 'the Team' were neither safe nor sound. When Honvéd, for whom many of the national side played, heard the news of the uprising while at a training camp outside the capital, they returned to Budapest.

Gyula Grosics later described how players who lived on the Buda side of the river – Puskás, Kocsis, Hidegkuti – had 'particularly scary' journeys home. 'They had to cross the bridges where the shooting was intense,' he told the *Spectator* in 1996. 'On the Friday, I ventured out and walked into a hail of gunfire. I was in a square with a statue of a Hungarian saint in the middle and I flung myself to the ground behind it and prayed like mad. The saint obliged, the shooting stopped. I ran.'

By the time the Soviets invaded in early November, most of Honvéd's players were in Spain, preparing to play Atlético Bilbao in the European Cup. Puskás defected, never to play for Hungary or Honvéd again.

SPARTA PRAGUE 6-2 RAPID VIENNA: EUROPE'S FIRST MAJOR FINAL
(1927)

Hugo Meisl, the son of a wealthy banker from Bohemia, resisted all attempts by his father to persuade him to forge a career in the family business. Instead Meisl joined the Austrian FA as an administrator, and in 1919 became selector of the national side, creating Austria's 'Wunderteam' of the 1930s.

But Meisl did not give up the day job, and in 1924 he suggested the setting up of an international tournament between central European clubs: the Mitropa Cup. He devised an innovative two-leg format and in July 1927 the cup was rubberstamped. Within months it was being contested by two teams apiece from Czechoslovakia, Hungary, Yugoslavia and Meisl's Austria.

Sparta Prague were the first champions. They only reached the final thanks to a coin toss against Budapest side Hungária. Meisl might have come up with the two-leg model, but he hadn't factored in teams finishing level after two matches. Sparta romped the final against Rapid Vienna. They won the first leg 6-2 at home, then lost the away leg 2-1 and were pelted with rotten fruit and stones for their trouble.

Italy soon joined the party, and in 1932 an Italian side won its first title under controversial circumstances. Having won the first leg of their semi-final against Juventus 4-0, Slavia Prague quickly went 2-0 down in the second leg and took to time-wasting to halt the slide. The crowd rioted, and Slavia refused to continue after a stone hit their keeper. After being trapped for hours in the changing rooms, both teams were informed of their disqualification. Bologna won the final on a walkover.

Mitropa organisers hoped British teams would deign to enter, but after World War II, the cup died off. Countries behind the iron curtain no longer competed and UEFA launched the European Cup. By 1980 it was a tournament for second-tier sides – which at least gave rise to the incongruous sight of Milan winning it in 1982.

OCTOBER 31

STADE OLYMPIQUE DE L'EMYRNE
ANTANANARIVO 0-149 AS ADEMA
(2002)

Stade Olympique de L'Emyrne were a team on the up. Having won their first Madagascan league title in 2001, the team from Antananarivo shocked the entire continent by advancing to the second round of the African Champions League. First they beat Olympique de Moka of Mauritius in an 'island derby' preliminary tie (twice postponed by political unrest in Madagascar). They then knocked out highly regarded Petro Atletico of Angola in the first round proper on penalties, after being forced to play a one-leg away tie due to the continuing civil unrest at home.

While they failed to reach the group stages of the competition, going down bravely 3-2 on aggregate to Costa do Sol of Mozambique, they were still in the hunt to retain their Madagascan title. The Malagasy league reached its denouement with a four-team, eleven- day round-robin playoff between SOE, AS Adema, US Ambohidratrimo and Domoina Soavina Atsimondrano.

SOE needed to win their penultimate match against DSA to have any chance of pipping Adema, who they faced in the final round of matches. But SOE were held to a 2-2 draw, the referee awarding DSA a controversial late penalty which was converted, denying SOE a chance of the title. So when SOE faced Adema, and an early decision went against them, their manager Ratsimandresy Ratsarazaka ordered his team to score some own goals in protest – which they did, 149 of them. Adema did not touch the ball for the rest of the game.

Ratsarazaka was suspended from football for three years, and banned from even attending the game during that time, while four of his players were suspended until the end of the season. Arbroath's famous 36-0 record was no longer intact – but at least Bon Accord were trying.

NOVEMBER

THE PROCURATOR-FISCAL CHARGES WOODS, ROBERTS AND MCAVENNIE
(1987)

'Old Firm' derby rumbles are ten-a-penny, but the on-pitch antics during the match between Rangers and Celtic at Ibrox on October 17, 1987 were so incendiary the Scottish courts got involved. Rangers had just won their first title in nine years, but had started off the new season as reigning champions badly. After twelve games they languished in fourth place, six points behind the leaders Hearts and – more importantly – four points behind Celtic. It was imperative they won when Celtic came to Ibrox, a fact betrayed by a particularly high-octane start, even by Old Firm standards.

After 16 minutes, Celtic striker Frank McAvennie clattered into Rangers goalkeeper Chris Woods. The two men went nose-to-nose, exchanging words and light slaps. Woods took McAvennie by the throat with his big glove, at which point his team mates Terry Butcher and Graham Roberts waded in. In the melee, Roberts crept up behind Woods and punched the Celtic player, but only Woods and McAvennie were sent off. Ibrox erupted as both sides became incensed and infused with a searing sense of injustice.

Almost as an afterthought, a match still had to be played out. It turned out to be breathless. Roberts went in goal and soon found himself picking the ball out of the net twice. Celtic's Peter Grant celebrated the second by crossing himself in front of the Rangers support. Ally McCoist pulled a goal back. Butcher, who had been booked for his part in the fracas, picked up a second yellow for lunging at Celtic keeper Allen McKnight. In the last minute, Richard Gough scrambled an equaliser. Before the final whistle, with the ball at his feet, Roberts conducted the crowd in the singing of sectarian chants. If any match deserved to be described as insane, this was it.

'This will have to go to the top of the house,' opined Scottish TV commentator Jock Brown on *Scotsport* the day after, displaying a clipped mastery of extreme understatement. And to the top of the house it did. Two weeks later, the Procurator Fiscal – Glasgow's public prosecutor – charged Woods, Roberts and McAvennie with 'behaviour likely to cause a breach of the peace'. Butcher's name was soon added to that list. 'It is certainly an unusual case,' explained a court spokesperson, 'but the case attracted a lot of adverse criticism.'

After an inquiry, which took up 218 hours of police time and 74 hours of the procurator fiscal's, McAvennie was found not guilty and Roberts not proven, while Butcher and Woods were found guilty and fined.

NOVEMBER 2

LIVINGSTON 5-0 DUMBARTON: JIM FALLON'S
HAPLESS REIGN ENDS
(1996)

Things were looking up for Dumbarton in the summer of 1995. Having just won promotion to the Scottish First Division thanks to a dramatic last-day victory over Stirling Albion, optimism was running high for the upcoming season. But then the manager who had guided them to promotion, Murdo MacLeod, was poached by Scottish Premier League side Partick Thistle. MacLeod soon came to regret his move; he took Partick down in his first season. That was nothing, however, compared to what was about to happen to his former club.

The 1995/96 season started well for Dumbarton. The managerless side won their first two games and stood joint top of the table. Then they appointed Jim Fallon one hour before their third league game of the season. That match was lost at home 4-0 – not quite the disaster it looks, considering it was against Dunfermline Athletic, who went on to win the title. But the result proved to be a harbinger of things to come as the team lost eleven of their next twelve matches. The one game they did win – 1-0 at home to Dundee United – was repaid with an 8-0 thrashing by the same team seven matches later. Strangely, that thrashing seemed to steady the ship, for all of two matches, both of which were drawn. Those would be the last points the club would gather all season. Dumbarton lost their last 19 games, ending the season having scored more points without a manager in two games (six points) than they did with Fallon during the subsequent 34 games (five).

Fallon – who had been given a new contract! – promised to regroup the following season. But a run of one win and eight losses from the first 12 games, culminating in a 5-0 shellacking by Livingston, saw him pick up his cards. Fallon's league record read: P46, W2, D5, L39. The minute Fallon left, Dumbarton won three of their next four games.

SPORTING LISBON 4-3 RANGERS: THE PHANTOM
PENALTY SHOOT-OUT
(1971)

The 1971/72 season was shaping up to be a hellish one for Rangers. The start to their domestic campaign had been a total shambles. Beaten twice by Celtic in the League Cup, Rangers lost five of their first six league games, only avoiding the shame of propping up the 18-team First Division by dint of having a better goal difference than East Fife. Their European campaign didn't start in much less humiliating fashion. Competing in the Cup Winners Cup, having been runners-up in the 1971 Scottish Cup final, Rangers were drawn with Rennes in the first round. After a tough-tacking display in France they were immediately accused of playing 'antifutbol' by Rennes manager Jean Prouff. Rangers scraped the home leg 1-0 at Ibrox and advanced to the next round.

Things looked up for the first 45 minutes of the second round against Sporting Lisbon. Rangers played their best football of the season to tear into a 3-0 half-time lead, but they were soon back into their old habits, letting the tie slip in the second half, the match ending 3-2. The return leg in Lisbon plunged Rangers into a blue funk. The team took nearly two days to arrive in Portugal due to an airport strike. With the scores 2-2 they let a 5-4 aggregate lead slip, allowing Sporting to force extra-time. Ronnie McKinnon broke his leg. Then, having gone into a 6-5 aggregate lead, they conceded another equaliser, six minutes from time. The match went to penalties, of which Rangers could only score one. Sporting's fans went wild. Rangers were out.

Or so everyone thought. Referee Laurens 'Lau' van Raavens had failed to apply the new away goals rule brought in that season. A *Sunday Mail* journalist watching from the stands came down to inform manager Willie Waddell, who in turn shook the referee's cage. Rangers were in fact through – and would go on to turn a shambolic season into one of the greatest in the club's history, reaching the final at the Camp Nou and beating Dynamo Moscow 3-2. Befitting a shambolic, rollercoaster season, captain John Greig lifted the cup in an ante-room after bottle-flinging Rangers fans went on the rampage. Plus ça change.

NOVEMBER 4

RACING CLUB 1-0 CELTIC: THE INTERCONTINENTAL CUP EXPLODES

(1967)

The Intercontinental Cup between the champions of Europe and South America had been becoming an increasingly fraught affair, ever since Milan and Santos crossed swords in 1963. When Argentina's Racing Club faced Celtic in 1967, it finally did what it had been threatening to do for a few seasons, and exploded.

In the first leg of the tie at Hampden on October 18, Jock Stein came onto the pitch to complain about the rough treatment meted out to Jimmy Johnstone. The complaint went unheeded by the referee. Celtic won 1-0, but the template had been set. The second leg on November 1 saw the Intercontinental Cup hit new heights of violence.

Before the game started in Buenos Aires, Celtic goalkeeper Ronnie Simpson was hit by a missile thrown from the crowd. He suffered a deep cut in his head and had to be replaced by John Fallon. Celtic took an early lead through a Tommy Gemmill penalty, after Johnstone was hacked down the box. While Johnstone continued to be kicked around the park like an empty beer can, Racing hit back with two goals to force a play-off. 'We don't want to play a third game,' said an angry Stein after the match, 'but we know we have to.'

The resulting match, three days later, was even more outrageous, being described by Reuters as: 'a bar-room brawl with soccer skills abandoned for swinging fists, flying boots and blatant body checking'. Johnstone was again hacked down and retaliated, causing a melee which resulted in Alfio Basile and Bobby Lennox being sent off. Johnstone was among four other players dismissed in the second half; John Hughes, Juan Carlos Rulli and Bertie Auld also walked – although Auld and Rulli refused to leave the field and amazingly were allowed to play on by a referee who had lost all control. Celtic, having had four men sent off, fined their players £250 each. The Racing players, who won the game 1-0, were all rewarded with a new car.

This tie effectively denied Jock Stein, who had led Celtic to the European Cup months earlier, a knighthood. 'His name was removed from the New Year's Honours list because of the unfortunate events in South America,' said a letter sent by the Scottish Office to Prime Minister Harold Wilson in 1970. 'The next year when Manchester United won the European Cup an immediate knighthood went to Matt Busby in the birthday list. Had we been able to move as quickly the previous year, Stein would have had his honour before the troubles in Argentina.'

NOVEMBER 5

OFF-PITCH INNOVATOR CHAPMAN RENAMES TUBE STATION
(1932)

Herbert Chapman's Arsenal were busy winning 7-1 against Wolverhampton Wanderers at Molineux, earning themselves another two crucial points to keep them top of the table, but on November 5, 1932 the more far-reaching action was going on at the underground train station situated next door to Highbury.

Ever since becoming Arsenal manager in 1925, Chapman had decided that Gillespie Road tube station would be better named after his new club. It was right next door to Highbury, and the station – on the otherwise busy Great Northern, Piccadilly and Brompton lines – was usually quiet, except on match days. He also privately reasoned that it would be a fantastic piece of marketing. The millions who used the tube every day would see Arsenal's name on the map.

With Arsenal having won the FA Cup in 1930 and the league in 1931, Chapman felt confident enough to raise the matter with the London Electric Railway in 1932. Despite the cost of reprinting maps and carriage posters, the LER agreed to Chapman's request, renaming the station Arsenal (Highbury Hill) in early November. The suffix – a sop to compromise by Chapman, as the LER had initially only offered to rename the station Highbury Hill – was dropped in 1960.

It was only one of many off-field innovations by Chapman. He was a prime mover in the introduction of numbered shirts. He erected a 45-minute clock at Highbury (and upon being told to take it down by the FA, simply replaced it with a standard one-hour timepiece, which would grace the Clock End until Highbury's demolition). He championed the use of floodlights for midweek fixtures – in those days they kicked off during working hours – and white footballs for increased visibility. And on the pitch? Chapman's greatest innovation was the use of a 'stopper' defender in his teams, whose sole purpose was to stay in the middle of the park and deal with long balls. Though according to some reports, the stopper was actually suggested to him by his captain, Charlie Buchan.

NOVEMBER 6

MANCHESTER UNITED REPLACE ATKINSON WITH FERGUSON
(1986)

At the start of November 1986, Ron Atkinson's Manchester United were ten points ahead of their nearest rivals Liverpool at the top of the First Division, enjoying the fruits of a run which had seen them win the first ten games of the season. Their campaign fell apart dismally, though. After going the first 15 games of the campaign unbeaten, United went on to lose 10 of the remaining 27. A hamstring injury to captain Bryan Robson was a major factor in their slump, but then so was the booze culture at the club which was to blame for a series of minor injuries which plagued the squad. Much to United's chagrin, their 19-year wait for a title was not ended and Liverpool won the double.

At the start of November 1987, Ron Atkinson's Manchester United were only out of the relegation places on goal difference. Crowds at Old Trafford were down – only 26,000 had watched United stammer to a dismal goalless draw in the League Cup against Southampton. In the replay on November 4, United were soundly beaten 4-1, an 18-year-old Matthew Le Tissier coming on to score Southampton's fourth. 'We can bounce back,' said Atkinson, but nobody was having it. United's dismal start cost him his job as he was sacked two mornings later.

Coming in later that day was Alex Ferguson, who had won three Scottish titles, four Scottish Cups, a Scottish League Cup and the European Cup Winners Cup with Aberdeen. Ferguson had been offered the Rangers job in 1983, then the Scotland post in the wake of Jock Stein's death and taking his country to the 1986 World Cup finals, but he had held out, saying he 'would like one really big job first, either in England or on the continent'. United gave him that chance. He opened his account with a 2-0 defeat at Oxford United.

Ferguson guided his new club to mid-table safety, then second place in 1987/88, his second full season. But his first big-money signings – Neil Webb, Mike Phelan, Jim Leighton, Danny Wallace – didn't work out. By January 1990, United were two points off the relegation zone, and the Old Trafford crowd unveiled a banner: 'Three years of excuses and it's still crap. Ta-ra Fergie'. With his job on the line, United travelled to Nottingham Forest for a third-round FA Cup tie they were expected to lose. Mark Robins scored the winner, and the rest is history.

EVERTON 0-1 LEEDS: THE BIRTH OF
THE 'DIRTY LEEDS' TAG?
(1964)

Don Revie's much-maligned Leeds United were capable of moments of exquisite beauty. Their 7-0 demolition of Southampton in 1972 culminated in a Billy Bremner-inspired 26-pass showboating sequence featuring four needlessly ostentatious backheels. Eddie Gray beat six challenges, two of them by the same men, to score a Maradonaesque ball-on-string effort against Burnley in 1970. But no amount of justifiable revisionism will ever change the perception of the side in the minds of most neutrals: they will forever be 'Dirty Leeds'.

Despite the raw talent on display, their decade-long dominance between 1965 and 1975 is chiefly remembered for their robust style of play, which first came to national attention three months after they gained promotion to the First Division. During a hot-headed match at Everton – one which became the first to be suspended for disciplinary reasons – the seeds of Dirty Leeds were sown.

After one minute, Fred Pickering was scythed down by Bremner. After four, Sandy Brown was sent off after reacting to a Johnny Giles studs-in-chest challenge. Brown had punched Giles in the stomach. The Everton crowd were incensed, more so when Leeds went one up through Willie Bell. When Bell and Derek Temple then knocked each other out challenging for a high ball on 36 minutes, and both teams squared up to each other, the crowd rained coins and cushions onto the pitch, forcing the referee to take the teams off the park for ten minutes to allow everyone to regain their composure. Fat chance. The remainder of the match was peppered with wild over-the-top challenges.

The nation was incensed. 'Leeds United must calm down; over-keen play will cost them friends and position,' advised a headline in the *Yorkshire Post*. It was not heeded, though neither was it 100% right. Leeds never won any popularity contests, but they did finish second in the league that year.

NOVEMBER 8

WERDER BREMEN 0-0 HANNOVER 69:
THE 32-MINUTE HALF
(1975)

In the wake of Graham Poll's infamous three-card trick in the 2006 World Cup, when the English official showed Croatia midfielder Josip Šimunić three yellows before issuing a red, a former FIFA referee rushed to offer some much-needed support to his beleaguered colleague. Wolf-Dieter Ahlenfelder, a retired Bundesliga official who took charge of several FIFA games during the mid-1980s, argued that mistakes were inevitable, as Poll and his ilk were being put under unreasonable pressure as a result of FIFA's diktats. 'The order has come down from on high to take out the yellow card if the players as much as blink,' wrote Ahlenfelder in the *Berliner Zeitung*. 'This World Cup has been over-refereed and first and foremost it is Blatter's fault.'

Sadly for the hapless Poll, the man going out to bat for him would have carried little weight in FIFA Towers. Ahlenfelder is primarily famous in his homeland for making the sort of hapless error which makes Poll look as equally reliable as Pierluigi Collina. In only his third game as a top-flight referee, Ahlenfelder blew up for half-time after only 32 minutes. He was only aware of his error after a linesman intervened – and even then, after adding what he assumed to be the remainder of the half, his whistle went 90 seconds too soon.

After the match – during which he also stuck his tongue out at a photographer – Ahlenfelder denied having been drunk, but did later admit to having 'a beer and a Maltese', the Maltese in question being Maltese Cross schnapps. 'We are men, we don't drink Fanta,' argued the chubby John Goodman look-a-like by way of defence. The DFB didn't swallow it, as it were, and punished Ahlenfelder with a small ban, perhaps bearing in mind his relative inexperience. He went on to referee for another 13 years. To this day, anyone in Bremen who orders an Ahlenfelder gets a beer and schnapps chaser. 'I'm proud of it,' says the man himself.

NOVEMBER 9

DUNDEE UNITED 5-0 ABERDEEN: WINDASS
SENT OFF THREE TIMES
(1997)

In 2006, on FIFA Fair Play Day, Bradford City striker Dean Windass marked the world governing body's officially designated jamboree of sportsmanship by grabbing Cheltenham Town's John Finnigan by the testicles. The victim, perhaps understandably, clumped his aggressor upside his head – and was sent off for his trouble. Fair play indeed.

It was apt that Windass celebrated the occasion in this manner, as he is infamous for being the only player in football to be sent off three times during a single match. This amazing feat was achieved during his spell at Aberdeen where, having picked up three red cards in his first season in Scottish football against Dundee, Dundee United and Motherwell, he went on to amass the same haul during the following season – in 22 minutes. He did this in a game at Dundee United. There must be something in the Tayside air which imbalances the cells in his head.

Having picked up a first-minute booking, another 21 minutes passed before Windass flew into another meaty challenge, picking up his second yellow card of the day. Referee Stuart Dougal sent him packing. But Windass didn't go quietly, choosing instead to launch into a robust one-sided debate over the matter with Dougal who, unimpressed, issued a straight red for foul and abusive language. Windass finally left the pitch in a raging stew, ripping a corner flag out of its moorings and tossing it to the floor. Dougal produced a third red.

In picking up three red cards, Windass had amassed a whopping total of 22 penalty points in one fell swoop, which equated to one point per minute played. He was suspended for seven weeks.

Aberdeen ended up losing the game 5-0, manager Roy Aitken getting the sack as a result. Windass's petulant performance could not be cited as a factor, however, as the Dons were 3-0 down after 21 minutes, a full 60 seconds before he departed.

TEAM BATH 0-2 CHASETOWN: 91-YEAR-OLD COACH SPOILS FOR FIGHT
(2007)

Team Bath had made the first round of the FA Cup for the first time in their history, and the Southern League Premier side had been rewarded for their achievement with a favourable draw at home to Chasetown, a division below them in the league pyramid. It was hoped that the touchline presence of their 91-year-old assistant coach and honorary president Ivor Powell – a former Welsh International and captain of Aston Villa – would spur them on to victory.

But Chasetown too had reached further in the competition than ever before, and were in no mood to take their eyes off the prize. In a pre-match oration described by one of the Chasetown players as 'Churchillian', manager Charlie Blakemore told his side that Team Bath were 'very very complacent' and there for the taking. 'Every challenge, smash! Get fucking in them! These lot don't know what's coming! They're fancy-danning it already. If I see any of you being nice and helping them up I'll bring yer off.' Which, while not quite up there with 'we will fight them on the beaches … if the British Empire and its Commonwealth last for a thousand years, men will still say this was their finest hour', is not far off it in sentiment.

The oratory seemed to do the job. Throughout the match Chasetown – who had travelled down to Bath with some 600 supporters for the game – were undoubtedly the better side. The most passion displayed by Team Bath came from Powell who, 15 minutes into the game, got so frustrated he threatened Chasetown coach Paul Jones with a raised fist. Team Bath's coach Andy Tilson had to step in and break them up. 'Ivor never got booked or sent off in his playing career but he always competed and spilled blood,' said Team Bath manager Ged Roddy. 'I think he might have been as frustrated as we were that we weren't going to war, and we needed to.'

Chasetown ran out easy winners. In the second round they forced Port Vale to a replay where they beat the league side 1-0. Away to Cardiff in the third, they were one minute from going in at half-time with a 1-0 lead over the Championship side but were pegged back. In the second half they were finally defeated 3-1 by a Cardiff side that went on to reach the final. Powell meanwhile ended the season by picking up an MBE for his services to the sport (football, not boxing).

NOVEMBER 11

FRANCE 2-2 SWITZERLAND: RAPPAN, INVENTOR OF 'THE BOLT', BOWS OUT
(1963)

Helenio Herrera and Internazionale made super-defensive football famous, or perhaps infamous, with their successful, stifling 'catenaccio' tactic of the 1960s. Catenaccio – literally 'the padlock' – won two European Cups for Inter, but while they (and later Italian football) would become synonymous with the style of play, it had its roots in 1930s Switzerland.

Karl Rappan was a not-particularly-distinguished forward for FK Austria Vienna and Rapid Vienna in the late 1920s, although he did win two caps for Austria. In 1931 he moved to Switzerland where he made his name as player-coach at Servette, before taking over the Swiss national side in 1937. At the time, the defensive WM formation – a tactic created by Herbert Chapman and Charlie Buchan at Arsenal in the 1920s which introduced an extra stopping defender – was sweeping the continent. Rappan took it on a notch, and created 'verrou' – 'the Bolt', or 'the Swiss Bolt' – which added a fourth defender and saw the team dropping deep, letting opponents have the run of the midfield but allowing them no space near goal.

The Bolt quickly worked wonders. At the start of the 1930s Switzerland were regularly shipping five or six goals, sometimes seven or eight, but that soon changed. They lost 4-0 at home to England in 1933. Five years later, just before the 1938 World Cup, they beat England 2-1. Then in the World Cup, the Swiss saw off a Nazi Germany side containing several Austrians.

Sometimes the Bolt would shear off – Austria famously beat Switzerland 7-5 in the 1954 World Cup – but Rappan didn't have a great talent pool to dip into. Under his auspices the Swiss competed in three World Cup finals: 1938, 1954 (as hosts, making the quarter-finals) and 1962. After an international career spanning four decades, Rappan bowed out in 1963 to lead Lausanne-Sports to two Swiss titles. It was left to Herrera to keep the Bolt's flame alive on the big stage.

NOVEMBER 12

ROY EVANS LEAVES LIVERPOOL –
THE END OF THE BOOT ROOM
(1997)

The legendary 'Boot Room' at Anfield, the control centre of Liverpool's domestic dominance through the 1960s, 70s and 80s, grew out of Bill Shankly's reign – but it had little to do with the man himself. Bob Paisley and Joe Fagan set up the tradition, along with fellow coaches Ronnie Moran and Reuben Bennett. 'It was somewhere we could talk and air our views,' explained Paisley of the fusty cubbyhole just up the corridor from the dressing rooms, 'and on match days a place to have a drink with visiting managers and backroom staff.' Guinness, brown ale and cheap scotch were served as tactics were discussed. Shankly would rarely pop in, preferring to let his subordinates brew their own ideas about the game.

The Boot Room served Liverpool well, though its dynasty would only stretch as far as two generations – Paisley then Fagan – before the Liverpool board looked further afield (albeit only as far as the pitch) and appointed Kenny Dalglish as player-manager in 1985. When Dalglish left six years later to be replaced by Rangers manager Graeme Souness, the days of the Boot Room were numbered metaphorically (its hand-me-down philosophy of slow but constant change was ditched by Souness in favour of immediate root-and-branch restructuring) and also physically, the room being demolished in 1993 when the Main Stand was renovated.

Souness's failure saw an attempt by the club to return to Boot Room values. Coach Roy Evans, who had been schooled in the tradition since the late 1960s, when Shankly decided he didn't quite cut it as a top-level full back, was installed as manager, and so nearly brought league success back to Anfield in a last hurrah. Evans's mid-90s side starring Robbie Fowler, Steve McManaman and Stan Collymore are remembered for their 'Spice Boys' decadence and ultimate failure, but few teams in the modern era could play as attractively. Too inconsistent, when it came to the crunch Liverpool were usually found wanting. The club brought in Gérard Houllier, fresh from winning the 1998 World Cup with France as technical director, as joint manager. The experiment was destined to fail. After a stuttering start to their 1997/98 campaign and a mind-numbing League Cup defeat by Spurs at Anfield, Evans decided enough was enough and quit, leaving Houllier in sole charge and closing the door on the Boot Room for the final time.

NOVEMBER 13

AUSTRIA 0-2 YUGOSLAVIA: YUGOSLAVS
QUALIFY FOR EURO '92 – FOR NOW
(1991)

The qualifiers for the 1992 European championships were shaped by political events from the start. In 1990, East Germany withdrew after the fall of the Berlin Wall, having been drawn in the same group as West Germany. After reunification, a united Germany side made up of players from both east and west entered their first major competition since 1934.

The USSR also qualified for the tournament, shortly before the break up of the Soviet Union. Russia decided to play under the banner CIS – the Commonwealth of Independent States – which excluded players from Estonia, Lativa and Lithuania, who had already formed separate national teams. After losing their last match of the finals 3-0 to Scotland, the 12 other state federations of the CIS decided it may be best to follow the independent model.

The biggest upheaval however regarded Yugoslavia, a republic which was also on the brink of collapse. They had finished first in Group Four, a point ahead of Denmark, and were one of the tournament favourites. Darko Pančev had been top scorer in the qualifiers with ten goals. But two weeks before Euro '92 began in Sweden, UEFA disqualified Yugoslavia after United Nations sanctions were placed on the Balkan states when civil war broke out.

The Danes were shocked and delighted to find themselves suddenly called back into the tournament – although they were not all sunning themselves on beaches at the time as the apocryphal tale tells it, but preparing for a friendly with the aforementioned CIS. The team started the tournament slowly, drawing with England and losing to hosts Sweden, but soon picked up their form, beating Michel Platini's France to reach the semi-finals, where they put out reigning champions Holland on penalties. The unlikeliest major championship win yet was achieved in the final, where the newly unified Germany – the world champions – were dispatched 2-0. But for once the story was personal rather than political. The second goal was scored, in a rush of emotion, by Kim Vilfort. Vilfort had spent the majority of the tournament at the bedside of his seven-year-old daughter who was dying of leukaemia.

ENGLAND 3-2 ITALY: THE BATTLE OF HIGHBURY
(1934)

When England met Italy in 1934, the stage was set for a fierce battle. Both teams considered themselves the best in the world, and Italy had just taken their chance to prove it by winning the 1934 World Cup. England, who had not deigned to enter the world championship, had never been beaten on home soil, despite losses in Czechoslovakia and Hungary that summer.

Italy's dictator Benito Mussolini was convinced his countrymen could lay waste England's proud record, so much so that he offered each player £150 and an Alfa Romeo car if they won. Italy's coach Vittorio Pozzo was not so sure, especially if they had to play during the English winter. The teams had first met in May 1933 at the Stadio Nazionale del Partito Nazionale Fascista in Rome, when the game ended in a 1-1, Arsenal's Cliff Bastin equalising an early Giovanni Ferrari goal. This time, the venue was to be a muddy ground in Highbury.

Bastin was selected for England again, along with six other Arsenal players including Wilf Copping, who according to newspaper reports had the foreigners running scared. 'Possibly the Italians were bewildered at the beginning of the struggle,' reported the *Guardian's* correspondent. 'They may have been nervous. They may have had a slight attack of football fright.' If they did, it was with good reason. Within minutes of kick off, Italian defender Luis Monti had his ankle broken by a nasty challenge from Ted Drake. By the 12th minute England had taken a 3-0 lead against the ten men with two goals for Eric Brook and one for Drake.

Italy fought back well, Giuseppe Meazza scoring two goals in four second half minutes and nearly completing a hat-trick only to be denied by the crossbar. And they had fought back literally. 'The Italians were very excitable,' reported the referee after the match. When the final whistle blew, injuries outnumbered the goals: English captain Eddie Hapgood suffered a broken nose, Ray Bowden could barely walk with an injured ankle, Drake had his legs 'shred to ribbons', Brook needed an x-ray on his arm, and Jack Barker had a strapped hand. All but Monti, however, made it to the team dinner.

Back home the Italians reported the game as a success, the team a 'platoon of gladiators'. In England, the FA were in less celebratory mood and considered banning all international matches.

NOVEMBER 15

SPARTA ROTTERDAM 1-1 FEYENOORD:
TREYTEL KILLS SEAGULL
(1970)

1970 was the greatest, yet most surreal, year in the history of Feyenoord. On May 6 they became the first Dutch club to win the European Cup, coming from behind to beat Celtic 2-1 in the San Siro final. Jock Stein's side had been hot favourites to win their second European Cup, and had taken the lead on 28 minutes through Tommy Gemmill, but Feyenoord captain Rinus Israel headed his side level three minutes later. The game went into extra-time and looked destined for a replay when, with three minutes to go, Coen Moulijn beat Billy McNeill to a long ball and scored the winner, lifting the ball gently past the keeper. More than 200,000 fans lined the streets of Rotterdam on Feyenoord's return.

Feyenoord were deposed as champions of Europe within five months. They went out on away goals in the first round of the following season's tournament against Romanian minnows UT Arad at the end of September, but by then they had become world club champions, beating Estudiantes in a spectacle-trampling orgy of 'antifutbol' (see July 22 entry).

But the year had yet to take its strangest turn. In November, during a derby against Sparta Rotterdam, Feyenoord keeper Eddy Treytel launched a goal kick and hit a seagull, killing it instantly. The dead bird was thrown behind the goal. After the game, Treytel took it home and had it stuffed. It now resides in the club's museum. In a comically petty postscript, Sparta have not let the matter lie, since claiming the bird is their property, as it was shot down over their stadium, then suggesting the museum piece is not the gull Treytel shot down in any case. Biologists are bickering over the matter to this day.

CHINA 4-0 NORWAY: THE FIRST WOMEN'S
WORLD CUP BEGINS
(1991)

The famous Dick, Kerr Ladies team did their best to keep their sport going after the small-minded mandarins of the Football Association effectively banned women's football in 1921. Playing representative friendlies against teams from France, Canada and the United States, they at one point styled themselves as 'The World's Champions 1917 – 1923'. Then in 1937 they played as Preston Ladies and beat Edinburgh Ladies 5-1 to win the Championship of Great Britain and the World. There would not be an official women's world champion team for another 54 years.

In the interim, there were several unofficial championships. The first notable attempt was the Coppa del Mondo, held in Italy in 1970 and won by Denmark, who beat the home side 2-0 in the final. England lost in the semi-finals, but did at least have the satisfaction of beating Germany along the way, something their male counterparts had been unable to do in their World Cup a month earlier in Mexico. Denmark repeated their trick of beating the hosts in the final a year later at the 1971 Mundial in Mexico.

It was at this point that the women's game started to pick up some serious momentum. While the FA finally lifted their draconian ban in 1971, part-time professional leagues were popping up around the world, most notably in Italy, the United States and Japan. FIFA tested the water with an Invitational Tournament in 1988, which Norway won, and launched the Women's World Cup in 1991.

The first World Cup goal was scored by Ma Li after 22 minutes of China's opening game against Norway. Norway, despite being stoved 4-0, went on to reach the final, losing to hosts USA, their striker Michelle Akers-Stahl becoming the first world star in the women's game (with the possible exception of Dick, Kerr's hotshot Lily Parr).

It is something of a shame that probably the most well-known image of FIFA Women's World Cups after five tournaments is that of USA defender Brandi Chastain, who took off her top to reveal a sports bra after scoring the winning penalty in her side's 1999 final shootout against China. Then again, the boys are still in control of the sports pages.

FRANCE 1-2 BULGARIA: GINOLA THE
EXOCET-FIRING MURDERER
(1993)

The final night of the 1994 World Cup qualifiers was an embarrassing one for two of Europe's giants. In Bologna, Graham Taylor's hapless England side were facing San Marino, hoping that Holland failed to win their last match in Poland and requiring a win themselves by a seven-goal margin to qualify. Their cause wasn't helped when, eight touches and nine seconds from the kick-off, England found themselves one down, Stuart Pearce's feathered backpass to David Seaman allowing Davide Gualtieri in to toe-poke home. 'And they've just kicked off,' commentated Jonathan Pearce on a London-based commercial radio station, 'and welcome to Bologna on Capital Gold for England versus San Marino with Tennent's Pilsner, brewed with Czechoslovakian yeast for that extra Pilsner taste and England are one down!' Nazi salutes apart, it was the most shameful moment in the national team's history. England scored seven, but Holland won 3-1 in Poznan and the jig was up.

Still, at least England weren't expected to qualify that day. Unlike France, who over in Paris were making England's implosion look like small beer. A month earlier, France could have ensured qualification with a win at home against a dreadful Israel side which had drawn two and lost five of its previous seven qualifiers. Leading 2-1 with seven minutes to go, France shipped two goals to lose 3-2. That still meant a draw at home to Bulgaria in the final game would see them through at their opponents' expense.

It was not to be. Eric Cantona had given France the lead, but Emil Kostadinov quickly levelled for Bulgaria. The French held out until 44 minutes and 40 seconds of the second half had elapsed. At which point, with France holding the ball by the corner flag near the Bulgarian box, David Ginola delivered a raking deep cross which aimlessly flew into space on Bulgaria's right wing. They swept up the pitch and 18 seconds later Kostadinov had roofed an effort into the right corner. Bulgaria were going to USA '94 and France were not. Facing the end of his reign, France manager Gérard Houllier accused Ginola of being 'the murderer' of French hopes: 'He sent an Exocet missile through the heart of French football and committed a crime against the team.' 'I am not a criminal,' responded Ginola. 'I have never stolen anything, I have never killed anyone. Everybody makes mistakes and people should be honourable enough to forgive them.'

The rift never healed. Bulgaria reached the semi-finals of the 1994 World Cup.

NOVEMBER 18

ENGLAND'S LAWTON JOINS THIRD-DIVISION NOTTS COUNTY
(1947)

Tommy Lawton had made an instant impact as a 16-year-old at Burnley, scoring within a minute of his debut against Tottenham and completing his hat-trick by half-time. It wasn't long before the big clubs were after him. By the end of the year Everton had signed him with a view to replacing Dixie Dean who, at 30, was nearing the end of his career. Dean acted as Lawton's mentor, and to good effect. By the time Lawton was 20 he had replaced the legendary Dean in the team, twice been the leading scorer in the First Division and had helped Everton to the 1938/39 league title.

During that season Lawton, whose main asset was his power in the air, scored 34 goals in 38 games and won his first cap for England, scoring on his debut. The only down side was getting his nose broken twice, both times by Arsenal's notorious midfield enforcer Wilf Copping, who had taken umbrage at the striker 'jumping too high'. Lawton was on the top of his game – but then came World War II.

After the league restarted in 1946, Everton suffered a poor season and Lawton was transferred to Chelsea. A good chunk of Lawton's career had been lost to the war, and he went on to lay waste to much of its remainder with some headstrong decisions. He quickly fell out with his manager at Chelsea, Billy Birrell, and still only 28 was sensationally transferred to Notts County – of the Third Division. On Boxing Day 1947, just over a month after he joined, County drew a huge 46,000 crowd for one of their matches.

Lawton went on a remarkable scoring run for England, scoring 22 goals in 23 games, but was dropped by coach Walter Winterbottom after a couple of poor performances. Late in his life however, Lawton maintained that his England career was ended simply because of a falling out with coach Walter Winterbottom, a chalkboard guru he referred to as 'that PT teacher'. 'Are you trying to tell me you're going to tell Neil Franklin how to play centre-half?' he claimed to have asked Winterbottom one day. 'And, God Forbid, Stanley Matthews how to play outside right? And me, you're going to tell me how to score goals?' Lawton's last England cap was awarded in 1948, while he was still only 29.

NOVEMBER 19

BOLTON 3-0 MANCHESTER CITY: TRAUTMANN'S FIRST GAME IN ENGLAND
(1949)

In October 1949 Manchester City made one of their most important signings of all time. German former prisoner of war Bert Trautmann was being lined up to replace the legendary Frank Swift in goal, and in time – but not without difficulty – would become one of the club's best-loved players.

As a soldier, Trautmann had been an escapee extraordinaire. He'd fled from the Russians, the French and the Americans, but when he fell into the hands of the British – literally, after diving over a hedge to escape the Americans – he ended up at a POW camp near St Helens in Lancashire. After the war, Trautmann, who had played football for the camp, joined St Helens as their goalkeeper, where he was spotted and snapped up by City.

Initially fans were unhappy the club had signed a German and protested against the decision, though Jewish leaders in Manchester were at pains to offer public support to Trautmann. He soon needed it after a shaky start, letting in three on his debut and, two weeks later, seven at Derby. But at Fulham in January, amid initial local protests over his presence, he eventually earned a standing ovation with a 'superlative' display in a 1-0 defeat. 'Even hardened pressmen could scarcely forbear to cheer,' cooed the *Manchester Guardian*.

He had secured his place in City affections, and did so again on a national scale in the 1956 FA Cup final against Birmingham. Trautmann had just been named Player of the Year and played the game of his life. Three minutes in, Don Revie put City 1-0 up. Birmingham soon equalised, but midway through the second half City scored two in five minutes; at 3-1 up they just needed to hang on.

Suddenly a chance fell to Birmingham's Peter Murphy. Trautmann smothered the shot but in diving at the ball collided with Murphy and fractured a bone in his neck. Unaware of the severity of his injury, and cradling his head in his hands, he fought on until the final whistle, somehow making two crucial saves. 'I couldn't see any of the players,' he later said. 'I know now that I made one or two more good saves but it must have been my subconscious taking over. Everything was a blur of black and white.' Triumph quickly turned to tragedy, however. Just three weeks after the cup final, Trautmann's six-year-old son was killed in a car accident.

GARFORTH TOWN 2-2 TADCASTER ALBION: SÓCRATES PLAYS FOR GARFORTH

(2004)

As far as qualifications go, former Brazil captain Sócrates had plenty. After playing languidly in midfield for Botafogo and Corinthians for the best part of a decade, he also scored 25 goals for Brazil in 63 appearances, playing with distinction in the 1982 and 1986 World Cups, and enjoyed a stint in Italy with Fiorentina. When he wasn't on the pitch, he found time to set up a pro-democracy political movement to protest against the military junta in Brazil; qualify as a doctor of medicine and philosophy; chain smoke; drink beer and maintain a beard. However, his most bizarre career move came when he joined Garforth Town of the Northern Counties East League First Division.

Garforth's manager Simon Clifford had been looking for some Brazilian blood to inject into the Yorkshire side, and when it transpired the 50-year-old doctor was game, Clifford invited him over. 'I put out a few feelers and Sócrates said he would be interested,' explained Clifford. 'He's a pretty principled guy and isn't interested in the money – which is just as well because we're not paying him. I'm told he's still in good shape, although he's still smoking. I'm pretty strict on discipline and smoking but I guess I can make an exception for him.'

A record crowd of 1,385 turned up to watch Garforth take on Tadcaster Albion, and were made to wait for the 78th minute to see the man in action, when he took off his tracksuit, three tops, and his coat, hat and gloves in order to amble onto the pitch (replacing Matt Higginbottom). After testing the goalkeeper with a 20-yard shot towards the end, Sócrates walked off at full-time and told the press, 'It was far too cold. The second I got out I had this incredible headache, I'm just not used to it. It was much faster than what I am used to. In Brazil games just aren't that fast.' It was Sócrates's first and last game for the club. He has since taken up chess.

NOVEMBER 21

CHILE VS USSR: USSR BOW OUT OF WORLD CUP
IN PINOCHET PROTEST
(1973)

In 1962 Chile reached the semi-finals of the World Cup they were hosting. It was their greatest-ever footballing achievement. They finished the tournament third, with a 1-0 play-off win over Yugoslavia. The achievement was all the more remarkable given the country was in turmoil after a series of devastating earthquakes. An anthem commemorating the feat, 'El Mundial de Sesenta y Dos' (The World Cup of '62), is still played regularly on Chilean national radio to this day.

In 1973, after beating Peru to top spot in their CONMEBOL qualifying group, Chile were in striking distance for a place at the 1974 World Cup in West Germany. They just had to beat the USSR in a two-legged play-off. The games were scheduled for September 26 in Moscow and November 21 in Santiago.

But on September 11, Chile's socialist leader Salvador Allende shot himself in the head while a coup d'etat led by General Augusto Pinochet was taking place. Pinochet set about destroying his opponents and Santiago's Estadio Nacional, where Chile had hosted the 1962 World Cup final, was used as a detainment and torture centre for refugees and challengers of his regime. The official death toll is 41 people but witnesses put the number much higher. Reports claim people starved to death in the changing rooms while bodies were left to rot. This, of course, was hidden from view when FIFA and the international press were allowed to visit in October.

On September 26, Russia and Chile drew the first leg of their tie in Moscow 0-0. However the USSR refused to play the return leg in Santiago in the wake of Pinochet's coup. FIFA, who had found the stadium fit for play, refused their request to a change of venue. On November 21, Chile turned up to a virtually empty ground and their captain put the ball in an empty net. Their opponents did not show up. Chile were awarded a walkover.

It was a short-lived victory. In West Germany, Chile drew with East Germany and Australia but were knocked out in the group stages – and returned to a country in the grip of a dictator.

ALI DIA GIVEN INTERNATIONAL CLEARANCE
TO BECOME A SAINT
(1996)

When Ali Dia showed up at Southampton in the middle of November 1996, nobody at the Dell had a clue who he was. Even the man who had signed him, Graeme Souness, had never seen him play. Souness had taken a gamble on who he had presumed was a Senegalese international on advice supposedly given by AC Milan and Liberia striker George Weah, apparently the player's cousin. But it wouldn't take long before everyone knew Ali Dia's name: 58 minutes to be precise.

Having been thrashed at Everton 7-1 the week before, Southampton were only three points off the relegation places and suffering a crisis of confidence. It was hard to work out exactly what was wrong, given that the strugglers had managed to embarrass reigning double champions Manchester United 6-3 less than a month earlier. Souness decided it was time to throw his curveball. Saints were about to play at home against Leeds, who were going through a sticky patch themselves, so he rushed through Ali Dia's paperwork with the FA. He would start on the bench.

After 32 minutes, the new boy got his chance. The club's best ever player, the legendary Matthew Le Tissier, came off with a bad thigh injury and was replaced by the worst the club will ever see. Ali Dia was so bad, his touch so lumpen, his positioning so inept, that Souness hauled him off in a fit of pique with five minutes to go. 'He ran round the pitch like Bambi on ice,' said Le Tissier. 'It was very embarrassing to watch.' After Dia's 58-minute cameo, Southampton had lost 2-0, George Graham enjoying his first win as Leeds manager.

An angry Souness gave one of his briefest post-match press conferences ever. With speculation mounting that, due to injuries, Dia might have to play at Oxford United in the League Cup in three days time, Souness grimaced: 'I sent him on today having never seen him play Premiership football. But I do not have any strikers. Am I enjoying this? Do you enjoy a kick in the balls?'

The story reached a grim end for Souness when it became clear George Weah didn't have a clue who Ali Dia was either. He had never played for Senegal and was certainly not his cousin. Souness had been duped. It turned out an anonymous caller had contacted the club and had been rather creative with Dia's CV. Dia turned up for treatment the morning after the match, and was told his contract was cancelled with immediate effect. He wound up at Gateshead where he scored two goals before being released.

BARCELONA 2-1 REAL MADRID: MADRID FINALLY KNOCKED OUT OF EUROPE
(1960)

Upon the inauguration of the European Cup in 1955, Real Madrid embarked on an incredible run of success. By the end of the 1960 tournament, they had won every single European Cup and never failed to win a European fixture at the Bernabéu. If one club wanted to end their reign more than anyone, it was eternal rivals Barcelona.

In the second round of the 1960/61 European Cup, the two teams were paired. Barcelona had just won their second *La Liga* title in a row under Helenio Herrera (though they had since parted company with the Argentinian manager). Madrid meanwhile had recently delivered their signature performance, thrashing Eintract Frankfurt 7-3 in the 1960 European Cup final. It would prove to be a controversial battle.

Both legs were refereed by Englishmen and on both occasions Real blamed the officials. For years, Barça had felt Real had benefited against them from official bias. The most notable occasion was during an 11-1 loss in 1943 when Franco's goons intimidated them before the match. This time, the decisions went against the European champions. In the first leg at the Bernabéu, Real were 2-1 up with three minutes to play when referee Arthur Ellis ignored a linesman flagging Sándor Kocsis offside, waved play on, then blew for a penalty when the Hungarian was fouled. Barcelona equalised and for the first time in the tournament's history, a team left Real's stadium unbeaten.

In the second leg, referee Reg Leafe disallowed four goals, three of them by Real. 'Leafe was Barcelona's best player,' said Real president Santiago Bernabéu after the match, a fact borne out by footage which offers little supporting evidence in the way of foul play. Real were out. Alfredo di Stéfano muttered darkly of a UEFA conspiracy, suggesting the ruling body were fed up with Real's domination of 'their cup'.

But Real would have the last laugh, beating Barcelona 5-3 in the Camp Nou two weeks later on their way to regaining the *La Liga* title. They then won five leagues in a row, a run which culminated in their sixth European Cup victory in 1966. Barcelona reached the 1961 final, only to lose to Benfica. They had to wait another 31 years to pick up their first European Cup.

NOVEMBER 24

BIRTH OF CHARLES MILLER, WHO BROUGHT FOOTBALL TO BRAZIL
(1874)

In downtown São Paulo there is a square called 'Praca Charles Miller', named after the man who brought football to Brazil. Charles Miller was born in 1874 into a wealthy Anglo-Brazilian family; his father had left Glasgow to work in the South American coffee industry. Charles, however, was packed off to a Southampton boarding school, where he spent his teenage years.

Miller quickly became proficient at both cricket and football, playing centre forward for the school team. Nicknamed 'Nipper', his goalscoring and dribbling skills brought him to the attention of some of the era's top teams. He was asked to play for St Mary's (who would later become Southampton) and once was invited to turn out for the Corinthians, who had turned up to play a fixture against a representative Hampshire side but were a man short. St Mary's hoped to keep hold of Miller, but in 1894 he returned to Brazil.

Miller had taken with him a couple of balls and the FA rulebook, and arrived in Brazil with a determination to win over the cricket-obsessed ex-patriots in the country. Soon enough he had drummed up enough interested men to stage the first game of football under 'Association Rules' and formed a football division of the São Paulo Athletic Club (SPAC), which had been set up in 1888 for Brits to play cricket. In April 1895 he arranged the first recorded match in Brazil, between men from the Railway and the Gas companies. The railwaymen won 4-2.

In December 1901, Charles helped form *La Liga Paulista de Football* along with four other clubs. The first three seasons saw his SPAC win the title. By now the word was spreading and within two years both Botafogo and Fluminese had been founded. Charles's interest in football faded in time – although he would still referee a Brazilian championship decider as late as 1949 – but his legacy remains. As well as a square, Charles even has a move named after him – the showboating backheeled cross known as the 'Chaleira'.

ENGLAND 3-6 HUNGARY: 'AGINCOURT IN REVERSE'
(1953)

The Aranycsapat – the Hungarian 'Golden Team' of Ferenc Puskás, Zoltán Czibor, Sándor Kocsis, Nándor Hidegkuti and József Bozsik – came to England in November 1953 as reigning Olympic champions and with a fearsome unbeaten record. But they were nervous. They had played poorly in a 2-2 draw against Sweden ten days before the match and according to defender Jenö Buzánszky, regarded Wembley as a 'holy place'. This would be the acid test.

England were still bruised after their 1950 World Cup performance, and not on best form. A month earlier they had been fortunate to preserve their long-standing unbeaten home record against foreign teams, a late penalty securing a 4-4 draw with a Rest of Europe side. Nevertheless, there was confidence. As the players walked out, captain Billy Wright turned to Stan Mortensen and, pointing at their lightweight boots, opined that England would be 'alright' because Hungary 'haven't even got proper kit'. Malcolm Allison remembers another overheard comment made from the stands, when Puskás came onto the field: 'Look at that little fat chap! We'll murder this lot!'

Oh dear. Within a minute the deep-lying Hidegkuti romped down the inside-right channel and thumped a shot past Gil Merrick in the England goal. Jackie Sewell equalised but Hidegkuti soon restored the lead, slamming the ball high into the net from 12 yards as six England players flailed around helplessly. Then came the game's signature moment. On the right-hand edge of the six-yard area, Puskás took delivery of the ball. Seeing that Wright was coming in to tackle from the side, Puskás pulled the ball back with his heel and hammered it home for Hungary's third, sending Wright sliding off the field, in the memorable words of *The Times* correspondent Geoffrey Green, 'like a fire engine heading to the wrong fire'. Puskás scored again before Mortensen pulled one back to make it 2-4 at half-time. In the second half, Bozsik added another and Hidegkuti completed his hat-trick. Alf Ramsey scored a consolation penalty.

'For two months the celebrations continued,' remembered Puskás. 'I tasted my country's wine in every city and village that I visited, and ate so much I really hate to think about it.' Meanwhile in England the post-mortem was being carried out. 'England were cut to ribbons,' announced *The Times* in a report headed 'The new conception of football'. 'It was Agincourt in reverse. English football can be proud of its past, but it must awake to a new future.' In May 1954, England travelled to Budapest having made no tactical tweaks whatsoever. They lost 7-1.

NOVEMBER 26

HEARTS MARCH TO WAR
(1914)

Heart of Midlothian were looking forward to the 1914/15 season. The previous campaign had seen them finish third in the league, setting a new club record of 54 points. With a philosophy of all-out attack, the team was tipped to win the title for the first time since 1897. Hearts began well, beating champions Celtic 2-0 in the opening match, and followed up the result with another seven successive victories.

But Britain had recently entered the Great War. Hearts immediately lost the services of two army reservists, George Sinclair and Neil Moreland. Then inside left Jimmy Speedie, influential in the opening day defeat of Celtic, decided to volunteer. Hearts kept going. After 16 games the team, built around the promising 21-year-old striker Henry Wattie, had lost only once and topped the table – but with tens of thousands dying in combat, the public mood was turning against footballers. 'When will the football players come?' read one poster.

Thirteen of them soon did, as Hearts marched en masse to the recruitment office and volunteered to fight. The club now had sixteen men in service, and club minutes record that 'the lead established by these gallant youths reverberated through the length of the land'. Within two weeks a record number of 600 fans followed the Hearts team to battle. Many died alongside their footballing heroes.

Back on the pitch, Hearts led the league for 35 out of 37 weeks, but the war took its toll and the club eventually faltered, finishing four points behind Celtic. It seemed unimportant. By the end of the war, seven Hearts players, including Speedie and Wattie, had been killed. And it wasn't until 1958 that the club would win the league again.

CALAIS RACING UNION FC 1-0 BÉTHUNE
(1999)

The Coupe de France gets serious in round seven. The regional rounds are over and most of the professional clubs are getting involved, so few paid much attention to Calais's win over Bethune when it happened. But Calais, from the non-league Championnat de France Amateur, France's fourth tier, were embarking on a cup campaign that would make them national heroes.

A 4-0 win over Dunkerque in the next round raised scarcely any more eyebrows. But then they beat a professional side, five-times Coupe de France champions Lille (slumming it in Ligue 2 at the time). A kind draw saw Calais ease past Langon-Castets-en-Dorthe – of the fifth tier! – to reach the last 16, where Ligue 2 Cannes were dispatched on penalties.

Calais – from the northern port well-known to British day-trippers – were suddenly in the quarter-finals, and now the country was paying attention. Drawn against top-flight Strasbourg, Calais went a goal behind after six minutes but amazingly turned it round by half-time and held on to win 2-1. 'It was a complete joke,' moaned Strabourg manager Claude le Roy. 'This defies the logic of football.'

They were in the semi-finals. No non-league side had ever reached the cup final, and that fact looked unlikely to be changed as the draw paired them with reigning league champions Bordeaux. Early editions of newspapers reported a Bordeaux win with the match yet to be completed, but Calais made fools of the French fourth estate with a 3-1 extra-time win.

The story of the final became a tragic fairytale. Jérôme Dutitre gave Calais an unthinkable 1-0 half-time lead against Nantes, only for Antoine Sibierski, later of Manchester City and Newcastle, to score twice in the second half – the winner a last-minute penalty.

Calais captain Reginald Becque lifted the trophy alongside Mickaël Landreau of Nantes, but looked none too happy doing so. Calais reached the quarter-finals in 2006, but the run, while still amazing, would never catch the public imagination in the same way. No non-league club has contested the FA Cup final since 1902, when Southampton lost to Sheffield United.

NOVEMBER 28

ROSS COUNTY 8-1 NAIRN COUNTY:
THE WORLD'S FASTEST HAT-TRICK
(1964)

When Bournemouth striker James Hayter scored three goals in two minutes and 20 seconds against Wrexham in February 2004, the hat-trick was reported as the fastest in the history of British football. Hayter could have been forgiven for thinking his achievement would be recognised for years, but it barely remained in the records for two months. The publicity surrounding Hayter's hat-trick energised former Ross County striker Tommy Ross, who scored three in 90 seconds during an 8-1 victory over Nairn County in the Highland League in 1964. Ross scored seven of County's goals in the match. At the time Ross assumed his claim to any record would be invalid. Only the referee had been keeping an eye on the watch that day, and it was believed a match had to have two timekeepers in attendance for the data to be considered official. As became clear in the wake of Hayter's treble, that wasn't the case.

A retrospective claim to the *Guinness Book of Records* was lodged and verified, and in April 2004 Ross's hat-trick officially replaced Hayter's British record. It also replaced both the official and unofficial world records (respectively James O'Connor's 2min 14sec hat-trick for Shelbourne against Bohemians in 1967 and Magnus Arvidsson's 1min 35sec effort for Hassleholm against Landskrona in 1995). It's a record unlikely to be superseded. 'When you scored in those days,' explains Ross, 'you just ran back to the halfway line and got on with it. The celebrations now take at least a minute and a half.'

Amazingly, November 28 of 1964 wasn't the only time that date went down in hat-trick history. On the very same day 35 years later, José Luis Chilavert became the first goalkeeper to score three goals in a game, converting three penalties for Vélez Sarsfield against Ferro Carril Oeste in a 1999 Argentinian league match.

JIMMY HILL, SOCCER PIONEER, TAKES
OVER AT COVENTRY CITY
(1961)

Third Division Coventry City's first-round FA Cup defeat at home to King's Lynn in 1961 was immediately christened the club's 'Black Saturday'. The *Coventry Evening Telegraph* described their performance in a 2-1 defeat – the only goal they managed against the non-league side being a comedy shank into his own net by a King's Lynn centre-half – as 'puny and deplorably inept'. Black Saturday did for manager Billy Frith, who was replaced by former Fulham striker and the man who saw off the minimum wage, ex-PFA chairman Jimmy Hill.

'A fresh approach is vital in the new and challenging times which now confront soccer,' explained Robins as he unveiled Hill, who did not disappoint on the field nor off it, where Coventry became the most innovative club in the country. Hill's ideas were legion. The home kit was changed to all-blue, City becoming the first team in the land to wear matching shirts and shorts. He coined the club nickname Sky Blues, and 'over a glass of gin and tonic' wrote the lyrics to the club anthem, the Sky Blue Song ('Let's all sing together / Play up Sky Blues'). The 'Sky Blue Express' ferried fans to away matches, keeping them entertained en route with live music, while the match programme became a fully-fledged magazine. The usual perfunctory PA announcements were jettisoned in favour of Radio Sky Blue, a pre-match show which kept crowds entertained and up to date with the latest news. Highfield Road became the first ground to have an electronic scoreboard, to relay closed-circuit pictures of away fixtures, and to offer hospitality packages. These were the beginnings of the modern game.

Meanwhile the club won two promotions in Hill's five full seasons to reach the top flight for the first time in their history. At which point Hill quit to take up a career in television. City's loss became TV's loss.

NOVEMBER 30

SCOTLAND 0-0 ENGLAND: THE WORLD'S
FIRST INTERNATIONAL
(1872)

In early 1870, FA secretary Charlie Alcock placed a notice in the Glasgow Herald newspaper suggesting a 'trial of skill between the champions of England and Scotland'. Calling for Scottish volunteers, he wrote: 'In Scotland, once essentially the land of football, there should still be a spark left of the old fire!' One member of the all-conquering Queen's Park team was selected by the FA to play alongside ten Scots from English public schools, and on March 5, 1870 the first ever representative fixture between the two countries was played.

There would be four more of these 'trials' by the end of 1871, but none were considered official as the English were selecting both sides. So the following year, Queen's Park, with a Scottish FA yet to be formed, entered negotiations with the FA themselves to arrange the world's first proper international. It would be played at the West of Scotland Cricket Club in Partick; the date, romantically, would be St Andrews Day.

Queen's Park goalkeeper and captain Bob Gardner selected the Scotland players. He ended up picking the entire Queen's Park XI, though he had wanted to play the unavailable Arthur Kinnaird (Wanderers) and the improbably monickered Lt Henry Waugh Renny-Tailyour (Royal Engineers). England, captained by Cuthbert Ottaway of Oxford University, drew their side from nine clubs including Sheffield Wednesday and Notts County.

In front of 4,000 spectators, Scotland ran out in blue shirts – Queen's Park's colours – and red hoods, while England wore white and sported caps. The Scots came closest to scoring, a Robert Leckie shot flicking the tape (which in those days acted as crossbar), but the match ended goalless. The game was the only 0-0 between the teams until 1970.

DECEMBER

DECEMBER 1

MONCHENGLADBACH 0-0 INTER: BORUSSIA FELLED BY DRINKS CAN
(1971)

Borussia Monchengladbach, a team built round the outstanding German midfielder Gunter Netzer, boasting dead-eye striker Jupp Heynckes and tenacious defender Berti Vogts, were one of the favourites for the 1972 European Cup. They set about proving it quickly. Having disposed of Cork Hibernians 7-1 on aggregate in the first round of the competition, they hosted Internazionale in the first leg of their second round tie at their Bokelberg stadium on October 20 – and thrashed a side containing Sandro Mazzola, Giacinto Fachetti, Roberto Boninsegna, Tarcisio Burgnich and Jair da Costa 7-1.

The result, however, did not stand. After 29 minutes of the game, with 'Gladbach 2-1 up, Boninsegna was felled by a drinks can thrown from the crowd and carried off. Mazzola handed the can to the referee, then Inter lost the match completely, shipping three more goals before half-time and another two in the second half. After the game Inter demanded UEFA award them the game 3-0. 'The rules are very clear in these cases and Borussia have to be penalised,' an Inter suit told the world's press. UEFA fined 'Gladbach the equivalent of £1,000 and ordered the first leg to be replayed in neutral Munich on December 1. In between, on November 3, Inter had won their home leg 4-2 (Boninsegna scoring, naturally), and so took to Munich a psychological advantage. They held out for a 0-0 draw, knocking a bitter 'Gladbach out – they had claimed Boninsegna was play-acting all along.

Who was right? UEFA claimed neutral observer Matt Busby had witnessed the striker unconscious in the Inter dressing room during the game. Then again, *The Times* carried testimony of a British supporter who was at the match and 'would not seem to have an axe to grind'. The fan was sure the can 'was either empty or virtually so, judging by its flight', that it hit Boninsegna on the shoulder, that Bonisenga considered his options for a split second before 'dramatically collapsing', and that one of his Inter team mates snatched a full tin of Coca-Cola from a fan before handing it to the referee 'with a great show of indignation'.

Still, much good it did Inter. They reached the final, only to be dispatched with ease with two goals from Ajax's Johan Cruyff.

DECEMBER 2

ARSENAL 3-0 LIVERPOOL: GUNNERS TURN
A HELLISH SEASON ROUND
(1990)

David O'Leary's record-breaking 622nd appearance for Arsenal was planned to be a celebration, but ended up in a brawl. The guests at Highbury on November 4, 1989 were Norwich City, who threw away a two goal lead to lose a pulsating match 4-3. Arsenal's winner came in injury time, Lee Dixon scoring from his own penalty rebound. The sight prompted Norwich to set about the celebrating Alan Smith, a scene ending in a 21-man brawl by the corner flag. (O'Leary did score his first Highbury goal for six years in the match, though.) Norwich were fined £50,000 for their part in the rumble, Arsenal £20,000. It was the first time the FA had held clubs directly responsible for their players. The precedent would have serious consequences for Arsenal the following season.

At Old Trafford on October 20, 1990, Nigel Winterburn went sliding in on Manchester United's Brian McClair. The two had history after Winterburn harangued the striker for missing a last-minute penalty in an FA Cup tie between the teams in 1988. The past resurfaced when McClair responded to the challenge by repeatedly kicking Winterburn in the back. Cue another 21-man brawl. On November 13, the FA fined both clubs £50,000 – and in an unprecedented measure docked United one point and Arsenal two.

The penalty left Arsenal eight points behind Liverpool in the title race, which looked an insurmountable deficit. But by the time they faced Liverpool at home less than three weeks later, they knew a win would take them to within three. Goals from Paul Merson, Dixon and Smith planted a seed of doubt in Liverpool heads. Their form became erratic, not helped by the shock resignation of Kenny Dalglish. Meanwhile the swing galvanised Arsenal, who went on to lose only one game all season, despite their captain Tony Adams being jailed for drink-driving in December. They ended the season champions, seven points ahead of Liverpool, despite their two-point deduction.

DECEMBER 3

REDKNAPP QUITS SOUTHAMPTON FOR PORTSMOUTH
(2005)

Harry Redknapp's first crack at football management was not a harbinger of the success he would later enjoy. Asked to take temporary control of Bournemouth in December 1982, the side he put out lost 9-0 at Lincoln. That result having somewhat ruined his chances of being given the job full-time, he was overlooked in favour of Don Megson. But within the year Megson was gone and Redknapp was promoted to manager. This time there would be no false start. Within two months of taking over in October 1983, Bournemouth had dumped holders Manchester United out of the FA Cup. By 1987, the club were Third Division champions.

It took some time before Redknapp got his chance in the top division. Having quit Bournemouth in 1991, exasperated at the lack of funds at his disposal, Redknapp became a coach at West Ham. When Billy Bonds walked out of the club in 1994, Redknapp took over, becoming the club's eighth manager since 1901. In his seven years at Upton Park he managed to stabilise a club notorious for yo-yoing between the top two divisions. In the six seasons before his appointment they had been promoted and relegated twice; after he left the club in 2001 they were relegated again within two years.

Redknapp resurfaced at Portsmouth, where he would eventually become a legendary figure, although his route to glory was unconventional. In 2003 he led the club into the Premiership – as West Ham went the other way – but walked out in 2004 after falling out with Portsmouth owner Milan Mandaric. To the horror of fans, he took over at rivals Southampton having earlier promised to 'never go down the road'. Redknapp was demonised, but forgiveness came after an unlikely chain of events. First, he ended the Saints' 27-year run in the top flight by taking them down. Then, angered at the Southampton board's ludicrous insistence on installing former England rugby union manager Clive Woodward as director of football, he walked out, straight back to Portsmouth. Fans were initially sceptical, but Redknapp was fully returned to favour by 2008, when his Pompey side won the FA Cup for the first time since 1939.

DECEMBER 4

DINAMO MOSCOW ENTERTAINED BY LONDON MAYOR
(1945)

At the end of an eventful tour of Britain, Dinamo Moscow were invited to dine with the Mayor of London. It was an opportunity to smooth over tensions and a chance for the Russians to finally sample some British fodder. Prior to their arrival, Dinamo officials insisted they would eat all their meals at the Soviet Embassy in Kensington, and even when they travelled out of the city they were sure to take their own eggs, chocolate drinks and butter. After a practice match in London, the hosts tried to tempt them with a lavish tea of 'chicken sandwiches and chocolate meringues', but the Russians decided not to attend. The visitors' reluctance to socialise aroused suspicions among Brits already wary of Stalin's Russia. In addition, Dinamo was run by Lavrenty Beria – the head of the KGB. A spokesperson for the team explained the 'mystery' surrounding the team, claiming they were just 'shy'.

Dinamo put on a brilliant display of football in all four matches and newspapers reports praised their 'Corinthian' spirit. Having drawn 3-3 against Chelsea in their first game they then took on Arsenal, who had drafted in two England players, one of whom was Blackpool's Stanley Matthews. This riled the Russians, who had specifically asked to play Arsenal and not England – but they went on to win the game 4-3, claiming it 'proved they were just about the best players in the world'. The losers used the excuse of heavy fog and rumours that, at one point, there were twelve Russians on the field.

Dinamo continued to shine in Scotland, earning a hard-fought 2-2 draw against Rangers. 'We must have them back next year,' said a TV commentator. The sentiment was unlikely to have been heard in Wales, where Cardiff City were thrashed 10-1. All in all, the Russians got a fair taste of Britain that winter: bad weather, bad food and a frosty reception.

DECEMBER 5

REAL SOCIEDAD 5-0 ATHLETIC BILBAO: BASQUES FLY FLAG POST-FRANCO
(1976)

The flag of the Basque Country, the Ikurrina (similar in design to the Union Flag, but in red, white and green), was designed in 1894 and for the first few decades of its existence was not a particularly potent symbol of the region. That all changed during and after the Spanish Civil War, when Basque identity was suppressed by General Franco and the flying of the Ikurrina was made illegal. It was occasionally seen at major events in the region, but usually quickly clamped down on by the civil guard. Those who unfurled it were sometimes killed for doing so.

The climate changed, of course, when Franco died in November 1975, albeit slowly. Spain's transition to democracy was a slow one and when Basque rivals Real Sociedad and Athletic Bilbao met in *La Liga* just over a year later, the Ikurrina was still illegal. So it was a politically memorable moment when Sociedad captain Inaxio Kortabarría and his Bilbao counterpart José Iríbar slowly marched towards the centre circle before kick off and unfolded the flag, before each taking a corner and holding it up to the 20,000 spectators in the Atocha stadium. 'The noise, already deafening, became a full-scale clamour,' reported local San Sebastian newspaper *El Diario Vasco*. That Sociedad went on to give their rivals a proper stuffing did not soften the impact of the first public display of Basque liberty since the 1930s.

The display did not stop the flag remaining controversial. In Bilbao a month later the civil guard fired rubber bullets at Basque demonstrators for unveiling the Ikurrina at a match. But it would only be a matter of weeks before the flag became legal. Then in 1981, the Basque Country took over *La Liga*. Real Sociedad snatched the title from Real Madrid with a goal 12 seconds from the end of their final match at Sporting Gijon. They retained it the following season, after which it was Bilbao's turn to wave the Ikurrina proudly as they landed two championships in a row of their own.

DECEMBER 6

EDWARD ELGAR SHOWS AN INTEREST IN WOLVES – AND WRITES CHANT
(1897)

There are not many football teams who can boast a famous classical composer among their most devoted fans. Equally, there are few players who can claim to have inspired a musician of such calibre to write a complex piece of music about the way they kick the ball.

Edward Elgar's interest in football began after a visit to see an old friend in Wolverhampton on December 6, 1897. The clergyman's daughter, Dora Penny, was sent to greet Elgar and his wife at the station and it appears Elgar and Dora hit it off immediately. 'Mr Elgar was left for me to look after,' recalled Dora in her book on the composer, *Memories of a Variation*. 'I quickly found out that music was the last thing he wanted to talk about. I think we talked about football. He wanted to know if I ever saw the Wolverhampton Wanderers play, and when he heard that our house was a stone's throw from their ground he was quite excited.'

From then on, Elgar started to frequent Molineux on a regular basis and was often seen riding to the ground on his bicycle eager to watch his favourite player, centre half Billy Malpass. In February 1898, he received a newspaper cutting from Dora describing how Malpass had 'banged the leather for goal'. The phrase instantly struck a chord in Elgar's head. He set the words to music. It is believed the piece was used in his composition *Caratacus*, and though some claim it to be one of the first football chants, it never really caught on in the stands.

In 1998, Wanderers unveiled a statue to Elgar at their ground before a pre-season match against Barcelona. Simon Osborn and the modern-day Malpass, Steve Bull, both banged the leather for goal in a 3-2 defeat.

AJAX 5-1 LIVERPOOL – THE ARRIVAL OF CRUYFF
AND TOTAL FOOTBALL
(1966)

Liverpool's 1966 championship winning team might have scored fewer goals than any champions since the war with the exception of Portsmouth in 1950, but only Arsenal in 1948 had been stingier in defence. In addition, in the European Cup to date they had only let in ten goals in twelve matches. They were not the sort of team to get turned over. Reflecting on their form, Bill Shankly went into their European Cup tie against Ajax brimming with confidence. 'All the questions have been answered,' he announced. 'Tomorrow is the day for the answers.'

But Ajax had a statistic of their own up their sleeve, as they were unbeaten in the Dutch league that season having scored 57 goals in 14 matches. Nevertheless, they still approached the tie with trepidation, as no Dutch team had yet made a mark in European competition. That state of affairs changed after 44 minutes. In a foggy Olympic Stadium, Ajax announced themselves, and Dutch football, to the world (even if half the stadium couldn't see what was going on). Cees de Wolf headed Ajax into a third-minute lead, a young Johan Cruyff added another on 17 minutes, before Klaas Nuninga scored two quick goals just before half-time. Nuninga's second was set up by Sjaak Swart who, in the fog, had earlier assumed the half was over and had to be sent back onto the pitch by a steward. Henk Groot added a fifth in the second half. Chris Lawler's last-minute consolation was anything but.

'We will win 6-0 at Anfield,' announced Shankly after the game. In his autobiography, he claims he made the comment in all seriousness, but Cruyff scored two in the return leg to see the Dutch side through. Ajax lost their quarter-final to Dukla Prague, but that wasn't the point. 'It was proof we were at international level,' said coach Rinus Michels. Six seasons later 'Total Football' had been honed to near-perfection, and Cryuff's Ajax had three European Cups to their name.

DECEMBER 8

DANNY BLANCHFLOWER SIGNS FOR TOTTENHAM
(1954)

Danny Blanchflower was the type of player who could turn a club's fortunes around. He was also the type of player who liked to do things his way, even if it meant stepping on the management's toes. Which is why Aston Villa put the Northern Ireland winger up for transfer in 1954 following a dispute over team tactics. Blanchflower was confused as to why the ball was rarely used in training sessions.

As soon as word spread that he was on the market, Arsenal and Tottenham, both struggling First Division sides, entered into a bidding war for the 28-year-old. Arsenal offered £28,500 but were outbid by Tottenham manager Arthur Rowe, who was determined to get his man at whatever price. In the end, Blanchflower was sold for £30,000, twice the price Villa had paid Barnsley for him.

Rowe soon stepped down as manager, and his successor Jimmy Anderson did not always appreciate Blanchflower's interference. Problems began with Anderson after Spurs lost an FA Cup semi-final to Manchester City in 1956. Blanchflower had reshuffled the team on the pitch in a vain attempt to find an equaliser and his on-the-hoof tinkering cost him the club captaincy. In 1958 Anderson made way for Bill Nicholson, who dropped Blanchflower – by now 32 and seen as a troublemaker – for Jim Iley. But Blanchflower's experience was soon missed, and he was reinstated as captain, destined to enjoy a spectacular Indian summer.

His intelligent promptings propelled Spurs to the double in 1961, the same year he became the first person to turn down an appearance on the BBC programme *This is Your Life*. 'Oh no it isn't,' he deadpanned, minutes before the programme went on air. It wouldn't be the last time he annoyed television executives, either. Employed as a commentator for CBS television in the USA during the mid-1960s, he proceeded to rubbish the quality of football he was witnessing. After an acerbic first season, he was not asked back, but Blanchflower was only ever interested in playing the game properly. 'The game is about glory, it is about doing things in style and with a flourish, about going out and beating the lot, not waiting for them to die of boredom.'

DECEMBER 9

WHITEHALL BANS NORTH KOREA ANTHEM
FOR 1966 WORLD CUP
(1965)

North Korea did not have too much trouble qualifying for the 1966 World Cup finals. With only one place offered to Africa, Asia and Oceania by FIFA, 16 countries withdrew in protest at the tournament's outrageously loaded structuring. So with Algeria, Cameroon, Egypt, Ethiopia, Gabon, Ghana, Guinea, Liberia, Libya, Mali, Morocco, Nigeria, Senegal, South Korea, Sudan and Tunisia all gone, and South Africa suspended by FIFA because of apartheid, this left Australia to play off against the Democratic People's Republic of Korea for the right to compete in England. Two matches were held in Cambodia in November 1965, the Koreans winning both easily, 6-1 and 3-1. Yet still they very nearly never made it to the following summer's finals.

The problem was that the United Kingdom officially failed to recognise the Democratic People's Republic of Korea. The Foreign Office initially threatened to deny the Koreans entry visas to the country, but that plan was nixed amid fears FIFA would take the finals away from England. So another plan was hatched. On December 9, the F.O. produced a report, entitled 'North Korean Participation In The Finals Of The World Cup' – which demanded the country be referred to as 'North Korea' and for their flag and anthem to be banned. Neither ban was workable, but while the flag diktat was overturned, the problem of the anthem was circumvented. National anthems were only played at the opening game and the final. It was a unique arrangement and one not since repeated. North Korea's anthem was never heard at the tournament.

Whitehall were no doubt happy to hear that the Koreans had been drawn in the group that played in Middlesborough, a long way from London. The squad were a local hit and are still remembered for their charm and politeness on Teesside. Their isolation obviously worked, too. The unfancied side beat Italy in one of the World Cup's most famous shocks and a rollicking PR triumph for 'North Korea'.

DECEMBER 10

ENGLISH LADIES FA FORMED IN WAKE OF FA BAN
(1921)

Thanks in no small part to the brilliance of the Dick, Kerr Ladies team, women's football exploded in popularity during World War I, a trend which showed no signs of abating once the men's Football League resumed in 1919. A game between Dick, Kerr and St Helens drew 53,000 to Goodison Park on Boxing Day 1920. An unofficial international between Dick, Kerr's England and France attracted a crowd of 25,000. During 1921, the team played 67 games in front of over 900,000 paying spectators.

The men became green-eyed, several club directors worrying that the women's game could eclipse the men's. Midway through 1921, Newcastle United refused to let the local women's team book St James' Park, even though two years earlier they had hosted a women's match which drew 35,000 and raised (in today's terms) over a quarter of a million pounds for war charities. The FA were concerned about the fact that the Dick, Kerr team played a series of charity matches to raise money for miners who had been locked out of their jobs when the pits were returned to private ownership at the end of March 1921. The fact that the women's charity exploits also highlighted how much money could be made from football meant that something had to be done. Battle lines were being drawn.

The FA launched a two-pronged attack on the women's game. A smear campaign accused the women of fiddling their expenses and cheating the charities they were raising money for. Meanwhile doctors provided spurious medical 'evidence' suggesting players would not be able to have children. 'I do not believe women are fitted for violent leg strain,' wrote a doctor in the *Lancashire Daily Post*. 'Football is much less suitable than lacrosse or hockey,' added the *Guardian*. On December 5, 1921 the FA used health concerns and financial impropriety to ban women from using men's pitches and officials. 'The game is quite unsuitable for females and ought not to be encouraged,' they said. Five days later a meeting of 25 ladies clubs in Blackburn founded the English Ladies FA which would keep the flame alight, though the game had suffered a serious setback from which it would take decades to recover. The FA did not apologise for their slight until 2008.

LIVORNO 2-1 LAZIO: DI CANIO'S FASCIST SALUTE
(2005)

When Livorno were promoted to Serie A in 2004, reaching the top flight of Italian football for the first time since 1949, conflict somewhere along the line was all but guaranteed. Livorno's fans style themselves as the most left-leaning in the country, often displaying banners and flags depicting Ché Guevara (sometimes, more contentiously, Joseph Stalin) so their stance was always likely to cause friction with some of Italian football's more right-wing supporter bases. Few would have guessed the most voluble opposition to their political posturing would come from someone on the pitch.

In retrospect, of course, that Lazio striker Paolo di Canio would become chief adversary of the Livorno support is not so much of a surprise. Di Canio was a member of Lazio's neo-Nazi ultras as a youngster, had a tattoo reading DVX (Latin for Il Duce) on his arm, and in his autobiography advanced the argument that Mussolini was a top chap because he made the trains run on time. After Lazio played host to Livorno in April 2005, a snarling di Canio presented the travelling fans with an unambiguous single finger. Then the season after, in the wake of a 2-1 defeat at Livorno, he antagonised them again with a palm-down, straight-arm salute to his own fans.

'I am a fascist, not a racist,' was di Canio's explanation. 'The salute is aimed at my people. I expect a robust defence from my club, otherwise I'm going to be really pissed off.' Happily Lazio did not agree, releasing a statement which distanced the club from 'any kind of racism or politicisation of football'. Having twice before seig-heiled at a Serie A match, against Roma and Juventus, this match marked the tipping point and di Canio was forced to promise never to salute again.

ITALY HONOURS MAZZOLA AND RIVERA
(1971)

After his debut for Internazionale as an 18-year-old in June 1961, for Sandro Mazzola the only way was up. Inter lost 9-1, a Serie A record (manager Helenio Herrera had fielded a team of youngsters to protest at a decision to replay a match which had been invaded by Juventus fans, and not award Inter the points.) Within three years the inside right was an integral part of the 'Grande Inter' side which won consecutive European Cups in 1964 and 1965.

Across the city, playing for rivals Milan, was creative midfielder Gianni Rivera. Rivera helped his club to the 1962 *Scudetto* as an 18-year-old and was the star of the sides which won the 1963 European Cup and regained the trophy in 1969, the year he became European Footballer of the Year.

But while both men were a part of Italy's success at the 1968 European Championship, they were considered too similar to be selected in the same line-up. By the time of the 1970 World Cup, it was decided by Italy manager Feruccio Valcareggi that each player would play 45 minutes per game, one taking over from the other. This policy was known as 'staffetta' – the relay – and it so nearly paid off for Italy until Valcareggi lost his nerve.

In the quarter-final against Mexico, Rivera replaced Mazzola at half-time. Rivera helped turn a 1-1 scoreline into a 4-1 rout. He was the hero again in the semi-final against West Germany, scoring the winner in extra-time. But in the final against Brazil, Mazzola started and did not come off. Rivera was sent on for the last six minutes of the match, by which point Italy were 3-1 down and as good as beaten.

The two men could not escape each other. The following year Mazzola was made Commander of the Order of Merit of the Italian Republic. But it was decided, in the interests of politics, to give the same medal to Rivera. Upon finding out, Mazzola was rumoured to have demanded a higher honour.

DECEMBER 13

WOLVES 3-2 HONVÉD: WOLVES 'CHAMPIONS OF THE WORLD'
(1954)

In 1954, the reigning champions of England, Wolverhampton Wanderers, inadvertently changed the face of European football forever. Taking advantage of the new floodlight technology, which had been given the go-ahead by the FA in 1951, Wolves staged a series of midweek Floodlit Friendlies against some of the best teams in world football. Racing Club, Moscow Dynamo and Spartak Moscow were all defeated in the most glamorous fixtures the country had ever seen. Wolves had even developed a special gold satin shirt to sparkle under the artificial glare.

Few, however, expected them to win their final Floodlit Friendly of the season. They were to face the mighty Honvéd of Puskás, Kocsis and Czibor. The Honvéd team contained six of the 'Magical Magyars' who had thrashed England 6-3 at Wembley in 1953 and 7-1 in Budapest the following June. On the evening of the match, Molineux was a mud pie of a pitch, deliberately waterlogged by Wolves manager Stan Cullis. An excitable 55,000 turned up to the game, which was also broadcast live on national television. Wolves initially failed to shine like their shirts, and were 2-0 down within 14 minutes, but as the Pathé newsreel commentator noted: 'The Wolves often take some time to warm up.'

Warm up they did. Four minutes into the second half, a Johnny Hancocks penalty made it 2-1. Then fourteen minutes from time, Roy Swinbourne scored two in twelve minutes to seal a famous victory. The following day's papers, desperate to put English football in a good light, were full of it. The *Daily Mail* named Wolves 'Champions of the World' while the *News Chronicle* hollered 'That's great, Wolves! Another boost for England: Honvéd Hammered!'

The 'hammering', of course, was debatable. But the English triumphalism had a positive effect. Two days later, *L'Equipe* editor Gabriel Hanot mooted the idea of an international championship to discover who the best team in the world really were. 'Before we declare that Wolverhampton are invincible, let them go to Moscow and Budapest,' he wrote. 'And there are other internationally renowned clubs: AC Milan and Real Madrid to name but two. A club world championship, or at least a European one.'

Within a year, UEFA had developed Hanot's idea and inaugurated the first European Cup. The tournament would subsequently prove Hanot's point: when Wolves first qualified for the European Cup in 1958/59, they were knocked out in the first round by Schalke.

NACIONAL 6-0 PEÑAROL – NACIONAL'S PERFECT SEASON
(1941)

With both clubs dating back to the end of the 19th century, Uruguay's *Superclasico* between Nacional and Peñarol is one of the oldest derbies in the world. It is also one of the most bitter, to the point that fans argue about which club was founded first.

Peñarol was initially set up in 1891 by British railroad workers and employees in Montevideo, but went under the English name of Central Uruguay Railway Cricket Club until it became a wholly Uruguayan concern in 1913. Nacional were founded in 1899, the first South American club set up by citizens of the continent itself as opposed to ex-patriots. Nacional do not recognise the CURCC as being the same club as Peñarol, therefore making them the oldest team in Uruguay.

The clubs quickly established themselves as the only show in town, sharing 22 of the 27 league championships in the amateur era. When football went professional in 1932, the duopoly *really* took hold. It took until 1976, when Defensor won the title, that the league was wrested from the teams' grasp. This level of domination is unprecedented in any other major footballing country.

While Peñarol can boast more titles, it is Nacional who retain most bragging rights. Uruguay's first ever victorious international, a 3-2 win over Argentina 1903, was an all-Nacional affair (albeit because CURCC refused to supply any players). Nacional supplied the majority of the players to Uruguay's 1924 and 1928 Olympic champion teams, plus the 1930 World Cup winning squad. In 1941, they delivered a perfect league season – winning all 20 games. They scored 79 goals along the way, including a 6-0 defeat of their arch-rivals. It remains the biggest margin of victory in a *Superclasico* to this day.

FLUMINESE 0-0 FLAMENGO: THE HIGHEST
CLUB ATTENDANCE
(1963)

Flamengo and Fluminese are the two biggest clubs in the most intense football city in the world, Rio de Janiero. The rivalry is fierce, and class-based. Fluminese was founded in 1902 by monied British ex-patriots and is seen as the establishment club, while Flamengo came into existence nine years later and quickly became the team of the people, thanks in part to the many black players who turned out for them.

With neither club owning a home ground of any significant size, both Flamengo and Fluminese took advantage of the gigantic state-owned Maracanã when it opened in 1950. And while neither club ever attracted the 200,000-plus crowd that witnessed Brazil's World Cup final debacle against Uruguay that year, it is no surprise that a 'Fla-Flu' derby would attract the largest audience ever to turn up to a club match in the world.

In the 1963 Campeonato Carioca (the Rio state league) the match between the two teams on December 15 gathered a recorded crowd of 177,656 paying spectators. The actual attendance, however, was reported to be as high as 194,603. Only two matches have ever attracted a larger crowd: the 1950 World Cup 'final' (which only *officially* drew 173,850) and a 1954 World Cup qualifier between Brazil and Paraguay (195,513). Needless to say, the game ended goalless.

The result was a shame, but does beg the question whether more amusement can be found in a smaller ground. On November 23, 1941, the Campeonato Carioca decider was played in Flamengo's tiny Gavea stadium, with only a 13,000 capacity. That day, Fluminese did not act in the aristocratic manner they usually affect. Only needing to draw, they spent the best part of the second half booting the ball out of the Gavea into a nearby lake.

DECEMBER 16

CRYSTAL PALACE 5-0 MANCHESTER UNITED: ROGERS SEES OFF O'FARRELL
(1972)

After the shambolic Wilf McGuinness era, Manchester United hoped for some stability. For a while, it looked like they had it under Frank O'Farrell, who had taken Leicester to the FA Cup final in 1969 and promotion two years later. Appointed in the summer of 1971, O'Farrell's United found themselves five points clear at the top of the table by December, the ageing triumvirate of Bobby Charlton, Denis Law and George Best enjoying a late revival.

Then the wheels came off. After a 5-2 victory over Southampton at the start of December, United failed to win any of their next eleven games. By the end of the season they had only won five more matches, finishing in eighth place, ten points behind champions Derby. Their form didn't get any better the following season. United lost their opening three fixtures, didn't win for nine, and by December, a year after topping the table, they were two points from bottom.

His team beginning to show their age, O'Farrell was beginning to regret not taking up the offer to sign the industrious Alan Ball from Everton when United were top of the league. He also had to deal with Best, whose drinking was a serious problem. When Best failed to turn up for a game at Norwich in early December, O'Farrell transfer-listed him. Less than a fortnight later, the board overruled him and welcomed Best back into the fold. O'Farrell's authority undermined, team spirit was shattered and United were thrashed by Crystal Palace, for whom Don Rogers was rampant and scored a spectacular solo goal.

'The match was lost before United took the field,' opined Jimmy Hill on ITV's *The Big Match* the day after. 'It was lost by Matt Busby and [chairman] Louis Edwards. By the way they have behaved this week they have cut the ground from under their manager's feet.'

Three days later, a pressured O'Farrell, who had taken to attacking journalists documenting the farce at Old Trafford with rolled-up newspapers, was sacked. He was replaced by Tommy Docherty, who would drag United clear of relegation, though their stay of execution only lasted 12 months.

NETHERLANDS 5-0 MALTA: THE UNLUCKIEST NON-QUALIFICATION OF ALL
(1983)

When Frank Rijkaard scored three minutes from time in Holland's final Euro '84 qualifying tie against Malta to wrap up a five-goal victory, his side's passage to the finals in France the following summer looked assured. The result meant they cemented their place at the top of their group ahead of Spain. Spain had one last game to play and could draw level on points, but with Holland enjoying a superior goal difference of 11, the result of the group looked done and dusted.

Spain's final game was also against Malta, a team they would have to beat by 11 clear goals to pip Holland on goals scored. But even though the Maltese were redefining the word hapless, having lost 8-0 to the Republic of Ireland in the game preceding the 5-0 Holland defeat, that was highly unlikely. Malta had never let in more than nine in 36 years of competitive football.

The game started badly for the Spanish. Defender Juan Señor missed a penalty on three minutes, then after Santillana opened the scoring Spain were pegged back by an equaliser on 24 minutes from Michael Degiorgio. Santillana completed his hat-trick by half-time but Spain were still nine goals short of their required total. But they got them. Hipólitó Rincón scored four, Santillana another, Antonio Maceda two in a minute, Manuel Sarabia made it 11-1 on 80 minutes. With four minutes to play, penalty villain Señor made amends for his miss by blasting home from close range. Spain had made it. Cue pitch invasion, forcing players to chase the crowd back into the stands.

It wasn't Spain's last escape act in the tournament. Defending champions West Germany were beaten to a semi-final place by Antonio Maceda's last-minute header – but their luck ran out in the final, goalkeeper Luis Arkonada fumbling Michel Platini's free-kick to gift victory to France.

DECEMBER 18

FIRST BALLON D'OR AWARDED TO MATTHEWS, THE CHAPLIN OF FOOTBALL
(1956)

At Wembley in May 1956, England beat an up-and-coming Brazil side 4-2. The Brazilian team contained four of the team who would go on to win the World Cup in Sweden two years later. Admittedly there was no Pelé or Garrincha in yellow yet, but it was still a satisfying result, especially as England missed two penalties as well. 'Make no mistake, these Brazilians are maestros,' wrote an excitable *Times* reporter. 'Wearing shirts of daffodil colour and the briefest of pale blue shorts, they might have belonged to a wood in springtime. Their gyrations, too, told of dance steps in wild woods with a special relish for flexibility and flourish. But this day it all faded against the solid oak of England.' Man of the match was Stanley Matthews, who had a hand in all the goals. 'Brazil were ever fearful of the pass to Matthews.'

The display effectively secured Matthews the first ever Ballon d'Or, an award for European Footballer of the Year set up by the respected *France Football* magazine and voted for by journalists across the continent. Winning the award was no mean feat, as he had pipped Alfredo di Stéfano, who had led Real Madrid to the first European Cup, by three votes, 47 to 44. Di Stéfano's team mate Raymond Kopa was third with 33 votes, Honvéd's Ferenc Puskás just behind in fourth with 32.

The *France Football* citation compared Matthews, surreally, to Charlie Chaplin. 'Even when he was forcibly marked his face didn't move,' wrote Gabriel Hanot, the journalist who helped launch the European Cup. 'He didn't laugh but he made the whole stadium laugh. After the Brazil match he was applauded like no other player ever had been, by both teams and officials. His gestures were comic and over the top. Chaplin and Matthews, two comic heroes of silent cinema, both English, two strings of a country with a natural sense of humour!' Nobody waxed lyrical like this about Michael Owen when he won it in 2001, did they?

DECEMBER 19

JULES RIMET TROPHY STOLEN FROM BRAZILIAN FA
(1983)

When the Jules Rimet Trophy was stolen from a London exhibition just before the 1966 World Cup, a spokesman for the Brazilian FA opined that such larceny 'would never have happened in Brazil. Even Brazilian thieves love football and would never commit this sacrilege.' Those words would come back to haunt the nation.

In 1970, Brazil became world champions for the third time. As a reward, FIFA allowed them to keep the 8lb Jules Rimet Trophy (a gold statuette of Nike, the Greek goddess of victory) forever. It was taken back from Mexico to the headquarters of the Brazilian Football Federation (CBF) in Rio de Janiero, where it was displayed in a bullet-proof glass and wood case in the foyer. Thirteen years later, on the evening of December 19, 1983, burglars entered the building and hacked through the wooden back of the cabinet with a crowbar, stealing the trophy. But this time Pickles the dog was not around to sniff it out.

A reward of £5,000 was offered for the cup by the Rio state bank, to no avail. 'The spiritual value of the cup is far greater than its material worth,' pleaded an emotional Giulite Coutinho, head of the CBF. 'I only hope it has not been melted down to be sold for its gold content.' Pelé was convinced this had indeed happened. 'It is not the fault of the thieves but of the authorities,' he suggested, 'because the people are desperate, without money and without food.' Three Brazilians and an Argentine were later tried and convicted for the theft.

For a while, there were rumours that the trophy stolen in 1983 had in fact been a bronze replica made in England after the 1966 theft – and that the English FA had only given the replica back at the 1970 World Cup, keeping the real thing themselves. So when the 1966 replica was auctioned in 1997 and fetched £254,000 – ten times its reserve price – some thought it must be the real thing, and the cup was safe. But it was later revealed that FIFA had taken a punt, just in case, and paid a hefty sum for an essentially worthless piece.

The original trophy was never found and it is thought Coutinho and Pelé's fears came true. In 1984, Brazilian president João Baptista Figueiredo was presented with a replica of the trophy, commissioned by the Eastman Kodak Company.

DECEMBER 20

HONVÉD 3-3 ATHLÉTIC BILBAO: A GREAT SIDE'S LAST COMPETITIVE GAME
(1956)

The national uprising in Hungary in October 1956 had a devastating effect on football in the country. The Honvéd team were caught up in the middle of the revolt, which lasted from October 23 to November 10. Ferenc Puskás was reported, at one point, to have been killed in the fighting. But the team remained alive and kicking, even with Soviet troops entering Budapest to quell the rioting. Honvéd were pleased to escape, travelling to Spain to take on Athlétic Bilbao in the first round of the 1956/57 European Cup.

Honvéd lost the first leg of the tie, 3-2 in Bilbao. With hostilities continuing back at home, it was impossible to stage the return leg in Budapest. So the team arranged to play their 'home' tie at the Heysel Stadium in Brussels. It was not a successful match for the Hungarian champions. Early on, their goalkeeper Lajos Farago was injured and with no substitutes allowed, Zoltán Czibor was forced to go in goal. Bilbao romped into a 3-1 lead, and despite Honvéd pulling level with late goals from Sándor Kocsis and Puskás, it was not enough to save their campaign. Honvéd were out and a great team had played its last competitive fixture.

The players opted not to return to Hungary. Sending for their families, they embarked on an unauthorised tour of Europe, playing friendlies in Italy, Portugal and Spain, before embarking on a tour of South America. Several of the squad decided to return to their homeland. Goalkeeper Gyula Grosics returned to Hungary to face a two-year ban. Others, including Puskás, Czibor and Kocsis, stayed away and ended up in the Spanish league after serving FIFA bans in the wake of their defections. Honvéd, their reign as one of the best clubs in Europe dramatically and unexpectedly over, would not win the Hungarian league again until 1984.

DECEMBER 21

CHARLTON 7-6 HUDDERSFIELD: SUMMERS SHINES IN GREATEST COMEBACK
(1957)

Charlton Athletic had been relegated from the First Division in 1956/57 having conceded 120 goals. Their display on the opening day of the following season proved they had not improved in defence over the summer. They had been 3-0 up at half-time at Huddersfield Town, but Bill Shankly's side replied with three second half goals to force a draw. It was a spectacular comeback, but nothing compared to the return fixture.

When the teams met again just before Christmas at a freezing Valley stadium, a similar goalfest looked unlikely for the first 17 minutes. Then Charlton's captain Derek Ufton dislocated his shoulder. In the days before substitutes, that meant the home side were forced to play the remaining 73 minutes with ten men, and by half-time Huddersfield had taken full advantage by scoring twice.

Charlton's left winger Johnny Summers pulled a goal back just after the restart, but Huddersfield quickly added three more and with just under half an hour to play, they were 5-1 up. Charlton immediately responded with two goals in two minutes. Their second of the afternoon was scored by Johnny Ryan from a Summers cross, the third by Summers himself. Summers then completed his hat-trick on 73 minutes, before scoring his fourth on 78.

The teams were level, 5-5, though not for long. Three minutes later Summers scored his fifth goal to put his team 6-5 up. Huddersfield managed an equaliser of their own with four minutes to play, but the momentum was all Charlton's, and with the clock on 90 minutes Summers crossed again for Ryan, who sealed the greatest comeback in league history. No team other than Huddersfield has scored six goals in a league match and lost.

It later transpired the heroic Summers had changed into some brand-new boots at half-time after his old ones had fallen to pieces. A notoriously one-sided left footer, he had scored all five of his goals with his right foot.

DECEMBER 22

THE START OF THE BIG FREEZE – AND THE BIRTH OF THE POOLS PANEL
(1962)

Three days before Christmas, a freezing fog enveloped Britain. Eighteen football matches were called off, with a further eight abandoned mid-game. The fixture card looked utterly decimated at the time, but although nobody knew it, there wouldn't be this much football again for over two months. By Boxing Day, the entire country had been covered in snow. Only 17 games were played on December 29. Come New Year's Day, not a single match was played. Five third-round FA cup ties went ahead on January 5, but with the country in the middle of a 'Big Freeze', battling -20° temperatures and 15-foot snowdrifts, the round didn't get completed until March 11.

The lack of matches wreaked havoc with the football pools, so Vernons, Zetters and Littlewoods acted quickly. A predictions system was put in place, and on January 26 the Pools Panel sat for the first time. The panel consisted of six men: former England players Tom Finney, Tommy Lawton and Ted Drake, former Scotland full-back George Young, former World Cup referee Arthur Ellis, and John Theodore Cuthbert Moore-Brabazon, 1st Baron Brabazon of Tara. Brabazon was a former Tory MP and aviation pioneer who, in 1909, strapped a wastepaper basket containing a piglet to the wing of a plane in order to prove that pigs could fly. Their deliberations were made behind closed doors at the Connaught Rooms in London, then announced live on BBC television. Of the 38 matches, the only predictions to raise eyebrows were Leeds to beat Stoke and Peterborough to win at Derby.

The weather slowly broke. There were eleven games on February 16, then 24 on February 23 – the most since the fog came down on December 22, and the first day the new Pools Panel wasn't required. By March 16 the first full league card since mid-December was played.

KEEGAN DECIDES TO LEAVE HAMBURG – TO JOIN JUVE OR BARÇA?
(1979)

During Kevin Keegan's final season at Liverpool in 1976/77, Juventus offered £1m for the striker, a huge fee at the time. So much did they want the player, they were prepared to wait two years for him until the Serie A ban on foreign imports was lifted, pay Keegan on top of the wages he would be earning at Liverpool in the interim, and give him the run of a local Fiat dealership while he was at it. Keegan was reportedly 'amused' by the offer but did not take it seriously. At the end of the season, having won the league and European Cup double with Liverpool, he left to play for Hamburg SV.

Keegan's stint in the Bundesliga was successful. Hamburg won their first German title since 1960 in his second season, and reached the European Cup final in 1980, where they lost to Nottingham Forest. Keegan also won the European Footballer of the Year award twice. But he was always planning to leave the club once his contract ran out, and in December 1979 announced his intention to move on. The only question was, where to?

Liverpool were interested in pairing him with Kenny Dalglish, but Keegan did not want to return to Anfield. Initially he was reported to have a preference for Juve, and had advised the club of his terms and conditions, which included being released for every single England game. But his wife Jean got cold feet, as Italy was suffering from a spate of kidnappings at the time. (Former prime minister Aldo Moro had, the previous year, been murdered by kidnappers.) He was then hotly tipped to move to Barcelona, but then in February 1980, Keegan announced he was returning to England, where only Chelsea had declared an interest. However he did not go to Stamford Bridge as 'they could not guarantee me First Division football' but, in arguably the biggest transfer shock since Tommy Lawton joined Third Division Notts County in 1948, Keegan joined Lawrie McMenemy's Southampton instead.

'I really think Southampton have got the potential to win the championship,' explained Keegan of his decision. Saints did indeed challenge for the title, coming second in 1983/84 – but only after Keegan had left for Newcastle in the summer of 1982.

SUNDERLAND 2-3 NEWCASTLE UNITED:
THE RIVALRY BEGINS
(1898)

The Football League was ten years old before the north-east's two biggest clubs met, but once they had done, they wasted little time in developing their rivalry. Sunderland had become the first new team to win admission to the league in 1890, replacing founder members Stoke, and had racked up three titles by 1895. Newcastle joined the new Second Division in 1893, taking five seasons to win promotion. Finally, on Christmas Eve 1898, it was on.

A crowd of 30,000 gathered at Roker Park, twenty special trains having been laid on to ferry Newcastle's support south. United were struggling in the relegation places, but quickly established a lead over their mid-table rivals and 'defensive tactics in the closing stages' secured a win to kick-start their season and they ended five points clear of trouble. The boot was on the other foot the following Christmas Eve, Newcastle throwing away a 2-1 half-time lead at home to lose 4-2.

The rivalry took a more sinister turn on Good Friday, 1901. Sunderland were chasing the championship and travelled to St James's Park. More than 35,000 fans were already jammed into the 25,000-capacity ground when even more supporters stormed the turnstiles. 'The scene was an unprecedented one,' reported the *Manchester Guardian*. 'The footballers got mixed up in the crowd, the rougher element of which commenced horseplay.' Flags and goals having been torn down, the police made baton charges and the game was called off. Sunderland won the rearranged match three weeks later, but lost the title to Liverpool by two points.

In December 1908 Newcastle lost 9-1 at home to Sunderland, who scored eight in the second half. The score still stands as a record in the derby, and a record top-flight home defeat. There was consolation for United though, as amazingly went on to romp the title. Ten years on from their first game, the teams had established a reputation for improbable inconsistency which would fascinate the country for the rest of the century.

DECEMBER 25

THE GAMES IN THE TRENCHES
(1914)

On the first Christmas Day of the Great War, an unofficial truce took place in the trenches. In their letters home, British soldiers mentioned how they shook hands with their German counterparts and swapped cigarettes. A Scottish brigadier described how the Germans 'came out of their trenches and walked across unarmed, with boxes of cigars and seasonable remarks. What were our men to do? Shoot? You could not shoot unarmed men.'

While a few still spoke of continued gunfire, most soldiers appear to have laid down their arms that day. Even more remarkable are suggestions that football matches were played in no-man's-land. A report in the *Manchester Guardian* on Boxing Day 1914 described how in one region 'every acre of meadow under any sort of cover in the rear of the lines was taken possession of for football.' A letter published on New Year's Day from a British Officer reads: 'I hear our fellows played the Germans at football on Christmas Day. Our own pet enemies remarked they would like a game, but as the ground in our part is all root crops and much cut up by ditches, and as, moreover, we had not got a football, we had to call it off.' A letter in *The Times* on the same day from a Major said a German Regiment 'had a football match with the Saxons [regiment], who beat them 3-2'.

In 1983 a former soldier of the Cheshire Regiment told of a match against the Germans started when 'the ball came from their side. I should think there were about a couple of hundred taking part. I had a go at the ball. I was pretty good then, at 19. Everybody seemed to be enjoying themselves. There was no sort of ill-will between us. There was no referee, and no score, no tally at all. It was simply a melee – nothing like the soccer you see on television.'

One match was played for a special trophy: a hare. 'The grey tunicked Germans the one side, and the kilted Jocks the other. The game was won by the Germans, who captured the prize. But more was secured than a hare. A sudden friendship had been struck up, the truce of God had been called, and for the rest of Christmas Day not a shot was fired along our section.'

DECEMBER 26

DICK, KERR LADIES 4-0 ST HELENS: WOMEN ATTRACT RECORD CROWD
(1920)

In October 1917, the works team of Preston-based munitions factory Dick, Kerr & Co. were in the middle of a terrible run of form. Enjoying some banter in the works canteen, one of the women at the factory, Grace Sibbert, suggested that the females at the company 'could do better'. Light-hearted bets at lunchtime ensued. If the 'boys' managed to put through one of the small cloakroom windows with a football, the 'girls' would buy them a packet of cigarettes; if the women managed it, they won chocolate.

One of the clerks at the company, Alfred Frankland, became impressed by the women's skill, and suggested to Sibbert that she and her friends form a team. Sibbert agreed, so Frankland organised a charity event at Deepdale, the home of Preston North End. The Great Holiday Attraction was held on Christmas Day 1917, drawing a crowd of 10,000 and raising £200 for a local hospital. Reports of the match suggest the crowd initially found the sight of the Dick, Kerr women playing football amusing, but quickly realised they could play. Dick, Kerr Ladies won the game 4-0 against a side from Arundel Coulthard Foundry.

Women's football quickly became extremely popular. Initially this was because the men were still at war and the Football League was suspended, but the game continued to flourish after the restart of the League in 1919. Frankland persuaded some of the country's top female players to join Dick, Kerr – including the women's game's first superstar, 14-year-old striker Lily Parr – and by 1920 the side represented England against a French team in the first unofficial women's international, which England won 2-0.

On Boxing Day a game between Dick, Kerr and St Helens at Everton's Goodison Park drew 53,000, with a reported 14,000 others locked out. But the popularity of the women's game was beginning to cause jealousy with the men. Within the year the FA had banned women's football, citing spurious health and financial reasons. The game continued but interest waned. The ban was finally lifted in 1971.

SÃO CAETANO 1-1 VASCO DA GAMA: BIG BLUES JOIN BRAZIL'S BIG BOYS
(2000)

Even by the standards of Brazilian domestic football, which reorganises itself annually by whim, the 2000 season was a total farce. In 1999, a rule had been introduced which relegated teams based on a rolling two-season performance. It was designed to help the big clubs avoid the ignominy of demotion, but by the end of the season Rio giants Botafogo were in the relegation zone. To avoid going down, they went to the sports justice courts to complain about a game played against São Paulo in which their opponents had fielded a player whose registration was gained using a false birth certificate. The court awarded Botafogo the points and Vasco da Gama went down instead.

Vasco had that decision overturned by the civil courts, but were banned by FIFA, who refuse to recognise teams appealing outside of their legal jurisdiction. So in order to keep Gama, FIFA and the Brazilian judicial system happy, the Brazilian federation organised a one-off trophy to replace the 2000 league: the Copa João Havelange. It was a mammoth tournament which, theoretically, could end with any team from four divisions winning the national championship. Given all this had come about as a result of the big boys wanting to ringfence their patch, there was only one possible outcome. São Caetano, who qualified for the final phase as runners-up of the second tier, reached the two-legged grand final.

They played Romário's Vasco da Gama and held them to a draw in the first leg. There would be no fairytale ending – after a second leg abandoned after a serious but non-fatal crowd crush (Vasco did a shameless victory lap of honour anyway), Vasco won the replayed leg 3-1. But São Caetano were permitted into the top division proper in 2001 – where they came runners-up again. Then, amazingly, the minnows reached the final of the 2002 Copa Libertadores, only to lose to Olimpia of Paraguay.

The Caetano dream soon died – along, tragically, with defender Serginho, who perished on the pitch against São Paulo in 2004. São Caetano knew of the player's heart condition but played him anyway and were docked 24 points as a result, robbing the team of Copa Libertadores qualification. All momentum was gone and within two years they were relegated back from whence they came.

DECEMBER 28

TEAMS SUFFER PAYBACK FOR AMAZING BOXING DAY GOAL GLUT
(1963)

There had obviously been plenty of festive cheer in the homes of England's professional footballers on Christmas Day 1963, for the scorelines of the Boxing Day fixtures were something to behold. An unprecedented 66 goals were scored in the First Division. The results read: Blackpool 1-5 Chelsea; Burnley 6-1 Manchester United; Fulham 10-1 Ipswich; Leicester 2-0 Everton; Liverpool 6-1 Stoke; Nottingham Forest 3-3 Sheffield United; Sheffield Wednesday 3-0 Bolton; West Brom 4-4 Tottenham; West Ham 2-8 Blackburn and Wolves 3-3 Aston Villa.

Though the scorelines were on the high side, many of them were not wholly surprising. West Ham had been tonked, but by the league leaders. Ipswich, who conceded ten, had already shipped 58 goals in 23 games. Stoke were struggling, and their opponents Liverpool were destined for the title. The only real surprise was Manchester United's capitulation at Burnley as they had started the day four points off the top of the table.

But if some of the Boxing Day scorelines raised eyebrows, the return fixtures two days later boggled the mind: Aston Villa 4-2 Wolves; Blackburn 1-3 West Ham; Bolton 3-0 Sheffield Wednesday; Chelsea 1-0 Blackpool; Everton 0-3 Leicester; Ipswich 4-2 Fulham; Manchester United 5-1 Burnley; Sheffield United 1-2 Nottingham Forest; Tottenham 0-2 West Brom.

For some, retribution had been swift. West Ham, who had lost 8-2 at home, won 3-1 at Blackburn. Manchester United, fresh from their 6-1 thrashing, nearly gave as good as they had got at Old Trafford with a 5-1 win. And most spectacularly of all, Ipswich avenged their 10-1 humiliation at Fulham with a 4-2 home victory over the Cottagers. It was one of their last acts of defiance, though. Ipswich, who had been champions in 1962, were relegated in last place having let in 121 goals.

SHEFFIELD 0-0 HALLAM: THE FIRST BATTLE
OF BRAMALL LANE
(1862)

Cricket was the crowd puller at Sheffield's Bramall Lane stadium. So when the ground's committee, seeking ways to make money, decided to host their first football match between Sheffield FC and Hallam, they hoped it would be an entertaining display of skill and sportsmanship to win the city's sporting cognoscenti over to an 'undignified' sport. Unfortunately, the ground's introduction to association football couldn't have been worse. The game would later be referred to, in one of the first match reports ever to be published in a newspaper, as 'the day the waistcoats came off and the fighting began'.

The match had been organised to raise funds for soldiers who had fought in the American Civil War, but the mood on the pitch was anything but charitable. Just after half-time, Sheffield founder and star player Nathaniel Creswick clashed with William Waterfall of Hallam. Although Creswick won the ball, he appears to have walloped Waterfall, who was holding him back, in the kerfuffle. The *Sheffield Independent* remarked how the Hallam player approached Creswick 'in the most irritable manner and struck him several times'.

This version of events was deemed 'unfair' by Hallam who fired off a letter to the paper. 'In the early part of the game,' they wrote, 'Waterfall charged the Major [Creswick], on which the Major threatened to strike him if he did so again. Later in the game, when all the players were waiting a decision of the umpires, the Major, very unfairly, took the ball from the hands of one of our players and commenced kicking it towards their goal. He was met by Waterfall who charged him and the Major struck Waterfall on the face, which Waterfall immediately returned.'

Apart from the aggression, there was little to animate the crowd, and after a gruelling three hours neither side managed to score. Much to the disappointment of Bramall Lane's committee, the spectators walked away decidedly unimpressed.

DECEMBER 30

RANGERS 7-0 HIBERNIAN: GAZZA BOOKS THE REF
(1995)

For over 17 years, there was one refereeing decision which stood head and shoulders above any other as the most pompous display of needless officialdom in the history of football: Clive Thomas's full-time whistle to prevent a Zico winner in a group match at the 1978 World Cup between Brazil and Sweden (see June 3 entry). It was a preposterous piece of petty posturing which had no peer, until the day SPL referee Dougie Smith dropped his notebook and cards midway through a game at Ibrox between Rangers and Hibernian.

Paul Gascoigne was the first to notice that Smith had left his cards on the turf. The Rangers midfielder picked them up and scooted after the referee with them. After grabbing Smith's attention, Gazza pulled out the yellow card, pretended to book himself and then flourished it at the referee. The 44,692 Rangers and Hibs supporters erupted with laughter – then pretty much as one with anger as the thin-lipped Smith took the cards from Gascoigne and immediately booked the player for his impudence. 'He might be able to take the fucking piss out of you,' the referee told Hibernian midfielder Joe Tortolano, who immediately questioned the decision, 'but he's not taking the fucking piss out of me.' Thanks to disciplinary points accrued in previous matches, the booking earned Gascoigne a two-match ban.

After the match, Rangers manager Walter Smith asked his refereeing namesake to reconsider and rescind the booking, but the official was having none of it. Poor Gordon Durie scored four forgotten goals amidst the furore. All this during the season of goodwill as well.

THE NASL DREAM DIES… ALONG WITH THE
NEW YORK COSMOS
(1984)

The New York Cosmos were drawing average crowds of 40,000-plus during the Pelé era between 1975 and 1977, occasionally enticing up to 70,000 people to The Giants Stadium, but once the Brazilian superstar retired the fans went with him. Attendances across the board in the North American Soccer League (NASL) had been higher when Pelé came to town, but once the Brazilian superstar had left, business plans slowly became unsustainable.

The NASL continued to attract big names – Johan Cruyff, Franz Beckenbauer, George Best, Gerd Müller and Rodney Marsh were among those who came and went – but none had the impact of Pelé. All were past their prime, and anyway the skills and influence of a Beckenbauer or Cruyff were considered too subtle to be understood by the majority of the USA's fledgling audience, where soccer was still a minority interest. The cost of their salaries soon began to outweigh the financial rewards on offer to franchise owners, and teams started going to the wall.

With no little irony, it also didn't help that the Cosmos only became truly dominant once Pelé had left. The Cosmos won the Soccer Bowl in 1978, 1980 and 1982, a state of affairs which further haemorrhaged interest in the NASL, which was seen as uncompetitive. When the franchise made a $5m loss in 1983, owners Warner Bros pulled out. In a desperate last throw of the dice, Cosmos asked Pelé to come out of retirement in 1984, but were denied.

By the end of the season, with only three other teams ready for 1985, the NASL demanded a letter of credit from Cosmos stating their willingness to compete the following season. The New Years Eve deadline was not met. Cosmos would have been thrown out of the league had they not left to become a touring concern. The league itself went out of business on March 28, 1985. The Cosmos did not have much longer to run themselves. On June 13, 1985 they played a friendly against striker Giorgio Chinaglia's old club Lazio. It degenerated into a fistfight and was abandoned. The Cosmos died there and then.

ACKNOWLEDGEMENTS

Thanks to our editors Jon Butler and Mark Searle. To our agents Annabel Merullo and Tom Williams at PFD. To Cris Freddi. To Helen Guthrie at Macmillan. To those whose help along the way will always be appreciated: Anushka Asthana, Denis Campbell, Alex Clark, Seb Costey, Elizabeth Day, Carrie Dunn, Ken Early, Javier Espinoza, Paul Farnaby, Simon Farnaby, Josy Forsdike, Ger Gilroy, Harvey, Dave Hewitt, Jessica Hopkins, Sean Ingle, Dan Jones, Tom Lamont, Tim Lewis, Sid Lowe, Alan McArthur, Alistair O'Neill, Dan Rookwood, Joel Rookwood, David Smith, Les Smith, Rob Smyth, Colette Soloman, Dave Spencer, Mark Townsend, Tom Walker, John Wright and Jessica Young. To everyone we work with at guardian.co.uk and the *Observer*. To the burglar who decided to steal everything except Rowan's laptop. To BBC Radio 3 for transmitting the nerve-calming *Late Junction*. To Alexander Ross Murray for all the years he talked football with Scott. To our families – Margaret Murray, and Lauren, Richard and Will Walker – for the invaluable love and support they have given us. And we did want to thank each other... but that would be too cheesy so we thought better of it.

BIBLIOGRAPHY

BOOKS

100 Years of Football The Fifa Centennial Book, Eisenberg C, Lanfranchi P, Mason T, Wahl A, Orion, 2004
100 Years of Scottish Sport, Baillie R, Mainstream, 1994
50 Years of the European Cup and Champions League, Radnedge K, Carlton Books, 2005
A Game For Rough Girls, Williams J, Routledge, 2003
Ajax: The Dutch, The War, Kuper S, Orion, 2003
Barca, A People's Passion, Burns J, Bloomsbury, 1998
Behind the Curtain, Wilson J, Orion, 2006
Bhoys, Bears and Bigotry, Murray B, Mainstream, 1998
Black Lions, Hinds R, Sportsbooks, 2006
Bob Paisley, Manager of the Millenium, Keith J, Robson Books, 1999
Book of Football Obituaries, Ponting I, Know the Score Publishing, 2008
Brilliant Orange, Winner D, Bloomsbury , 2000
Calcio, Foot J, Forth Estate, 2006
Complete Book of the World Cup 2006, Freddi C, Harper Sport, 2006
Daily Telegraph Football Chronicle, Barrett N, Carlton Books, 2004
Encyclopedia of British Football, Cox RW, Russell D, Vamplew W, Routledge 2005
Encyclopedia of British Football, Soar P, Willow, 1987
Engineering Archie, Inglis S, English Heritage, 2007
England Managers The Toughest Job in Football, Glanville B, Headline, 2007
European Ritual, King A, Ashgate, 2003
FA Cup Giant Killers, Harrison P, Tempus, 2007
Fear and Loathing in World Football, Armstrong G, Giulianotti R, Berg 2001
Ferenc Puskás, Captain of Hungary, tr de Major A, Stadia, 2007
Fields of Glory, Paths of Gold, Connolly K and MacWilliam R, Mainstream, 2005
Football Against the Enemny, Kuper S, Orion, 1996
Football Grounds of Britain, Inglis S, Harper Collins, 1996
Football Strangest Matches, Ward A, Anova, 2007
Football: The First Hundred Years : the Untold Story, Harvey A, Routledge, 2005
Fowler: My Autobiography , Fowler R, Maddock D, MacMillan, 2005
Freedom of Expression and Freedom of Information, Beatson J, Cripps Y, Williams D, Oxford University Press, 2000
Futebol: A Brazilian Way of Life, Bellos A, Bloomsbury, 2002
Great Football Headlines, Michael O'Mara Books, 2002
Hand of God: The Life of Diego Maradona, Burns J, Bloomsbury, 1997
In a League of their Own! The Dick, Kerr Ladies 1917–1965, Newsham G, Scarlett Press, 1997
Jack and Bobby, McKinstry, Harper Collins, 2002
Keane: The Autobiography, Keane R, Dunphy E, Michael Joseph, 2002
Kicking and Screaming, Taylor R and Ward A, Robson Books, 1995
Manchester City's Cult Heroes, Clayton D, Know the Score, 2007
Match: The Complete Book of Football, ed Hunt C, Hayden Publishing, 2003
Morbo, Ball P, WSC Books, 2001
Moving With The Ball, Lanfranchi P, Taylor M, Berg, 2001
My Father and Other Working Class Football Heroes, Imlach G, Yellow Jersey Press, 2006
My Favourite Year, ed Hornby N, Cassell, 1993
News of the World Football Annual, Bateson B and Sewell A, Invincible Press, various years
Official History of Arsenal, Soar P and Tyler M, Hastings Hilton, 1996
Out of his Skin, Hill D, WSC Books, 2001
Premiership, Horrie C, Simon and Schuster, 2002
Rothmans Football Yearbook, Rollin J and Rollin G, Headline, various years
Scoring for Britain: International Football and International Politics, 1900-1939, Beck P, Routledge, 1999
Soccer in a Football World, Wangerin D, WSC Books, 2006
Sport and Identity in the North of England, Hill J, Williams J, Edinburgh University Press, 1996
Sport, Harris T, Yellow Jersey Press, 2007
Sport, Sectarianism and Society in a Divided Ireland, Sugden J, Bairner A, Continuum, 1993
Story of the World Cup, Glanville B, Faber and Faber, 2005
Striking for Soccer, Hill J, Peter Davies, 1961
Sunday Times Illustrated History of Football, Nawrat C and Hutchings S, Octupus Publishing, 1998
The Ball is Round, Goldblatt D, Penguin, 2006
The Complete Encyclopedia of Football, Radnedge K, Carlton Books, 1998
The Dick Kerr's Ladies, Jacobs B, Constable and Robinson, 2004
The FA Cup The Complete Story, Lloyd G and Holt N, Aurum Press, 2005
The First Black Footballer, Vasili P, Frank Cass, 1998
The Fourth Olympiad, Cook T, British Olympic Association, 1909
The Global Sports Arena: Athletic Talent Migration in an Interdependent World, Bale J, Maguire J, F. Cass, 1994
The Guiness Football Encyclopedia, ed Hart G, Guiness Publishing, 1995
The People's Game, Walvin J, Mainstream, 1994
The Perfect Ten, Williams R, Faber and Faber, 2006
The World Cup Strangest Moments, Seddon P, Robson Books, 2005
Tor!, Hesse-Lichtenberger U, WSC Books, 2002
Ward's Soccerpedia, Ward A, Anova, 2006
Wembley Stadium of Legends, Tomsett P and Brand C, Dewi Lewis Media, 2007
When Saturday Comes The Half Decent Football Book, Lions A and Ronay B, Penguin 2005
White Storm 101 Years of Real Madrid, Ball P, Mainstream, 2002
World Football Yearbook 2002-3, Goldblatt D, Dorling Kindersley, 2002

NEWSPAPERS

Accrington Observer
China Daily
Daily Mail
Guardian
Independent
Independent on Sunday
International Herald Tribune
Irish Examiner
New York Times
Newcastle Journal
Nottingham Evening Post
Observer
Stockport Express
Sunday Herald
Sunday Times
The Times
Yorkshire Post

PERIODICALS

Champions
Der Spiegel
FourFourTwo
Spectator
Time
Vanity Fair
When Saturday Comes

WEBSITES

bbc.co.uk
cafc.co.uk
cbcsports.ca
espn.com
fa.com
le.ac.uk
liverpoolfc.tv
offthetelly.co.uk
soccerlens.com
uefa.com
wisa.org.uk